Mediating Culture
in the
Seventeenth-Century German Novel

Mediating Culture

in the

Seventeenth-Century German Novel

Eberhard Werner Happel, 1647–1690

Gerhild Scholz Williams

The University of Michigan Press
Ann Arbor

Published in the United States of America by
The University of Michigan Press
Manufactured in the United States of America
♾ Printed on acid-free paper

2017   2016   2015   2014   4   3   2   1

A CIP catalog record for this book is available from the British Library.

Library of Congress Cataloging-in-Publication Data

Williams, Gerhild Scholz, 1942–
    Mediating culture in the seventeenth-century German novel :
  Eberhard Werner Happel, 1647–1690 / Gerhild Scholz Williams.
       pages   cm
    Includes bibliographical references and index.
    ISBN 978-0-472-11924-0 (cloth : acid-free paper)—ISBN 978-0-472-12010-9 (ebook)
    1. Happel, Eberhard Werner, 1647–1690—Criticism and
  interpretation.   2. Happel, Eberhard Werner, 1647–1690—Sources.
  3. Happel, Eberhard Werner, 1647–1690—Characters.   4. German
  literature—Early modern, 1500–1700—History and criticism.
  5. German fiction—Early modern, 1500–1700—History and criticism.
  6. German literature—Social aspects—History—17th century.   7. Heroes
  in literature.   8. National characteristics, German, in literature.   9. Gender
  identity in literature.   10. East and West in literature. I. Title.
  PT1737.H18Z73   2013
  833'.5—dc23
                                                    2013044601

Contents

❦

Preface

৯.

Parle afin que ie te voye
—Madame de Scudéry, *Ibrahim* (1641)

Seventeenth-century German literature is increasingly attracting the critical attention of scholars, who survey a variety of early modern texts in the context of culture, gender, class, media and translation studies, and, of course, history. To this we might add celebrity studies,[1] or its seventeenth-century iteration, which explored and exploited the fame and notoriety of media stars like Imre Thököly (1659–1705) and Marshal Schomberg (1615–90), whom we will meet in chapter 2. Recent inquiries into what Doris Bachmann-Medick and others have called "cultural turns" have also opened exciting avenues for the study of texts that, in the past, were often set aside as mere epigones or unwieldy amalgamations in print, variously called *Theatra, Universalbibliotheken, Pandecten*, commonplace books, or novels.[2]

Eberhard Werner Happel (1647–90),[3] much like his contemporaries, delighted in turning out endless series of novels, and in the process of collecting, reordering, and reorganizing knowledge, he provided, in writing, space for the permutations of history and fiction much prized by his readers.[4] He

1. Joseph A. Boone and Nancy J. Vickers, eds., "Celebrity, Fame, Notoriety," special issue, *PMLA* 126, no. 4 (2011).

2. Gerhild Scholz Williams, *Ways of Knowing in Early Modern Germany: Johannes Praetorius as a Witness to His Time* (Aldershot: Ashgate, 2006), 11.

3. Gerhard Dünnhaupt, ed., *Personalbibliographien zu den Drucken des Barock*, Hiersemanns bibliographische Handbücher 3 (Stuttgart: Hiersemann, 1991); Walter Killy with Hans Fromm, eds., *Literaturlexikon: Autoren und Werke deutscher Sprache*, vol. 4 (Gütersloh: Bertelmanns Lexikon, 1989), 653–55.

4. Sylvie Thorel-Cailletteau, "The Poetry of Mediocrity," in *The Novel*, vol. 2, *Forms and Themes*, ed. Franco Moretti (Princeton: Princeton University Press, 2006), 71–74.

excelled as much as a journalist as he did as a writer of knowledge literature, a fact recently explored in breadth and depth by Flemming Schock.[5] Moreover, with the help and support of librarians and technicians, scholars have made significant progress in digitizing and investigating the massive encyclopedic and novelistic writings of this period while parsing their role in knowledge production and dissemination and thus their subsequent impact on the public discourse.[6]

While mostly neglected throughout the Enlightenment and the nineteenth century, Happel attracted a bit of critical attention in the 1930s, when Gerhard Lock devoted a study to Happel's "courtly-gallant novels."[7] Lock contributed to critically confining Happel and his novels within a concept that, as we will see, did not at all do justice to his writerly distinction. The seventeenth-century designation of "gallant," according to McCarthy, "originally referred to the polished manners and correct demeanor of educated aristocratic men toward others, especially toward women." While this aspect is present in much poetry and many novels of the time, it is by no means a dominant feature of Happel's novels.[8] Moreover, Lock's suggestion that Happel was satirized by contemporaries because of his "gallant" style lacks documentation. In fact, quite the opposite was true, as we will see in the reaction of contemporary writers discussed later in this study.[9] I intend to show that to pigeonhole Happel as a mere writer on gallant topics is to seriously misread him. My proposed reevaluation of Happel's novels will be aided by

5. Flemming Schock, *Die Text-Kunstkammer: Populäre Wissenssammlungen des Barock am Beispiel der "Relationes Curiosae" von E. W. Happel*, Beihefte zum Archiv für Kulturgeschichte 68 (Cologne: Böhlau, 2011).

6. Pamela H. Smith and Benjamin Schmidt, eds., *Making Knowledge in Early Modern Europe: Practices, Objects, and Texts, 1400–1800* (Chicago: University of Chicago Press, 2007), introduction. A selection of two hundred *Theatrum* texts has been digitized (along with its secondary literature) by a project funded by the Deutsche Forschungsgemeinschaft, started at the University of Darmstadt, and transferred, with Nikola Roßbach to Kassel (with cooperation of the Herzog August Bibliothek, Wolfenbüttel): *Welt und Wissen auf der Bühne: Die Theatrum-Literatur der Frühen Neuzeit; Repertorium*, ed. Nikola Roßbach and Thomas Stäcker with Flemming Schock, Constanze Baum, Imke Harjes, and Sabine Kalff (Wolfenbüttel: Herzog August Bibliothek, 2011), http://diglib.hab.de/edoc/ed000132/startx.htm.

7. Gerhard Lock, *Der höfisch-galante Roman des 17. Jahrhunderts bei Eberhard Werner Happel* (Würzburg: Konrad Triltsch, 1939).

8. John A. McCarthy, "The Gallant Novel and the German Enlightenment (1670–1750)," *Deutsche Vierteljahrschrift für Literaturwissenschaft und Geistesgeschichte* 59 (1985): 49; Lock, *Der höfisch-galante Roman*.

9. "Es ist sehr wohl möglich, daß [Christian] Reuter sich mit seiner Satire besonders gegen die Romane Eberhard Werner Happels wandte" (It is quite possible that Reuter directed his satire against the novels of Eberhard Werner Happel). Lock, *Der höfisch-galante Roman*, 19.

the fact that the study of novels has emerged as part of the current general interest in and curiosity about how the production of knowledge impacted seventeenth-century narrative.[10] In addition, explorations of national identity formation, gender and sexualities, Western European encounters with neighbors to the east, and confrontations with non-European and non-Western powers and cultures (most challenging among them the feared and admired Turk) have all invigorated early modern studies and are continuing to open new and exciting perspectives into the past.[11]

I intend to contribute to this critical discourse in several ways. This study aims, first, to be an exploration of the narrative wealth and multiversity of Happel's work. It is, second, an examination of Happel's novels as illustrative of seventeenth-century novel writing in Germany. Finally, it is an investigation of the synergistic relationship in Happel's writings between the booming print media industry and the evolution of the German novel.

---

10. Fritz Wahrenburg, *Funktionswandel des Romans und aesthetische Norm: Die Entwicklung seiner Theorie in Deutschland bis zur Mitte des 18. Jahrhunderts*, Studien zur allgemeinen und vergleichenden Literaturwissenschaft 11 (Stuttgart: Metzler, 1976); Johannes Burckhardt and Christine Werckstetter, eds., *Kommunikation und Medien in der Frühen Neuzeit*, Historische Zeitschrift, Beiheft 41 (Munich: Oldenbourg, 2005).

11. James Tracy, ed., *The Rise of Merchant Empires: Long-Distance Trade in the Early Modern World, 1550–1750*, Studies in Comparative Early Modern History (Cambridge: Cambridge University Press, 1990); Lynne Tatlock, "Selling Turks: Eberhard Werner Happel's *Turcica* (1683–1690)," *Colloquia Germanica* 28, nos. 3–4 (1995): 307–37; Gabor Agoston, "Information, Ideology, and the Limits of Imperial Policy: Ottoman Grand Strategy in the Context of Ottoman-Habsburg Rivalry," in *The Early Ottomans: Remapping the Empire*, ed. Virginia Aksan and Daniel Goffman (Cambridge: Cambridge University Press, 2007), 75–103.

Acknowledgments

❧

Newspapers have played an important role in my life as far back as I can remember. So have novels ever since I picked the first one off the bookshelf in my parent's home in Germany. As a teenager, I thought I might like to be a journalist. Instead, I entered the academy, studied comparative literature, and specialized first in medieval and later in early modern German and French literature and culture. As I progressed in my chosen field, I discovered that this period, specifically the seventeenth century, gave birth to one of my favorite media—namely, newspapers as we understand them today. Moreover, in the course of my research on the prolific journalist/writer Johannes Praetorius (1630–80), I realized that news reports exerted an extraordinary influence on his literary production. Through my work on Praetorius, I found my way to another hugely successful writer of the period, Eberhard Werner Happel (1647–90), who, like Praetorius, also excelled in journalistic writings. Beyond this, however, Happel produced lengthy and immensely popular novels, many, though not all, based on news reports. Happel's novelistic masterworks have attracted and kept my attention for the past several years, eventually resulting in the study you have before you.

As is always the case with a multidisciplinary and multimedia research project, many debts have been incurred, which I would like to acknowledge with much gratitude. First, I am thankful to Washington University's generous research support in both time and money, without which this project could not have been undertaken. I was able to significantly advance this work during two sabbatical leaves. The resources of Washington University's Olin Library provided materials on-site and access to resources elsewhere, through the library's excellent loan services and the expert assistance of Brian Vetruba.

This project, as others before it, has benefited from Carol Jenkins's incomparable research and editorial skills. John Morris once again, lent his impeccable editorial assistance as I moved toward completion of the volume. I have worked with both of them in productive and enjoyable cooperation for many years. Without Jill Edwards's professional support and warm friendship, many tasks might have never seen completion.

Having discovered Happel's novels much earlier, my colleague and friend Lynne Tatlock supported this project through her own research on this author. Moreover, she supplied me with a copy of the *Ungarische Kriegs-Roman*, all six volumes of it. This generous act of sharing made it possible for me to do much of the work in my St. Louis home.

Regular research sojourns at the Herzog-August-Bibliothek, Wolfenbüttel, Germany, moved the project forward at a steady pace. I am happy to express my deep gratitude to the library's professional and helpful staff, particularly Jill Bepler, Volker Bauer, and Christian Hogrefe.

I would like to thank Megan Armstrong for first introducing me to her group of "Ottomans," scholars researching the Ottoman/European interaction in the early modern Mediterranean.

I am indebted to the ever helpful and knowledgeable Holger Boening, director of the Institut für Deutsche Pressforschung at the University of Bremen, Germany. He and Volker Bauer hosted a conference on early modern media at the Herzog August Bibliothek through which I met a number of helpful colleagues in the field. Following this conference, Holger Böning introduced me to Albert Gelver, whose tireless sleuthing and copying provided me valuable newspaper materials from the holdings of the institute. Albert Gelver put me in touch with Peter Bode, who made available to me a copy of Fürst Abaffi's *Manifesto*. I am most grateful to all of them.

My colleagues Magnus Ressel, Markus Friedrich, Wolfgang Kaiser, and Anna Busquets Alemany permitted me access to their research, some of it yet to be published. My book is infinitely richer because of their generosity. At a conference on the topic of outsiders (*Aussenseiter*) that was hosted by Rudolf Schlögl and held in Konstanz, Germany, I met colleagues whose research on pirates and corsairs proved to be very important to this book. My colleague from Down Under, Matthew Glozier, alerted me to his monograph on Friedrich von Schomberg, thus introducing me to information that I otherwise would have missed.

During the last ten or so years, my colleague and friend Flemming Schock, expert in all things Happel, helped me in ways too numerous to count. He provided information about online and print resources. He patiently and reliably shared with me his deep knowledge of seventeenth-century news and novel writing. In the end, he and Gerhard Dünnhaupt rendered the most valuable help: they read the complete manuscript and made numerous suggestions for changes and corrections that significantly improved the book.

I thank the anonymous readers at the University of Michigan Press for their endorsements. My warmest expressions of appreciation go to Ellen Bauerle and Alexa Ducsay of the University of Michigan Press for their expert support. For Ellen and me, this is a reunion of sorts. She and I worked together several years ago on my first publication with the press.

Finally, I dedicate this book to Mark S. Wrighton, chancellor of Washington University in St. Louis, and to Edward S. Macias, former provost at Washington University, for their tireless work in the service of making WU a great institution and for being unfailingly supportive of the scholarly side of my dual appointment as a member of the administration and the Faculty of Arts and Sciences.

I gratefully acknowledge permission from the following publications: "Staging the News: The Theater of Passions and Politics in Eberhard Werner Happel's *Dess Englischen Eduards* (1690/1)," in *Dimensionen der Theatrum-Metapher in der Frühen Neuzeit: Ordnung und Repräsentation des Wissens*, ed. Flemming Schock et al. (Hannover: Wehrhahn, 2008), 369–89; "Grenz-gänger: Fiktive Begegnungen mit historischen Helden (Emmerich Töckely und Friedrich von Schomberg)," in Volker Bauer and Holger Böning, Die Entstehung des Zeitungswesens im 17. Jahrhundert: Ein neues Medium und seine Folgen für das Kommunikationssystem der Frühen Neuzeit. Bremen: edition lumière, 2011, 269–81; "Romancing the News: History and Romance in Eberhard Happel's 'Deß Teutschen Carls' (1690) and 'Deß Engelländischen Eduards' (1691)," in Mara R. Wade, ed., *Gender Matters: Discourses of Violence in Early Modern Literature and the Arts* (Rodopi); "Early Modern Translation and Transfer: Mixing but (Not) Matching Languages," which will appear in a collection edited by Bethany Wiggin.

Abbreviations

৯

AR   *Der Academische Roman* (1690)
AT   *Der Afrikanische Tarnolast* (1689)
BM   *Der Bayrische Max* (1692)
EE   *Der Engelländische Eduard* (1691)
ER   *Europäische Relation*
FC   *Der Frantzösische Cormantin* (1687)
IM   *Der Insulanische Mandorell* (1682)
IS   *Der Italienische Spinelli,* sometimes also the *Italiänische
       Spinelli* (1685)
KB   *Türckis. Estats- und Krieges-Bericht* (1683–84)
KC   *Kern-Chronica* (1690)
NM   *Nordische Mercurius*
OB   *Der Ottomanische Bajazet* (1688)
RC   *[Hamburger] Relations-Courir*
SQ   *Der Spanische Quintana* (1686)
TC   *Der Teutsche Carl* (1690)
TE   *Theatrum Europaeum*
ThEx *Thesaurus Exoticorum* (1688)
UK   *Der Ungarische Kriegs-Roman* (1685–97)

ONE

Setting the Stage

ℰ

Happel's Novels

Between the invention of movable type and the birth of the Internet, the development that had the most lasting impact on human communication was the emergence of the periodical press: the regularly delivered daily, weekly, and monthly news reports that began to be published in Germany during the first decade of the seventeenth century.[1] The periodical press profoundly affected the national and international exchange of ideas and transfer of news. Its impact can be seen in written texts of all kinds, particularly in the newly emerging and increasingly popular narrative genre of the novel. The news media were to play an unusually important role in the German novel of the seventeenth century, rendering it fertile ground for the examination of mutual influences. Moreover, to explore the interaction of multiple European and non-European cultures reflected in the great variety of print media in the seventeenth century is especially fitting at the present time, when globalization is on everyone's mind and in everyone's discourse.[2] The seventeenth century is acquiring new currency in our thought exactly

1. Carsten Prange, *Die Zeitungen und Zeitschriften des 17. Jahrhunderts in Hamburg und Altona: Ein Beitrag zur Publizistik der Frühaufklärung* (Hamburg: Hans Christians, 1978), 9–16; Holger Böning, *Welteroberung durch ein neues Publikum: Die deutsche Presse und der Weg zur Aufklärung; Hamburg und Altona als Beispiel* (Bremen: Edition Lumière, 2002), 13–25.

2. The bibliography is endless and growing daily. Here are a few of the most recent entries: Jürgen Osterhammel and Niels P. Petersson, *Globalization: A Short History*, trans. Dona Geyer (Princeton: Princeton University Press, 2005); Margaret C. Jacob, *Strangers Nowhere in the World: The Rise of Cosmopolitanism in Early Modern Europe* (Philadelphia: University of Philadelphia Press, 2006).

because current globalizing energies touch almost all economic, political, and cultural environments. They resonate with the contemporary reader because we see them emerge already in the baroque, in the early modern colonizing ambitions that pushed European powers to aggressively broaden their reach across their borders to distant lands. Striving for economic wealth and political power by subjugating (or, at the very least, gaining influence over) faraway countries and cultures, European hegemonic ambitions competed for resources of all kinds: gold, spices, hardwood, silk, and especially slaves, the human capital whose labor was perceived as indispensable in the increasingly competitive world market.[3]

In the latter half of the seventeenth century, Eberhard Werner Happel was one of the authors whose writings recorded this early modern race toward European global dominance. A tireless producer of news collections, histories, and multivolume novels, many of which melded conventional seventeenth-century convoluted fictions with contemporary events and personalities, Happel reflected on the cultural dynamics of his time, which are often reminiscent of those of our present day. From his media-rich observation point in the bustling and powerful merchant city of Hamburg, he reported on a German Empire that was politically fractured and threatened by endless wars, by the voracious trading and colonizing appetites of its neighbors Sweden and Denmark, and by the growing imperial ambitions of France, the Netherlands, England, and the Ottoman Porte.[4]

---

3. The literature on the early modern Atlantic and Mediterranean slave trade is vast. Some of the most recent studies are Salvatore Bono, *Piraten und Korsaren im Mittelmeer: Seekrieg, Handel und Sklaverei vom 16. bis 19. Jahrhundert*, trans. Achim Wurm (Stuttgart: Klett-Cotta, 2009); Douglas R. Burgess Jr., *The Pirates' Pact: The Secret Alliances between History's Most Notorious Buccaneers and Colonial America* (New York: McGraw-Hill, 2008); Robert C. Davis, *Christian Slaves, Muslim Masters: White Slavery in the Mediterranean, the Barbary Coast, and Italy, 1500–1800* (London: Palgrave Macmillan, 2004); Suraiya Faroqhi, *The Ottoman Empire and the World around It* (London: Tauris, 2007); Murray Gordon, *Slavery in the Arab World* (New York: New Amsterdam Books, 1989); Robert C. Davis, *Holy War and Human Bondage: Tales of Christian-Muslim Slavery in the Early Modern Mediterranean* (Santa Barbara, CA: ABC-CLIO / Praeger, 2009); Claire Jowitt, *The Culture of Piracy, 1580–1630: English Literature and Seaborne Crime* (Aldershot: Ashgate, 2010).

4. About Hamburg as a thriving media market, see Flemming Schock, *Die Text-Kunstkammer: Populäre Wissenssammlungen des Barock am Beispiel der "Relationes Curiosae" von E. W. Happel*, Beihefte zum Archiv für Kulturgeschichte 68 (Cologne: Böhlau, 2011), 34–46; Kai Lohsträter, "Alles Kriegstheater? Das 'Theatrum Europaeum' im Kontext der Kriegberichterstattung des 17. Jahrhunderts," paper delivered at Interdisziplinärer Workshop des DFG-Projekts "Welt und Wissen auf der Bühne: Die Theatrum-Literatur der Frühen Neuzeit," March 12–13, 2011, University of Kassel, Germany; Günther Dammann, "Fakten und Fiktionen im Roman bei Eberhard Werner Happel, Schriftsteller in Hamburg," in *Hamburg: Eine Metropolregion zwischen*

Produced mostly after Happel settled in Hamburg,[5] his novels document the political sense and the romantic sensibilities of his time. They were so widely read and popular that one of his publishers, Matthaeus Wagner of Ulm, continued to produce and sell new titles under Happel's name for several years after the author's death.[6] This study will explore Happel's astonishing intellectual, cultural, and social reach as he guided readers across the European continent and beyond, to the Near East, the Far East, Africa, and Asia.

Wann ich/ ein jener Weltweise/ gefraget würde/ wie mein Vatterland hiesse/ würde ich ihm antworten: Die Welt. . . . Solchem nach habe mir die Welt zu meinem Vatterland erkohren. . . . Darum sollen wir unsern Sinn auf keinen Ort allein wenden/ sondern uns dessen bescheiden/ daß wir nicht einem Winckel zu- oder angebohren/ und daß vielmehr die gantze Welt unser Vatterland sey. Wann aber die gantze Welt mein Vatterland/ so thue ich ja nicht übel/ wann ich den Ruhm der gantzen Welt/ nach meinem Vermögen/ außbreite. Was ist fürtrefflicher als die Welt/ du magst ein Stück loben was dier beliebet/ so wirst du solches an einem Theil der Welt am besten thun können.[7]

Früher Neuzeit und Aufklärung, ed. Johann Anselm Steiger and Sandra Richter, Metropolis: Texte und Studien zu Zentren der Kultur in der Frühen Neuzeit (Berlin: Fink, 2012), 461–66; Christian Meierhofer, "Allerhand Begebenheiten: Happels *sogenannte Europaeische Geschicht-Romane* als Wissensfundus," in *Polyhistorismus und Buntschriftstellerei: Populäre Wissensformen und Wissenskultur in der Frühen Neuzeit*, ed. Flemming Schock, Frühe Neuzeit 169 (Berlin: De Gruyter, 2012), 230–53.

5. "Everhard Gverner Happelius, ein Hesse von Geburth/ hat lange Zeit in Hamburg privatisiret" (Eberhard Werner Happel, a Hessian by birth, has lived as a private writer for a long time in Hamburg). Gottfried Zenner, ed., *Novellen aus der gelehrten und curiösen Welt* (Frankfurt am Main: Augustus Boetius, 1692), 67.

6. One of those is *Der Sächsische Witekind/ Oder so genannter Europaeischer Geschicht-Roman, Auf Das 1692. Jahr; In welchem/ Nach Ahrt deß Italiänischen Spinelli, Spanischen Quintana, Frantzösischen Cormantins/ Ottomanischen Bajazets/ Teutschen Carls/ Engelländischen Eduards und Bayrischen Max, in einer Liebes- und Helden-Geschichte/ die Denck-würdigsten Begebnüssen/ Kriegs- und Politischen Staats-Sachen/ Glücks- und Unglücks- auch hohe Todes-Fälle/ Hoch-Fürstliche Bey- lager/ Schlachten/ Belager- und Eroberungen/ etc. dieses Jahrs unparteyisch beschrieben werden* (Ulm: Matthaeus Wagner, 1692), *Vorrede*.

7. "If I were to be asked by anyone what is my homeland I would respond: The World. . . . In this way I have chosen the world as my home. . . . That is why we should not devote our mind entirely to one place; rather, we should understand that we don't belong to only one little corner, rather that the whole world is our home. If, however, the whole world is my home, it behooves me that I present [to you] the whole world to be best of my ability. What would be better than the world; you can praise what you wish [of the world], you will find that you praise it best."

Reading only one of Happel's novels, his *Weltbürgertum*, would make his self-consciousness and self-confidence as a citizen of the world immediately apparent. Happel's life in Hamburg, that prosperous and intellectually vibrant island, at once both urban and urbane, surrounded by the turmoil of multiple regional wars, profoundly affected his narrative reach. It prompted him to write, though in the German language, a distinctly European novel spanning wide geographies and plumbing significant political and emotional depths.

> Die Welt ist und bleibt ein Allgemeines *Theatrum* und Schauplatz aller Welt-Händeln/ auf welchem Jahr auß/ Jahr ein/ den Aufmercksamen vnd Wissen-Begierigen das Jenige/ was da und dorten sich zuträget/ vnd zwar vielfaltig/ was schon zu andern Zeiten sich ereignet/ von Neuem/ nur mit diesem Unterscheid vorgestellet wird/ daß zwar die Sache an sich selbsten/ biß an wenige Umstände/ fast die Vorige/ vnd nur von andern Personen/ oder in andern Ländern außgeübet/ vnd Menschlicher Beurtheil- und Anschauung vor Augen gestellet wird.[8]

Happel participated in this world on many levels: intellectually, professionally, and economically.[9] From his geographic good fortune as a resident of Hamburg flowed yet another advantage (as Flemming Schock has persuasively argued): namely, that Happel successfully made use of Hamburg's media wealth, which, along with access to the rich store of newspapers produced in Hamburg and elsewhere, included public libraries and private book collections. His contemporary Gottfried Zenner says as much when he comments that Happel settled in Hamburg "wegen der guten Bibliothecen als auch der Verleger halber" (because of the good libraries and also because of the publishers).[10] In his *Ungarische Kriegs-Roman*, Happel gratefully acknowledges the riches of one of those libraries in particular, that of Mayor

---

Eberhard Werner Happel, *Mundi Mirabilis Tripartiti: Oder Wunderbaren Welt In einer kurtzen Cosmographia Fuergestellet*, vol. 2 (Ulm: Daniel Bartholomaeus, 1708).

8. "The world is and remains a general *Theatrum* and a stage for all world activities (actions), on which year after year everything that is new and exciting is presented according to all the particulars which only change in small ways in that we put before you all human judgment and opinions of different persons and countries" (*EE* I: *Vorrede*).

9. For an overview, see Böning, *Welteroberung durch ein neues Publikum*, 73ff.; Uta Egenhoff, *Berufsschriftstellertum und Journalismus in der Frühen Neuzeit: Eberhard Werner Happels Relationes Curiosae im Medienverbund des 17. Jahrhunderts*, Presse und Geschichte 33 (Bremen: Edition Lumière, 2008); Schock, *Die Text-Kunstkammer*.

10. Zenner, *Novellen aus der gelehrten und curiösen Welt*, 67.

Julius Surland (1657–1703), one of the most distinguished among the many Hamburg book collectors. The dedication (*Zuschrifft*) of August 12, 1687, praises Surland's library as a "herrliche Bibliothec" (beautiful library) that, as it continued to grow, would become one of the most famous ("curieusesten" [most amazing]) in the world.[11]

Hamburg was also occasionally home to the well-known writer Philipp von Zesen (1619–89), who, in 1642, founded the *Teutschgesinnte Genossenschaft* in an effort to advance the German language toward literary distinction at a time when the market was very much dominated by all things French. A few decades later, Johann Rist, founder in 1658 of the Elbschwanenorden, became, like Happel, a journalist and a writer of novels.[12] Of equally great importance for Happel and his writer colleagues was the arrival in Hamburg of Georg Greflinger (1618–77), who, aside from his work as a historian, translator, and poet, gained fame as one of the first news editors. He founded the *Nordische Mercurius*, a newspaper that would be the source of many of the news reports that found their way into Happel's novels.[13] Hamburg's energetic media market was connected to all the important European news centers, ensuring a reliable and uninterrupted supply of news and newspapers.[14] Thus, it is not surprising that the first media theorist, Kaspar Stieler (1632–1707), though not a resident of Hamburg, was, like Rist, a member of one of the most renowned German literary societies, the Fruchtbringende Gesellschaft, and a frequent visitor to the city. Here he published his groundbreaking and frequently quoted definition of the news media, the *Zeitungs-Lust und Nutz* (1695).[15]

Scholars in the field of media studies have devoted a great deal of attention to the emergence of newspapers and newspaper collections and their influences on early modern communication, literature, and culture. Happel figures very large in such research, with several recent studies centering on Happel's news writings. Both Uta Egenhoff and Flemming Schock, for example, have analyzed Happel's famous nonfiction work the *Relationes*

---

11. Schock, *Die Text-Kunstkammer*, 45; Eberhard Werner Happel, *Der Ungarische Kriegs-Roman*, 6 vols. (Ulm: Matthaeus Wagner, 1685–97), II: dedication.

12. Rist went to school in Hamburg, and after several years as pastor in Wedel (not far from Hamburg), he joined other writers in Hamburg as one of the most important religious poets of the time (Schock, *Die Text-Kunstkammer*, 48).

13. Schock, *Die Text-Kunstkammer*, 48.

14. For a detailed introduction, see Wolfgang Behringer, *Im Zeichen des Merkur: Reichspost und Kommunikationsrevolution in der Frühen Neuzeit*, Veröffentlichungen des Max-Planck-Instituts für Geschichte 189 (Göttingen: Vandenhoeck und Ruprecht, 2003).

15. Böning, *Welteroberung durch ein neues Publikum*, 33, 96, 113, 57, 34.

Curiosae (1681–91), taking a close look not only at the work itself but at the cultural environment from which it emerged.[16] Setting aside Happel's work as a novelist, both scholars, following Carsten Prange, focus almost exclusively on his journalistic achievements. Holger Böning has opened our eyes to the burgeoning influence of the Hamburg media market in the seventeenth century. Without their important and pioneering contributions to the research in early modern news printing, none of the most recent work would have been possible or even thinkable.[17]

In *Novel Translations*, her significant study of the evolution of the German novel within the European context, Bethany Wiggin mentions Happel only in passing.[18] In comparison, in his book on the Hungarian uprising and European power politics in the second half of the seventeenth century, Béla Köpeczi offers a detailed review of the six volumes of Happel's *Ungarische Kriegs-Roman* (1685–98).[19] Köpeczi praises Happel's historical and political accuracy and acuity, while blaming those same traits for suffocating the novel's central love story, which Köpeczi calls "psychologically insufficiently grounded" (nicht genügend begründete Liebesgeschichte).[20]

These scholars are of the same mind when highlighting Happel's extensive use of multiple media in his writings, foremost among them news reports, news collections as well as chorographies,[21] and travel writings. Regarding the latter, we know that having studied at the University of Kiel and because of Kiel's closeness to the court of Holstein-Gottorp, Happel was familiar with and frequently made use of the widely popular writings of the traveler and explorer Adam Olearius (1603–71), who famously journeyed through Persia and Russia in the service of the Duke of Holstein-Gottorp. Though

---

16. Egenhoff, *Berufsschriftstellertum und Journalismus in der Frühen Neuzeit*; Schock, *Die Text-Kunstkammer*.

17. Prange, *Die Zeitungen und Zeitschriften*; Böning, *Welteroberung durch ein neues Publikum*; Holger Böning, "Weltaneignung durch neues Publikum: Zeitungen und Zeitschriften als Medientypen der Moderne," in *Kommunikation und Medien in der Frühen Neuzeit*, ed. Johannes Burkhardt, Historische Zeitschrift Beiheft 41 (Munich: Oldenbourg, 2005), 105–37.

18. Bethany Wiggin, *Novel Translations: The European Novel and the German Book, 1680–1730*, Signale: Modern German Letters, Cultures, and Thought (Ithaca: Cornell University Press, 2011), 113–14.

19. Béla Köpeczi, *Staatsräson und Christliche Solidarität: Die ungarischen Aufstände und Europa in der zweiten Hälfte des 17. Jahrhunderts* (Vienna: Böhlaus Nachf., 1983), 353–61.

20. Ibid., 354.

21. "Chorography was a rather peculiar early modern genre that combined history, geography, topography, natural history, antiquities, and genealogies with socioeconomic, political, and cultural descriptions of a particular region." Barbara J. Shapiro, *A Culture of Fact: England, 1550–1720* (Ithaca: Cornell University Press, 2000), 69.

Olearius was no longer among the living by the time Happel came into his own, Happel's frequent mentions make clear that he was familiar with him,[22] not only as a writer but also as a patron of the university and a tireless collector on behalf of Holstein-Gottorp's cabinet of wonders (*Wunderkammer*). Moreover, the foreword of the *Thesaurus Exoticorum* (1688) identifies travel writings as important sources for his books.[23]

Of special importance to this analysis is the fact that Happel mined newspapers for much of the information employed in his novels. News items are woven into the narrative structure as his characters spend considerable time reading, commenting on, and reacting to them.[24] For example, the novels' narrative progress is often driven by news reports about the activities of corsairs and pirates. These seagoing profiteers, whether outlaws or legally sanctioned, made the coastal areas of Europe and the seas beyond unsafe for travelers, merchants, peasants, and fishermen, whom they pursued and captured, either to sell as slaves or to retain for ransom.[25] Likewise present both in newspapers and in Happel's novels is the century-long conflict between the German and Ottoman empires, the struggle for hegemony over eastern Europe, and the quest for the control of Hungary.[26] In addition, Happel fills many pages describing and decrying the religious conflict that affected the whole of Europe after the French revoked the Edict of Nantes (1598) in 1685, driving many French Protestants to seek refuge in neighboring countries or overseas colonies.

Of utmost importance to this study is the fact that Happel's creative life-span corresponds to the beginning of a vigorous trans-European discussion about the nature of the novel and novel writing—the relationship between fact and fiction, between history and romance, and between the rapidly growing community of novel writers and readers in France and England. In this, Happel follows the advice that his near contemporary Sigmund von Birken (1616–64), a famous and successful writer, had directed at the readers of Herzog Anton Ulrich's (1633–1714) six-volume novel *Aramena*. In a preface to the reader ("Vor-Ansprache zum Edlen Leser"), Birken confirms

---

22. Happel mentions Olearius in the *Academische Roman*: AR, 65.

23. *ThEx, Vor-Rede*.

24. For a first exploration of the "newspaper novel" theme, see my "Staging the News: The Theater of Passions and Politics in Eberhard Werner Happel's *Dess Englischen Eduards* (1690/1)," in *Dimensionen der Theatrum-Metapher in der Frühen Neuzeit: Ordnung und Repräsentation des Wissens*, ed. Flemming Schock et al. (Hannover: Wehrhahn, 2008), 369–89.

25. See chapter 3.

26. Köpeczi, *Staatsräson und Christliche Solidarität*, 354–68.

that both histories and novels have their uses, but he contends that more praiseworthy than either are those novels combining history and fiction, novels that Birken calls "Geschichtgedichte und Gedichtgeschichten." Such works offer, according to Birken, a most useful and entertaining pastime ("ein recht-adelicher und dabei hochnützlicher Zeitvertreib"), as opposed to mere histories, which, though useful, tend to bore and even disgust the reader ("jedoch zuweiln mit eckel gelesen").[27] In his address to the reader ("Vor-Ansprache zum Edlen Leser"), the preface to his *Teutsche Rede-bind und Dichtkunst* (1679), Birken reviews the history/fiction dichotomy in greater detail: "die Gedichtgeschicht-Schriften/ behalten zwar die wahrhafte Historie mit ihren haupt-umständen/ dichten aber mehr neben-umstände dazu/ und erzehlen die Sachen nicht in der Ordnung wie sie sich zugetragen" (the fiction-history writings keep to the truth of the historical events, but they add to it events that are not narrated as they unfolded).[28] Setting these up against fiction, he continues, "die Geschichtschriften/ die Geschicht-gedichte/ tragen entweder eine wahrhafftige Geschichte unter dem fürhang erdichteter Namen verborgen . . . oder sind ganz erdichtete Historien" (the historical writings either hide true stories under fictional names . . . or are completely invented narrations).[29]

How much this discussion was on Happel's mind is apparent in the frequency with which he addressed the topic of these narrative dichotomies and their impact in the prefaces of his novels. Finally, careful examination of Happel's novels reveals that the dramatic play with gender and social and national identities is ubiquitous on both sides of his repeatedly elaborated duality of fact and fiction.

Happel about Happel

What little we know of Happel's life comes from two sources, both products of his own pen. He briefly comments on his life's challenges in his own voice in his address to the reader when he reviews the circumstances, creation, and publishing history of the novel *Der Afrikanische Tarnolast*.[30] In addi-

---

27. Anton Ulrich Herzog von Braunschweig-Lueneburg, *Die durchleuchtige Syrerinn Aramena* (1669), pt. 1, ed. Blake Lee Spahr, facsimile of the first edition (Bern: Lang, 1975), *Vor-Ansprache zum Edlen Leser*. I am grateful to Professor Dünnhaupt for this information.
28. Ernst Weber, ed., *Texte zur Romantheorie*, vol. 1 (Munich: Fink, 1974), 89.
29. Ibid., 81.
30. Eberhard Werner Happel, *Der Afrikanische Tarnolast* (1689), ed. John D. Lindberg, 4

tion, a comment published shortly after his death points to the *Academische Roman* (1690) as a hidden source for his biography ("seiner Jungend Lebens-Lauff hat er in den *Academischen Roman* verdeckter Weise beschrieben" [a description of his youth he hid in the story of the *Academische Roman*]).[31] More detailed information about the *Tarnolast's* gestation is contained in a fictional autobiography embedded in the novel *Der Teutsche Carl*, also published in 1690. According to the accounts given in both novels, Happel came to writing by happenstance in 1666, at nineteen years of age, when he sought relief from melancholy at a time when things did not look especially promising for him: "[M]eine *Melancholischen* Gedancken zu vertreiben/ ich/ nachdem ich meine *Academische Scripta* und *Lectiones repetiret/* die übrige Zeit auf eine andere Weise zu versüssen gedachte. Nemlich/ meine Gedancken und Sinne *applicirten sich/* da ich kaum das neunzehende Jahr meines Alters überschritten, zu einem *ROMAN*, und solchem nach habe ich damahlen diesen *TARNOLAST* begonnen" (In an effort to drive away my melancholy thoughts and to sweeten the time after my academic work and having repeated my lessons. That is, when I was barely nineteen years old my thoughts and my mind turned to a novel, and so I started the *Tarnolast* in those days).[32]

One year later, poverty would drive Happel from his home, his family, and his studies.[33] He finished the *Tarnolast* in 1670, while living in Hamburg, and deposited it with printer/publisher Johan Naumann, hoping that it would soon reach his reading public. But Naumann tarried over the publication until his death made it impossible. Nineteen years passed before the *Tarnolast* was issued by the print shop of Matthaeus Wagner in Ulm, who would also publish several of Happel's subsequent novels. As Happel jokingly comments in the *Tarnolast's* preface, it was high time, as the book threatened to become his "Opus Posthumum." He was right: he died in 1690.

The basic narrative ingredients characteristic of Happel's style are already in place in the *Tarnolast*, his first novel. In his later novels, however, Happel becomes a more disciplined, more knowledgeable, and stylistically more adventurous writer. Looking back on his earlier writings, a mature Happel

vols., Bibliothek des Literarischen Vereins in Stuttgart 305–8 (Stuttgart: Anton Hiersemann, 1982).

31. Zenner, *Novellen aus der gelehrten und curiösen Welt*, 67.

32. Happel, *Der Afrikanische Tarnolast*, address to the reader.

33. "Nachdem ich aber etwas mehr/ als ein Jahr/ darüber zugebracht/ kam ein neuer Sturm/ der mich über Berg und Thal auß meinem Vatterland hinweg risse" (*AT: Vorrede*).

comments critically on his occasional slips into his native Hessian dialect: "Du wirst . . . zwar einen mercklichen Unterschied finden/ inmassen Er [*Tarnolast*] mit dem Hessischen *Dialect* hin und wieder angefüllet" (You will find a bit of a difference in that the *Tarnolost* is filled, here and there, with a Hessian dialect [*AT: Vorrede*]).

Between 1666 and 1690 (and even beyond), many and varied publications were to follow upon Happel's "first conceived" work ("am ersten empfangen worden"). Judging by comments from contemporaries, Happel's writings enjoyed great popularity and sold well. When the *Afrikanische Tarnolast* finally reached booksellers in 1689, the novel had the good fortune of attracting the attention of one of the great minds of the late seventeenth century, the philosopher, scholar, and literary critic Christian Thomasius (1655–1728),[34] who devoted a much-quoted review to Happel's first novel, praising the author's ability to effectively convey to the reader the otherness of Prince Tarnolast's African culture and upbringing.[35]

Happel offers additional information about the vagaries of his life and art in the fictionalized biography recounted in installments by Baldrich, one of the characters in the *Teutsche Carl* (1690).[36] Once again, Happel mentions the hardships of laboring over his first novel for about a year, at which point his family's poverty forced him to leave his native Hesse.[37] In the *Carl*, he speaks about himself in the third person, adopting the pseudonym "Kirchberg" by combining part of the name of his birthplace, Kirchhain, with part of the name of the place where his father had served as Lutheran pastor, Rauschenberg. (In the following discussion, I will refer to the protagonist as Kirchberg/Happel.) This autobiographical sketch tells the story of a man who had "sein Leben lang seltzame Ebentheuer außgestanden" (in his life had many remarkable experiences [*TC* I: 70]), the first of which involved his schooling. As a pastor's son, Kirchberg/Happel was destined for the academy, despite the fact that he profoundly disliked school as a boy—so much so that he lied, cheated, and repeatedly fled his boarding school in an effort to return to his village and his parents. He much preferred roaming the countryside with peasant boys to learning lessons at school. The fact that

34. Christian Thomasius, "Eberhardi Guerneri Happelii Africanischer Tarnolast," in *Freimütige, lustige und ernsthafte, jedoch vernunftsmässige Gedanken oder Monatsgespräche . . .* , ed. Christian Thomasius (1689; repr., Frankfurt am Main: Athenaeum, 1972), 697–806.

35. Ibid., 731, 737.

36. Eberhard Werner Happel, *Dess Teutschen Carls/ Oder so genannten Europäischen Geschicht-Romans auf das 1689. Jahr* (Ulm: Matthaeus Wagner, 1690).

37. Ibid., 134.

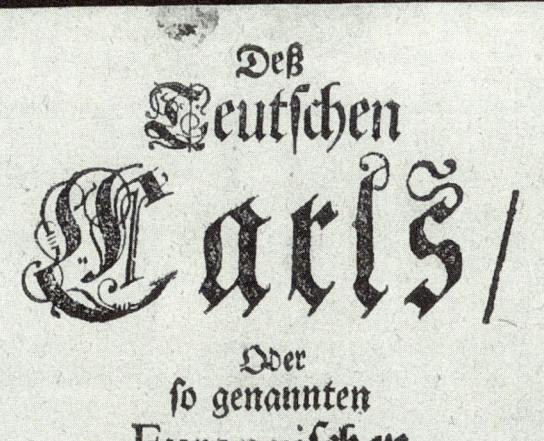

Deß
Teutschen
Carls/
Oder
so genannten
Europæischen
Geschicht- ROMANS,
Auf
Das 1689. **Jahr/**
Dritter Theil.
Worinnen
Unter
Einer angenehmen Schreib-Art/
nach Weise der vorigen Geschicht-Roma-
nen/ angeführet und abgehandelt werden/ die
Merck-würdigsten Fürfälle und Begebenheiten jetzt-
besagten Jahrs/ auch andere Lesens-würdige
Materien von allerhand Sachen;
Aufgesetzet
Von
Everhardo Gvernero Happelio.

U L M/
Druckts und verlegts Matthæus Wagner/ 1690.

Fig. 1. Eberhard Werner Happel's *Dess Teutschen Carls/ Oder so genannten Europäischen Geschicht-Romans auf das 1689. Jahr* (Ulm: Matthaeus Wagner, 1690) (Herzog August Bibliothek, Wolfenbüttel)

school was a social leveler ("Schul wuste keinen Unterschied der Classen") and therefore offered one of the few opportunities for social and economic advancement in the rigid early modern class system little impressed the boy Kirchberg/Happel.

Nevertheless, the boy's father prevailed, and, at age sixteen, Kirchberg/Happel was sent on to the University of Marburg to study first medicine and then law and mathematics.[38] To supplement his income, Kirchberg/Happel intermittently worked as a tutor while also laboring over the *Afrikanische Tarnolast*.[39] Before he ever finished any degree, however, his father had to follow a call to another parish financially less profitable than the one he left behind (*TC* I: 98). The attendant scarcity of funds prompted Kirchberg/Happel to interrupt his studies. He and a fellow student and cousin decided to "walk a hole into the world," taking along nothing but a change of shirts and half a French crown, all the money Kirchberg/Happel's mother could spare her son (*TC* I: 138). They found themselves begging for sustenance from local clergy along the way, with varying success.

The vagaries of their wanderings make for interesting reading, offering a finely drawn description of the life and state of mind of two young, very poor students on the road. Securing a meal and a place to sleep presented a constant challenge. They had to depend on the charity of strangers—the local pastor or chaplain, a generous peasant, or the occasional helpful innkeeper. Not always able to find food and shelter, the two journeying students frequently suffered from hunger and cold. They wandered through Thuringia; they saw Erfurt and Jena and spent time in Magdeburg, noting that the city was still scarred by the devastating siege of 1631. Eventually, the two companions had a falling out and went their separate ways. Kirchberg/Happel turned to Hamburg/Harburg, where he supported himself once again by tutoring. Three years later, he moved on to the University of Kiel, where, as we read in the novel, his fine reputation as a teacher ("die Zahl seiner Discipeln wuchs von Tag zu Tag" [the number of his pupils grew daily]) earned him a more lucrative teaching position, including a salary, along with the mere room and board he had heretofore been forced to

---

38. Eberhard Werner Happel, *Der Insulanische Mandorell (1682)*, ed. Stefanie Stockhorst, Bibliothek seltener Text in Studienausgaben 12 (Berlin: Weidler, 2007), 645–46.

39. "[D]a ihm die Zeit Anfangs ziemlich lang werden wolte/ dannenhero setzte er sich nieder/ und fienge an/ einen ROMAN zu schreiben. Herbst 1666, 19 Jahre alt . . . zurück zum Vater ohne Geld; dann mit einem Verwandten in die Welt" (Since time was heavy on his hands, he sat down and began to write a novel. In the fall of 1666 he returned to his father as he was broke; then he left again with a relative to explore the world [*TC* I: 137]); *AT* I: *Vorrede*.

accept (*TC* I: 204).[40] Duke Frederick III of Holstein-Gottorp was interested in learning and trade and also in a lavish lifestyle, which he supported by securing a piece of the Oriental and Muscovite silk and hardwood trade for his tiny principality.[41] He was also renowned for his patronage of the University of Kiel and of Adam Olearius. Throughout his journeying days as a student, Happel continued to work on the *Afrikanische Tarnolast*.[42] At this point, owing to the frequent interruptions in his education brought about by his financial hardships, Kirchberg/Happel was eleven years senior to most of his fellow students.

By the mid-sixties, Kirchberg/Happel left the University of Kiel for a financially and socially more profitable teaching position at a wealthy court in the country, close to the ducal court of Holstein-Gottorp.[43] Life was good at this court: Kirchberg/Happel was given a horse to ride and a reasonable salary and was living as if in Utopia (*TC* I: 206). Unfortunately, Holstein-Gottorp was part of Sweden at the time, and when Denmark broke with Sweden ("brach mit Schweden/ zu deß Kaysers und Römischen Reichs Vortheil" [*TC* I: 206]), his patron left for Vienna, and Kirchberg/Happel returned to Hamburg.

In the end, Kirchberg/Happel overcame his many familial and personal challenges and achieved happiness and success as a writer/journalist in Hamburg, where he was granted residence rights (*Bürgerrecht*) in 1685. He lived in the city until his death in 1690; his travel plans, as Flemming Schock tells us, apparently came to naught. Beyond what Happel conveys in these novels about his life and beyond the list of publications he provides in the novel *Der Spanische Quintana*, in the forewords to several other novels, and in part 2 of the *Mundus Mirabilis Triparti*, this is essentially all we know about him. We do know, however, that his novels were bought and read by enough people that he was able to support himself and his family with his earnings as a writer. Gottfried Zenner mentions with admiration the many books, especially novels, that Happel had published by the time of his death, as well

40. According to Schuwirth, Happel did not teach there: Theo Schuwirth, *Eberhard Werner Happel (1647–1690): Ein Beitrag zur deutschen Literatur des 17. Jahrhunderts* (Marburg, 1908).

41. Samuel H. Baron, ed., *The Travels of Olearius in Seventeenth-Century Russia* (Stanford: Stanford University Press, 1967), introduction, 3–30.

42. "[D]aselbst arbeitete ich von neuem/ auch in meinem *miserabelsten* Zustand . . . an dem angefangenen *TARNOLAST*" (even in my horrible state there I began work anew on the *Tarnolast* [*AT* I: III]).

43. "Sein Patron hielt eine Tafel und Hof/ wie ein mächtiger Reichs-Graf. . . . Er war ein Holsteinischer von Adel" (his patron kept his estate like a powerful duke. . . . He was of Holstein nobility [*TC* I: 206]).

as Happel's enthusiasm for his writing. Commenting on the *Academische Roman*, Zenner notes that Happel "hat seine Bücher-Lust in dieses Wercks ersten Vorrede contestiret/ vnd gewünschet in eine öffentliche grosse Bibliothek gesetzt zu werden" (had articulated his love for books in the preface of this work and noted that he would love to become part of a large public [he probably meant "well-known"] library).[44] It is surprising, then, that Happel fell from readers' favor with startling swiftness by the early eighteenth century, leaving later authors like Eichendorff to characterize his novels as confused and confusing, a "Mischmasch"—a fate that Grimmelshausen, Gryphius, and Opitz, only a few of Happel's contemporaries, managed to escape.[45]

History and Romance / Fact and Fiction

Eberhard Werner Happel went very deliberately about constructing his seemingly unstructured works. The prefaces of almost all of his novels mention an overarching theme, a methodology even, according to which he organizes his narratives: namely, the amalgamation of fact and fiction (*Geschichte* [*historia*] and *Romanisirung*). To this must be added a second theme that is based on a concept of performance: Happel's texts, whether novels or news compendiums, are meant to teach the young through performances on the virtual stage that is the world. This theme (one could call it a mission) is based on Happel's conviction that those ignorant of history are like the blind vainly searching in the dark for directions.[46] This teaching mission, the presentation of the fullness of the human drama—war and peace, crime and punishment, love and hate—unfolds, as I will describe in greater detail, on Happel's world stage in print ("Theatro oder Schau-Platz"), highlighting the theatrical quality of all of his work. Extending the metaphor, Happel goes even further, describing the stage of his works as a mirror in which is reflected the theater that is the world ("Dinge . . . welche auff den Theatris, als in einem Spiegel/ praesentirt wird" [*ISI: Vorrede*]). His playing with identity confusions based on gender, class, and nationalities adds, as we shall see, to this theatricality, this staged quality.

The preface to volume 1 of Happel's novel *Der Spanische Quintana Oder*

---

44. Zenner, *Novellen aus der gelehrten und curiösen Welt*, 67.

45. See Schock, *Die Text-Kunstkammer, Epilog*, 365–81.

46. "[W]ie blinde Leute/gleichsam im Finstern tappen" (*SQ* I: *Vorrede*); "Ohne dieselbe tappen wir im Finstern" (*FC* I: *Vorrede*).

Sogenannter Europaeischer Geschicht-Roman Auf Das 1686. Jahr presents several of the themes that reveal the interaction of news media, history, and fiction characteristic of Happel's novels in general and of his historical novels, his *Geschicht-Romane*, in particular.

> Hoch- und vielgeneigter Leser. Allhier bekommest du den 1. Theil unsers so genannten Spanischen Quintana zu sehen/ und in diesem und dessen übrigen Theilen wird dir alles das Remarquableste/ so in und um Europa in diesem jetzt lauffenden 1686. Jahre . . . vorgelauffen/ unter einer angenehmen *Romanisirung* fürgestellet/ also/ daß fürnehmlich die zarte Jugend auf diese Weise gute Wissenschafft um die Geschichten dieser Zeit bekommen wird. . . . Die *Historie* ist ein solch nützlich Werck/ daß wir ohne dieselbe/ wie blinde Leute/ gleichsam im Finstern tappen würden/ darum ist es hoch nothing/ daß man die *Geschichten unserer Zeit* fleissig aufzeichnet/ welches von diesem auf dies/ von jenem auf andere Weise geschiehet. Ich habe mir die *Romanische Weise* hiebey am bequemsten düncken lassen/ und lebe der Versicherung/ es werde der geneigte Leser seine Belustigung haben in Durchlesung dieses Quintana, eben also/ wie bey unserem Spinelli, bey Gelegenheit seine Ergötzung finden. (Emphasis mine)[47]

These often-repeated comments speak to the duality of spinning pleasant love stories, *Romanisirung(en)* or fiction, and embedding them into facts, *historia*.[48] Never missing an opportunity to promote his work, Happel

---

47. "Dear Reader, here I offer you the first part of our *Spanische Quintana*, where you will find everything assembled which is in Europe in this current 1686th year . . . all gathered within the fictional action so that the tender youth will, in this way, be introduced to the good sciences and history of the present time. . . . History is such a useful work that without her we are like the blind unable to find our way. Therefore it is important that we diligently record the stories of our times, which one does this way, another that way. I have found that the way of telling a romance is the most comfortable [way to do this], and I am assured that my reader will find enjoyment in perusing the *Quintana* just as he did with our *Spinelli*."

48. Compare the introduction of *Der Engelländische Eduard* (*EE* III: *Vorrede*): "Es bleibet aber der Author nicht nur bey der blossen *Romanisirung*; sondern ist bemühet/ unter diesem Liebes- und Helden-Gedicht/ auch die vornehmste Handlung und Verrichtungen so wol in Kriegs- als auch in andern Sachen . . . ohne Zusatz/ oder Jemanden Nachtheil/ wie es einem *Historico* geziemet/ Unpartheyisch . . . mit einzuflechten" (The author does, however, not rest with simple fictionalizing; rather, he tries to combine tales of lovers and of heroes with reports on important actions and activities as well as with tales of war and other things . . . without adding anything that [would be] to anyone's disadvantage, just as it is the duty of an historian, namely, to be neutral).

reminds his readers how much they had enjoyed the novel dealing with the events of the preceding year, the *Italiänische Spinelli*.

Here and elsewhere, Happel further subdivides the category "history" into the "descriptions of many kingdoms and countries and . . . the most memorable events that took place in Europe . . . [in 1690], the year just past" (*EE* I: *Vorrede*).[49] Supporting his claim to truthfulness on the part of the author/*Historico* and to neutrality as a narrator, Happel insists that nothing even remotely untrue could have slipped into his narrative.[50] Rather, he relates only "what is taken from reports generally considered authentic and publicly available" (*EE* III: *Vorrede*). As for the romance (*Romanische Außziehrung*), he leaves it to the acuity of the reader to separate romance from fact—in this case, from historical fact.[51]

Happel's novels present a challenge to the modern reader's perseverance. He mixes and matches multiple media; blends romance with newspaper accounts, geographies, chorographies, and biographies; and incorporates voyages to distant shores, encounters with strange peoples, and detailed reports on worldwide political and economic developments with discussions of wonders and science. That said, these novels are treasure troves of information, providing myriad insights into the culture and thinking of the second half of the seventeenth century.[52] They bear witness both to the vigorous and profitable media market, which intended to entertain and instruct, and to the vibrancy of fiction writing and fiction reading in German-speaking countries. Indeed, these novels move along the "news-novel-axis," the influence of news reporting on novel production, which Lennard Davis identifies as characteristic of the early modern English novel.[53] Consequently, as

---

49. This is much like the introduction to the *Teutsche Carl*: "[E]ine und jede andere vorfallende Historische Merck-würdige Begebenheiten an ihrem Ort/ und zu ihrer Zeit/ auf Historische/ das ist/ Unpartheyische Weise/ eingeführt werden/ und zwar Alles unter einem Lieblichen Helden-Roman, welche Schreibens-Art/ so viel ich annoch mercke/ den meisten Liebhabern meiner Wercken am Besten gefallen" (All noteworthy historical events, where and when they occurred, are presented and reported according to the manner of historical writing, that is, without taking sides, all of it presented in a lovely heroic novel according to the manner of writing that I know most pleases the lovers of my work [*TC* I: *Vorrede*]).

50. "[J]edoch unpartheyisch/ und zumahl nicht/ jemand im geringsten zu touchiren/ hierinnen finden" (You will find it here, however, very impartial and not in the least touched up [changed] [*Der Frantzösischen Cormatin, Vorrede*]).

51. "[S]ondern denen sonsten für *Authentisch* gehaltenen Berichten und *publiquen* Schrifften zumessen" (however, always part of authentic reports and public documents [*EE* III: *Vorrede*]).

52. Brean Hammond and Shaun Regan, *Making the Novel: Fiction and Society in Britain, 1660–1789* (New York: Palgrave Macmillan, 2006), 16.

53. Catherine Gallagher, "The Rise of Fictionality," in *The Novel: History, Geography, and*

an exceedingly popular novelist, Happel might be seen as belonging to the group of early modern writers whom William Warner defines as "entertainers and media workers, rather than as authors."[54] Happel's novels deliver outspoken testimony to the force of the rapidly expanding print media market in Hamburg, which, even during the volatile seventeenth century, kept itself politically and economically intact by playing its geographic and diplomatic cards right, thus staying out of the power plays between Denmark, Sweden, France, England, and the German Empire.[55] The importance of Hamburg as the quartermaster to northern and central Europe prompted the powers needing weapons and supplies for the endless military altercations of the seventeenth century to see to it that none exerted exclusive control over the city.

News and Newspapers

The women and men who populate Happel's novels keep on the move as they adjust and respond to changes in their personal lives. They are frequently compelled to escape unwanted parental censure and sexual attention by admirers of both sexes or to search for a long-lost lover/husband/friend, all of which forces them repeatedly to hide their identities behind cross-dressing, changes of name or identity, or all three at once. They are repeatedly torn from their surroundings by pirates or robbers and sold as slaves many times over before fortuitous events lead them back to their loved ones. As Happel's characters move through these trials and tribulations, they habitually mention *Zeitungen*, *Avisen*, and *Relationen*, always sent recently from somewhere else, as the media conveying to them global as well as local news items. These newspapers make their voluntary or involuntary peregrinations less distressing by providing a comforting presence no matter where the characters end up. In fact, his characters' frequent experience of being shipwrecked, lost, or captured is made all the more traumatic by the absence of newspapers. Being taken prisoner often means being cut off from news, which deepens the feeling of isolation, as the German Schenck, a character in the *Quintana*, learns: "Während seiner Gefangenschaft hatte Schenck

---

Culture, ed. Franco Moretti (Princeton: Princeton University Press, 2006), 340, citing Lennard Davis, *Factual Fictions: The Origins of the English Novel* (New York: Columbia University Press, 1983).

54. William B. Warner, *Licensing Entertainment: The Elevation of Novel Reading in Britain, 1684–1750* (Berkeley: University of California Press, 1998), xiii.

55. Schock, *Die Text-Kunstkamme*, 71, 72.

keine Möglichkeit/ auf neue Zeitungen zu schlagen [*sic*]" (During his captivity, Schenck had no opportunity to read a newspaper [*SQ* I: 394]). To be without news was truly to be nowhere. Conversely, the comfort level of the novels' characters is significantly raised by the reality that an increasingly tight-knit communications network—of which the imperial postal system had become the most important part—made news available in most places.

By midcentury, the extensive gathering and wide distribution of news depended largely on the ever-widening net of postal routes and newly established postal centers emerging first in the German Empire and then all over Europe.[56] We find this cultural reality emphasized in the lives of Happel's characters in the *Eduard*, where the articles released on the occasion of Emperor Joseph's election and coronation are quoted in full in the first volume. Item 34 contains detailed instructions as to how the office of the imperial postmaster (*General Erb-Reichs-Postmeister*) should be administered and who should be appointed to this office (*EE* I: 264). While the instructions consist mostly of wording meant to ensure the unimpeded transport of letters and packages across the German Empire, they also affirm that the imperial post office and all its local stations and representatives were to remain unencumbered by any pressure or interference from local authorities.[57]

Returning to his often-expressed notion of the world as a theater, Happel underscores the staged quality of these novels and their news content by having newspapers announced, expected, brought into a room, or received with welcoming comments as part of the narrative ambiance.[58] Serving as important props, newspapers affect the characters' movements and actions. *Zeytungen* are interminably requested, argued over, or quoted as having been read somewhere by someone not currently present. Moreover, characters like Spinelli, the protagonist of the novel bearing his name, read the news to one another for information and enjoyment: "Spinelli schüttelt den Kopff/ als Klaur dies Zeitung herlase/ und bekannte freymüthig/ daß er von dem Englischen Könige eine gantz andere Meinung jederzeit gehabt" (Spinelli

---

56. Wolfgang Behringer, "Veränderung der Raum-Zeit-Relation: Zur Bedeutung des Zeitungs- und Nachrichtenwesens während der Zeit des Dreissigjährigen Krieges," in *Zwischen Alltag und Katastrophe: Der Dreissigjährige Krieg aus der Nähe*, ed. Benigna von Krusenstjern and Hans Medick, Veröffentlichungen des Max-Planck-Instituts für Geschichte (Göttingen: Vandenhoeck und Ruprecht, 1999), 39–81.

57. "[D]aß Unser General-Obrist-Reichs-Postamt in seinem effect erhalten/ und zu dessen Schmählerung nicht vorgenommen/ verwilliget/ oder nachgesehen" (That our general imperial post office be supported and nothing be taken away or reduced (from its authority) [*EE* I: 264]).

58. "[H]eutigen Tages das *Europäische Theatrum* Denckwürdiger Glückes-Wechseln" (The noteworthy changes in fortune in the European theater [*EE* I: 1]).

shook his head as Klaur was reading the paper and admitted readily that heretofore he had harbored a very different opinion of the English king [*IS* IV: 104]). To some degree, reading the news seems also to deconstruct class barriers, at least temporarily. Innkeepers are described as reading newspaper items to their noble patrons: "Nun muß ich/ fuhr jener (der Wirt) wieder fort / meinen Herren etwas fürlesen/ worauß zu sehen/ daß etliche geringere Herren in Verfolgung der Religion bey ihren Unterthanen eben so streng sind/ als der König von Franckreich" (Now I have to read to you, the land-lord continued, something which will tell you that some lower-level lords persecute their subjects just as vigorously as the king of France [*SQ* I: 398]).

During an especially trying episode in his life, the Englishman Eduard expresses his displeasure with the unrelenting stream of bad news (here about England's battles with the Dutch) by insisting that he is sick of the papers ("nunmehr solcher Zeytungen ganz überdrüssig" [*EE* III: 187–88]). Later in the narrative, however, we find Eduard leaving his traveling companions because he wants to read the news just arrived from home about events in England, France, and Ireland.[59] Yet another innkeeper provides Eduard and his companions with several newspapers containing news about the Turk ("am folgenden Tag kam der Hauß-Wirth mit allerhand Zeytungen" [*EE* I: 204]). At one point, Happel even identifies one of his newspaper sources, *Die Venetianische Fama, oder wochentliche Donnerstags-Zeitung* (the *Venetian-ische Fama*, or weekly Thursday paper), "mit allen möglichen Eintragungen von Trontheim, Stockholm, Zürich, Metz, Venedig, Rom, . . . Paris, am 18. September. . . . Auch aus der Türckei und Constantinopel. Die Zeitung ist genau so arrangiert wie die Nachrichten gekommen sind" (with all kinds of news from Trondheim, Stockholm, Zurich, Metz, Venice, Rome, . . . Paris, on September 18. . . . Also from Turkey and Constantinople. The newspaper is exactly organized as the news arrives [i.e., chronologically] [*EE* IV: 204]). This newspaper, according to one of the characters, was produced at the court by a number of "smart people" ("viele kluge Köpfe").

News awaits Happel's travelers upon their arrival at a new town or coun-try, no matter how distant or remote, suggesting that Happel's characters, locales, and events are interconnected by vast and reliable information net-works. An example from the *Spinelli* demonstrates how the news is woven into the novel's action.

---

59. "Eduard hatte sich indessen von der Compagnie abgesondert/ und sein Divertissement in unterschiedlichen eingelauffenen neuen Zeitungen gesucht" (In the meantime, Eduard had left the group and looked for his entertainment in various newspapers [*EE* III: 386]).

Inzwischen kam deß Klauers Diener von Post-Hause/ und brachte allerhand geschriebene und gedruckte Zeitungen/ worinn sich folgende Materien unter anderm funden: Tod der Königin von Dänemark; Probleme in Ungarn mit den Türcken; Tod des Bischofs von Eichstädt (Illustration des Leichenzuges); Uber Londen kamen auß Neu-Jorck in Virginien Brieffe/ daß man daselbst in Bekehrung der Wilden sehr avancire/ und daß die Übersetzung der Bibel in ihre Sprache schon viele unter ihnen so weit kommen/ daß man ihren das Predig- und Vorlese-Amt anvertrauen können. Es sollen zu dem Ende schon über 300. Kirchen gestifftet seyn in selbigem Land. In Thüringen habe zwei Diebe viele Kirchen, Schlösser und Höfe bestohlen. In den Gemächern/ darinnen die Leute geschlaffen/ hätten sie gessen/ getruncken/ und getantzet/ ja gar auff Instrumenten gespielet/ ohne daß jemand davon erwacht wäre. Ihrer Abkunfft nach gabe sie sich vor Schinders-Knechte auß; aus Paris Verschüttungsunglück; aus Ungarn, aus Rotterdam eine Mißgeburt (*IS* II: 5–6).[60]

News reaches the characters wherever they roam in their search for adventure and as they demonstrate prowess in battle or bed, when they are forced to flee predatory fathers or relatives or are diverted during their travels by violent storms, unscrupulous pirates, and the ubiquitous robbers.

Especially stimulating to the seventeenth-century "news junkie" are the big cities, where news from all corners of the globe is collected and disseminated. According to the innkeeper of a Dutch guesthouse where Eduard and his friends briefly lodge, news is nowhere more industriously gathered than in Amsterdam, the bustling and wealthy Dutch merchant city.[61] Here, reports from all across Europe, Africa, the East Indies, and the West Indies

---

60. "In the meantime, Klaur's servant arrived from the postal station with many [hand] written and printed newspapers which contained the following news: the death of the queen of Denmark; problems in Hungary with the Turks; the death of the bishop of Eichstätt (illustration of the funeral). Through London we get news from New York in Virginia that the conversion of the natives is making good progress and that the translation of the Bible into their language has progressed so much that natives can actually be employed as readers. To this end, more than three hundred churches have been established in this region. In Thuringia, two thieves have robbed many churches, castles, and farms. And in the rooms where people slept, they have eaten, drunk, danced, and made music without anyone ever waking up. According to them they were executioners' helpers. From Paris we hear about an accident by suffocation; from Hungary and Rotterdam about a freak birth."

61. Faruk Tabak, *The Waning of the Mediterranean, 1550–1870* (Baltimore: Johns Hopkins University Press, 2008), 176–81. Tabak repeatedly points to the emergence of Amsterdam as Europe's most important news hub.

find eager distributors and consumers.⁶² *Gazetten* and *Avisen* arrive daily, to the delight of a public remarkably astute about the variety and veracity of news.⁶³

This innkeeper is clearly a seasoned consumer of news, able to distinguish (as is Eduard) between the hunger for sensational and salacious news and the wish and need to be properly and reliably informed about important events.⁶⁴ In view of such readerly discernment, it is obvious that not all news media are created equal: *Gazetten*, also called *Gassenzeitungen*, gratified the reader's thirst for the sensational and are distinguished from "rechtschaffenen und wichtigen Kriegs- und Staats-Sachen," the appropriate type of information for the nobleman who insists on timeliness as well as on the reliability of the information ("Zweifels-frey von allem guten Bescheid geben" [*EE* I: 209]). Another comment on the sometimes questionable veracity of some news reporting comes from Eduard's friend Siegfried, a German cavalier. Crossing the English Channel in the company of several upstanding companions of different nationalities, he converses with them about weather phenomena, specifically the reports about wondrous rains that fill seventeenth-century news reports (*EE* III: 34).⁶⁵ The companions review reports of such events at length, finally reaching the conclusion that most of them are lies.⁶⁶ Such discriminating comments indicate that the news is not only consumed but also critically assessed for content and veracity.

This understanding corresponds to the media theorizing of Happel's contemporary Kaspar Stieler, mentioned previously, whose definition of a newspaper is frequently quoted: "Das Wort: Zeitungen kommt von der Zeit/ darinnen man lebet/ her und kan beschrieben werden/ daß sie Benachrichtigungen seyn/ von den Händeln/ welche zu unserer gegenwärtigen Zeit in der Welt vorgehen/ dahero sie auch Avisen/ als gleichsam Anweisungen

---

62. "[W]ie er (der Wirt) dann eben diesen Nachmittag mit unterschiedlichen Avisen seine Gäste versah" (as the landlord this very afternoon provided his guests with different kinds of newspapers [*EE* I: 280]).

63. "Aus Rom/ Türckey/ Ungarn und Preussen lauffen allerhand Zeitungen ein" (Many newspapers arrived from Rome, Turkey, Hungary, and Prussia [*EE* I: 293]).

64. "Es hat nicht die Meynung/ mein Herr Wirt/ antwortet darauf Aimir, als ob wir allein Begierde hätten/ *Gazetten* und Gassen-Zeitungen zu wissen/ sondern unser Verlangen ist von rechtschaffenen und wichtigen Kriegs- oder Staats-Sachen dieser Lande einige Nachricht zu haben" (It is not my opinion, dear landlord, that we want to read the boulevard press; rather, we would like to receive news about important matters of war and state in this country [*EE* I: 208])

65. Shapiro, *Culture of Fact*, 86–104.

66. "Gleichwie aber an vielen betrüglichen Zeitungen von dergleichen Wunder-Regen/ so da und dorten sich sollen ereignet haben/ kein Mangel" (There is no shortage in these kinds of cheating newspapers of such wondrous rains that happened here and there [*EE* III: 41]).

genannet werden. . . . Gedruckte Erzehlungen . . . ohne gewisse Ordnung und Beurteilung: zu ersättigen des Lesenden Neugirigkeit."[67] Stieler confirms the important position attained by this new medium in the context of the early modern communication networks since its first appearance in Germany early in the seventeenth century. The prominent role played by news production and consumption in European politics and culture by the end of the century affirms that newspapers were reaching an extended readership that had come to insist on a regular and reliable supply of information about noteworthy events from places near and faraway. The new medium brought things worth reading about (*Leßwürdigkeiten* [*EE* III: 394]) in line with things worth seeing or remembering (*Sehenswürdigkeiten* and *Denckwürdigkeiten* [*EE* III: *Vorrede*]). Happel's contribution to the culture of things worth seeing and experiencing is, of course, his monumental collection of news, the *Relationes Curiosae*.[68]

Newspapers provided important stimuli that broadened the mental horizon of the reader, who was, as is the case in Happel's novels, also frequently a traveler.[69] In his novels, news keeps characters on the move. In fact, travel, either voluntary or involuntary, is often prompted by reading about events in faraway places. For example, reading the news encourages male characters to enlist in the various European wars. In response to what they read, they sometimes change sides and allegiances in favor of a general they admire or in reaction to changes in the fortunes of any given conflict. Their choice of less-martial travel destinations appears similarly motivated: the characters read about this or that exciting town or court and decide to go there and check it out.

Happel further contextualizes the news by supplementing the informa-

---

67. "The word *newspaper* hails from 'news' of the times in which we live, and it can be described as a publication that brings the news of events that take place in our time. Therefore they are also called *Avisen*, that is, 'information.' [These are also] printed stories presented without any formal order or judgment [as to priority] meant to satisfy the reader's curiosity [thirst for news] [2]." Cited in Erich Strassner, *Zeitung*, Grundlagen der Medienkommunikation 2 (Tübingen: Niemeyer, 1997).

68. Schock, *Die Text-Kunstkammer*.

69. "[N]eben den großen Unkosten/ auch einer gefährlichen Rayse dahin/ überheben/ wann er uns dieselbe . . . durch eine Beschreibung gleichsam vor Augen stellet" (aside from the great cost there is also danger associated with such travel . . . which he presents to us in his report [*EE* III: 223]). Happel had mentioned this before, for example, in the *Thesaurus Exoticorum* (3v), where he notes that traveling is expensive and dangerous, that it therefore makes sense to read books instead, and that reading about foreign countries and people is a more efficient use of time ("er kan auff einmahl so viel und mehr sehen/ als er mit vielen Jahren und Reisen wird erkundigen können").

tion with many lengthy and detailed reports on the culture, history, and geography of a given locale, as was typical of early modern chorography.[70] These reports are usually delivered by a character, always male and very often German, who is either from or very familiar with the specific area or country. After he finishes his recitation, the audience invariably compliments and applauds him on his knowledge and narrative skill.

The German Novel

With the notable exception of the works of Grimmelshausen, the German novel of the seventeenth century has only recently begun to emerge from the shadow of French and English "birth-of-the-novel" narratives. This attitude persists as a truism in literary criticism, to such an extent that, in a conference paper on the theory of the novel, Franco Moretti proposed that the German novel between Grimmelshausen and Goethe had missed the aesthetic turn executed by French, English, Italian, and Spanish national literatures, in that "quantity never turn[ed] into quality."[71] This statement must not go unchallenged. The shadow cast by Grimmelshausen and Goethe, two giants of German letters, is beginning to recede somewhat as work on the reenvisioning of seventeenth-century German prose production and the evolution of print media gets underway.[72] It makes sense to place Happel's novels right where Marina Warner puts the "elevation of the novel as a conscious cultural project that gives 'the' novel an objective character." Warner continues, "[The novel] offers an instance of an effective intervention in the direction of media culture through an expansion of the concept of literature." The first French and British novelists may have been, according to Warner, the "early and formative players" in the story of "the beginning of early modern print entertainment." During the second half of the seventeenth century, however, Happel most certainly participated vigorously in this "print entertainment" as an important player in "a market-driven competition" that pressed him to produce a readable and thus salable product.[73]

Happel found support for this ambitious undertaking in the Hamburg

---

70. Shapiro, *Culture of Fact*, 65–69.

71. Franco Moretti, "Theory/History," 7 (paper presented at the conference "Theories of the Novel," Brown University, October 2007). I am indebted to my colleague Bob Hegel at Washington University for sharing this paper with me.

72. Wiggin, *Novel Translations*, 6n4.

73. Warner, *Licensing Entertainment*, xiii.

publisher Thomas von Wiering (1640–1703), for whom Happel produced his journalistic and historical writings, and in Matthaeus Wagner of Ulm, who published most of Happel's novels (and continued to publish under Happel's name even after the author's death). The vigorous growth of the market for novels and newspapers made it possible for German writers like Happel to live by their craft, because, by their own admission, they observed closely and reacted to what their readers wanted to consume: "dahero invitire ich billich einen curieusen Liebhaber sothaner Romanen/ die allemahl ihr gewisses Absehen haben/ in Zeiten an sich zu bringen/ das geringe Geld wird keinen gereuen/ und ist solches nicht zu achten gegen dem Nutzen/ den Klein und Groß darvon haben wird" (Therefore, I invite any reader of these novels who is interested to spend some time to not regret the small amount of money [they spend for the book] because this is nothing compared to the benefit for young and old).[74] The change that led to the success of these novels and their authors must be sought in the fact that increasing numbers of readers craved novels despite the distaste—disgust even—that contemporaries frequently directed at such works and their reading, especially when women were the readers. The antinovel polemics affected the way later generations looked at these novels, disdained as long-winded, multivolume mishmashes of history and romance.[75] Clearly, however, such criticism did not dissuade most readers, as sales, particularly of Happel's works, confirm.

In an earlier study, I have shown that such popularity with readers also provided notoriety and income for the Leipzig journalist/writer Johannes Praetorius (1630–80), whose "ways of knowing" led him to new "ways of telling."[76] Praetorius's publications, enormous in volume and expansive in the amount of knowledge collected and reorganized, presented to his literate (but not necessarily learned) audience a wealth of information about the political, social, and intellectual environment in which they lived, including the turbulence caused by the many wars punctuated with periods of uneasy peace. As acute an observer and diligent a writer as he was, Praetorius never attempted to write novels.[77] My study of Praetorius and his oeuvre led me

---

74. *OB* I: *Vorrede*.

75. Merio Scattola, "Roman und praktische Philosophie in der Tradition der Gelehrtengeschichte," in *Kultur der Kommunikation: Die europäische Gelehrtenrepublik im Zeitalter von Leibniz und Lessing*, ed. Ulrich Johannes Schneider, Wolfenbütteler Forschungen 109 (Wiesbaden: Harrassowitz, 2005), 299–301. See also Wiggin's discussion of Gotthard Heiddegger's (1666–1711) invectives against the novel: Wiggin, *Novel Translations*, introduction.

76. Gerhild Scholz Williams, *Ways of Knowing in Early Modern Germany: Johannes Praetorius as a Witness to His Time* (Aldershot: Ashgate, 2006), 1.

77. For a small tract about a woman's lying-in period, fictional but not novelistic, see Ger-

to Happel, who employed in his novels some of the same news sources used by Praetorius and, it appears certain, some of Praetorius's writings. Moving from Praetorius to Happel provided me an adventure in cultural, linguistic, and historical "turns." As Bethany Wiggin notes in *Novel Translations*, exploring these texts assists us in attending to and hearing "the voices, writers of novels, drowned out by the critics-censors," voices who have "quite interesting things to say."[78]

Happel's Way of Telling

Any doubt that Happel had interesting things to say or that he was preeminent as a writer of novels among his contemporaries must be put to rest on the basis of the observations of Christian Thomasius, a distinguished scholar/philosopher and one of the most astute observers of the late seventeenth-century German novel and French-German literary influences. He commented in detail on the *Afrikanische Tarnolast* (1689) in his *Monats-Gespräche* (1689), commending this novel, as I have already noted, for its verisimilitude as well as its author's ability to construct his characters according to the time and social space they occupied.[79] In fact, Thomasius, with his strong endorsement of the novel's successful narrative strategies, highlighting Happel's melding of history and romance (*Liebesbegebenheiten*), brushes aside any criticism that this genre might not be able to teach about history and human nature: "Menschen [wären] allezeit Menschen/ und auch die grösten Helden sind menschlichen Schwachheiten unterworfen. Sie ässen/ träncken/ schlieffen/ liebten/ hasseten/ erzürneten sich/ u.s.w. wie andere Leute. . . . und sey dannenhero der Herr Happel vielmehr zuloben/ daß er von seinen Helden überall Menschheit vorblicken lassen" (People are always [just] people, and even the greatest heroes have human weaknesses. They eat, drink, sleep, love, hate, get angry, etc. just as other people. . . . And therefore

---

hild Scholz Williams, ed., *Mothering Baby: On Being a Woman in Early Modern Germany; Johannes Praetorius's "Apocalypsis Cybeles: Das ist Eine Schnakische Wochen-Comedie (1662),"* Medieval and Renaissance Texts and Studies (Tempe: Arizona Center for Medieval and Renaissance Studies, 2010).

78. Wiggin mentions Happel as the translator of Huet's tract on the novel: Wiggin, *Novel Translations*, 6.

79. Wilhelm Vosskamp, *Romantheorie in Deutschland: Von Martin Opitz bis Friedrich von Blanckenburg*, Germanistische Abhandlungen 40 (Stuttgart: Metzler, 1973), 103–20; John A. McCarthy, "The Gallant Novel and the German Enlightenment (1670–1750)," *Deutsche Vierteljahrschrift für Literaturwissenschaft und Geistesgeschichte* 59 (1985): 66.

we have to praise Herr Happel for letting us see the humanity in his heroes [731]).[80]

Thomasius's vigorous defense of the *Tarnolast* found a strong supporter in Nikolaus Gundling (1671–1729), who praised the novel's closeness to human nature, in which truth and fiction are always inextricably linked.[81] Gundling confirms Thomasius's opinion when he says that "aus des Happels (Everh. Guer.) Africanischen Roman. Vieles Lernen können; So gar in Politischen Dingen" (from Happel's African novel we can learn much, even in things political).[82] His pronouncements precede by several decades Gotthard Heidegger's harsh criticism of novel writing and novel reading.[83] Novels, Gundling observes, teach the reader to discriminate between truth and illusion. No matter whether narratives were created long ago or more recently, Thomasius confirms in turn, the reader will draw from them lessons about virtue and morality.[84]

In his novels, Happel defines his vision of the world and his mission as a writer.[85] He belongs to what Jane Newman so aptly calls the "heterogeneous citational community," whose many-layered sources hail from all areas of late seventeenth-century print media.[86] Multiple systems of meaning and knowledge intersect and converge as Happel constructs his expansive *Welttheater*, on whose stage romance plays out against the backdrop of traditional knowledge systems. As these knowledge systems evolve, they give life to and make room for new ways of comprehending the world. This world is Happel's stage, and he populates it with his memorable characters for the benefit of all who want to know, learn, and be entertained. Happel articulates a view widely shared by his contemporaries, who habitually refer to the world as a stage. People and events come and go, thus affirming that life is mutable and transitory and that "what we see depends on where we stand and how we

---

80. See also Fritz Wahrenburg, *Funktionswandel des Romans und aesthetische Norm: Die Entwicklung seiner Theorie in Deutschland bis zur Mitte des 18. Jahrhunderts*, Studien zur allgemeinen und vergleichenden Literaturwissenschaft 11 (Stuttgart: Metzler, 1976), 148–50.

81. Scattola, "Roman und praktische Philosophie in der Tradition der Gelehrtengeschichte," 303.

82. Ibid., 311.

83. Wiggin, *Novel Translations*, 3.

84. Scattola, "Roman und praktische Philosophie in der Tradition der Gelehrtengeschichte," 306.

85. Lynne Tatlock, "*Thesaurus Novorum*: Periodicity and Rhetoric of Fact in Eberhard Werner Happel's Prose," *Daphnis* 19, no. 1 (1990): 112–13; Tatlock, "Selling Turks."

86. Jane Newman, *The Intervention of Philology: Gender, Learning, and Power in Lohenstein's Roman Plays*, ed. Paul T. Roberge, University of North Carolina Studies in the Germanic Languages and Literatures 122 (Chapel Hill: University of North Carolina Press, 2000), 4.

look."[87] Furthermore, Happel's novels are mirrors in which each reader finds reflected what he or she wishes to see. On Happel's stage, the "discourses of fact"[88] are juxtaposed with the sensuality and sexuality of romance, a mixture that contributed to Happel's sales successes. The *Italienische Spinelli* (1685) demonstrates how Happel joins the metaphors of the *Theatrum* with that of the mirror to articulate the urgency that prompted him to write about the amazing events of his recent past.

> Auf einem *Theatro oder Schau-Platz* stellet man für allerhand sothane Veränderungen deß Menschlichen Glückes/ allerhand Liebes- und Helden Thaten/ See- und Land-Schlachten/ Mordthaten/ Listen und Behendigkeiten; man kan aber nicht so viel/ durch menschliche Witz ersinnen und erdencken/ daß sich nicht von weit mehrere Dinge und in viel einer grösseren Verschiedenheit auf dem Erdboden/ welche auff des *Theatris, als in einem Spiegel/* praesentirt wird . . . Gleichwie aber ich keine Fleiß spahre/ was die Einrichtung dieser Materie dienet/ also wendet der Verleger auch grosse Unkosten auf einen reinen Druck und gute Kupfferstücke zu diesem Wercklein/ welches/ mit Gottes Segen/ mit der Zeit zu einem grossen Tractat *erwachsen und von Vielen mit Verlangen wird gesucht werden*; . . . welches ich nicht sage/ meine Arbeit zu preisen; Nein/ ich kenne meine Schwachheit/ sondern ich bin versichert/ daß die *Wichtigkeit der Sachen/* die sich zu unserer Zeit/ da wir unter den listig- und klügesten Leuten leben/ begeben haben/ und noch zutragen werden/ einen jeden Liebhaber der Historischen Wahrheit anlocken wird.[89] (*IS* II: *Vorrede*; emphasis mine)

The juxtaposition of truth and fiction, history and romance, and reality and illusion, as well as the theatricality of his writing, make Happel's novels

---

87. Ibid., 6.

88. Shapiro, *Culture of Fact*, 4.

89. "On this theater or stage are presented the vagaries of human fortune, many deeds of love and heroism, sea and land battles, murders, deceits and trick; there is nothing so strange that the human mind [wit] can make up that we cannot find somewhere on this earth which are presented in the theater as in a mirror. . . . I have not spared any effort concerning this material, just as the publisher has not spared any costs related to printing and illustration [engravings] for this work, which, in due time and with God's blessings, will have grown into an important work that is sought after by many [readers]. . . . Which I do not say to praise my work. No, I know my own weaknesses, rather, I am assured that the importance of the events that are happening in our days, as we live among the smartest and most informed people, will attract many a lover of historical truth."

early modern multimedia entertainment spectacles. As I have already noted, they not only earned him Thomasius's praise for the expert blending of love stories and history but also caught the attention of the periodical writer Gottfried Zenner.[90] Briefly reviewing Happel's oeuvre up to and including the *Eduard*, Zenner praises Happel as an author whose many books, including his geographies and universal histories, he recommends to the reader because of their wide range over knowledge of all kinds.[91]

Happel's reason for telling his stories echoes that of the famous Frankfurt engraver, editor, printer, and publisher Matthaeus Merian (1593–1650): "weil dann nicht weniger von Jugend auff ich mir vorgenommen haben/ in diesem *THEATRO* oder Schaw Platz der Geschichten der Welt mich zu üben" (because I have wanted, since my youth, to practice in this theater or stage of the world's stories).[92] Merian's vast news compendium, the *Theatrum Europaeum*, provided Happel with much information for his own voluminous writings. Like Merian, Happel considered himself a neutral ("unpartheyisch") teller of tales who wrote for readers fully capable of distinguishing fiction from fact, or, as he puts it, "romanische Außzierungen" from "eigentliche Geschichte" (*EE* III: *Vorrede*). In this, he followed the seventeenth-century custom of many writers and publishers, who stressed their rejection of any defined ideological position.[93] This narrative neutrality enters into Happel's novels, becoming part of the characters' habitus, when, for example, we hear the German Klaur in the *Italienische Spinelli* insist that he will describe the most noble powers and alliances governing Europe

90. Thomasius, "Eberhardi Guerneri Happelii Africanischer Tarnolast," 790; Zenner, *Novellen aus der gelehrten und curiösen Welt*: "In den Liebesgeschichten hat Happel allegationes artig mit den Umständen der Geschichte gemischt."

91. "Beschreibet er das Universität Wesen/ welche Bücher denn allerseits bey jungen und curiösen Gemüthern viel Lust und Nutzen schaffen; die Curiositäten in etlichen Tomis in folio sind auch bekandt/ und machen dieses Mannes Schrifften insgesamt ein eigene Bibliothecam curiosam aus/ wie denn der Autor Happelius mit Mart. Zeilero und Hr. Erasm. Francisci kan verglichen/ und mit gutem Recht unter die Polygraphos und Polyhistores dieser Zeit gezehlet werden; ob er gleich wie obbemelte beyde seine Sachen in Teutscher Sprache geschrieben hat" (He describes university life, and which kind of books served young and inquiring minds; the curiosities of many volumes are known and they are presenting this man's writings as his own library of things worthwhile knowing [curiosities]. For that reason, one can compare Happel to writers like Zeiler and Erasmus Franscisci, and one is justified in counting him among the polygraphs and polyhistors of his time, even though he wrote his works in German). Zenner, *Novellen aus der gelehrten und curiösen Welt*, 70–71.

92. Matthaeus Merian in the first volume of his *Theatrum Europaeum* (1618–1718), I, *Vorrede*.

93. "Hierauff erfolgen unpartheyischen Gegenbericht," in Lohsträter, "Alles Kriegstheater?," 6.

only as historical facts, free of any national passion ("Jedoch müsset ihr euch dabey versichert halten/ daß ich blosserdings historisch gehe/ und von keiner Passion weiß/ es ist mir ein Potentat so lieb/ als der andere" [However, I assure you that I only proceed historically, that I do not follow any passion. I like one ruler as well as the next] [*IS* I: 123–24]). Happel repeats this assertion in part 3 of the *Spinelli*: "Anjetzo berichte ich/ daß diejenigen Erzehl- und Beschreibungen/ welche bey ihrem dato von Jahr oder Tag angezeichnet sind/ allesamt für Historische oder wahrhafftig sind zu achten" (I now bring you those descriptions and narratives that have been reported in their day, and all have been found historically sound and true [*IS* III: *Vorrede*]).

Such authorial gestures allowed Happel to develop what Warner, referring to Eliza Haywood's early eighteenth-century fiction, calls "formula fiction": novels that address a reader who is "plural in terms of interests" with a "polymorphous liability to be hooked by many zones of readerly enjoyment."[94] Merian, Happel, and Praetorius represent a trend in seventeenth-century publishing in that they carefully assessed their readers' desires and interests in order to satisfy them in pursuit of increasing sales. In different ways, all three fed off the same sources, early modern news reports contextualized by chorographies and knowledge literature (*Wissensliteratur*) of all kinds.[95] These media provided the materials that ultimately made these writers, at least in their time, famous (and, in the case of Merian, rich).[96] Directed at a general reader, this type of fiction contributed to the success of serials popularized in England by novelists such as Aphra Behn. Happel's own version of serialization, his penchant for multivolume print productions, began with his first novel, the *Afrikanische Tarnolast*, which proved so attractive and popular that, as previously noted, readers coveted novels published under Happel's name even several years after his death.[97] Save for the sixth volume

---

94. Warner, *Licensing Entertainment*, 89.

95. Happel praises Wagner's publication of Zeiler's mammoth encyclopedia, in *BM* IV: 312: "Herrn Zeilers Epistolische Schatz-Kammer/ wird als ein sehr gutes Buch gerühmt." Martin Zeiler, *Herrn Martin Zeillers/ Wolseeliger Gedächtnüß Epistolische SchatzKammer: Bestehend Von Siebenhundert und Sechs Sendschreiben/ Worinnen Allerhand köstliche Schätze/ unterschiedlicher Künsten und Wissenschafften/ schöner anmutiger und nutzlicher Historien/ lehr-reicher Fragen . . . zu finden seynd* (Ulm: Matthaeus Wagner 1683).

96. Marion Kintzinger, *Chronos und Historia: Studien zur Titelblattikonographie historiographischer Werke vom 16. bis zum 18. Jahrhundert*, Wolfenbütteler Forschung 60 (Wiesbaden: Harrassowitz, 1995), 70.

97. "Happel's name functions in these subsequent publications more like a brand name than a designation of original authorship." Lynne Tatlock, "The Novel as Archive in New Times," *Daphnis* 37, nos. 1–2 (2009), n25).

of the *Ungarische Kriegs-Roman*, these posthumous novels were sold without correcting for authorship; that is, Happel continues to be identified as the author of books he could not have written.[98] Therefore, for purposes of this study, I, too, will consider these posthumous publications (except for the *Portugalische Clara*, published in 1710) as part of a single corpus.

The baroque penchant for formal and generic excess, overwhelmingly present in the art forms employed by Happel's contemporaries, also finds expression in his novels. Most often working in series of four books of four hundred or more pages each, Happel comments on wars, nationalist passions, expansionist and colonizing ambitions, scientific curiosity, and wondrous events. Against this backdrop, the historical, cultural, and geographic education and the emotional maturing and sexual confusions of Happel's characters unfold before us as they travel across many European and non-European landscapes and cityscapes. During endless rounds of hide-and-seek played with gender and social and national identities, the characters never tire of putting on disguises and taking new names and new personalities, always challenging the reader to remember who is doing what, when, where, and to whom. Thus, the peripatetic lives of the actors provide as rich a panorama as the world in turmoil through which they—and we—travel.[99] The modern reader enters these novels, these "histor[ies] written in the present tense,"[100] through multiple refractions that give them the "capacious form, [the] generic mixture that 'contains multitudes' of earlier writings."[101]

98. The anonymous continuator writes in the preface to the sixth volume: "Nachdem aber die Wagnerische Erben dennoch diese Buch nicht also ligen lassen/ sondern der curieusen Welt gerne gantz darreichen wollen; als habe ich es mir endlich gefallen lassen/ selbiges zu continuiren . . . ob ich gleich wol weiß/ daß meine Arbeit deß seeligen Happelii nicht gleich kommt" (After the heirs of Wagner decided not just to let go of this book, but felt that the interested reader [world] should see it, I have taken it upon myself to continue the work . . . even though I know that my work cannot be compared to that of the blessed Happel).

99. "[N]eben einer kurtzen/ jedoch accuraten Beschreibung deß Königreichs Groß-Brittannien/ allerhand andere wichtige Sachen/ von grossen Verräthereyen/ mächtigen Kriegs-Verfassungen/ grausamen Feld- und See-Schlachten/ namhafften Eroberungen/ Neue Verbündnüssen/ Königl. Heyraten/ hohen Todes-Fällen/ wunderlichen Geschichten/ seltsam verwickelten Liebes-Intriguen/ . . . neben vielen Merck- und Leßwürdigkeiten" (aside from a short but accurate description of the kingdom of England, many other important details of great treachery, powerful wars, cruel land and sea battles, famous victories, new treaties, royal weddings, important deaths, wondrous tales, strange love intrigues . . . along with much that is worthy of remembering and reading [*EE* I: *Vorrede*]).

100. Sam Tanenhaus, "History, Written in the Present Tense," *New York Times*, March 4, 2007), 4, 11–13.

101. Hammond and Regan, *Making the Novel*, 18.

In true kinship with the audience, Happel's characters are readers as well, eagerly consuming much disparate information along with contemporary opinions, judgments, and prejudices.

Happel's interest in the emerging genre of the novel, both as fiction and as criticism, prompted him to insert a German translation of Pierre Daniel Huét's *Traité de l'origine des romans* (Letter on the origin of novels, 1670)[102] into his novel *Der Insulanische Mandorell* (1682).[103] Huét's tract provides the theme for the English cavalier Prince Mandorell's long conversation with the Oriental Prince Covvatiar about the nature and history of the novel. Mandorell advises the prince to read novels not only for enjoyment but also for their excellent learning.[104]

While Happel's novels lost their attraction to the reading public after the mid-eighteenth century, Thomasius's review of the *Tarnolast*, previously mentioned, and Happel's use of Huét's tract are routinely cited in studies of the origins of the German novel,[105] keeping his name alive in early modern literary studies. In addition, the novels' densely woven content meets our current interest in seventeenth-century "cultural turns."[106] As noted, there has recently been renewed interest in Happel's collections of news (the *Relationes Curiosae*, the *Kern-Chronica*, the *Türckis. Estats- und Krieges-Bericht*, and the *Thesaurus Exoticorum*), in the volumes on contemporary news and history, and in what would now be called ethnography.[107] Moreover, the

---

102. Pierre-Daniel Huet, *Traite de l'origine des romans: Faksimiledrucke nach der Erstausgabe von 1670 und der Happelschen Uebersetzung von 1682 mit einem Nachwort von Hans Hinterhaeuser* (Stuttgart: Metzler, 1966).

103. Happel, *IM*, 431–71.

104. "Nichts kann den Verstand FORMIEREN und bequem machen/ der Welt zu dienen/ und sich darin zu schicken/ alß die guten Romanen/ diese sind fromme Lehrmeister/ welche denen von der Schule folgen/ und welche sprechen und lesen lehren auff eine weit lehrsamere und durchdringendere weise/ alß die/ so in der Schule lehren" (Nothing can better form and adjust one's mind and serve the world and all that is in it better than good novels. These are perfect teachers which are like those in school and teach us to speak and to read in a more effective way than even those [teachers] in school [*AT* I: 473]).

105. Vosskamp, *Romantheorie in Deutschland*, 72–77; Wahrenburg, *Funktionswandel des Romans und aesthetische Norm*, 149–51; McCarthy, "Gallant Novel," 47–78.

106. Doris Bachmann-Medick, *Cultural Turns: Neuorientierungen in den Kulturwissenschaften*, Rowohlts Encyclopädie 55675 (Hamburg: Rowohlt, 2006), 7–58. For a recent publication dealing with Thomasius's role in the evolution of literature and poetics of his time, see Manfred Beetz and Herber Jaumann, eds., *Thomasius im literarischen Feld: Neue Beiträge zur Erforschung seines Werkes im historischen Kontext* (Tübingen: Niemeyer, 2003), 35–59.

107. Eberhard Werner Happel, ed., *Türckis. Estats- und Krieges-Bericht (1683–1684)* (Hamburg: Thomas von Wiering, 1685); Happel, *Thesaurus Exoticorum*; Happel, *Historia Moderna*

Fig. 2. Eberhard Werner Happel's *Thesaurus Exoticorum* (1688) (Herzog August Bibliothek, Wolfenbüttel)

advertising for the "Continuation der Historischen Kern-Chronica" in the *Relations-Courir* (1684) signals Happel's wish to sell his works as well as the desire of the public to buy them. Furthermore, he also announces the sale of past issues to the interested reader.[108]

As is apparent from the attention he paid to Huét, Happel was aware that, by choosing the novel form, he was engaging with a newly emerging medium whose authority was first acknowledged by the French and whose roots reached back to antiquity. Insisting on the novelty of the novel, which he designates here as "so-called" (presumably because of the newness of the long prose narrative),[109] he comments repeatedly on the importance of joining history and fiction for the edification and enjoyment of the reader.

> Wie sonsten die so genanten Romanen nummehro auch in Teutsch-land sich gewaltig mehren/ und aber biß dato meines wissens noch niemand in unserer Mutter-Sprache von dem Uhrsprung und unter-schied der Satyrischen/ Fabelhafften/ Historischen und Romanischen Schrifften geschrieben/ alß habe mir insonderheit angelegen seyn las-sen/ des Frantzösischen M. HUETS Brief/ darin Er die Materie vom Uhrsprung der Romanen gar artlich abhandelt/ in verschiedenen Capitteln des dritten Buches einzuführen/ welches dem Leser hof-fentlich nicht Unangenehm seyn wird.[110]

Thus, Prince Mandorell is not only conversant in many languages but also exceedingly well read. Wanting to combat his lovesickness by traveling the

---

Europae, Oder eine Historische Beschreibung dess Heutigen Europae (Ulm: Matthaeus Wagner, 1692); Happel, *Kern-Chronica der merckwürdigsten Welt- und Wunder-Geschichte*, 2 vols. (Hamburg: Thomas von Wiering, 1690).

108. "[O]b jemand einig von den vorhergehenden Jahren haben möchte/ er die noch man-glenden [*sic*] andere Jahre darzu bekommen kan" (Should anyone desire to get past issues [of this paper], he can readily obtain them [Z 100/1685/18/8]).

109. "[S]ogenanter Roman" (so-called novel): literally speaking, the novel for Happel and Huét is not really "so-called," since their word is *Roman* or *roman*. The word is much older than the seventeenth century—in the Middle Ages, it referred to a verse narrative. Happel, like Huét, employs this new kind of long prose narrative without ever talking about the novel versus other forms. He only repeats the distinction between history and fiction, between "historia," or "Ge-schichte," and romance ("romanische Handlungen, romanisiren").

110. "As the so-called novels are now also appearing more frequently in Germany, but since, until now, no one, to my knowledge, has looked at their origin and at the difference between satiric, fantastic, historical, and romance writings, therefore I have taken it upon myself to intro-duce the French letter of M. Huet in several chapters into the third book, which I hope will not be unpleasant to the reader." *IM, Vorrede*; also 572–629.

world, he goes to America, where he instructs Prince Covvatiar in the practice of learning languages by reading novels (*IM* II: 573). Happel's personal
dislike of school, to which he alluded in his autobiographic notes, surfaces
once again: according to Mandorell, novels are "fromme Lehrmeister/
welche denen von der Schule folgen/ und welche sprechen und lesen lehren
auff eine weit lehrsamere und durchdringendere weise/ alß die so in den
Schulen lehren" (devout teachers who follow [after] those in the schools and
who teach speaking and reading much more effectively and intensively than
those who instruct in schools [*IM* II: 628]).

When we contemporary readers engage with these rather lengthy narratives, we marvel at Happel's exemplary execution of Huét's and Thomasius's
narrative prescriptions. Far from merely constructing tales about romantic
and familial complications—the hallmark of the gallant novel[111]—Happel
inserts his pleasant, albeit convoluted, stories ("allerhand annehmlichen
Romanisirungen" [*Vorrede*]) into the "hard news" of the day, which filled the
pages of the popular press of the time.[112] The narrative universe thus expands
geographically, historically, dramatically, and emotionally.[113] Eagerly pursuing the uncertain paths of loves lost and found, incestuous longings, mistaken identities, and sex in various locales with (for some) frequently changing partners, the reader follows Happel's characters through voluminous
pages packed with detailed accounts of politics, wars, economics, science,
international treaties, royal and imperial weddings, births and deaths, and
preternatural wonders, as well as with stories of the simple life, rude manners, and lax morals of the lower classes. Happel's construction of verisimilitude relies on the print media as witness, diminishing the importance of the
educated and highly born as witnesses.[114] The transnational media events
of the times—wars, revolutions, and wonders brought to the characters via

111. As a designation for seventeenth-century novels, the term *gallant* refers to a certain
courtly way and style of interacting (love intrigues, language use). See Conrad Wiedemann, *Der
galante Stil 1680–1730*, Deutsche Texte 11 (Tübingen: Niemeyer, 1969).

112. Volker Meid, *Die deutsche Literatur im Zeitalter des Barock: Vom Späthumanismus zur
Frühaufklärung, 1570–1740*, Geschichte der deutschen Literatur von den Anfängen bis zur Gegenwart 5 (Munich: Beck, 2009), 567–71; Böning, "Weltaneignung durch neues Publikum,"
105–34.

113. Hans Geulen, *Erzählkunst der frühen Neuzeit: Zur Geschichte epischer Darbietungweisen und Formen im Roman der Renaissance und des Barock* (Tübingen: Lothar Rotsch, 1975);
Bachmann-Medick, *Cultural Turns*, 35.

114. Reviewed in Stefanie Schmitt, *Inszenierungen der von Glaubwürdigkeit: Studien zur Beglaubigung im späthöfischen und frühneuzeitlichen Roman*, Münchner Texte und Untersuchungen
zur Deutschen Literatur des Mittelalters 129 (Tübingen: Niemeyer, 2005), 10.

the ever-present *Zeytungen*—keep characters and readers alike on the move across the European continent and beyond, serving as an introduction to this world for untraveled youth.[115]

Like Praetorius, Happel, ever the practical writer living by his craft, alerts his audience to the fact that he is mindful of his readers' pocketbooks, for which reason he makes his publications available at a reasonable price ("deß geringen Geldes"). Similarly, Johannes Praetorius had pointed to the modest size of his publications as especially attractive to the thrifty shopper.[116] Both Happel's novels and Praetorius's news publications include news about the Great Fire of London (1666); the giant's tooth found in Krems, Austria, in 1645; the likelihood of procreation between animals and humans; and the effect of bleeding corpses on the murderer.[117] Concerning the scientifically and philosophically fascinating issue of procreation resulting from sexual intercourse between animals and humans, Happel refers to Olearius and Conrad Gessner (1516–65), though he is generally more reticent than Praetorius in identifying the sources from which he so liberally borrows (*EE* III: 346). It has been suggested that this oversight may have arisen from the fact that novels, as works of fiction, did not demand any clear marking of sources, leaving Happel less compelled to list his in any detail. This suggestion, however, is undercut by Schock's observation that the news reporting of the *Relationes Curiosa* proves Happel to be as acquisitive as Praetorius, often to the point of plagiarism, with scant attention paid to source disclosure.[118]

115. "[D]ie Romane . . . bilden die affecten fast alle miteinander so lebhaffte für, daß ein junger Mensch, der sonst noch wenig Gelegenheit hat in die Welt zu gucken, sich dieselben ja so deutlich imprimiren, als ingemein ein Mensch sich die Idee eines frembden Thiers, daß er abgemahlet siehet, eindrückt" (novels . . . form the affections in such an effective way that a young person who otherwise has no opportunity to see the world can imagine things [with their help] just like a person can form an idea about a foreign animal that he sees in a drawing [painting]). Quoted in McCarthy, "Gallant Novel," 64–65.

116. "[D]u wirst leichtlich vermuthen/ . . . was für eine kostbare Menge der Tractaten heraußgekommen sey/ von denen neulichsten Feuer-Ruthen: als davon nunmehr alle Buchladen angefüllet seynd/ und ihre Käuffer erwarten: welche aber wegen der grossen Curiosität kaum alles an einem Ort antreffen: oder wenn sie es je angetroffen haben/ schwerlich bezahlen können: . . . Sintemal die Anzahl der Stücke leichtlich ein par ziembliche Quart/ Bünde machen/ und schier etliche Wochen zum durchlesen erfordern solten. Aber wo ist die *patientz* darzu? Ich halte viel von der *concentration*, und Sumerischen Berichte eines weitschweiffenden Wercks." Johannes Praetorius, *Adunatus cometologus; Oder ein Geographischer Cometen Extract* (Leipzig: Johann Wittigau, 1665), 3.

117. Williams, *Ways of Knowing*, 74–75.

118. Flemming Schock, "Reading Others: Intertextuality in Early Modern Popular Writing (Eberhard Werner Happel's *Relationes Curiosae*)" (unpublished manuscript). I am grateful to Flemming Schock for sharing this unpublished work.

In a review of his writings in general, then, it can be said that Happel makes liberal use of the ubiquitous print media, though he remains vague as to specific sources employed.

Finally, all novels produced during the last third of the seventeenth century in Germany, including Happel's, provide an inestimable source of knowledge about a period in history very much akin to our own in the overwhelming excesses in art, literature, and accumulation of knowledge.[119] They thus deserve the same degree of critical attention that French, English, Spanish, and Italian novels have received.[120] The time for an in-depth study of Happel's novels has come, not only for scholars and students of the early modern period, but for all who are curious about what the vigorous production of German novels in the second half of the seventeenth century can tell us about the development of the novel, the culture that prompted its production, and its place in literary and media history. Happel's portrayal of his turbulent and swiftly changing world cannot help but remind twenty-first-century readers of their own world; exploring his, we will learn much about ours. The study of German literature between 1670 and 1750, which John McCarthy, more than twenty years ago, wistfully called "a bit murky," will come alive in this process.[121]

Hence, this study proposes to give Happel's novels the attention and scholarly scrutiny they deserve based on their popularity and girth and their cultural, historical, and literary modes of presentation. To this end, I will explore several of Happel's novels, specifically his historical novels (*Geschicht-Romane*), bringing to light their narrative sophistication and the dynamism and variety of their "cultural turns."[122] I will address the structural and interpretive challenges posed by these narratives, including those published within a year or two after his death, to allow the *Engelländische Eduard* (1691), the *Bayrische Max* (1692), and volume 6 of the *Ungarische Kriegs-Roman* to be included in his oeuvre.[123] In the course of this investiga-

---

119. "Even in the seventeenth century, people felt overwhelmed by what Leibniz called 'the horrible mass of books.'" Jeffrey Nunberg, "Data Deluge," review of *The Information: A History, a Theory, a Flood*, by James Gleick, *New York Times Book Review*, March 20, 2011, 10. See also McCarthy, "Gallant Novel," 51–61.

120. "Here is why the German case is so interesting: more novels published here than anywhere else in the world . . . and yet, between Grimmelshausen and Goethe, a century where quantity never turns into quality." Moretti, "Theory/History." See also Franco Moretti, ed., *The Novel*, vol. 2, *Forms and Themes* (Princeton: Princeton University Press, 2006).

121. McCarthy, "Gallant Novel," 48.

122. Bachmann-Medick, *Cultural Turns*, 7–27.

123. Two years after Happel's death, the 1692 novel *Der Sächsische Witekind* makes a point

tion, we will come to see Happel's significant literary talent, and we will have the chance to admire his ability to synthesize impressive amounts of information as well as his surprisingly subtle understanding of human nature and social interaction. We will learn about pirates and robbers, university life, contemporary politics and celebrities, cross-dressing and sexual confusion, foreign peoples and European power struggles—in short, about matters large and small that attracted readers of the later seventeenth-century Europe to the novel, as they continue to do for readers of novels today.

The Chapters' Progression

To demonstrate how effectively Happel employed the attention fixed by the media on historical figures and the interaction of such figures with his fictional characters, chapter 2 will focus on two men who repeatedly surface in his novels and as subjects of widely disseminated media reports: the rebellious and charismatic Hungarian count and general Emmerich (Imre) Thököly (1659–1705) and the intrepid Frederick, first Duke of Schomberg (1616–90). Thököly attempted to liberate Hungary from both the Ottoman Turk and the German emperor and to achieve religious tolerance for his country in the process. After the king of France renounced the Edict of Nantes in 1685 in order to unite the realm under one faith, Gallican Catholicism, Schomberg, as marshal of France, refused to abandon his Calvinist faith and consequently lost all he had gained during many years of service to the French crown.

Happel approaches these historical celebrities and their extraordinary lives in several ways:

1. Fictional characters ask each other for information about historical events and people. The person addressed responds by supplying the information either by drawing on personal experiences

---

of recalling for the reader the titles of his novels, no doubt to profit from his popularity: "In welchem/ Nach Ahrt deß Italiänischen Spinelli, Spanischen Quintana, Frantzösischen Cormantins/ Ottomanischen Bajazets/ Teutschen Carls/ Engelländischen Eduards und Bayrischen Max, in einer Liebes- und Helden-Geschichte/ die Denck-würdigsten Begebnüssen/ Kriegs- und Politischen Staats-Sachen/ Glücks- und Unglücks- auch hohe Todes-Fälle/ Hoch-Fürstliche Beylager/ Schlachten/ Belager- und Eroberungen/ etc. dieses Jahrs unparteyisch beschrieben werden." Eberhard Werner Happel, *Der Sächsische Witekind/ Oder so-genannter Europaeischer Geschicht-Roman. Auf das 1692. Jahr* (Ulm: Matthaeus Wagner 1692).

or by reading from a recently delivered newspaper (*Quintana,
Spinelli, Eduard*).

2. Fictional characters and historical persons interact as part of the
   narrative. For example, Thököly's exploits come into view in the
   most carefully narrated historical details in the six volumes of the
   Ungarischen Kriegs-Roman.[124]

3. Happel further amplifies the factual/fictional mode of telling
   by multiple use of reports taken from other media, most notably
   newspapers/reports of the years treated in his novels, as well
   as broadsheets and news compendiums like the *Theatrum
   Europaeum.*

Chapter 3 will broaden this book's narrative and geographic scope as I
explore the roles of pirates, robbers, captives, and slaves in Happel's novels.
Their treatment exemplifies his reporting of the more sensational side of hard
news, testifying to the reading public's tremendous interest in contemporary
social, political, and economic news items. Happel's *Geschicht-Romane* offer
many tales about the marginal groups (*Randgruppen*) of robbers and pirates.
In fact, Happel's predilection for mixing facts and fiction becomes especially
apparent when the action of his lengthy novels is moved along as the protagonists, be they men or women, encounter robbers and pirates who capture,
buy, and sell them as slaves or ransom them as their captives.

In chapter 4, remembering Happel's often-repeated dichotomy of fact
and fiction, history and romance, I will turn to romance and gender confusions and examine the passions that impel Happel's fictional characters as
they pursue each other and their dreams across the landscapes and cityscapes
of Europe and beyond. Always in danger of potentially violent encounters
with the Other, whether in the form of parents who turn out not to be parents, strangers, or people thought to be friends, Happel's characters meet,
separate, and meet again, all the while exploring new and familiar spaces
for the readers, who themselves need not leave the comfort of their reading
chairs. The exploration of the structural and interpretive challenges posed
by the interaction of news and romance, politics and passion, will reveal

---

124. Tatlock, "Novel as Archive," 353–71. The *Ungarische Kriegs-Roman* appeared in six
volumes from 1687 to 1697, covering the years 1683 to 1689.

that news events influenced the characters' actions as much as the challenges brought about by mix-ups in gender, culture, and class.

In this book's conclusion, I will return to the proposal articulated in the beginning: namely, that the synergy of many textual forms—of news and novel, history and fiction—significantly advanced the evolution of the novel in seventeenth-century Germany as well as western Europe generally.

TWO

"The Court of Public Opinion"

Fictionalizing Encounters with Historical Heroes (Imre Thököly and Friedrich von Schomberg)

꽃

Roger Boylan discusses a contemporary author's (Ken Follett's) approach to fiction in terms that seem to recall the seventeenth-century novel and particularly Happel's *Geschicht-Romane*: "Multiple plot strands woven through a vast tapestry of times past. In this huge panorama, empires rise and fall, wars break out and characters of varying social backgrounds live mostly happy or mostly unhappy lives."[1] Happel, too, concocts his novels—as vehicles of knowledge transfer—from a mixture of history and romance, making romance all the more engaging and instructive by introducing detailed accounts about military and political celebrities of his time. For this chapter, I have selected two political figures, General Thököly and Duke Frederick of Schomberg, outsized even in the context of the seventeenth century, to demonstrate how effectively Happel employed the attention fixed by the media on historical figures and how he constructed their interaction with his fictional characters.[2] During the second half of the century, these men

---

1. *New York Times Book Review*, October 3, 2010, 22.

2. EE III: XXIII: death of Friedrich, Herzog of Schomberg. Friedrich Hermann (or Frédéric-Armand), first Duke of Schomberg (originally Schönberg) (December 1615 or January 1616–July 11, 1690), was both marshal of France and a general in the English army. Count Imre Thököly de Késmárk (Thököly/Tököly/Tökölli Imre in Hungarian, Mirko Thököly in Croatian, Imrich Tököli in Slovak) (April 25, 1657–September 13, 1705) was a Hungarian statesman, leader of an anti-Habsburg uprising, prince of Transylvania, and (briefly) vassal king of Upper

were the subjects of countless news reports, which found their way, in turn, into news collections such as the *Theatrum Europaeum* (1633–1738), Happel's *Türckis. Estats- und Krieges-Bericht* (1683–84), and the *Thesaurus Exoticorum* (1688).[3] Both men appear as actors in Happel's novels and in conversations among the novels' characters.

Different in many particulars, the two men shared two important attributes that contributed to their success as well as their eventual demise: both were gifted leaders of men, and both were deeply devoted to their faiths (Lutheran and Calvinist, respectively). Schomberg was a soldier for hire, a gifted military mind of international fame, with little demonstrable attachment to the land of his birth, Germany. Thököly, a member of the Protestant Hungarian nobility and a man deeply influenced by his national and religious identity, devoted most of his adult life to the liberation of his homeland from Ottoman and German domination and to the establishment of religious tolerance, if not the removal of Catholic dominance.

Following the vagaries of these two men as reported in the contemporary news media, we cannot help but acknowledge the quickly rising power of these media. These men dominated the daily content of the media, if not the daily headlines (there were none).[4] Testifying to the popularity and reach of news reports is the notice in the *Europäische Relation* of March 7, 1685, alerting the public to fact that collections of newspapers in single volumes were available for sale. For example, one volume gathered together news stories from 1683 to 1685 dealing with the "Uhrsprung des Ungerischen Krieges . . . exact beschrieben . . . in 40. auf 56. Bogen groß mit 21. Kupfer geziehret" (origin of the Hungarian war . . . exactly described . . . in forty to fifty-six sheets decorated with twenty-one copper engravings [*ER* 21: 168; Z

Hungary. See Bryan Cartledge, *The Will to Survive: A History of Hungary* (New York: Columbia University Press, 2011), 112–15. The visual history of the Ottoman wars (1683–1685) has recently been published as volume 11 of Paas's monumental work: John Roger Paas, ed., *The German Political Broadsheet, 1600–1700*, vol. 11, *1683–1685* (Wiesbaden: Harrassowitz, 2011).

3. Eberhard Werner Happel, *E. G. Happelii Grösste Denckwürdigkeiten der Welt oder so genannte Relationes Curiosae*, vol. 3 (Hamburg: Thomas von Wiering, 1687); Happel, *Thesaurus Exoticorum. Oder eine mit Aussländischen Raritäten und Geschichten Wohlversehene Schatz-Kammer Fürstellend Die Asiatische, Africanische und Americanische Nationes . . . Darauff folget eine Umständliche von Der Tuerckey Beschreibung . . . und sein verfluchtes Gesetz-Buch oder AKORAN* (Hamburg: Thomas von Wiering, 1688); Happel, ed., *Türckis. Estats- und Krieges-Bericht*, nos. 1–137 (Hamburg: Thomas von Wiering, 1683–84). He published other encyclopedic works not immediately relevant to this study.

4. In 1650, the Leipzig book trader Timotheus Ritzsch launched the *Einkommende Zeytung*, which appeared six times a week. See Gerhild Scholz Williams, *Ways of Knowing in Early Modern Germany: Johannes Praetorius as a Witness to His Time* (Aldershot: Ashgate, 2006), 113–14.

19/1685/E.R.]). Happel's ability not only to access but also to produce information in multiple forms was to prove a boon to his professional success.

Reading through many copies of newspapers from 1683 to 1686 and reviewing a number of broadsheets from the same time period make clear that, then as today, certain names commanded news writers' and presumably readers' attention more insistently than others. These were the stars, the celebrities, of early modern news culture. Introducing his lengthy novel about the Turkish wars, the *Ungarische Kriegs-Roman* (1685–97), Happel explains in the foreword to the first of the novel's six volumes that this novel should be taken as a journal in which are described in great detail the memorable circumstances that dominated the Europe of his day, here the interminable war between the Ottoman Turk and the German Empire. Added to the narrative are reports about historical and contemporary events and personages, all of which are embedded in tales of romance, which had previously pleased his readers.[5] To keep his readers "on message," Happel periodically interjects reminders into his novels about his factual/fictional "ways of telling." For example, in the *Bayrische Max*, he expresses his wish that "[w]ir werden hoffentlich nicht unrecht thun/ wann wir uns wieder einmahl ein wenig erkundigen/ was indessen da und dort Notabels in der Welt vorgegangen/ damit so wol dem *Geschicht- als Liebes- und Helden-Roman* seine Gebühr geschehe" (hopefully, we will not be remiss if we look here and there to find what noteworthy events have been happening so that we do justice to both, history and fiction [*BM* II: 165]).[6]

As Happel combines information gleaned from all areas of late seventeenth-century print media, most frequently from newspapers, his novels give voice, as mentioned in chapter 1, to Newman's "heterogeneous citational community," the chorus of print products rehearsing much similar information.[7] This community increasingly relied on newspapers for information about local, national, and international events, responding to the public's need to keep abreast of the ever-changing contemporary military and political "informationscape." From its inception, the newspaper's rise

5. "[E]inem absonderlichen Journal, als darinn dieser jüngste Türcken-Krieg sehr genau beschrieben ist" (a special journal wherein the most recent Turkish wars are described in great detail [*UK* I: *Vorrede*]). Eberhard Werner Happel, *Der Ungarische Kriegs-Roman*, 6 vols. (Ulm: Matthaeus Wagner, 1685–97).

6. Happel, *Der Bayrische Max Oder so genannter Europaeischer Geschicht-Roman Auf Das 1691. Jahr* (Ulm: Matthaeus Wagner, 1691).

7. Jane Newman, *The Intervention of Philology: Gender, Learning, and Power in Lohenstein's Roman Plays*, ed. Paul T. Roberge, University of North Carolina Studies in the Germanic Languages and Literatures 122 (Chapel Hill: University of North Carolina Press, 2000), 4.

Der
Ungarische
Kriegs-ROMAN,
Oder
Außführliche
* * * * * * * * * * * * * * *
* * * * * * * * * * * * * * *
Beschreibung /
Deß jüngsten
Türcken-Kriegs /
Wobey
Aller darinnen verwickelter Ho-
her Potentaten Länder / Macht / und
Herrschafft / absonderlich aber eine curieuse
Beschreibung von Ungarn/Persien/ und Türckey/ zusamt
denen denckwürdigsten Belagerungen und blutigsten Feld-
Schlachten so die Türcken Zeit ihrer Herrschafft zu jedermanns
Verwunderung vorgenommen und erhalten haben.

Unter einer anmuthigen Liebes- und Helden-
Geschichte auf Romanische Weise in einer reinen unge-
zwungenen Teutschen Redens-Arth verfasset und mit allerhand
Nutz- und ergötzlichen Historischen/Politischen und dergleichen leß-
würdigen Sachen angefüllt /
Von
EVERHARDO GVERNERO HAPPELIO.
Mit schönen Kupffern gezieret.

ULM /
Druckts und verlegts Matthäus Wagner / 1685.

Fig. 3. Eberhard Werner Happel's *Der Ungarische Kriegs-Roman* (1686–97)
(Herzog August Bibliothek, Wolfenbüttel)

in readership and distribution was driven equally by European power politics, the century's endless wars, and all manner of national and international political conflagrations. Moreover, the reading public's need to know grew apace with an indefatigable hunger for the entertainment gleaned from the more sensational news about wonders, scandals, and crimes. By the last quarter of the seventeenth century, the time of the Turkish wars and Happel's most productive period, monthly, weekly, and daily newspapers had formed a communication network that reached across the European continent and the Far East and Near East and all the way to the New World.[8] In fact, Happel's fascination with the Hungarian-Ottoman story prompted him to include news details about this centuries-long conflict not only in many of his historical novels but also in his *Relationes Curiosae* (1681–91) and in other collections of news and curiosities, such as the *Thesaurus Exoticorum* (1688) and the *Türckis. Estats- und Krieges-Bericht* (1683–84). Noting how often newspapers are mentioned in Happel's novels, it is clear that reading newspapers was rapidly becoming not only an indispensable form of entertainment but a social imperative for men and for women, if one wanted to hold one's own in conversation. In short, reading and discussing news are inextricably bound to the narrative progression of Happel's historical novels, as news reports prompt characters to act, react, comment, and converse about items that catch their attention.

In the course of this chapter, I will show that the synergies between contemporary news writing and Happel's novels significantly contributed to Happel's popular success and to his readers' increasing sophistication as knowledgeable consumers of the contemporary media.

Multimedia Settings: Framing the Stars

In his factual/fictional style of writing, Happel typically employs media that present comparable and often identical information, thereby demonstrating the varieties of ways, forms, and levels of reception beyond his fictions at which news was consumed, circulated, and redeployed.[9] Two tangible

---

8. Béla Köpeczi, *Staatsräson und Christliche Solidarität: Die ungarischen Aufstände und Europa in der zweiten Hälfte des 17. Jahrhunderts* (Vienna: Böhlaus Nachf., 1983), introduction; Wolfgang Behringer, *Im Zeichen des Merkur: Reichspost und Kommunikationsrevolutions in der Frühen Neuzeit*, Veröffentlichungen des Max-Planck-Instituts für Geschichte 189 (Göttingen: Vandenhoeck und Ruprecht, 2003).

9. These boundaries come impressively into view in volumes 12 and 13 of the *Theatrum Eu-*

examples of the considerable narrative impact of items in the news are the revocation of the Edict of Nantes and Thököly's Turkish imprisonment by the Pasha of Grosswardein (now Oradea, Romania), both in 1685. These events, to which I will return in this chapter, generated significant national and international media coverage concurrent with their appearance in Happel's novels.[10] This media attention highlighted the fact that Friedrich von Schomberg, grandee of Portugal and marshal of France, achieved renown not only for his military brilliance but also for resigning his post and forsaking his sizable fortune after King Louis XIV's vow to re-Catholicize France. Imre Thököly's rebellion against the German Empire and his intermittent and frequently problematic association with the Ottoman Turk, the Sublime Porte,[11] were judged by his contemporaries and by Happel as complicated and difficult to impossible to assess in their personal depths and political consequences. But at base, both men chose to defend what we today would call inalienable rights: namely, sovereignty of action and freedom of religious expression.

Providing narrative context for his novels' action, Happel arranged other historical actors around these two men. Though important in themselves in contemporary terms, these characters owe their presence in Happel's novels to the actions of these two men and media stars. Such is the case with King Louis XIV of France, whose role highlights Friedrich von Schomberg's steadfast faith. Other examples are Thököly's wife, Ilona Zrinyi, and the imperial field marshal General Caprara, who engaged with each other in a delicate fictional/factual pas de deux at the siege of Munkàcz, the all-but-invincible fortress that Ilona Zrinyi valiantly defended from 1685 until 1688.[12]

---

ropaeum (1691, 1698), which gather the "Denck- und Merkwürdigste[n] Geschichten/ Welche/ ihrer gewöhnlichen Eintheilung nach/ und verschiedenen Orten durch Europa . . . vom Jahr vom 1687. biß 1691 [XIII]. sich begeben und zugetragen" (title page). Volume 12 covers the years from 1679 to 1686.

10. Köpeczi, *Staatsräson und Christliche Solidarität*, introduction. Köpeczi's review of Thököly's actions as he struggled between the Ottoman Turk and the German Empire is based on French and Dutch pamphlets, newspapers, journals, historical and geographical handbooks, and contemporary fiction. By Köpeczi's own admission, a review of the German, Italian, and English sources would have been overwhelming. Even with this caveat, it has to be said that Köpeczi's study represents a valuable source of factual information pertaining to the Hungarian story.

11. The Sublime Porte is the open court of the sultan, led by the grand vizier; its name derives from the gate to the Topkapi Palace in Istanbul, where the sultan held the greeting ceremony for foreign ambassadors.

12. Count Aeneas Sylvius de Caprara (1631–February 1701), also known as Enea Silvio or Äneas Sylvius von Caprara, was an Austrian field marshal of Italian descent. He served under Charles V, Duke of Lorraine, against the Turkish advance into Hungary, soon winning distinction

It should be clear by this point that Thököly and Schomberg represent fortuitous choices if one intends to demonstrate Happel's masterful merging of history and romance. They appear as part of the narrative action or are topics of conversation in all of the *Geschicht-Romane* published between 1685 and 1690. Moreover, Thököly occupies center stage in the first and fourth volumes of the *Ungarische Kriegs-Roman*, the six-volume novel portraying the evolving Hungarian crisis with singular historical accuracy. In the context of their media-driven notoriety, Schomberg and Thököly take on many of the characteristics that we associate with contemporary celebrities, in that their actions (in the case of Thököly, one could almost speak of antics) populate and sensationalize Happel's novels as much as they did newspapers and broadsheets of their day.[13] As per Joseph Boone and Nancy Vickers in their recent special issue of *PMLA*, Schomberg and Thököly perform their celebrity status just as we observe in celebrities today. They are part of a "deep history" of notoriety and fame; they demand a gaze—even in an age before photography, their faces are known from countless broadsheets and pamphlets; they perform according to their self-assigned mission; they reside in the public sphere; they act on a stage that is more cosmopolitan than parochial, more subject to public opinion than their personal reflection; and, finally, they invite close readings. Happel's integration of these celebrities into his novels confirms that what was true then is true today: "like love, celebrity is something we cannot live with or without."[14]

Structuring the Encounters

As noted in chapter 1, Happel employs three approaches when weaving reports about these historical figures and their lives into his *Geschicht-Romane*: fictional characters ask each other about historical events or people, fictional and historical figures interact with each other, and Happel makes frequent use of reports taken from other media. These narrative approaches to the fictional characters' encounters with their historical counterparts make

---

after the siege of Neuhaeusel from July 7 to August 17, 1685, resulting in its capture. In 1689, Caprara became commander in chief of imperial forces in the region until his retirement in 1696, serving as vice president of the Imperial War Council until his death in February 1701.

13. While not giving an exact number of broadsheets, Köpeczi provides an exhaustive list, including publication venues beyond the German-speaking areas, at the end of his book: Köpeczi, *Staatsräson und Christliche Solidarität*, 387–408.

14. Joseph A. Boone and Nancy J. Vickers, "Introduction: Celebrity Rites," in "Celebrity, Fame, Notoriety," special issue, *PMLA* 126, no. 4 (2011): 906–8.

them come to life in ways that deepen the reader's understanding not only of their historical roles but also of the personal and professional challenges they faced. While the historical players do not emerge as "individuals" in the modern sense of the word, the nuanced narrative portraits suggest an emotional response and, on occasion, even empathy on the part of the reader. In other words, because of Happel's "way of telling," his presentations of Schomberg, Thököly, and other historical figures interacting with them have greater emotional resonance than is found in the most voluminous news compendium of the seventeenth century, the *Theatrum Europaeum*, which, especially in volumes 11, 12, and 13 (1686, 1691, 1698), reports on many of the same events and persons portrayed in Happel's novels. As the editor of volume 13 puts it (aptly describing the practice in all twenty-one volumes), he gathered the most noteworthy stories of the period, or the "Denck- und Merkwürdigste[n] Geschichten/ Welche/ ihrer gewöhnlichen Eintheilung nach/ und verschiedenen Orten durch Europa . . . vom Jahr vom 1687. biß 1691 [XIII]. sich begeben und zugetragen" (most memorable and amazing stories, which according to their customary assignments took place and happened in places all across Europe during the years 1687 to 1691 [title page]). But unlike the gathering and reporting style that characterizes the *Theatrum*, Happel's choice of genre, the novel, allows him to put flesh on the bones of distant historical persons, bringing the drama of their lives close to the reader as he moves beyond the polemics of religion or politics to the human interactions played out against the backdrop of history in the making. This is not to deny the public excitement generated by contemporary news accounts of the persecution of the French Protestants after the revocation of the Edict of Nantes or the course of Thököly's rebellion. But as Happel melds facts with the fiction of chance meetings, loves lost and found, distances traveled, and challenges conquered, he engages his public emotionally and intellectually on a level that news accounts alone could never deliver.

The events and experiences governing Thököly's and Schomberg's lives certainly qualify as memorable and noteworthy. Detailed newspaper accounts followed both men, informing readers of their whereabouts and their personal trials and tribulations. The newspapers of most interest to us are those that would have been available to Happel in Hamburg, where he produced his novels until his death in 1690: the *Nordische Mercurius*, the *Relations-Courir*, the *Europäische Relation*, the *Europäische Fama*, and the *Altonaische Relation*,[15] all of which devoted much space to Schomberg and

---

15. These began appearing in Hamburg in 1664 and were undoubtedly read by Happel and the editors of the *Theatrum*. See Holger Böning, *Welteroberung durch ein neues Publikum: Die*

Thököly, as did the *Theatrum*. Volume 13 of the *Theatrum* did not appear until 1697, but the news reports in it correspond to the historical backdrop of volume 6 of the *Kriegs-Roman*, which was written and published by an anonymous continuator. The factual information presented in the two works overlaps to such an extent that common news sources for both have to be assumed.

The aforementioned three modes of blending facts and fiction (fictional characters talking about historical characters on the basis of news reports, fictional and historical characters interacting in the story, and novels relating information gleaned from newspapers or from news compendiums) offer Happel (and his continuators) several narrative options. First, he is able to critically assess and comment on the stars' personalities, their military and political actions, and, to some extent, their emotional states. He sheds light on their impact on European politics of war and peace and on the importance to their lives' stories of their deep and abiding—even militant—faith, which shaped their loyalties, their actions, and finally their fate. Relying on his impartiality as a writer of history, which he never tires of emphasizing, Happel was able to highlight their sometimes contradictory character traits without giving the impression that he was passing personal judgment. Employing news sources (whose authors he almost never identifies), Happel avoided, for the most part, any direct expressions of authorial admiration or censure, allowing his readers to view and assess these personalities for themselves. This approach offered him the freedom to present the diverse, sometimes paradoxical aspects of an action or an actor without abandoning his self-proclaimed perch of neutrality, the role of *Historico*, for which he was praised even after his death.[16] In the same way, this strategy invites readers to arrive at their own understanding of what motivated these larger-than-life actors as they crossed cultural, geographical, and historical limits and

---

deutsche Presse und der Weg zur Aufklärung; Hamburg und Altona als Beispiel (Bremen: Edition Lumière, 2002), 40, 55, 58. Böning reviews in detail the exact dates as well as the possibility that some of these newspapers may have appeared earlier than the surviving documents claim. See Böning, ed., *Deutsche Presse: Bibliographische Handbücher zur Geschichte der deutschsprachigen periodischen Presse von den Anfängen bis 1815*, vol. 1 (Stuttgart: Frommann-Holzboog, 1996), 19–46; Günther Dammann, "Fakten und Fiktionen im Roman bei Eberhard Werner Happel, Schriftsteller in Hamburg," in *Hamburg: Eine Metropolregion zwischen Früher Neuzeit und Aufklärung*, ed. Johann Anselm Steiger and Sandra Richter, Metropolis: Texte und Studien zu Zentren der Kultur in der Frühen Neuzeit (Berlin: Fink, 2012).

16. "Dem Happelio, dem besten Geschicht-Schreiber dieser Erden!" (To Happel, the very best historian in the world). In Eberhard Werner Happel, *Historia Moderna Europae, Oder eine Historische Beschreibung dess Heutigen Europae* (Ulm: Matthaeus Wagner, 1692), *Voransprache*.

boundaries and, in Thököly's case, just as often transgressed the limits of the accepted political and religious order. It also allows Happel to transport his readers to distant lands, where they encounter foreign cultures, different languages, and unfamiliar peoples and customs, on which Happel only occasionally passes judgment.

In addition, confronting the more mundane perspective of income generation, his stratagem of using and repeatedly reusing contemporary news stories in his *Geschicht-Romane* satisfied his readers' expectations, with which, according to his own words, Happel was quite familiar: "Nachdem ich gesehen/ daß mein jüngst publicirter so genannter nicht Christl. Potentaten Kriegs-Roman/ nicht allein bald aufgekaufft/ sondern auch in eine außländische Sprache übergesetzt/ und von jedermänniglich beliebet worden/ hat mich solches angefrischet/ gegenwärtigen Ungaris. Kriegs-Roman fast aus eben demselben Grunde einzurichten/ und nicht zweiffelend/ es werde der geneigte Leser einigen Gefallen daran haben" (After I have seen that my most recent novel, the so-called *Christl. Potentaten Kriegs-Roman*, has not only sold out but has also been translated into a foreign language and is popular with everybody, I have been inspired to write this *Ungarische Kriegsroman* according to the same template, hoping to please my reader).[17] Clearly, his readers were as much consumers of newspapers as they were devotees of novels, the success of the former leading to the popularity of the latter.

The Two Men and Their Times

Judging by the intense media interest and Happel's sales successes, Thököly and Schomberg were already European legends during their lifetimes. They towered over ordinary mortals as they shaped the events that, in both cases, would spell their demise. Both men embody striking examples of how seventeenth-century pan-European conflicts, the hegemonic ambitions of the major European powers, and the instability of political and personal alliances affected all players: the rich, the poor, the average, and the extraordinary. As Thököly and Schomberg move through these novels, we learn as much about their military competence and political skills (or occasional lack thereof) as about their religious allegiances, even passions. We recognize their charisma, we empathize with their personal choices, and we

17. Happel, *Der Ungarische Kriegs-Roman*, I: *Vorrede*

glimpse the character traits that made them effective leaders (if, in the case of Thököly, a controversial one). We also come to know them as examples of two opposing, quintessentially baroque personality types. Thököly, who equally opposes Ottoman-Muslim and Habsburg-Catholic domination of his homeland, is a rebel, a malcontent, and a hero of the partisans of an emergent Hungarian nationalism. Schomberg, passionately Calvinist to the core, comes across as the personification of the early modern transnational European military leader, seemingly unmoved by nationalist passions, bringing military success to the sovereigns of all faiths who engaged him in their service.

Imre Thököly (1659–1705): Rebellion and the Dream of an Independent Protestant Hungary

Thököly and the Hungarian story (or, as Heinz Duchhardt calls it, the "Problemzone Ungarn"[18]) appear in several of Happel's novels and news publications, with special detail and drama in the six-volume *Ungarische Kriegs-Roman*. Happel specifically addresses his public's "wish to know" when he explains his long preoccupation with Thököly: "[I]nmittelst habe ich diese Ungarischen Materie etwas umständlich zu beschreiben keine Bedencken getragen/ weil die Augen von gantz Europa nach dessen verworrenen Zustand anjetzo gerichtet stehen" (In all this I did not hesitate to describe the Hungarian matter in some greater detail, because the eyes of all of Europe are currently directed at these affairs [*UK* I: 460]). Driven from his northern Hungarian homeland, Thököly, in his effort to lead the Protestant Hungarian nobility in the fight for national liberation and freedom of religion, had turned alternately to Constantinople and the other European powers, France and Poland most notable among them, for support against Vienna.[19] Ultimately, his ambition was to free Hungary of both the Turk as well as the Catholic Roman emperor. Later generations, depending on their point of view, have judged his life either tragic or pathetic, but it surely was a

---

18. Heinz Duchhardt, *Europa am Vorabend der Moderne, 1650–1800*, ed. Peter Blickle, Handbuch der Geschichte Europas 6 (Stuttgart: Eugen Ulmer, 2003), 254–55.

19. *Wöchentlicher Extraordinari Friedens- und Kriegs-Curier*, April 24, 1685: "Durch einen gewissen Curier hat man verstanden/ daß nach Dantzig grosse Wechsel aus Franckreich abgeschickt/ und eine grosse Summa Gelds dem Teckely zur Fortsetzung seiner Treulosigkeit zu übermachen anbefohlen worden" (A certain messenger made known that a check was sent from France to Danzig to help Thököly to continue his acts of betrayal [Z 98/1685/Fr.-XII/8]).

Warhaffte Eygendliche
Abbildung und Conterfey
Des Fürtrefflich-Tapfferen
Ungarischen Helden Teckeli.

MICHAEL TECKELY

Fig. 4. Imre Thököly (1659–1705) (National Library, Budapest, Hungary)

life of personal and historical drama, one profoundly affected by the vagaries of European power politics.

Thököly and the Hungarian events also filled many pages of contemporary newspapers devoted to events of the years 1683 to 1687 (*Nordische Mercurius, [Hamburger] Relations-Courir, Europäische Relation, [Altona] Europäische Fama*, and *Altonaische Relation*), as well as the already mentioned *Krieges-Bericht*, the *Thesaurus Exoticorum*, and volumes 12 (1679–86) and 13 (1687–91) of the *Theatrum Europaeum*.[20] Although volume 13 did not appear until seven years after Happel's death in 1690, we can assume that his anonymous continuator in volume 6 of the *Ungarische Kriegs-Roman* made use of these periodical publications as Happel had done before him. A comparison of Happel's novels to compendiums such as the *Theatrum* and his own *Thesaurus Exoticorum* (1688) demonstrates not only how quickly news publications had become indispensable for writers of different narrative genres but also how newspapers, journals, broadsheets, and letters almost immediately found their way into both news media and the novel. The eyes of all of Europe were trained on Hungary (*UK* I: 460), and the public, eager to be informed, read Happel's novels as enthusiastically as it did newspaper accounts. Mindful of this news hunger, Happel stresses the urgency of undertaking his new publishing venture, the *Ungarische Kriegs-Roman*, by citing the great popularity of an earlier novel of his, the *Christlichen Potentaten Kriegs-Roman* (1680), as the impetus for writing the *Ungarische Kriegs-Roman*.[21] The new project was to deal year by year with the triangulated pan-European struggle among the Ottoman Turk, the empire, and the rebellious members of the Protestant Hungarian nobility. The result would be, once again, a fictionalized *Zeitgeschichte* representing the major military and cultural challenges of the day.

While Thököly does play a leading role in the *Ungarische Kriegs-Roman* (to which I will return shortly), he also turns up in several of Happel's earlier novels, specifically those *Geschicht-Romane* that chronicle the years concurrent with the *Ungarische Kriegs-Roman*.[22] In the *Italienische Spinelli* (1685),

---

20. Matthaei Sel. Erben Merian, ed., *Theatri Europaei Continuati Dreyzehender Theil/ Das ist: die Fortsetzung Denck- und Merckwurdiger Geschichten/ Welche/ ihrer gewohnlichen Eintheilung nach/ an verschiedenen Orten durch Europa . . . vom Jahr 1687, an biss 1691. sich begeben und zugetragen . . .* , vol. 13 (Frankfurt am Main: Johann Goerlin, 1688), 2, 4, 9, 11, 38, 257, 373, 647, 1022, etc.

21. *UK* I: *Vorrede.*

22. Happel himself enumerates his novels in the *Frantzösische Cormantin* (1687), where he

for example, the narrator cautions that even after the Turk had been routed at the siege of Vienna, one should not take his power lightly.[23]

The *Teutsche Carl* of 1690, the year of Happel's death, presents an elaborate discussion of the failing strategies employed by Thököly as he struggles to gain greater power in Hungary by finding a niche between the Turk and the empire. Thököly also surfaces, more insistently fictionalized, in the *Bayrische Max*, a novel published two years after Happel's death, in 1692, but still under his name. The preface (*Vorbericht und Anrede*) advertises the novel to the "Hoch- und Viel-Geehrte Leser" as another in the series of *Geschicht-Romane*, written because it seemed (according to the editor) that the reader had taken a special liking ("sonderbares Belieben") to this kind of novel (*BM* I: *Vorbericht*). This *captatio benevolentiae* is, again, followed by a list of the *Geschicht-Romane* published prior to the *Bayrische Max*. The preface remained unsigned, but the preceding dedication (*Zuschrifft*) to Maximilian Emanuel of Bavaria identifies the writer as Happel's longtime publisher, Matthaeus Wagner of Ulm. Not knowing for certain who actually wrote the novels appearing after 1690, we can conjecture that up to and including the *Eduard* and the *Carl*, the books may have been sketched out in manuscript by Happel himself and completed by Wagner or may have been written by an anonymous author following the popular template provided by Happel's earlier novels. Whereas the anonymous author acknowledges writing volume 6 of the *Ungarische Kriegs-Roman* to complete the series after Happel's death, no such clarification is offered in the *Bayrische Max*.

While the *Geschicht-Romane* from the *Spinelli* forward make episodic mention of Thököly and his travails, the count takes center stage in the *Ungarische Kriegs-Roman*. In other words, Happel's work and, with it, the development of the count as a character in the *Geschicht-Romane* evolve alongside his major oeuvre, the *Ungarische Kriegs-Roman*, as he himself mentions in *Bajazet* (1688). Alluding to this novel's fourth volume, he reveals,

mentions the *Italienische Spinelli* (1685) and the *Spanischen Quintana* (1686). Published posthumously in 1693, the *Sächsische Witekind* adds the *Ottomannische Bajazet* (1688), the *Teutsche Carl* (1690), the *Engelländische Eduard* (1691), and the *Bayrische Max* (1692) to the list.

23. "Gleichwohl muß man den Barbarischen Hund nicht allzu gering schätzen . . . Inmassen die Printzen und Hospordarn von Siebenbürgen/ Wallachei und Moldau mit ihrer Mannschafft zu ihm stossen müssen/ wann er es ihnen befiehlet/ ja selbst der Graf Thököly stehet jetzo mit einer ziemlichen Macht zu seinem Geboth (We must not underestimate the barbarian dog . . . inasmuch as the princes and nobles of Transylvania, Wallachia, and Moldavia must join forces with him [the Ottoman] when he orders it, and even Count Thököly is now under his command [*IS* I: 146]).

"Schier-künfftig hast du auch zu sehen den Vierdten Theil/ oder Beschluß dieses Romans/ welchem so dann auf dem Fuß gleichsam folgen wird der Fünffte oder Letzte Theil des Ungarischen Kriegs-Romans/ in dessen Außfertigung wir jetzo begriffen sind/ und sobald derselbe seine Endschafft erreichet" (In the future you will see the fourth chapter or end of this novel, upon which will immediately follow the fifth and last part of the *Ungarische Kriegs-Roman*, which we are in the process of completing and which will soon reach its end [*OB* III: *Vorrede*].) At Happel's death, however, the war in Hungary was still far from over. The continuator tells us that he felt compelled to scatter the characters once again in search of further adventure, so that they could be reunited at the end of the sixth and final volume (though still predating the end of the war, which finally concluded in 1699).

Happel makes Thököly part of the narrative of the *Geschicht-Romane* in the three ways previously mentioned. The *Spinelli* and the *Quintana* report mainly on events gleaned from the available newspapers: the sieges of Neuhäusel, Belgrade, Ofen, and Gran and the destruction of the important bridge at Esseck. They also report repeatedly on Thököly's imprisonment at Grosswardein as well as about his subsequent transport to Adrianople (*IS* II: 351–71; IV: 330–40). More specifically, documents that we encounter in the *Quintana* are quoted almost verbatim in the *Theatrum*, whose editors, in turn, had gleaned them from contemporary newspapers. One such document is a letter addressed by Thököly's wife, Ilona, to Field Marshal Caprara on November 28, 1685. A copy appears in the *Quintana* (I: 109–11) as well as in the *Theatrum* (XII: 843). In the letter, Ilona implores Caprara to lift the siege of Munkács, which she had been holding since 1685 while her husband tried to secure financial and military support in his struggle for Hungarian independence. Signaling her strength and her resolve, she insists that should Caprara not be willing to honorably lift the siege, she would not be afraid to continue her resistance ("Ich erschrecke vor der Last der Waffen nicht"). Acknowledging that Thököly had been abandoned by many of his former allies, she continues, "Was mich anlanget/ werde ich die Treue/ die ich Gott und meinem Mann schuldig bin/ nicht brechen" (As far as I am concerned, I will not betray the faith due God and my husband [*SQ* I: 106, 107]). The narrative repeats essentially what we find reported in the daily press about Ilona's resolve and steadfastness.

The fate of Thököly and his wife also comes up in the *Frantzösische Cormantin*, which recounts a widely reported episode of the war: the hanging of four of Thököly's supporters in the town of Eperis. At this point, Ilona, still holding Munkács, continues to express confidence that aid from the

Porte would soon turn things to the better, even if the suffering was great at the moment: "Obgleich man jetzo etwas leyden müsse/ so würde doch Gott bald helffen/ indeme der Türck mit großer Macht herauß kommen/ erst sich die eingenommenen Plätze erobern/ und hernach durch ihren Herrn den TÖCKELY helfen wurde" (Even if we have to suffer now, God will help soon in that the Turk will approach in great force, conquer the places taken, and, in due course, come to the help of their lord, Thököly [*FC* II: 251]).

As is the case in the *Cormantin*, contemporary events are usually narrated in response to informational questions asked by one character of another, who then reports what was read in the newspapers that are constantly cited, alluded to, or read aloud. While these reports are not given to emotive commentary (at this point, op-ed pages belong to the distant future), some emotional content can be detected between the lines, such as in an allusion to Ilona's anxiety about her husband's struggles. One of the rare comments about her marriage to the much younger Thököly, who had by then emerged as the leader of the *Kuruc* rebels, makes reference to the public's interest in and censure of her actions as well as to the fact that Field Marshal Caprara would not take her word for Thököly's willingness to compromise, "weil aber dies Damen intrigiren . . . und den [*sic*] Haß gegen den unvergleichlichen Hauß Österreich geneugsam bekandt ist . . . damit daß sie dem Tökely geheurathet/ da er schon lange der Auffrührer ihr Rädelsführer gewesen" (but because the ladies are spinning their intrigues and their hatred of the house of Austria is well-known . . . because of that she married Thököly, because he had long been the leader of the rebels [*ER* 99: 786–87]).[24]

Other, equally dramatic encounters between Happel's readers and these actors emerge in the *Bayrische Max*. Pursuing military honors, Max, the protagonist, joins the imperial forces in their fight against the archenemy, the Turk (*BM* II: 92). On a reconnaissance mission, Max happens upon "Töckelische mit Türcken und Tartarn vermischte starke Parthey" (Thököly's men mixed with Turks and Tartars [*BM* II: 93]). (Newspapers frequently mentioned Turks and Tartars as part of Thököly's army.[25]) The soldiers—or rebels, as Max calls them—take him prisoner. In camp, he meets a Ger-

---

24. Caprara's attitude toward her is described as "daß sie also dem Herrn Feld-Marschall keine Brillen wieder verkauffen können" (that they would not be able to sell any eyeglasses to the field marshal [i.e., make a fool of him]).

25. As in the contemporary press, "Tartars, Turks, and malcontents" is a stock phrase in nearly all of the novels. For example, we read in the *Relations-Courir*, "Aus Nieder-Ungarn continuiret/ daß die Türcken/ Tartarn und Rebellen in 50 000 starck" (*RC* 5 [1685]: January 11; Z 100/1685/4/6).

man who persuades him to change sides and, like him, serve in Thököly's army. Although distressed at the suggestion by this otherwise good German ("dieser sonst prave Teutsche") that he become a traitor, Max consents to temporarily join the rebel army, for pragmatic, if not patriotic, reasons (*BM* II: 108). This information agrees with news reports that tell of two hundred Germans who served in Thököly's army and retreated with him in 1685 to the German border after the surrender of Eperis (*ER* 78 [1685]: 619). It had been Thököly's misfortune—reported in great detail in the *Relations-Courir* of September 18 and October 8, 1684, as well as in the *Nordische Mercurius* of April 14, 1685—that imperial troops had overrun his encampment at Eperis.[26] This important event also found its way into the *Ungarische Kriegs-Roman*, where General Schultz is quoted as writing to Graf Geiger that with "Göttlicher Hülffe den Töckeley samt seiner völligen Reuterey von hier auß seinem Quartier gejagt/ und Halß über Kopff biß unter den Wald verfolget/ viel niedergemacht/ seinen Schlitten/ samt seinen besten Kleidern/ und ander Bagage, ingleichen abermal seine geheime Cantzley" (with God's help I chased Thököly and his troops from their encampment and pursued them in a wild chase into the woods, killing many and capturing his sled with his best clothes and all of the other baggage, including his secret correspondence [*UK* III: 167]).[27]

Thököly himself barely got away with just the clothes on his back, but his secret plans concerning Eperis and Ofen fell into enemy hands, those of General Schultz. Ingeniously mixing fact and fiction, Max's subsequent encounter with Thököly serves as an effective device to introduce the reader to this controversial and contradictory personality. Like Cergely, one of the main characters in the *Ungarische Kriegs-Roman*, Max finds the general to be nothing like what he had expected. Instead of a warlike, irreverent rebel, he meets an attractive, friendly, and polite gentleman who shows great empathy with Max's hesitation to join the rebel army, an act that might force him to march against the imperial forces.[28] After giving his word that he would not leave camp without permission, Max, to his astonishment and appreciation,

---

26. "[D]ann in jüngst eroberten Cantzley/ Sachen Töckelys/ hat man Brieffe gefunden/ welche von grosser Consideration" (recently letters have been found in Thököly's belongings that are of great importance [Z 20/1685/30/2]).

27. "[S]einen Schlachtplan/ der in seiner Cantzley gefunden wurde,/ womit der Plan dem kayserlichen vor Ofen verraten war" (*UK* II: 523); "Das gantze Teckelysche Lager ist samt allen/ was darinnen gewesen . . . Teckely selbst soll/ wie die Gefangenen berichten/ kaum in den Schlafhosen davon kommen seyn" (*RC*, Z 100/1684/82/1).

28. "Einen ansehnlichen/ sondern zugleich auch verständigen freund- und höflichen Herrn" (a respectable as well as reasonable, friendly, and polite lord [*BM* II: 109]).

finds himself free to move about: "Dergleichen unverhofftes Tractament hätte ich mich nimmermehr versehen" (*BM* II: 109). His positive assessment of the count is clouded only by the fact that Thököly had risen up against the emperor and was thus fighting against Christians. Nonetheless, when Max meets several of the Turkish officers and a few Tartars among Thököly's troops ("so wackere und prave Leuthe/ daß ich mich höchstens vewundern mußte"), he voices his astonishment that people frequently called barbarians are, though strangers with unfamiliar customs, superior to his countrymen in virtues and morals ("die uns doch in guten und rühmlichen Sitten in vielen Stücken vorgeben" [*BM* II: 109]).

In the foreword to the first volume of the *Ungarische Kriegs-Roman*, the author reminds his readers that along with the most accurate descriptions of the recent hostilities between what the *Nordische Courier* called the "Bluthund" or Turk[29] and the German Empire, he will, true to his often-articulated mission, deliver geographical and cultural facts on countries near and far. Following the formula of his publishing success, these reports will be embedded in the "gewöhnliche Romanis[che] Erfindungen," which have pleased the reader in the past ("welche dem geneigten Leser noch allemal gefallen haben" [*UK* I: *Vorrede*]). It will be remembered that he had elsewhere recommended himself to his readers as a *Historico*—in fact, as the best history writer in this world ("dem Happelio, dem besten Geschicht-Schreiber dieser Erden")—a point of pride he intends to keep in his narrative focus.[30] True to this self-proclaimed expertise, he promises reports about such media events as coronations, weddings, deaths, and funerals of members of the imperial family and the nobility and about heroic battles and bloody sieges ("viel von den allerblutigsten Schlachten/ so zwischen Türcken und Christen/ oder ihren anderen Feinden fürgefallen sind" [many of the most bloody battles that have taken place between Turks and Christians and their enemies] [*UK* I: *Vorrede*]).[31]

---

29. "[D]en Erbfeind Christl. Nahmens den Türckischen Bluhthundt" (the deadly enemy, the Turkish bloodhound [*Nordische Courier*, September 11, 1683])

30. Happel, *Historia Moderna Europae, Voransprache*. Also in the *BM*: *Vorbericht und Anrede*: "Er [Happel] wird sich befleissigen/ die vornehmste Begebnüsse dieses abgewichenen Jahres/ ohne Partheylichkeit/ *Fide historica* . . . anzuführen" (He will try to describe the events of the past year without partiality and simply with historical faithfulness [BM I: *Vorbericht und Anrede*]). Also see *BM* III: *Vorrede*.

31. To this must be added the reports about violent and strange weather events and bloody crimes that the characters tell each other when they gather to share a meal at home or in one of the many guesthouses or as they travel in search of adventure or each other: see I, 5 (imperial diet in Augsburg); IX (coronation of the emperor; privileges of the Crown); XII (relationship

In the course of reading the *Ungarische Kriegs-Roman*, we learn not only about Imre Thököly's life and fate but also about that of his father, Istvan, Count of Kessmark (1623–70), a recently installed magnate with rich land-holdings in Upper Hungary.[32] The elder Thököly had fallen under suspicion of having conspired against the emperor in the struggle over the sovereignty of Protestant Hungary.[33] The resulting imperial attention led to the loss of title, land, and wealth.[34] In the novel, Balassi, Imre Thököly's secretary, who often appears in news accounts (generally nameless), insists on Istvan Thököly's innocence ("Es wuste dieser Herr gar nichts von dem Complot, Rath und Anschlägen" [This lord knew nothing of conspiracy, counsel, or betrayals] [*UK* I: 336]).[35] The same opinion is advanced in the chapter on the "Herkunft des Grafen Thököly," as reported in the *Thesaurus Exoticorum*.[36] Reading contemporary press reports, however, makes it clear that public opinion was divided on the question of the senior Thököly's guilt or inno-

between the emperor and the electors); XVIII (the Golden Bull); II, 8 (death of the Herzog of Lothringen).

32. Köpeczi, *Staatsräson und Christliche Solidarität*, 33, 190. Magnates were wealthy and influential ennobled families in Transylvania (and also in the kingdom of Poland). Paul Lendvai, *The Hungarians: A Thousand Years of Victory in Defeat*, trans. Ann Major (London: Hurst, 2003), 138.

33. "Zuflucht von Antitrinitariern bei dem Grundherrn Istvan Thököly in Käsmark" (Refuge of the Antitrinitarians at the castle of Istvan Thököly in Käsmark), in Marta Fata, *Ungarn, das Reich der Stephanskrone, im Zeitalter der Reformation und Konfessionalisierung: Multiethnizität, Land und Konfession, 1500–1700* (Münster: Aschendorff, 2000), 201. To this day, whether or not Istvan participated in the uprising has not been determined.

34. Erasmus Francisci puts it this way: "Ich will nochmals unterdessen/ für meine Wenigkeit/ diesen älteren Tökli keiner empörlichen Verständniß bezüchtigt haben; sondern nach wie vor/ die rechte Beschaffenheit hiervon lieber von andren erlernen/ als andere dieselbe zu lehren mich erkühnen" (I do not want to accuse the older Thököly of a rebellious mind, but rather leave this assessment to those who know better rather than to take upon myself to teach others). Erasmus Francisci, *Der blutig-lang-gereitzte/ endlich aber Sieghafft-entzündete Adler-Blitz Wider den Glantz deß barbarischen Sebels/ vnd Mord-Brandes* (Nuremberg: Johann Andreae Endters, Seel.Söhne, 1684), 226.

35. In the *Wöchentlicher Extraordinari Friedens-und Kriegs-Curier* of March 7, 1683, he is mentioned as Sermay [Z 98/1683/Fr.-Eo I/ 2]; in the *Europäische Relation* of 1685, he appears as Bebnehasy, who is described as being held in Vienna while a courier is sent to Thököly (*ER* 81: 642; [Z 19/1685/E.R.]). Francisci mentions Balassi several times as having negotiated and carried messages for Thököly (*Der blutig-lang-gereitzte*, 40, 53, 306).

36. *ThEx*, 376. See http://diglib.hab.de/drucke/gv-2f-26/start.htm-. One of the many broadsheets about Thököly's life puts it this way: "Erst von dessen (Emmerichs) Herrn Vater/ dieser hieß Stephan Thököly de Keßmark. . . . Er hielt sich auf in Ober-Ungarn/ auf seinen Gütern/ und wußte von denen Zusammenrottungen . . . gar nichts oder das wenigste" (Of his [Emmerich's] father, whose name was Stephan Thököly of Keßmark. . . . He mostly stayed in Upper Hungary on his estates and had no or very little knowledge of the rebellions).

cence, as indeed was Happel himself. Recent histories of seventeenth-century Hungary offer a more nuanced assessment of the count's involvement. They identify Istvan as one of the coconspirators in the rebellion against the empire in response to Vienna's ruthless persecutions of Protestant nobles and clerics and to the invalidation of the Hungarian constitution of 1673.[37] The elder Thököly died in 1670 or 1672, during the siege of his castle, and his landholdings and wealth were then confiscated by the emperor. Stories (if not history) have it that Imre Thököly, only fourteen at the time, escaped across the Polish border disguised as a woman.[38] He eventually joined Prince Apafi (1662–90), ruler of the autonomous region of Transylvania (*Sieben-bürgen*) (*ThEx* 4, 17–18). Because Apafi paid tribute to the Sublime Porte, the region enjoyed relative calm and semi-independence.[39] Though divided in their opinion about what motivated the younger Thököly's later actions, specifically his relationship with the Sublime Porte, his contemporaries as well as more recent historians unanimously praised his talents as a military leader and his brilliance as a tactician, even if later assessments of Thököly's role in the power struggle between the Habsburgs and the Sublime Porte would prove his actions disastrously wrongheaded.[40]

But before all this came to pass, before his father lost all he owned and all over which he ruled, young Imre was raised with all the privileges accorded his station. He was well tutored in the fine arts and literature at the Atheneum at Eperis, where he completed his studies in 1669, imbued with a passionate Protestant faith and well trained in the arts of war. As previously noted, Eperis would come to haunt him almost twenty years later. On February 1, 1687, death sentences were passed on four of Thököly's fellow rebels: "und aufs neue [ihres] Eydes ungeachtet/ sich mit der Rebellischen TÖCKELISCHEN PARTHEY und Faction eingelassen/ viel Botschafften hin und hergeschicket/ und empfangen" (and not minding their oath, they joined Thököly's rebellious party, sending many emissaries back and forth [*FC* II: 252]).[41] The judgment of Cormantin (the protagonist of the novel

---

37. Lendvai, *Hungarians*, 138; Fata, *Ungarn*, 274.

38. "Schickt seinen Sohn EMERICUS THÖKLY IN Bauernkleider nach Siebenbürgen, von da; verfolgt, aber auf dem Weg von einem guten Freund in polnische Frauenkleider gesteckt" (send his son Emericus Thököly in peasant clothing, from there; pursued on the way, a friend put him into women's dress). Francisci, *Der blutig-lang-gereitzte*, 223.

39. Mihaly Apafi I (1662–90), prince of Transylvania. See Lendvai, *Hungarians*, 140–41; Köpeczi, *Staatsräson und Christliche Solidarität*, 16–18.

40. László Kontler, *A History of Hungary: Millennium in Central Europe* (New York: Palgrave Macmillan, 2002), 179–80.

41. [A]uf Mungatz an die TÖCKELIN geschrieben/ über die grossen Drangsaalen/ die sie

that bears his name) on this event is, for Happel, uncharacteristically blunt: "Das war/ sprach CORMANTIN jetzo/ dieser boßhafftigen Leuten ihr verdienter Lohn" (This was, said Cormantin, the deserved reward for these evil people [*FC* II: 252]).

In the *Ungarische Kriegs-Roman*'s fictionalized story of Thököly's life, his emissary and secretary, Balassi, reports that the young Thököly had successfully championed the Protestant religion against several "Römischgesinnte," excelling in not only theological but also secular studies and argumentation (*UK* I: 340). At this age, he was not yet the rebel he would become but a committed and diligent student who, still innocent of rebellion against the Habsburg crown, expected to regain his patrimony in land and wealth. For the time being, fortune was on young Thököly's side, providing him with the resources his patrimony could not. He inherited large landholdings from his cousin Graf Rhaddai Ferentz (Rhodai Ferentz), who died without a male heir (*UK* I: 340).[42] Additionally, he came into possession of considerable wealth upon the death of his mother. Lastly, while in his very early twenties, he benefited from his marriage to Ilona Zrinyi, the wealthy widow of Prince Ragotzki, a member of one of the most illustrious and powerful families in Hungary (*UK* I: 341).

Despite the inauspicious and turbulent years of his earlier youth, these fortuitous events gave Thököly the resources that enabled him to think seriously about reclaiming his patrimony and supporting the cause of Protestant Hungary or, less loftily, the establishment of Hungary as a religiously tolerant nation. Several times, but never with success, he appealed to the imperial court in Vienna for redress of his grievances. According to the *Nordische Mercurius*, his emissary was informed that any income from properties whose owners had betrayed their loyalty to the emperor would be

---

außstehen müssen/ und wie ihnen zu Eperis übel ergienge. . . . Worauff die TÖCKELIN zu Eperis/ wie sie mit Freuden gehöret/ daß man gegen ihren Herrn/ und sie TÖCKELIN zu Eperis wol gesinnet sey/ und obgleich man jetzo etwas leyden müsse/ so würde doch Gott bald helffen/ indeme der Türck mit großer Macht herauß kommen/ erst sich die eingenommenen Plätze erobern/ und hernach durch ihren Herrn den TÖCKELY helfen wurde" ([he] wrote to Mungatz to the Thökölin about the great distress which they had to suffer and how badly it had gone in Eperis. . . . After which the Thökölin told them how well they were disposed toward her and her Lord. And in spite of the fact that they had to suffer now, God would help in that the Turk would come in great force and reconquer the places they had lost and, after that, would come to the help of her lord Thököly [*FC* II: 252]).

42. "[A]ls er [Thököly] kaum in Siebenbürgen ankommen/ nach weniger Zeit/ sein Herr Vetter Graf Rhodai Ferentz und zwar ohne männlichen Erben starb (when he, Thököly, had barely arrived in Siebenbürgen, his cousin Rhodai Ferentz died without male heirs). *ThEx*, Leopold I, 17.

confiscated and employed for war expenses ("Kriegs-Nothwendigkeit" [*NM*, Vienna, October 24, 1683]). Thököly was turned away even more insistently when another of his emissaries ("ein gewisser Gesandter") suggested to the Herzog of Lothringen that Thököly might be useful in negotiating a peace with the Porte, "welches ihnen alles contra ausgeschlagen/ und dabey bedeutet worden/ ohne Verzug das Gewehr wieder ihren König niederzule-gen/ und gegen den Erbfeind mit allem Eyfer zu ergreiffen" (which they all rejected while indicating that he should promptly put down the guns directed against the king and take them up with all due passion against the archenemy [*NM*, Linz, October 26, 1683]). In other words, he was advised to surrender without voicing any further demands. Of course, he did not. The newspapers never tired of repeating that it was the arrogance with which he articulated his demands in the face of the established order that hardened the attitudes of the imperial negotiators. Throughout 1685, we find reports in the *Europäische Relation*, for example, that pointed to his weakening posi-tion, such as a note from March 5 saying that "hofft man/ daß des Teckely Macht ehisten abnehmen/ und seine Adherenten zum vorigen Gehorsam übergehen werden" (one would hope that Thököly's power was waning and that his followers would return to their previous loyalties [i.e., to the emperor] [*ER* 19 (1685): 146]).[43]

After unsuccessfully appealing to Vienna, Thököly turned to the Porte for assistance. The sultan confirmed Thököly's right to his ancestral lands and, assuring Thököly of his support, bestowed on him the titles "count" and, later, "prince." Accepting the former title but rejecting the latter, Thököly combined expectations for his future as the leader of the Protestant Hun-garian nobility with defiance of the emperor, practicing the *Realpolitik* that media reports followed with their often caustic comments on his actions, his whereabouts, and his partisans. His asking the Porte for help introduced important moral questions that would be repeatedly raised in the media and throughout this lengthy novel. Was turning to the infidel Turk for assistance justified if Thököly or any other nobleman felt rebuffed by what he under-stood as his emperor's denial of justice? Should Thököly be condemned as a malcontent, a rebel; or must his struggle for Hungarian freedom be admired and honored as patriotic, pious, and personally righteous? Were those who followed Thököly's leadership justified in turning against a ruler—in this case, the German emperor Leopold I—if, as the rebels alleged, this ruler acted against the nobility's freedoms and privileges ("wofern sie etwas wieder

---

43. Z 19/1685/E.R.

deß Adels Freyheiten und Gerechtsame zu thun sich unterwinden" [*UK* I: 341])? Finally, was it permissible or tolerable to raise weapons against the divinely established authority of the emperor and, in the face of the Ottoman threat, to shake the foundations of the social, political, and religious order? Had his countrymen, again and again characterized as given to warfare and strife, decided to follow Thököly as their leader because he inspired them with dreams of a sovereign and Protestant Hungary or, as others insisted, to help them better rob and pillage in the name of such "freedom" (*UK* I, 1: 369)? While keeping writers for seventeenth-century newspapers as well as Happel busy, the answers to these questions remain both elusive and pertinent to this day.

Given the ambiguities implicit in Thököly's shifting strategies and uncertain actions, it is not surprising that even Constantinople viewed Thököly with some misgivings: the sultan muses, in Happel's words, "[W]as vor Händel machet ihm der Rebellische Töckeli? Dieser ist zwar ein Bundsgenoß/ oder vielmehr ein neulich angnommener Vasall . . . aber er bleibt gleichwol ein Rebell" ([W]hat kind of trouble does the rebellious Thököly bring to him? Though he is an ally or, better, a recently appointed vassal, he remains a rebel). He seems to have been quite aware that Thököly's secret dealings with the Porte ("heimliche Estats-Interesse" [*UK* I: 71]) were prompted more by his need to secure support against the emperor ("rechtmässigen Herrn") than by any devotion to the Ottoman or the Qur'an (*UK* I, 1: 71). A news flash from Vienna (April 19, 1685) supports this assessment. After asserting that it was becoming increasingly challenging for Thököly to find a place to rest, the report confirmed that "[d]ie Pforte trauet ihm auch nicht viel mehr/ vielmehr ist er daselbst heimlich in grossen Ungnaden/ weil er für den Ursacher gehalten wird/ dieses für die Mahometaner so unglücklichen Krieges" (the Porte did not trust him much; in fact he had secretly fallen into great disfavor in this, for the Turks, so unfortunate war [i.e., the defeat at Vienna in 1683] [Z 19/1685/E.R.]).

To the contemporary reader, however, it is clear that Thököly's notoriety as a character in a novel and his celebrity as a person dominating the news were not due purely to the political and military turmoil and the fascination of the reading public with his actions. Rather, they were influenced and fanned by the relentless media attention fixed on him, as a review in the *Nordische Mercurius* and similar publications circulating during the years 1683 to 1686 suggests. Assessing only a fraction of the events that supplied news content for these years, we note that news available to Happel clearly showed a western European bias toward the empire, frequently picking up news items that identified Thököly as a malcontent or rebel and describing him as a man between the fronts, alternately rejected by both the Porte and the empire. But in some of the many contemporary broadsheets that commented on the events as much as they reported them, more ambivalent opinions can be found about Thököly and the public's abiding interest in his activities, his flamboyance, and his eventual downfall.[44] These broadsheets alternately call him a "Fürtrefflich-Tapfferen Ungarischen Helden," the "Ungarischen Ertz-Rebellen," or "der Ungarischen Malcontenten Haupt- und Anführer."[45] Depending on whether the reports are partial to Emperor Leopold I or supportive of Hungarian political independence and religious self-determination, Thököly is either condemned as a rebel and a malcontent or praised as a hero for standing up against the German emperor, whose policies regarding Hungary's Protestants were considered despotic and arbitrary by the writers of these latter tracts.

The pride Happel took in his role as an impartial *Historico* is evident in the way his fictions mediate between the extremes and the contradictions that dominated the media. In the *Ungarische Kriegs-Roman*, this mediation becomes apparent to the reader through one of the novel's fictional protagonists, the mysterious Albanian nobleman Cergely (*UK* I: 87), whose travels the reader follows across six volumes and ten years of struggle with the Ottoman Turk. After having heard much about Thököly, Cergely (and, with him, the reader) is looking forward to meeting the famous man in person. Along the way, the often ambiguous news reports that Cergely had read and his conversations with various traveling companions put forward both sides of the media reactions to Thököly, constructing a striking—if conflicting— portrait of the man.

Carefully creating an aura of authenticity, Happel introduces Ferenc Balassi (mentioned previously), Thököly's confidant and emissary and possibly a fictional stand-in for one of Thököly's historical secretaries. An unnamed man identified by this title appeared on several occasions in the *Nordische*

44. Gisela Cenner-Wilhelmb, "Feind oder zukünftiger Verbündeter? Zur Beurteilung der politischen Rolle der Emerikus Thoekoely in den grafischen Blaettern seiner Zeit," in *Das Osmanische Reich und Europa 1683 bis 1789: Konflikt, Entspannung und Austausch*, ed. Gernot Heiss and Grete Klingenstein, Wiener Beiträge zur Geschichte 10 (Munich: Oldenbourg, 1983), 54–70. Cenner-Wilhelmb's essay suffers, as does much of the research on Thököly, from confusion about exactly when he turned where for support.

45. I thank Roger Paas for sharing his treasure trove of images with me; they have appeared as the eleventh volume of his magnum opus, *Das politische Flugblatt* (2010). Köpeczi's book also offers a number of excellent images in the appendix (pp. 391ff.).

Mercurius.[46] According to news reports, Thököly's secretary was captured at Pressburg (now Bratislava, Slovakia) in 1683 along with the Protestant postmaster and mayor of the town ("so beyde Lutherisch") and accused of having assisted Thököly in his secret flight from the town on August 22, 1683. The *Relations-Courir* of September 2, 1685, told of yet another secretary, named Syrmay, who was said to have gone over to the enemy and asked for pardon.[47] On September 11, the *Mercurius* informed its readers that "Töckelisch Gesinten bösen Gemüther" (bad people who hold with Thököly) had spread false rumors that the Turk had taken Vienna ("daß Zeitungen und Nachrichten einkommen/ daß die Türcken sich der Stadt Wien bemächtiget hätten" [newspapers and news had come in reporting that the Turk had taken Vienna]). Two years later, after the surrender of Eperis,[48] Thököly's secretary (unnamed but most likely Syrmay), mentioned in other press reports as having surrendered to Vienna, was now reported to have been sent to Vienna to ask for the imperial pardon. A news clipping from September 30, 1685 (*Relationes Curiosae*), has both of Thököly's secretaries, Syrmay and Bethnehasi, in Vienna trying to negotiate a pardon in exchange for a surrender of all places still under his command. The paper's wry comment suggests that Thököly is in no position to negotiate: "so ist doch wegen dieser condition kein Perdon zu hoffen" (the condition offered does not suggest hope for a pardon).[49] Another paper explains that the request was denied because the decision had come too late ("allzuspäth") and because of Thököly's supposed close relationship with the Porte ("sintemahlen er bey der Pforten eben in solchem aestim . . . befindet" [since he seems to be [again] esteemed by the Porte] [*ER* 77 (1685): 609; Z 1/1685/E.R.]). In September of 1685, a person now identified as "Teckelische Secretarius Bethnekasy" was reportedly making suggestions—not taken terribly seriously—about how to defeat the Turks. In fact, Bethnehasi was being kept under surveillance ("und wird unterdessen . . . fleissig verwachet") due to imperial mistrust [*ER* 80 (1685): 626; 81 (1685): 642)].[50] Adding to the contradictory news coming out of Hungary is the information on November 1, 1685, in the *Relations-Courir* that the

---

46. "Und wird unterdessen dahier (Caschau) befindliche Teckelische Secretarius Bednehasy fleissig verwachet" (And in the meantime, Thököly's secretary, Bethnehasi, who is here now, is well guarded [*ER* 81 (1685): 642; Z 19/1685/E.R.]). See Köpeczi, *Staatsräson und Christliche Solidarität*, 355.

47. "Des Töckely geheimer Rath/ Secretarius und Haupt-Rebell Syrmay ist mit 10 Pferden übergangen umb Kayser Perdon bittend/ gestern allhier (Vienna) arrivirt" (Z 100/1685/82/5).

48. Now Prešov, Slovakia.

49. Z 100/1685/98/7.

50. Z 19/1685/E.R.; Z 19/1685/E.R.

sultan had offered "des Töckelys General Bethnehasi Töckelys 'Stelle.'" But he was too much of a coward and instead delivered Caschau (now Košice in Slovakia) to Vienna and asked for pardon "den er auch erhalten." Furthermore, Bethnehasi offered to deliver to the emperor all other places and officers remaining under Thököly's command.[51] Two years later, in 1687, the ambiguous and contradictory news about Thököly's dealings with the Porte continues, reflected in yet another news item. The paper blames Thököly's alleged loss of troops on his having lost the support of the Porte and reports that his wife was secretly seeking an imperial pardon.[52]

To return to Happel's narrative, Balassi meets the fictional Cergely and his companions as they journey through Hungary in search of Thököly. Raising many morally and politically charged questions about loyalty, national pride, and religious freedom as he converses about the count, Balassi urges Cergely to look to additional sources of information in the many available tracts and daily newspapers ("von denen Zeitung . . . fast täglich gelesen wird") for a more balanced review of the life and times of the "brave and devout Thököly" (*UK* I: 342). According to Balassi, Thököly was being exonerated in the court of public opinion—a conclusion not necessarily shared by the careful reader of the contemporary press.

Balassi is not only an admirer but also a coconspirator. The reader discovers that this learned and well-traveled man is on a secret mission for Thököly ("Politische Heimlichkeiten" [*UK* I, 1: 303]), a mission that might involve King Louis XIV of France and might be prompted by Thököly's anticipation that France and Portugal could be persuaded to support him in his quest for the liberation of Hungary (*UK* I: 311). Balassi reminds his listeners that in 1677 and 1678, when Thököly was not yet twenty, he had already assembled around him a group of horsemen called *Kuruc*.[53] With their help, Thököly had defeated the imperial forces in 1679/80 and forced them to surrender parts of Upper Hungary.[54] These bold military strikes brought him early fame, providing the groundwork for his later ambition and, so he hoped, ultimately for the creation of an independent Hungary. At this

---

51. Z 100/1685/116/8.

52. "[W]eil der Töckely seine Credit bey der Pforte ziemlich verlohren . . . und die Töckelin selbst fängt an bey so gestalten Sachen den Kayserlichen Pardon zu suchen" [*Relations-Courir*, Z 100/1687/78/6].

53. *Kuruc* comes from the Turkish word *kurudsch*, meaning "rebel" or "insurgent" (Lendvai, *Hungarians*, 138, 543).

54. Miklós Molnár, *A Concise History of Hungary*, trans. Anna Magyar (Cambridge: Cambridge University Press, 2001), 129–30.

earlier juncture, Thököly was supported by King Louis XIV, by the king of Poland, and by Count Apafi of Transylvania as, together, they formalized an anti-Habsburg alliance that brought two thousand French soldiers by way of Poland to Transylvania.[55] In the 1680s, Apafi changed sides, abandoning Thököly's cause and accepting the imperial pardon with the assurance that he would continue as the ruler of Transylvania.[56] In fact, on April 1, 1685, a news item in the *Relations-Courir* highlighted Thököly's precarious situation. General Schultz, one of the imperial military leaders whose name is mentioned repeatedly in novels and newspapers as the action proceeds, had come upon ("ertappet") one of Thököly's supply camps. The news was followed by the information that Thököly had sent an emissary to the Porte for assistance in revoking Apafi's requisition of Thököly's possessions and holdings in Transylvania (*RC* 22 [1685]: April 1; Z 100/1685/22/7). Shortly thereafter, on May 29, news was circulating about Thököly's great distress: he could not hope any longer for Turkish help, and many of his followers were leaving him to accept the emperor's pardon.[57]

As they travel along, Cergely, Balassi, and another fictional traveler— Michael Claudi, a *Rittmeister* from Saxony and, as it turns out, a spy in the service of the emperor—converse at length about the personal and hegemonic interactions of the various players, be they historical or fictional. To pass the time, Balassi reviews Thököly's biography with the keenly listening Cergely and the skeptical Michael. Balassi's tone is positive and admiring, and his account is almost completely based on a widely circulating version of Thököly's biography used by Happel in his *Thesaurus Exoticorum* (1688) (*UK* I, 1: 344).[58] The biography, beginning with Thököly's father's fall from imperial grace and the son's flight via Poland to his relatives in Transylvania, depicts a young man undaunted by the difficult hand that fortune has dealt him and his family. While he possesses all the virtues of a noble youth, one shines most brilliantly of all: Thököly's devotion to his Protestant faith (*UK* I, 1: 339). Balassi puts into words one of the underlying themes of this lengthy novel: that Thököly's life and his struggle, his sporadic alliance with

---

55. Lendvai, *Hungarians*, 139.

56. Ibid., 140–41.

57. "Der Teckely stehet in grosser Consternation, weilen er nicht allein von den Türcken nichts mehr zu hoffen/ sondern seine Adhaerenten sich von ihm abzusondern suchen" (Thököly is very upset not only because he has lost all hope with the Turk but because his followers are beginning to leave him [*RC*, April 29, 1685; Z 100/1685/26/7]).

58. *ThEx*, 95–97. It also appears throughout Francisci's tract on the Turkish-Hungarian conflagration: Francisci, *Der blutig-lang-gereitzte*.

and fealty to the Turk, were largely framed in the context of the vigorous Protestant opposition by parts of the Hungarian nobility to domination by the Catholic emperor, as well as their deep resentment toward the Jesuits.

Balassi's narrative contradicts much of the negative information found in many contemporary press reports. This contradiction further heightens the reader's curiosity about this extraordinary man, while also signaling what is the hallmark of news reporting, namely, the occasional inconsistencies that arise from the need to get the news to press quickly. The journalistic ambition to satisfy reader curiosity as swiftly as possible finds expression in the writer's comment that the little tract ("Tractaetlein") was "in Eyl zusammengeschrieben, und denen begierigen Zeitungs-Lesern mitgeteilet worden" (written down in a great hurry so that it would reach the eager readers).[59]

In Balassi's description, Thököly is handsome, brave, learned, and polite: "Ein schöner wolgestalteter noch junger Herr von etwa 29. Jahren/ von lieblich roth und weissem Angesicht/ etwas wenigen Barths und bräunlicher Haare/ erhabenen und pöltzigten Augen" (A beautiful, well-built, still young man of twenty-nine years with a lovely red-and-white face, a bit of a beard and light brown hair, dignified and dark [?] eyes [*UK* I, 1: 342]). Following almost verbatim the information provided in the *Thesaurus Exoticorum*, the novel portrays him as being at the top of his world, physically attractive, a strong and decisive leader, admired by his followers, and a central figure in the battle against the emperor's rule in 1681.[60] The papers and the novel repeatedly note that Thököly was able to persevere in the pursuit of his cause mainly because his marriage to Prince Ragotzki's widow, Ilona Zrinyi, gave him access to her vast fortune and thus a power base in Upper Hungary.[61] In 1681, increasingly alarmed at escalating Hungarian militancy and Thököly's growing army of followers, Emperor Leopold I employed a diversionary tactic. He called a meeting of the Hungarian estates, the Diet of Ödenburg, where he agreed to restore the division of power between the estates and the Crown and to grant the Protestants permission once again to practice their religion.

59. Anon., *Warhafftige Eigentliche Original Bildnüs Nebst Denkwürdiger und Ominöser auführlicher Lebens-Beschreibugn/ des gebohrnen Ungarischen Grafen Nunmehro aber/ von Ottomannischen Porten/ bereits erklärten Fürsten Emerici Tökeli . . . Dabei zu finden auch das Manifest und Bildnüs Abaffi des Fürsten aus Siebenbürgen . . .* (1683). Cited in Köpeczi, *Staatsräson und Christliche Solidarität*, 264. I am grateful to Albert Gelver and Dr. Bode from the Institut Deutsche Presseforschung, University of Bremen, Germany, for making a copy of the pamphlet available to me (SDC12239).

60. Fata, *Ungarn*, 276.

61. Kontler, *History of Hungary*, 180.

Thököly chose to stay away from the diet and, in defiance of its compromise, published a manifesto calling on the Hungarian people to support the cause of a free Protestant Hungary.[62] He allied himself instead with the Sublime Porte, consenting to a short-lived appointment as prince of Upper Hungary. He did, however, reject the Porte's offer of the royal crown of Hungary, choosing instead to place his hope and trust in the trans-European intrigues and conflicts that pitted the Porte against Habsburg and both against France. He hoped, it appears, that the national conflicts born of the struggle for European hegemony would, in the end, further the cause of his own national ambitions.[63]

While Cergely listens with rapt attention to Balassi's exposition, the Catholic Michael Claudi ("der Ungarische Michael . . . als ein eyffriger Catholic" [the Hungarian Michael . . . a devout Catholic])[64] becomes increasingly agitated. Imre Thököly may have been virtuous and devout in his younger years, he says, but by now he had turned into nothing better than a rebel, "a man of a different stripe" (*UK* I, 1: 345). Claudi maintains that though Thököly had repeatedly asked for an imperial pardon, he had done so with such arrogance and with so many conditions that it was impossible for the emperor to accede.[65] The *Relations-Courir* of May 6, 1685, agreed with this assertion, writing that Thököly could not receive an imperial pardon by way of the intercession of the Polish king because there was no assurance that he would return to his duty to the empire.[66] Two years earlier, the *Mercurius* had written that Thököly's behavior at the siege of Vienna so irked the Polish king and the emperor that an emissary was sent to inform Thököly "daß es in seiner [the emperor's] Macht stündte/ demselben innerhalb 24. Stunden gäntzlich auszurotten und zu vertilgen/ weiln dann gegebener Thököly zu Catholischer Resolution sich nicht bequämen/ sondern die Vergleichs-Sache und Implorierung des Kayserl. Pardons in eine weitläufftigkeit ziehen wil" (that it was in his [the emperor's] power to totally crush and obliterate him within twenty-four hours because the selfsame Thököly did not want

---

62. Köpeczi, *Staatsräson und Christliche Solidarität*, 50.

63. Kontler, *History of Hungary*, 180.

64. At an earlier point, Michael appears as a Saxon.

65. "Auß Ober-Ungarn verlautet/ daß der Teckely von seinen Conditionen nicht abstehen . . . sondern er habe [an die Pforte] geschrieben/ denen Bassen zu Erlau und Waradin zu befehlen/ ihm auff sein Begehren zu assistiren" (From Upper Hungary we hear that Thököly will not give up on his demands . . . rather he is supposed to have written [to the Porte] to order the Pashas of Erlau and Waradin to assist him if he needs it (*NM*, Linz, October 30, 16??).

66. "Es scheinet aber/ daß Ihre Mayestet. seiner Begehren kein Gehör geben werde" (It appears that His Majesty is not paying him any heed [Z 100/1685/37/5]).

to assent to the Catholic resolution, rather he wants to drag out at length the offer of accommodation and imperial pardon [*NM*, Breslau, October 22, 1683]). Two weeks later, the same newspaper reported that the pope urged the emperor "Accommodation . . . zu benehmen und ihn zu absoluter Submission zu disponieren" (to deny him [Thököly] the accommodation [pardon] and force him into absolute submission [*NM*, Wels, October 30, 1683]). Thököly and his rebel followers were evidently confident that the Porte would defeat the empire in 1683; the empire's victory caught not only Thököly but also much of Europe completely by surprise.

Realizing that neither Michael's nor Balassi's opinion could be accepted as gospel ("für Evangelia halten kunte"), Cergely poses, once more, the basic moral question "ob es einer christlichen Nation erlaubt sey/ bey den Türcken wider ihre Christliche Obrigkeit/ Schutz zu suchen" (whether a Christian nation was permitted to seek protection from the Turks against the Christian authorities [*UK* I, 1: 346]). Balassi responds by directing Cergely and the reader to a widely circulated *Manifest* (1681) about the age-old rights and privileges of the Hungarian people: "darinn genugsam fürgestellet wird/ auß was Ursachen die Ungarische Stände grossen Theils bey der Ottomanenischen Pforten Schutz zu suchen . . . und die Waffen zu ihrer Defension zu ergreiffen genöthiget worden" (in this it is sufficiently demonstrated why the Hungarian estates sought protection from the Ottoman Porte . . . and why they were forced to take up weapons in their defense [*UK* I, 1: 346]). The novel reproduces the *Manifest* in its entirety and attributes it to Prince Michael Apafi I of Transylvania (1632–90). This *Manifest*, which also circulated as a pamphlet published in 1683,[67] is a passionate and eloquent declaration in support of Hungarian sovereignty and freedom of religious expression (*UK* I, 1: 346–66) and against the emperor's disdain toward the Hungarian estates and his unjustified and undeserved breach of faith against the Hungarian Protestant nobility.[68] The *Manifest* outlines the reasons why some members of the Hungarian estates had sought protection with the Ottoman Porte and why they were justified in doing so. It closes with bitter allegations of ancient liberties trampled and religious freedom suppressed and, in the end, passionately invokes the "Hungarian" Jehovah, who would ensure that, in due time, freedoms lost would be restored and the enemy would be vanquished (*UK* I, 1: 366; *Manifest*, 14).

This expression of Apafi's patriotism, however, is undercut by a "Rela-

---

67. Anon., *Warhafftige Eigentliche Original Bildnüs*.
68. Köpeczi, *Staatsräson und Christliche Solidarität*, 355.

tion oder Kundschafft" reported in the *Nordische Mercurius* on February 10, 1685, which suggested that Apafi (through his secretary, Michael Telecki) had secretly contacted the emperor to confirm his oath of loyalty to him. The *Relation*, described as a copy of an anonymous letter that, along with Thököly's baggage, had fallen into enemy hands, warned the Porte against the action of Prince Apafi and his secretary, Telecki, who had also negotiated with Vienna and Poland for help against the Porte. Moreover, the writer reminded the Porte that Prince Apafi, while having declared his allegiance to the Porte to ensure the independence of his realm, had never actually lifted a finger in the Porte's support ("noch niemahl zu Dienst des grossen Sultans den Säbel entblößet"). The writer went on to recommend that if the Porte were to insist on backing Apafi, the prince should be asked to send his troops but should be told to stay away from the battle ("weil wir ihn selbst sehr verdächtig halten" [because we find him very suspicious]). He may have been right. On April 22, 1684, the *Nordische Mercurius* reported that Apafi's emissaries had approached Vienna with the offer of peace negotiations ("Friedens Mediation"), only to be rebuffed. On September 26 of the same year, the *Relations-Courir* told of a visit by one of Apafi's emissaries to the Porte, supposedly to defend his "Principal" against accusations of disloyalty.[69] In short, not only in the daily press but subsequently in Happel's novels, Apafi's and Thököly's stratagems vis-à-vis the Porte—and, by extension, vis-à-vis Vienna—were contradictory and were ultimately revealed as unsuccessful exercises in *Realpolitik*.

Though Michael listens to Balassi's narrative of Thököly's life "mit wundersamer Gedult" (with amazing patience), he remains unmoved by the rousing language of the *Manifest*, which seems to him suspicious and disingenuous ("verdächtig und erdichtet"). He points out that thoughts are free until they lead to actions punishable under the law ("Gedanken sind so lange Zoll frey/ bis sie durch Worte oder That selber offenbahren/ alsdann warden sie gemeiniglich straffbahr/ wann sie böse sind" [*UK* I: 367, 269]).[70] Although Michael has, for reasons not revealed at this point in the narrative, "gone over to the Turk," he insists that his devotion to His Majesty, the German emperor, was so deeply rooted that he could never deny it, even in the midst of Turkey ("mir [ist] der Respect gegen Se. Kayserl. Majest. So tieff eingewurtzelt/ daß ich desselben auch mitten in Türckey nicht werde in

---

69. Z 100/1684/77/8.

70. He continues, "Aber meine Gedanken sind gut/ und gründen sich auf die reine unverfälschte Warheit" (But my thoughts are honorable and are founded on the untainted truth, discursively not decisively [*UK* I: 367]).

Vergeß kommen lassen" [respect for His Imperial Majesty is so deeply rooted in my person that even in the very middle of Turkey I would not forsake it] [*UK* I: 367]).[71]

The reader remains in suspense as Cergely and Balassi turn to Michael for the counternarrative about Thököly, the rebel and malcontent. Michael begins by firmly maintaining the veracity of his version and his right to speak it, asserting that his "tongue must be as free under a free sky as Lord Balassi's had been" (*UK* I: 367). He begins by criticizing the stories circulating about Thököly ("theils erdichtet, theils allzupartheyisch" [as in part made up, in part much too partial]), and he calls the *Manifest* suspicious and the motives of the rebels whitewashed. They do not desire freedom and rights, he says; rather, they want simply to plunder and rob ("die Leute schätzen und aussaugen" [to pressure and oppress the people] [*UK* I: 369]). As bandits from all over Germany and eastern Europe (Croatia, Bohemia, Silesia, and Poland) joined (as the newspapers reported) Turks and Tartars (*NM*, Linz, March 27, 1684), Thököly's men wanted only to exploit the sweat and blood of the common people—a far cry from fighting for "Religion und Landes-Freyheit." Widely circulating news reports described Thököly's followers as a ragtag group of mercenaries ("Erzt-Rebellen"), often denouncing them as worse than the Turk himself, as they were said to steal children and sell them into slavery as well as to plunder and steal for their "Sold" (pay).

Michael pauses in his diatribe against Thököly for a moment to reassure his audience (and the reader) that he believes Thököly himself to be very much opposed to the brutal behavior of his men, going so far as to punish and even execute those whom he caught committing violence. But since he could control only those closest to him, the rest essentially did as they pleased (*UK* I: 378). In the end, Michael opines, rebellion unfailingly leads to the loss of order, discipline, even civilization, no matter how noble the cause may appear to be. In Michael's estimation, there was no country in the world whose wars had devoured more people and whose earth had drunk more blood than Hungary. Again, such assertions force the reader to wonder why Michael had "gone Turk," but he will not divulge this information until he has discharged his duty to deliver a message to the man he so obviously disdains, Imre Thököly (*UK* I: 386).

When, in the novel's first volume, the three men arrive at Thököly's camp, Cergely, along with the reader, finally meets the notorious leader (*UK*

---

71. A rather ambiguous character, the fictional Michael "went Turk" yet remained loyal to the emperor.

I, 1: 392), in the midst of a multinational force of about twenty thousand men. The count is resting close to Neuhäusel,[72] awaiting news from the Ottoman Porte that Balassi is to deliver. Setting up this fictional encounter with as much historical accuracy as possible, Happel has Thököly politely welcome Cergely, who immediately takes a liking to him. Thököly's ambiguous personality, as reflected in many media reports and eloquently described in Balassi's and Michael's conflicting portraits, becomes instantly apparent. Although Cergely finds him polite and handsome, eyes ablaze with courage, he also acknowledges that Thököly appears to be consumed by the ambition to rise above the station of a mere Hungarian count ("in seinem Hertzen einige Ehrsucht hegete/ und mehr als ein ungarischer Graf wolte geehrt werden" [UK I: 392]).

Cergely compares Thököly to Gustavus Adolphus of Sweden, who, after his untimely death in 1632, had become a European legend, a Protestant saint of sorts. Holding onto his admiration, yet compelled to acknowledge historical reality, Happel's Cergely separates the leader from his men, noting that much as he admired the count and enjoyed his company, he was little pleased with Thököly's officers and his men, calling them "von tückischem und grimmigem Gesichte/ von schlechter Conversation und grausamer Conduite" (of mean and cruel countenance, of bad speech and cruel conduct [UK I, 1: 394]). Cergely appears to echo a news report of August 15, 1683, wherein the Polish king had accused Thököly's troops of "sengen und brennen" (burning and destroying) in Moravia and Austria. If such behavior were to continue, the king was quoted as saying, he would destroy Thököly's landholdings in Hungary. Upon receiving this threat, the report says, Thököly had apologized for the actions of his undisciplined troops ("sehr undisciplinirtes Volck"). The anonymous commentator noted that one could trust that Thököly would hold still while waiting to see if any support was forthcoming from the Groß-Vezier (grand vizier) (NM, Imperial Army camp at Angern, August 15, 1683). Two years later, the Relations-Courir of July 19, 1685, reported Thököly's flight to Munkács and, from there, to Caschau,[73] all in the hope that the two emissaries he had sent to the Pasha of Erlau would be able to secure support for him. This hope was in vain, the paper reported, as quite the opposite was the case: "hat der Bassa des-

---

72. Part of Turkish Hungary after 1664, Neuhäusel was the "most beautiful and earliest example of a walled city in the Italian Renaissance style." Fata, Ungarn, 177.

73. Munkachevo (Ukraine); Kosliše (Slovakia).

sen Bündnüß gleich zerrissen/ dem Vornehmsten von ihne Stranguliren/ und die anderen 2 arrestiren lassen" (the pasha immediately tore up this contract and had the most noble strangled and the other two arrested [Z 100/1685/58/5]).[74] The imperial general Schultz was in hot pursuit, and we read two months later, in the *Europäische Relation* of October 11, 1685, that the plunder gathered by Thököly's army was being distributed to the general's men ("weil Zeitwehrender Rebellen viel Raub dahin gebracht worden" [because the rebels had gathered much plunder in this place]).

Happel's Thököly, be he hero, rebel, or malcontent, is clearly an intriguing individual. For a short period of time, he participated in the complicated challenge to Ottoman and imperial dominance in eastern Europe, fighting against overwhelming odds in a dispute in which the European powers sometimes united against the Turk and sometimes directed their aggressive struggles for European hegemony against one another.

In October of 1685, Thököly, whom the Porte considered partly responsible for their defeat at the siege of Vienna in 1683, appealed for Turkish support at the siege of Caschau. What followed was a sensation in the European media world and cause for much speculation. The reporting on the event is contradictory: a note from October 30 stated that Thököly had been taken prisoner by the Turks and brought in "Banden und Eisen" (bound and in irons) to Grosswardein.[75] His wife was said to have fled to Poland along with all her worldly goods, only to be robbed of them by brigands en route.[76] The former piece of news turned out to be half true, the latter completely false. Thököly had in fact appealed to the Pasha of Grosswardein for help with the siege of Caschau. The pasha had welcomed him, invited him to a sumptuous meal, and then abruptly declared him a prisoner, saying that while he sympathized with Thököly's plight, he was acting on the order of Constantinople (*ER* 89 [1685]: 707). Before he was to be transported to Adrianople, Thököly was granted permission to write to his wife. This is the origin of Ilona's letters, which, in Happel's novel, become the topic of discussion between the historical Field Marshal Caprara and the fictional Cergely. A news report from Vienna on April 19 of the same

---

74. The same was reported by the *Relations-Courir* of November 1, 1685.

75. The most detailed news report of the trap that had been set for Thököly is in the *Relations-Courir* of November 4, 1685: "Eigentliche und ausführliche Relation von der Übergabe der Stadt Caschau und Arrestirung des Töckley" (Z 100/1585/118/ 4–6).

76. *ER* 89 (1685): 700; Z 19/1685/E.R.

year confirmed the Porte's secret distrust of Thököly,[77] and a beautifully engraved broadsheet from 1685 accused the Turk of betrayal: "Vorstellung der erbärmlichen Tragödie/ welche der Bassa von Groß-Waradein mit dem Weltberuffenen Hungarischen Haupt-Rebellen Graf Emerich Teckely/ allda im Monat Octobr. Dises 1685. Jahres gespielet/ in dem er denselben prächtig eingeholet/ freundlich empfangen/ tyrannisch angesprenget/ und endlich in Ketten und Banden geschlossen" (The description of the pathetic tragedy that the Pasha of Grosswardein inflicted on the world-renowned Hungarian rebel leader Count Emmerich Thököly in October 1685. He had accompanied him with great splendor, welcomed him in a friendly way, [then] cruelly attacked him, and finally bound and chained him). In the end, Thököly and his wife, like the Ottoman forces, were forced to leave Hungary. By 1699, Sultan Mustapha II abandoned Turkish rule over all of Hungary, including Transylvania. Three months later, in July, the *Europäische Relation* (54: 425) told readers that Thököly had appealed in vain for help from Poland, the Porte, and Transylvania, which put him into such despair that he offered to "turn Turk" if they only would support his struggle.[78]

There were other challenges before Thököly and his wife reached the end of their journey. After his release from Turkish captivity in 1686, Thököly is described in the novel by a Dalmatian nobleman as on the run: "vergleicht sich derselbe einem verschüchterten Stuck Wild/ welches in der Irre herumwallet" (he can be compared to a traumatized deer wandering through the wilderness [*UK* IV: 185]). This reflects a note in the *Relations-Courir* (1685) describing him as the "hin und her vagirenden Töckely" (the Thököly who is wandering around aimlessly), who should give up his high expectations and accept the imperial pardon ("mit dem Kayserl. Pardon amplictiren solle" [*RC* 105 (1685): Vienna, October 7; Z 100/1685/102/6]). We read the same in the *Europäische Relation* from Vienna for April 15, 1685: "[Thököly] von einen Ort zum andernen herumb vagierete/ und Niemanden mehr trauete" (Thököly wanders around from place to place not trusting anybody [Z

---

77. "Die Pforte trauet ihm auch nicht viel mehr/ vielmehr ist er daselbst heimblich in grossen Ungnaden/ weil er für den Ursacher gehalten wird/ dieses für die Mahometaner so unglücklichen Krieges" (Z 19/1685/E.R.).

78. "Welches alles ihn sehr jrre und verzweiffelt machete und so weit gebracht/ daß er den Türcken anbietet zur Versicherung seiner Treu ihre Religion anzunehmen" (All of which confused him and drove him into despair to the point that he offered his conversion to the Porte [Z 19/1685/E.R.]).

19/1685/E.R.]). He was, in fact, still scheming to liberate Munkács.[79]

For a brief moment during 1685, media and reader attention turned with intense interest from Thököly to the Thökölin—his wife, Ilona. Cergely, the charming, irresistible gentleman "to whom no one in the whole world could deny anything," wants to hear more about this remarkable woman, particularly about her courageous defense and ultimate surrender of the fortress of Munkács in 1688. We read about her negotiations with the emperor for a capitulation that would allow her to abandon the besieged property but not its contents or her and her husband's possessions. Leopold, in turn, instructed her to forgo all contact with her husband. Meanwhile, we read, in the novel and in the media, about Thököly's efforts to communicate with her. Two of his letters survive and are quoted in full in the novel.[80] While Thököly remains in detention with the Pasha of Grosswardein (1685–86), one of his letters reassures her that the sultan will support him anew in his struggles to liberate his country and his wife. For this reason, he explains, he is keeping close to the sultan and his deputies. A second letter confirms his optimistic assessment. He expresses continued faith in his cause, a faith that, at this point, seems quite foolhardy.

Despite the long odds against her, Ilona held on to Munkács from 1685 to 1688. This did not stop rumors circulating in newspapers that she had sent the keys to the castle to General Caprara in 1685. Nothing could have been further from the truth, as the skeptical writer confirmed: "so ist doch von dar noch keine Nachricht eingelauffen" (no news has arrived yet from there [*ER* 91 (1685): 722; Z 19/1685/E.R.]). Equally false were reports of November 1, 1685, that "des Töckely 2 fürnehmsten Herschaffts-Festungen/ Potach und Mongatsch freywillig nebst 8 à 9000 Mann/ so dem Töckely gehörig gewesen/ an Ihro Kayserl. Mayest. Übergangen/ und in Dero Devotion sich ergeben" (Thököly's most noble forts/castles Potach and Munkács have voluntarily surrendered to His Imperial Majesty along with eight to nine thousand of his men).[81] Shortly thereafter, upon Thököly's arrest by the Pasha of Grosswardein, Field Marshal Caprara turned to Munkács, expecting that a siege would prompt the Thökölin to submit to imperial mercy ("sich der

---

79. Kontler, *History of Hungary*, 181.

80. *UK* IV: 185.

81. *RC*, Z 100/1685/116/6. Two weeks later, we read in the same newspaper that the news about Munkács is uncertain ("keine sichere Nachricht/ ob die Töckelin mit ermaleten Hn. Gen. Feld-Marschall Caprara die Übergabe Capitulation geschlosssen" [*RC*, November 15, 1685; Z 100/1685/123/7]).

Kayserl. Gnade desto ehender submittiren werde" [*RC*, November 8, 1685; Z 100/1685/120/6]).[82] Reports appeared in the *Europäische Relation* that she was distraught over the imprisonment of her husband and, bereft of any counsel, reportedly pleading with the Polish king to intercede with the emperor on her behalf (*ER*, November 18, 1685; Z 19/1685/E.R.). Such an intercession, the writer surmised, would hardly be granted ("sie wird selber solches schwerlich erhalten" [it is doubtful that she will be granted this request]). A month later, on December 6, the paper reported that she had changed her mind and, contrary to what had been reported, now insisted that her husband had voluntarily gone to Adrianople and would return with a strong relief force ("mit einen starcken Succurs wieder zu kommen"). Therefore, she would not surrender Munkács. The reporter noted, with some consternation, that she had "gar unseren Leute/ so etwas nahe kommen/ mit Stücken zurück getriben" (even driven back our troops, who had come too close with cannons [*ER* 98 (1685): 777]). Completely frustrated with the "Halsstarrigkeit der Töckelin" (headstrong attitude of the Thökölin) and long before she handed over Munkács, Caprara found himself compelled ("genöthiget") to declare her and her followers rebels, thus making her goods and property free for the taking.[83] Moreover, he gave orders to lay siege to Munkács with three thousand men ("berennen und einzuschliessen"). Even more interesting is his plan to send Bethnehasi so that he could convince her to surrender and accept the imperial pardon.[84]

The delicate pas de deux between the empire (as represented by Field Marshal Caprara) and the Thökölin put both of them most effectively into the spotlight of public attention, in the media as well as in Happel's novel. After raising the dramatic tension of his narrative by mixing factual and fictional meetings, contacts, and conversations, Happel could not let pass the chance to construct an encounter between the novel's protagonist, Cergely, and this extraordinary woman. Joining Caprara's besieging army encamped outside of the walls of Munkács, Cergely expresses his curiosity about the

---

82. *RC*, Vienna, November 4, 1685: "Eigentlicher und ausführliche Relation von . . . Arrestirung des Töckely" (Z 100/1685/118/4).

83. "Indessen hat der Herr General Caprara anhero geschrieben/ daß er wegen anhaltender Halsstarrigkeit der Töckelin genöthiget worden/ sie sambt ihren Anhang für Rebellen zu erklären/ und seinen unterhabenen Trouppen ihr Leib Leben und Guet frey zu geben" (In the meantime, General Caprara has written that because of the unyielding attitude of the Thökölin he would declare her life and goods free for the taking [*ER* 103 (1685): 819; Z 19/1685/E.R.]).

84. "[U]nd hat indessen den Bethnehasi zu ihr gesandt/ damit sie die Extrema nicht erwarten/ sondern zeitlich sich ergeben/ und der Kayserl. Clementz sich theilhafftig machen solte" (*RC*, November 29, 1685; Z 100/1685/131/6).

famous fortress and the woman who holds it under her command. Ilona, referring to her family connections, calls herself Princess Ragozi (Ragotzki) and insists that Munkács was part of her patrimony as a member of one of the oldest and most powerful families of northern Hungary and thus is not under the control of the emperor at all (*UK* IV: 193). Cergely and Caprara converse about the astounding fortress and its valiant defender. Clearly, the woman whom Caprara calls "eine unvergleichliche Dame" equally fascinated both the general European public and the reading one. In his conversations with Cergely, Caprara expresses his admiration for her steadfastness and devotion to her unfortunate ("unglückselig") husband. As he reads the couple's letters (which actually were intercepted), Caprara describes how he had repeatedly asked her to surrender, urging her to consider her precarious situation.

Caprara's comments and Thököly's letters touch the reader, expressing a side of the couple's relationship that we have not heard or seen before. Thököly's tenderness for his beleaguered and besieged wife demonstrates an affection that can be read as analogous to his devotion to his beleaguered country. For a moment, their failing mission recedes into the background as Happel allows us to see the couple's mutual love, and the fictionalized account of their romance offered here resonates with the historical facts familiar to the reader.[85] As is the case repeatedly in factual-fictional encounters of his characters, Happel does not separate the one from the other but, rather, melds romance with history, lending greater depth and definition to both.

Increasingly eager to know more, Cergely presses Caprara for permission to read Ilona's response to Caprara's demand of surrender. Moved and impressed by her dignified defiance, Cergely decides that he is eager to meet her in person. Of course, only the universe of the novel allows for such a meeting. Consequently, Happel constructs a typical fictional surprise as he arranges the encounter, introducing a new character, Alonso, a long-lost friend of Cergely who surfaces among Caprara's troops.[86] Alonso brings reports of Thököly's address to the Hungarian estates on January 29, 1686. Still in denial of the military, political, and personal realities facing him, Thököly had opened this address with the words "wir Imre Thököly von Gottes Gnaden/ und auß sonderbarer Clementz deß Türckischen Kaysers/ Fürst in Ungarn" (we, Imre Thököly, by God's grace and the clemency of

---

85. *TE* XII: 843; *UK* IV: 193–201.

86. Alonso appears as "verstossener König" and is most likely King Alfonso VI of Portugal (1643–83).

Zrinyi Ilona arczképe és névaláírása.

Fig. 5. Ilona Zrinyi (1643–1703) (Austrian National Library, Vienna, Austria)

the Turkish emperor prince in Hungary), thus reminding the estates of their obligations to him (*UK* IV: 202).

In his fictional universe, Happel does what he promised his readers he would do: he joins history with *romanische Handlung*, the "action of romance," to enhance their reading pleasure. He moves Cergely, Alonso, and the reader ever closer to an imagined encounter with Thököly and Ilona. When it at last occurs, it involves not polite conversation across the dinner table but a face-off in (cross-dressed) combat (*UK* IV: 209ff.). Two knights from the fortress challenge two knights from the besieging army to a duel. The challenge is presented by a young boy in white wearing a wreath of laurels around his head. Caprara reacts with suspicion, while Cergely responds with great excitement, eager to accept the challenge. He points out that he is free to engage in single combat if he wishes, since he is a volunteer soldier, not a member of the imperial army, and is therefore not under Caprara's authority.[87]

Disguised as a trumpeter, Cergely enters the fortress to deliver his acceptance of the challenge to the princess. Welcoming him, she shows him around the fortress, where he meets a man dressed in green Turkish garb whom he feels he has seen before but cannot place. This is, of course, Thököly himself, who, in the *Spanische Quintana*, is described as moving around in Transylvania and along the border of Turkish territory with a small group of followers generally dressed in the green of Ottoman nobility (*SQ* 243).[88]

The next day, Cergely and Alonso meet the two knights as they come down from Munkács, and they engage in vigorous and valiant combat. Cergely and Alonso both prevail, and after the defeated pair acknowledges the victors' superior fighting skills, the four separate. According to their prior agreement, Cergely accompanies his opponent off the field and away from Munkács. Only at this point does he recognize his opponent as Thököly, now free to escape the siege. From the conversation they share before they part, Cergely (and the reader) gain a deeper understanding of Thököly, his courage, and his superior intellect. After they part, Cergely grants Thököly a long enough lead to ensure that Caprara will not be able to catch up with him (*UK* IV: 230).

---

87. It is interesting to note that one of the characters in the *Ungarische Kriegs-Roman*, the African cavalier Zolfiar, shares this pride in his independent status as a fighter (*UK* V: 365).

88. "While social, political, and above all, economic innovation swept the West, the Ottoman Empire remained steeped in sterile ceremonial. The color of robes and of slippers, the cut of sleeves, the shape of turbans, the length of beards defined in scrupulous detail the difference between one set of officials and others." Ronald Segal, *Islam's Black Slaves: The Other Diaspora* (New York: Farrar, Straus and Giroux, 2001), 116.

There is, in fact, no historical record of Thököly ever visiting his wife during the siege of Munkács. To the contrary, according to a news report from Vienna of November 28, 1683, when Thököly wanted to withdraw to the fortress, his stepson—Ilona's son from her first marriage and not a supporter of Thököly—refused him entrance.[89] In 1685, another report from Vienna (October 21) stated that he had left Munkács and, unable to find refuge anywhere, did not know where to turn.[90] Happel constructs this encounter in such a way that the reader meets Thököly after he has been weakened but not yet defeated in his cause. Furthermore, the report given in the *Quintana* describes Thököly as publishing, on April 2, 1686, a proclamation affirming his authority over parts of Transylvania, because he is once again in good standing with the sultan.[91] While more and more magnates and towns accepted defeat and, with it, the imperial pardon, Thököly remained, despite news reports to the contrary, a significant *Störfaktor*, a fact that Happel conveys in his construction of this fictional encounter and escape.[92]

Turning from Cergely to Alonso, the other combatant, we follow him and his opponent into the castle of Munkács, where we meet several gentlemen who entertain Alonso until a lady "with heroic mien" enters the room. As she greets Alonso, she reveals that she had been his challenger ("sehet ich bin euer Gegner gewesen/ und habe in vollen Küriß mit euch gekämpft" [behold, I have been your opponent and fought with you in full cuirass] [*UK* IV: 231]) and that Cergely's opponent had been Thököly. At first speechless and then profoundly apologetic for not having yielded victory to her, Alonso

89. "Graf Thököly hat sich zwar nach Mongatsch retiriret/ den Winter allda in Sicherheit zu bleiben/ weil aber sein Stieffsohn ihm das Schloß gesperret/ ist er darauff nach Siebenbürgen gewichen" (Count Thököly has retreated to Mongatch, to stay safe during the winter, because his stepson has refused entry to the castle. After this he has returned to Transylvania).

90. "Weil dem Teckely sein beängstigtes Gewissen ihm nirgends Ruhe lasset/ als hat er sich auß Mungatch gemacht/ sonder Wissen/ wohin er seinen Cours genommen habe" (Because Thököly cannot find any rest for his anguished conscience he left Mungatsch without any information where he may have gone [*ER* 85 (1685): 674]; Z 19/1685/E.R.]).

91. The proclamation represents a reassurance of his power and a threat to those who would dare to resist him (*SQ* II: 242). "Sonsten ist der Thököly bey den Türcken wieder in zimlichem Ansehen/ und gehet er stets grün gekleidet. Die Türcken geben ihm den Namen Cziliak-Vezier, welches einen Bassa oder Haupt vom Stern bedeutet/ wodurch sie einen Führer oder Wegweiser bedeuten wollen" (Otherwise, Thököly is back in the good graces of the Turk, and he usually goes around dressed in green. The Turks are calling him Cziliak-Vizier, which means to them a leader or advisor [*SQ* II: 243]). Thököly is moving around acting as if still in power, while many of his followers abandon him. The contradictory news reports are, in fact, a reflection of the situation.

92. Lendvai, *Hungarians*, 142.

praises Ilona's martial prowess as well as her ability to defend the fortress against such overwhelming odds. The historical Ilona Zrinyi, extraordinarily courageous in real life, metamorphoses into one of Happel's powerful and daring fictional heroines, as adept at combat as at polite conversation.

A delicious meal is served, signaling that the fortress remains fully supplied with food and drink. Alonso marvels at the wealth and luxury of the castle, and the countess points out that the family's treasure is securely kept at Munkács, a fact that explains how she could mount such a passionate and long-lasting defense.[93] She points out that they have access to sufficient water, food, and munitions for a lengthy siege (which was, indeed, to last for three years). At the end of the meal, Ilona bids Alonso good night. The next morning, she presents him with a beautiful ring in memory of their combat.

Back in camp, Cergely and Alonso recount their adventures to Caprara, who is as delighted at the outcome as he is furious about having let Thököly slip away. But he accepts that, as a knight and gentleman, Cergely, given the trust placed in him and Alonso by Thököly and Ilona, could never have betrayed them (*UK* IV: 243).

Happel's novel, like contemporary press reports and, much more soberly, the *Theatrum*, follows Thököly as he advances his cause by fostering, among his followers and his imperial opponents, a reputation as a great military leader with a stellar political future. In the end, he would be defeated as much by the unexpected rout of the Porte outside Vienna in 1683 as by the emperor's political astuteness in extending amnesty to all those willing to abandon Thököly and his cause. An excerpt from the "General Perdons, welchen I. Kays. Mayst. allen Ungarischen Rebellen anbietet" (general pardon that His Imperial Majesty offers to all Hungarian rebels) appeared in the *Relations-Courir* from Vienna on January 25, 1684 [Z 100/1684/9/5]. But it must be recognized that Thököly's attempts to work both sides of the conflict and thus control politics to his own advantage yielded only brief success.

Historians have suggested that Thököly was by no means "exclusively a hanger-on of the Ottoman Empire" but was sincere in his determination to liberate his "Fatherland from the Turk" as well as from the Germans, as indicated in a November 1681 diary entry by his wife.[94] She, for one, was convinced

---

93. This is also mentioned in the *Quintana*; it must have been an important news item: "Hat noch das Schloß Mongatz, wo er seine Gemahlin und den Rest seines Vermögens verwahrt" (He is still in possession of the castle Mongatz, where he keeps his wife and the rest of his wealth [*SQ* II: 242]).

94. Lendvai, *Hungarians*, 140.

that he made common cause with the Turk for purely pragmatic reasons: he needed help against Catholic Vienna's rule over Hungary, and no other power would oblige him, neither France nor Poland nor Russia nor England.

Thököly stayed away from the Turkish siege of Vienna, seeking instead to enlarge his holdings in southern Hungary: "der Thököly bey sich habenden Rebellischen Ungarn/ Türcken und Tartaren in etliche 60.000 Mann starck . . . eingefallen/ und darinnen sengen und brennen sollen" (Thököly and his rebels, Hungarians, Turks, and Tartars, around sixty thousand men . . . have attacked and burned and destroyed [areas in southern Hungary] [*NM*, Breslau, September 11, 1683]). Despite Thököly's political maneuvers, the Turkish defeat on September 12, 1683, became the turning point not only in the struggle between the Porte and Vienna for dominance in the Balkans but also in Thököly's career.[95] To pacify the Hungarian estates in the wake of his victory, Leopold II, now dealing from a position of strength, went so far as to offer amnesty to the Hungarian rebels.[96] Many of them accepted, including, as previously noted, Prince Michael Apafi I of Transylvania, which had long been an Ottoman protectorate. Things had indeed changed, as the *Nordische Mercurius* noted on October 21, 1683: "[D]aß das Glück und die Conjunctur [sich] nun geändert hätten/ deßgleichen suchen viel andere abgefallene und untreu gewordene Ungar. Magnaten an wiederumb den Keys. Perdon/ da es dann scheint/ daß alles in der Güte mögte beygeleget werden" (fortune and the stars have changed. For this reason many have left the Hungarian magnate and returned to the imperial pardon because it appears that everything could be solved in good grace [*NM*, Vienna, October 21, 1683]). We read in the *Relations-Courir* of February 24, 1684, five months later, that a high-ranking Hungarian official had pressed Thököly to acknowledge his mistakes and fall in repentance at the feet of His Imperial Majesty, Leopold II. Thököly reportedly rejected this recommendation, insisting that he would find support with the Porte.[97] Already in March of the same year, some of the rebels seemed to assess the situation differently from their leader. They arrived at the imperial headquarters at Neusohl wishing to accept the pardon and indicating that others would follow.[98]

---

95. Ibid., 141.

96. Fata, *Ungarn*, 278.

97. "[H]at dem Kayserlichen Hofe remonstrirt/ daß er (the official) abermahl dem Teckely zugeschrieben/ und ermahnet/ damit er seine begangene Fauten breuen/ und zu Ihrer Kayserlichen May. Füssen fallen solle . . . daß er (T) resolvirt wäre/ sein Heil unter deß Groß-Sultans Protection zu suchen" (Z 100/1684/18/5–6]).

98. "Dieser Tage sind 18 Rebellen allhier angekommen/ welche umb Kayserlichen

Once again, in 1685, the *Nordische Mercurius* confirmed that many men had left Thököly and accepted the offer of imperial mercy ("sich der Kayserl. Gnade und Barmhertzigkeit zu ergeben vorgiebet"). Moreover, a Hungarian deserter declared that Thököly's army would soon disband because the troops and their leader despaired for lack of support ("weilen sie nirgends her einige Assistance zu gewarten/ und der Teckely selbst desperiret" [*NM*, Vienna, September 6, 1685, 72:1685, 569; Z 19/1685/E.R.]). Two stories in the *Relations-Courir* (September 23 and 30, 1685) confirmed that Thököly's secretary (here again unnamed)[99] had been sent to Vienna to be informed that the rebels who had appealed ("anflehen") for imperial pardon would be granted it. Thököly, however, would agree to such an arrangement only if he was to be installed as "Fürst in Ober-Ungarn," a demand the emperor was unwilling to fulfill (Z 100/1685/94/5). After repeated appeals to the emperor for restitution of his properties and reestablishment of religious toleration had been rejected, Thököly turned for support elsewhere. Following their defeat in 1683, however, the Porte also regarded him as too unreliable for further cooperation.

By the end of the novel, Cergely (and no doubt many a reader) has changed his mind about this thought-provoking figure. Thököly, driven out of now Habsburg Hungary, is still active in neighboring areas. Not yet defeated, he lays siege with an army of Turks and Tartars to the castle Novigrad in Serbia along the Danube (*UK* VI: 558). "Whatever the newspapers tell us," muses Cergely, it appears that Thököly, though without obvious means of support, does seem to have money, possibly conveyed by the French, in whose interest it remains to deal with a distracted empire and a weakened Porte. At this point, not unlike Max in the *Bayrische Max*, the novel's disillusioned characters echo the opinion of news reports, namely, that Thököly is nothing but a traitor and murderer ("Verräther und Mord-Brenner"), the leader of a marauding band of mercenaries (*UK* VI: 519). Nonetheless, the struggle over Hungary among the Ottoman Porte, the German Empire, and the Hungarian Protestant nobility continues to preoccupy the news. A conspiracy in Cronstadt intended to severely damage the imperial forces was thwarted, though Cronstadt went up in flames.[100] The assumption ("geme-

---

Pardon bitten/ versichernd/ daß mehr folgen werden" (*RC*, March 31, 1684; Z 100/ 1684/ 28/4).

99. The secretary is here unnamed but is identified in the *Relations-Courir* as one of two who appear together on one occasion: Syrmay and Bethnehasi (*RC* 96 [1685]: Vienna, September 30; Z 100/1685/98/6).

100. Brasov (Romania).

ine Rede") was that Thököly started the fire, although this could never be proven. The damage to his reputation, however, had been done. By the late nineties, he was driven into exile in Nicomedia, where he and Ilona died, in 1705 and 1703, respectively.[101]

Thököly became at best a distraction for the emperor, viewed with mistrust as an on-again, off-again ally of the Sublime Porte. Protestant Europe, however, having witnessed the persecution of the French Huguenots, which climaxed in the early to mid-eighties, saw him as a valiant defender and supporter of the Protestant cause, a hero whose international standing grew exponentially with the distance from the action on the ground in faraway Hungary—at least until the atrocities associated with rebellion became too numerous to bear.[102]

Friedrich Graf von Schomberg (1615/16–1690): Military Glory and Religious Persecution (*Waldenser/Thalleute*)

The Persecution of the Protestants as a Media Event

Just as Imre Thököly's destiny is inseparably linked with the vagaries of Hungarian religious tolerance and national identity, so is the life of the peripatetic Friedrich Hermann (or Frédéric-Armand), first Duke of Schomberg (originally Schönberg), inseparable from the religious turmoil that defined France at this time. In the newspapers of the 1680s, especially in 1685, Hungary and France, religion and politics, Schomberg and Thököly regularly shared what we would now call the headlines, thereby providing Happel with the materials for his *Geschicht-Romane*. This symbiosis is advanced to such a point that in a fictional dialogue between the Duke of Lorraine and Schomberg published after Schomberg's death in 1690, Schomberg comments on the relationship between France, the Porte, and the importance of Transylvania to both the empire and the Porte. The posthumous assessment of Thököly's importance put into Schomberg's words signals the writer's assumption that the marshal presumably had intimate knowledge of Hungarian matters.[103]

---

101. *UK* VI: 519–20; *TE* XIII: 261.

102. Cenner-Wilhelmb, "Feind oder zukünftiger Verbündeter?," 55.

103. E. le Noble, *Les Ombres de Schomberg et de Lorraine*, has Schomberg talking about who should rule Transylvania, Thököly or Apafi's young, ineffectual son. Schomberg opines, "Der eine ist ein berühmter Feldherr, der sich einen Namen gemacht hat, trotz fürchterlicher Schicksalsschläge . . . Ich kenne den Adel von Siebenbürgen; und es gibt unter ihnen wenige, die nicht

By inserting contemporary news reports published in Hamburg and Altona into his novels' encounters between the celebrities and his own fictional characters, Happel's nuanced, historically compelling, and emotionally engaging enactment of Schomberg's life highlights the story of the persecution of the French Protestants. The tales he heard from the refugees who daily arrived in Hamburg must have been of even greater immediate impact on his writing. A note from January 4, 1685, in the *Relations-Courir* said as much. It told of a ship being readied in Amsterdam with food and other necessities to transport refugees to Hamburg, from where they would travel to the places they had chosen for their future homes.[104]

Long before the Huguenots were put in great peril by the formal revocation of the Edict of Nantes (1587) by the Edict of Fontainebleau on October 22, 1685, the persecutions of *Waldenser*, or, as they often appear in Happel's novels, *Thalleute*, had driven significant numbers of Protestants from the valleys of Piedmont into Switzerland, the Netherlands, Germany, and England.[105] *Glaubensflüchtlinge*, as the title of a recently published collection of essays about confessional migration aptly calls them, constituted a migration that significantly affected many countries in western and central Europe.[106] Not unlike Thököly's rebels and malcontents, the *Reformierten* engaged the European and specifically the German newspaper and pamphlet readership for decades with tales of oppression, suffering, and eventually resettlement across many European countries.[107]

In 1655, a massacre in Piedmont left many dead, and great numbers of

---

einen Fürsten, wie es Tekeli nach Abstammung und Wert ist, einem schwachen Kind vorziehen würden . . . Sohn eines Vaters, der durch Schlauheit, Betrug und Verrat in die Position seines Herrn erhoben wurde" (The one is a famous military leader who has gained a reputation in spite of a very challenging fate . . . I know the Transylvanian nobles; among them are few who would not prefer a prince like Thököly in heritage and worth instead of a weak child . . . son of a father who reached a position of power through cleverness, cheating, and betrayal). Cited in Köpeczi, *Staatsräson und Christliche Solidarität*, 207–8.

104. "Allhier wird ein Schiff verfertiget/ welches mit Proviant und andern Nothwendigkeiten versehen ist/ . . . umb die Frantzösische entwichene Reformirten/ . . . nach Hamburg über zu bringen/ von dannen sie nach den Orthen/ wohin sie selber wollen/ ihnen abzureysen freystehet" (Z 100/1685/147/8).

105. Susanne Lachenicht, *Hugenotten in Europa und Nordamerika: Migration und Integration in der Frühen Neuzeit* (Frankfurt am Main: Campus, 2010), prologue, 27–43.

106. Joachim Bahlcke, ed., *Glaubensflüchtlinge: Ursachen, Formen und Auswirkungen frühneuzeitlicher Konfessionsmigration in Europa* (Berlin: LIT, 2008), V–VI.

107. *300 Jahre Hugenotten in Hessen: Herkunft und Flucht, Aufnahme und Assimilation, Wirkung und Ausstrahlung: Ausstellung, Museum Fridericianum, Kassel, 12. April bis 28. Juli 1985* (Kassel: Weber und Weidemeyer, 1985).

the survivors fled into neighboring Protestant Switzerland. A lengthy tract on the "bloody and barbarous Massacres, Murders, and other unheard of cruelties" committed by the "Duke of Savoy's Forces, joined with the French Army, and several bloody Irish Regiments" was published in London the same year.[108] Numerous publications would follow documenting the seemingly endless series of atrocities that the Protestants had to endure.[109] On October 22, 1685, the revocation of the Edict of Nantes made religious persecution the official French state policy, widespread and vigorously implemented. The Most Christian King's move toward religious uniformity was prompted by his absolutist ambition to establish a French form of Catholicism, known as Gallicanism, in his realm.[110] The revocation presented thousands of French Protestants with very limited options: they either had to abdicate their Protestant faith and submit to rebaptism or suffer untold indignities that often escalated into cruelties and brutalities.

Even before October 22, 1685, the papers talked almost daily of the repression and antagonism directed toward Protestants. The *Relations-Courir*, reporting from Paris on February 4, 1684, reads that an edict went out to the press ("unter die Presse") on the basis of which nine to ten Reformed churches in Provence, Languedoc, and Vivarez (i.e., Vivarais) were to be demolished (Z 100/1684/11/3). A lengthy report from Paris dated January 19, 1685, leaves no doubt that the king meant business when he vigorously moved toward the Catholicization to be codified in the revocation a few months later. After their effort at fighting the demolition of their church with legal means, not only were the citizens of the town of Puy Laurez (in Languedoc) ordered by the Parliament of Toulouse to proceed, but the king prohibited the use of their academy. Four faculty members had to flee, the assumption being that their possessions would be confiscated.[111]

---

108. *Matchlesse Crueltie, declared at large in the ensuing History of the Waldensians. . . . Wherein is related their Original and Beginning. . . . Likewise, Hereunto is added an exact Narrative of the late Bloody and Barbarous Massacres . . .* (London: Edward Brewster, at the Crane in Pauls Church-yard, 1655).

109. Ibid.

110. Matthew Glozier, *Marshal Schomberg (1615–1690), "The Ablest Soldier of His Age": International Soldiering and the Formation of State Armies in Seventeenth-Century Europe* (Brighton: Sussex Academic Press, 2005), 106.

111. "[D]er König . . . [hat] dem Parlement Ordre ertheilet/ nicht allein die ermelte Kirche zu demoliren/ sondern auch den Reformirten den Gebrauch der Accademia allda verbothen." In case of resistance, "4 Professoren ermleter Accademie gestraffet werden sollten/ welche sich aber/ als sie davon Nachricht bekommen mit der Flucht salviret/ es dörfften aber ihre Güter conficirt werden" (Z 100/1685/7/3–4).

A report of May 1, 1685, told of the forcible rebaptism ("Abschwerung") of two young children and the destruction of Protestant churches ("weil ihre Kirchen zu Steinhauffen gemachet" [*ER* 35 (1685): 270; Z 19/1685/E.R.]). On October 29, we read that no pen could describe the devastation and "our daily suffering" in the city of La Rochelle.[112] The *Relations-Courir* had already noted on June 22 that the churches of Rouen and Caen had been closed and that pastors were prohibited, under threat of arrest, from coming within twenty miles of these towns (Z 100/1685/47/3). From the same town, it was reported that people had to travel for days, in the middle of winter, to find a church and a pastor to have their children baptized ("Imnittelst man diesen Winter mit grosser Betrübniß gesehen/wie diese Leute ihre Kinder zu taufen gantze Tage lange reisen müssen" [Z100/1685/21/2]). In May, word had come from Paris that Protestants in the service of His Majesty's Navy were henceforth forbidden to worship in front of the mainmast and had to pray in front of one of the smaller masts. The fine for singing hymns was five hundred gold pieces (*Gulden*) (Z 100/1685/33/3). Aside from rebaptism, either voluntary or involuntary, pastors were forbidden to conduct worship (*ER* 88 (1685): 701; Z 19/1685/ R.R.). On August 3, the same paper presented thirteen articles formulated by the clergy and approved by the king that were to serve as the template for the treatment of Protestants (*ER* 62 (1685): 494–95); Z 19/1685/E.R.). A day after the revocation, on October 23, 1685, the word from Paris was that all Reformed churches had to be closed, no religious services would be tolerated across the land, and any clergy failing to abjure their faith within thirty-one days would either have to leave the country or face conscription into the galleys (*ER* 85 [1685]: 672; Z 19/1685/E.R).

Friedrich von Schomberg's swift reaction to the revocation left little doubt of either his awareness of the repressions already suffered by his fellow Protestants or his commitment to defend the faith in strongly worded statements. Together with the marquis de Ruvigny, the deputy-general of the Huguenots in France, he published a *Humble Petition* to be presented to Louis XIV. With the revocation, the marquis de Ruvigny, as the representative of the Protestants in France, lost his annual income of twelve to fifteen thousand pounds annually.[113] Although this document (which was immediately translated into English) proved unsuccessful, it did express Schomberg's outrage at the measures directed against the Huguenots, which

---

112. Z 100/1685/116/2.

113. *RC*, October 29, 1685; Z 100/1685/114/5.

FRIDERICUS DUX DE SCHOMBERG*etc.*

Fig. 6. Friedrich von Schomberg (1616–90) (Herzog August Bibliothek, Wolfenbüttel)

foreshadowed his actions to follow.[114] When a growing number of Protestants were beginning to think about organized resistance, they turned to the marshal as their potential leader. He declined, however, and the king praised him for his faithfulness.[115]

Schomberg's state of mind seems to have been of great interest to the readership of the European newspapers. He appears repeatedly in the papers, especially those published toward the end of 1685. The *Relations-Courir* of December 21, 1685, mentioned several discussions ("Unterredungen") that Schomberg had with the king. On December 25, it is insinuated by those who wanted to see him abandon his religion that he might change his mind ("wancken"), but the insinuations proved false.[116] According to the *Relations-Courir* of September 7, 1685, the king even went so far as to advise Schomberg to discuss the differing religious precepts ("Religions-Puncte") with the archbishop of Paris. But the weakness of the cleric's argument only strengthened Schomberg in his Protestant faith.[117] Clearly, his steadfastness was unassailable.

From News to Novel

Happel was most likely familiar with the various tracts addressing the oppression of the Protestants as well as with the news reported in the media. The newspapers mentioned were published in either Hamburg or nearby Altona,[118] and he was also able to read English pamphlets (which, in any case, were later translated into German). As we observed in Happel's treatment of Thököly and the Hungarian story, the news seamlessly entered his novels, especially those written between 1685 and 1690. The news provided, once again, the *historia*, the stage, on which the *romanische Handlung* played

---

114. Glozier, *Marshal Schomberg*, appendix, 200–207; Friedrich von Schomberg and marquis de Ruvigny, *The Humble Petition of the Protestants of France Lately presented to His Most Christian Majesty* (London: L. Curtis, 1685).

115. "[D]aß er [the King] mehr wuste als was in dem Brife stünde/ woran er doch sonderlich Vergnügen/ wegen dessen [Schomberg's] Treue" (Z 100/1685/10/4).

116. "Daß der Marschal de Schombert auch wancken solle/ streuen diejenigen aus/ die es gerne sehen/ aber es ist noch wenig apparentz darzu" (Z 100/1685/143/4).

117. "[M]ehr und mehr in seinem Glauben gestärcket worden/ und dahero in demselben beständig zu bleiben beschlossen" (Z 100/1685/88/3–4).

118. Holger Böning's publications on the Hamburg mediascape and Flemming Schock's book *Die Text-Kunsthammer* are indispensable resources for reviewing Happel's life and work in Hamburg.

out, creating the context for the story of Friedrich von Schomberg's life, courage, and heroism and, of course, the context for Happel's novel.

Born in Heidelberg to illustrious Palatine nobility, Schomberg gained fame early as a gifted and courageous military leader. He was widely praised for his exceptional intelligence, as well as for his skill at learning languages: "Le Duc de Schomberg devint si habile dans les Langues, qu'on lavoit de la peine a discerner qu'elle etoit la sienne proper, & quoy qu'il n'eut sejourne que peu d'annees en Angleterr, il avoit portant apris & retenu la beaute & la purete de cette Langue quand il revient" (The Duke of Schomberg is very facile with languages, so much so that it is difficult to discern whether he speaks his native language or another one. Even after spending only a little time in England, he mastered the beauty and purity of that language upon his return).[119] Schomberg spoke French, German, and English fluently—an English nobleman, the Earl of Clarendon, praised Schomberg's Protestant faith as much as his fluency in English, and Schomberg was described in another instance as a Frenchman (*sic*) with excellent English skills.[120] He was also competent in Dutch, and the ease with which he adapted to the culture of Portugal when in the service of the Portuguese crown was credited to his ability to readily master that the Portuguese language as well.[121]

Recounting the duke's biography, Rheinwald, a fictional character in the *Engelländische Eduard*, affirms the widely held public admiration of this amazing gift: "Der Hertzog von Schomberg wurde in den Sprachen so fertig/ daß man schwerlich darvon seine Mutter-Sprach unterscheiden konte" (The Duke of Schomberg was so accomplished in speaking [foreign] languages that one could hardly make out the difference between his own and other languages [*EE* III: 359]). Schomberg also excelled in diplomacy: "Mais il s'etoit si bien instruit des secrets de toute l'Europe, qu'il scavoit ceut de touts les Cours, & n'etoit pas moint proper le Cabinet, qu'il le fut dans la suite pour la guerre" (But he was so well informed about all the secrets of the European powers that he knew everything at all courts and as much about

---

119. Hippolyte DuChastelet de Luzancy, *Abbregé de la Vie du Frederic Duc de Schomberg . . . Par Monsr. de Luzaney, Ministre d'Harwich & Chapelain du feu de Duc de Schomberg* (La Haye: Jean Aelberts, Marchand Librairie, près la Cour, 1690), 10. This is a translation of the original *Panegyrick to the Memory of his Grace, Frederick, late Duke of Schonberg*, published in 1690 by DuChastelet de Luzancy in London.

120. Glozier, *Marshal Schomberg*, 58, 62.

121. "In regard of his particular long experience here, and knowledge of the language, to be the ablest commander as to this war." Sir Richard Fanshaw, quoted in Glozier, *Marshal Schomberg*, 58.

the cabinets in the course of war).[122] His gifts served Schomberg well as he pursued his military career in the service of multiple countries and sovereigns. Few famous lives put the interminable transcontinental wars fought by multinational armies into better relief.

Schomberg's life as a soldier with geographically and politically diverse appointments reflects the waxing and waning of European power politics.[123] In this, he resembles Thököly, who variously courted the support of Poland, France,[124] and the Sublime Porte.[125] However, Schomberg's career, unlike Thököly's, unfolded within the cultural framework of western Europe's military, religious, and political loyalties. Despite his changing international assignments and allegiances, his honor was never questioned, and his reputation remained untarnished to his death. In this, too, he was unlike Thököly. Schomberg appears to have been a man without any ambiguity whatsoever, in his character or his actions. Thököly's actions, while doubtless completely genuine in their origins and leaving no uncertainty about his desire to liberate Hungary and gather its people under native rule, came in for harsh public criticism.

Like Thököly's army, the armies under Schomberg's command were multinational, among both the officers and the enlisted ranks.[126] Along the way, his service was rewarded with many titles and promotions, with money and land. When this wealthy, powerful, and admired grandee of Portugal and marshal of France gave up everything and left his adopted France forever, the European media world was bound to take notice. The trajectory of his career had inexorably moved him to the point where his religious loyalties had to come into conflict with his professional ambitions.

---

122. DuChastelet de Luzancy, *Abbregé de la Vie du Frederic Duc de Schomberg*, 11.

123. Happel comments that "Catalonien und Flandern haben diesen Helden/ als Marschallen von Frankreich/ kennen lernen" (Catalonia and Flanders have gotten to know this hero as marshal of France [*EE* III: 364]). Matthew Glozier's chapter titles indicate the major locations of Schomberg's service: the Netherlands, France, Portugal, England, and Ireland. He also served, albeit briefly, in Brandenburg.

124. Hints that France might provide financial support for Thököly appear periodically in the press, such as in a report from Vienna on January 26, 1687: "Der Tökely hat wieder grosse Geld-Remissen bekommen" (Z 100/1687/16/7).

125. *RC*, Vienna, February 27, 1684: "Teckely mit den seinigen aber lebet indessen von Türckischen und . . . [*sic*] Geldern/ wie der dann dessen unlängst eine grosse Summa überkommen" (Z 100/1684/18/7).

126. In addition, Happel mentions many international commanders, such as the Duke of Lotharingia, Prince Eugen of Savoy, Generals Caprara and Carrara, Schultz, Häusler, Leslie, and many more, all of whom show up in his novels. See John Childs, "'For God and for Honour': Marshal Schomberg," *History Today* 38, no. 7 (1988): 49.

Schomberg's contemporaries read about him in various *Zeytungen* and in the eulogies and biographies circulating after his death in 1690. They also met him in the fictional universe of Happel's *Geschicht-Romane*, in several of which he appears in person and in conversations. His story is contextualized and fictionalized with the most historical detail in the *Spanische Quintana*, the *Frantzösische Cormantin* (1687), the *Teutsche Carl* (1690), the *Engellän-dische Eduard* (1691), and the *Bayrische Max*, whose characters comment on the marshal's itinerary and actions.[127] Observations about him are often as brief and as factually neutral as the news bulletins from which they were clearly derived.[128] At other times, the narratives convey Schomberg's color-

---

127. The *Eduard* reviews the events of 1690 and, therefore, could have been at least begun by Happel himself. The *Max* deals with 1691, announcing in the frontispiece that it has been written following the model of previous *Geschicht-Romane* by E.G.H. ("nach Weise der bißheri-gen Geschicht-Romanen/ beschrieben werden/ von E.G.H."). No mention is made of Happel's death in the previous year.

128. In addition to what has already been mentioned, a few additional examples might suf-fice to affirm the marshal's ubiquitous presence in the media.

(a) *Ordinary Reichs-Zeitung* (Vienna), August 6, 1678: "Marschall de Schomberg/ so von seinen Völckern 4000. Mann nach Braband zur Luxemburgischen Armee abgeschickt/ stehet jetzo bey Reckem/ hat umb Masyck alle Dörffer vnd Kirchen außgeplündert. Die Allijrte Armee/ darzu das Chur-Brandenburgische Regiment zu Pferde/ von General-Major Eller/ jetzo zu Chrucier stehend/ stossen soll/ hat sich auß der Gegend von Jülich nach Geyden-Kirchen gezogen/ dem Feinde zu folgen" (Marshal Schomberg, who sent four thousand of his men to Brabant to the army of Luxembourg, is now standing close to Reckem [Renkum?]. Has plundered all vil-lages and churches around Masyck. The allied army as well as Major General Eller's Brandenburg cavalry regiment now stationed at Chrucier has left the area of Jülich and turned to Geilenkirchen in pursuit of the enemy [2]); August 17, 1678: "Gestern soll ein Theil der Schombergischen Armee über die Brücke seyn/ vermuthlich die Wachten daselbst zu verstärcken" (It was said that yesterday part of Schomberg's army went across the bridge, probably to strengthen the guards [1]).

(b) In brackets: "So mit 3000. Mann von dem Schombergischen Corpo" (with three thousand men of the Schomberg corps [2]).

(c) "[S]o ist Befehl ergangen/ an den Spanischen Unterthanen sich zu erholen/ wie auch/ daß Marschall de Schomberg mit Monsr. Luxemburg sich conjugieren soll" (An order went out to recover whatever possible from the Spanish subjects as well as that the marshal was going to join the Duke of Luxembourg [3]); *RC* (Hamburg), 1689: "Yorck, 11. May . . . Man sagt/ daß etliche Regimenter zu Fuß zu Wasser und Lande auch im Anzuge begriffen/ und sich mit jetztgemeldeter Reuterey zu Pferde conjugieren sollen/ und werden dieselbigen biß auff 22000 Mann vergrössert/ und so man mehrere von nöthen haben möchte/ soll der Herzog von Schomberg als Generalissimus mit den übrigen folgen" (It was said that several regiments were ap-proaching on land and on sea; they would join the cavalry and thus increase the army up to twenty-two thousand men, and if more are needed the Duke of Schom-berg will follow as general with the remaining [soldiers]) [a.a.O.]; "Haag, 23. May

ful life and career, his successes, and his changing fortunes, so typical of the complex times in which he lived.

Just as Thököly's life story articulated the emerging Hungarian nationalism and militant demands for religious tolerance in the face of powerful Catholic European and Islamic Ottoman interests, Schomberg emerged as a heroic military professional whose career mirrored the quickly changing pan-European alliances and hostilities and whose inner compass was very much guided by his fervent Calvinism. However, the two men differed not only in their personalities but also, more significantly, in their personal attitudes toward their faith. Until the revocation forced him to take a public stand, Schomberg's commitment to his faith was intensely private and did not affect his career decisions. He served Catholic and Protestant sovereigns with equal professionalism, for which he was amply rewarded. In this, he differed from Thököly's more overtly political and militant religiosity. Remaining a constant, appearing in nearly all reports about Schomberg, and following him into Happel's novels is the admiration for his unshakable Calvinist faith and the respect for his strategic brilliance and personal courage—even among those who did not fully support his cause.[129] The public admiration for Thököly, as reflected in the media and in Happel's novels, began to fade when faced with relentless reports of his resistance against the emperor and the ill behavior of the rebels or malcontents among his troops.

Schomberg makes his first personal appearance in Happel's novels in the *Spanische Quintana* in 1686, though the plight of the Protestants had already been a frequent subject of conversation among the actors of the *Italienische Spinelli*, published a year earlier. A declaration issued by the king of Denmark assuring the freedom of religion for all faiths introduces the plight of the French who sought refuge in his realm (*IS* II: 14). Spinelli and his friends decry the destruction of Huguenot churches and express outrage at the ill

---

Mit jüngst eingelauffenen Brieffen hat man Zeitung/ daß der Französische Intendant das angehaltene sehr köstliche Schiff/ so des Marschals und Herzogs von Schomberg Sohn gehöret/ ungeachtet des Königs von Frankreich deshalben ertheilten Passes/ confisciret" (With the letters that have arrived most recently it was made known that the French commander has stopped and confiscated a most luxurious vessel that belonged to the marshal's and duke's son, in complete disregard of the passports that had been issued by the king of France).

129. Reports of his personal bravery even found their way into the newspapers. The *Relations-Courir* of April 27, 1685, told of his courageous defense of a man who had been attacked in a church over a property dispute. The disagreement had reached such a point that the Duke de la Force "den Degen in der Kirche gezücket/ es ist aber solches durch etlich von Adel und den Mareschal de Schomberg wieder beygeleget worden" (Z 100/1685/34/5).

treatment of Protestants, which Spinelli calls worse than the treatment of the Jews (*IS* II: 198). The very direct relationship between media and novel emerges when Klaur, one of the many German characters whom Happel credits with exceptional political acuity and learning, points to the declaration addressed to all Protestants that had been recently drafted by the French clergy and had found the support of the king. This very series of "Articulen," together with the king's assent, to which had been added a few royal exceptions, was reported verbatim in the *Europäische Relation* of August 3, 1685, from Paris. Later in the narrative, attempting to raise his listeners' empathy for the plight of the French Protestants, Klaur describes the harassment of the faithful in great detail: "Es ist nöthig/ meine lieben Freunde/ daß ich euch die wahre Beschaffenheit der gedruckten Reformirten ein wenig besser vor Augen stelle/ vielleicht möchtet ihr da besser urtheilen/ daß man ihnen Unrecht thut/ und allzuscharff mit ihnen verfähret" (It is important, my dear friends, that I put before your eyes the true nature of the oppression of the Reformed people. Then maybe you can better judge for yourselves how much they are being wronged and how harshly they are being treated [*SQ* IV: 64]).[130] Subsequently, Spinelli picks up a letter dated September 5, 1685. It contains a copy of a report "wegen der harten Verfolgung der Reformirten selbigen Königreichs" (because of the harsh persecution of the Protestants in this very kingdom), detailing the misery of the persecuted ("der elende Zustand") (*IS* IV: 71–82). The novel ends with the German Klaur's tearful reading of the revocation: "Als Klauer weiter lesen wolte/ giengen ihm die Augen über/ denn er kam auf eine Hertz-brechende Materie (Behandlung der Reformirten). Edict von Nantes 1598, Edict von Nimes 1629 alle revocirt und widerrufen" (When Klaur wanted to continue reading, his eyes teared up because he came upon a heartbreaking matter [the treatment of the Reformed people]. The Edict of Nantes [1598] and the Edict of Nîmes [1629] were all revoked and annulled).[131] That this report is immediately preceded by information about Thököly's imprisonment on October 15, 1685, and subsequent transport to Adrianople by the Pasha of Grosswardein ("in listiger Weise") reveals, once again, how closely Happel watched the news and how quickly it found its way into his novels (*IS* IV: 333).

---

130. This is followed by the complete directives against the Protestants (*SQ* IV: 64–71) as outlined in the *Europäische Relation*.

131. This is followed by "Sr. Aller-Christl. Maj. Edict, welches das Vebott/ kein öffentlich Exercitium der Reformirten protestirenden Religion in seinen Königreich zu halten/ in sich begreiffe" (His Most Christian Majesty's Edict, which prohibited any religious exercise by (those of) the Reformed Protestant religion in his kingdom [*IS* IV: 335–40]).

The *Spanische Quintana* introduces Schomberg in the context of the strife that had developed over the complicated diplomatic wrangling between Portugal, France, Spain, and England. From 1652 to 1658, Schomberg, then serving in the French army, had successively been commissioned captain and *maréchal-de-camp*, lieutenant general, and colonel of a regiment of German infantry.[132] In Portugal, the struggle for independence was to last from the signing of the Peace of the Pyrenees in 1659 until official recognition by the Peace of Westminster in 1668. As reported by Rotalino, one of the *Quintana*'s fictional characters, Schomberg and a number of French officers who had surreptitiously joined him fought under Portuguese command and, in 1668, defeated the Spanish in a decisive battle: "Inmassen Frankreich des Pyrenaischen Friedens ungeachtet zuließ/ daß der Graff von Schomberg und viel ander Frantzosen in Portugisische Dienste gingen; welche in ein und anderer Schlacht die Spanier hart geschlagen" (Inasmuch as France allowed, in total disregard of the Peace of the Pyrenees, Duke Schomberg and many other French troops to go into Portuguese service, defeating the Spanish in a number of battles [*SQ* II: 409–10]). Schomberg had made his first contacts with the English during the Portuguese-Spanish conflict. To hide his connections with France—forbidden under the Peace of the Pyrenees of 1659—his contract was negotiated in England with the help of James II, whom he would later help defeat as commander of the army in the service of William of Orange.[133]

Trying to do justice to the complicated three-step between Portugal, Spain, and France, which also intermittently involved the Netherlands and England, Happel has Rotalino voice his—and presumably Happel's—insistent impartiality. Rotalino advises his listeners that he will tell the story as if he were a neutral observer, a stranger, not a native-born Portuguese: "Ich will vielmehr einen Historicum abgeben/ davon einem Dinge unpartheyisch redet/ ja ich will itzo kein gebohrener Portuguise/ sondern so lange ein Frembder seyn/ und als ein Frembder von Portugal in der Ferne reden" (I will act as a historian who talks about things without taking sides. In fact, [for this reason] I don't want to be a born Portuguese but rather act as a foreigner talking about Portugal as a foreigner [*SQ* II: 372]).[134] Rotalino's report

---

132. Glozier, *Marshal Schomberg*, xvi; Childs, "'For God and for Honour,'" 46.

133. Childs, "'For God and for Honour,'" 47.

134. A comparable pronouncement about the neutrality of the historian comes from the German Klaur in the *Spinelli*. Asked about the most powerful potentates in Europe, he prefaces his response by saying that he thinks only historically, far from any nationalist passion ("daß ich blosserdings historisch gehe/ und von keiner Passion weiß/ es it mir ein Potentat so lieb/ als der andere" [*IS* I: 124]).

follows the chorographic model we have come to expect from Happel: we hear much about Portugal's history, geography, trade, and colonial ambitions in the East Indies and of the character and personality of her people. Even the stereotypical early modern anti-Semitism makes its appearance: "[S]ind sie insgemein sehr streng und grausam/ dem Geitz und Wucher sind sie sehr ergeben/ und haben Gelds zusammen zu raffen/ alle Winckel der Welt durchgekrochen. Einige wollen sie beschuldigen/ daß sie sehr arg und boßhafftig sind/ weil ihnen von dem vielen Judenblut/ so unter diese Nation vermischet/ anhencken soll" (they generally are cruel and severe, given much to usury, and rake together money exploring all corners of the world. Some people accuse them of being mean and nasty because they have much Jewish blood, which has been mixed into this nation [*SQ* II: 376]).

Rotalino dwells with special affection on Portugal's prowess as a seafaring and trading nation, attributing the wealth of this small country to its fleet's ability to procure goods and raw materials from faraway China (Macao), Brazil, and Africa. Rotalino's assumed narrative neutrality also confirms what the European public of the time knew of Marshal Schomberg, whose military and diplomatic brilliance served many different sovereigns. Thanks to his skills as a military leader, Portugal was now at peace, its independence and sovereignty assured. Schomberg's very success, however, had cost him his job, as Portugal no longer required his military genius. He contemplated offering his services once again to France, but he feared that with anti-Protestant sentiments heating up, he would not be given the chance there to advance his military career.[135] Still, he made France his home and, in 1669, married a French Huguenot, Susanne d'Aumale, and purchased the lordship of Coudert near Paris. A few years later, in 1673, Louis XIV, pragmatist that he was, commissioned Schomberg to lead French troops in battle once again. After this, his ascent through the ranks of the French military was swift. In 1674, he became commander in chief of the French army. In 1675, Louis XIV promoted him to marshal of France, while intermittently attempting to convert him to Catholicism.

But if Schomberg, after accepting the military and political honors granted him, expected a peaceful life, this hope was soon to be dashed. In January of 1686, after rejecting all suggestions that he convert to Catholicism after the revocation of the Edict of Nantes, he refused to attend the procession marking King Louis XIV's celebration of the unification of his subjects

---

135. "My plan is to pass from here (Portugal) to France, but because of my religion I do not foresee any future." Quoted in Glozier, *Marshal Schomberg*, 70.

under one faith, sealed with the Edict of Fontainebleau. Schenck, the *Quintana's* resident German know-it-all, reviews the main points of this edict as they had appeared ad infinitum in the daily press: "[D]ass keinem Protestanten Hilfe, Essen, Unterkunft gewähert werden sollte, dass alle gemeldet werden sollten im fernen Nachforschung zu tun. Kranke und Sterbende nur nach katholischem Glaubensbekenntnis absolviert, wenn nicht, nicht begraben, wenn genesen, dann hingerichtet. Weiter Torturen und Gewalttaten gegen Adlige und Bauern, die nich von ihrem Glauben ablassen wollten" (that no help, food, or dwelling must be offered to the Protestants, and that everyone who did this should be reported. The sick and the dying should be treated with Catholic rites; if not, they must not be buried. If they recover, they should be executed. Additional brutalities would be directed against the nobility and against peasants who expressed their unwillingness to leave their faith [*SQ* I: 344]). The *Relations-Courir* of October 15, 1685, confirmed that horrible atrocities had been committed: cheeks had been branded; noses, ears, and women's breasts had been cut off ("Es sind auch unterschiedliche Persohnen/ welche nicht abfallen wollen/ theils auff den Backen gebrandtmahlet/ theils Nasen und Ohren/ und die Weibsbilder die Brüste abgeschnitten" [Z 100/1685/102/8]). With the "cataclysmic decision"[136] to forcefully reestablish the Catholic faith in the Gallican tradition as the state religion, Louis officially condoned this renewed vigorous and violent persecution of French Protestants.

In reaction, after trying to change the king's resolve, Schomberg gave up everything—wealth, station, and rank[137]—and left France, first trying to return to Portugal and then moving to Brandenburg, whose elector welcomed him with open arms. It was noted in the *Relations-Courir* (Cologne, May 30, 1687) that the king of France approved Schomberg's decision to

---

136. Matthew Glozier and David Onnekink, eds., *War, Religion, and Service: Huguenot Soldiering, 1685–1713*, Politics and Culture in North-Western Europe, 1650–1720 (Aldershot: Ashgate, 2007), 4.

137. "Der Marschall de Schomberg ist am übelsten dran/ massen ein solcher Herr bei Hofe gar leicht vermisset wird; bisher hat er sich noch aufgehalten/ ob es der Länge Stand halten solte/ muß der Zeit geben. . . . Der König hat mit dem Schluß des Jahres alles unter einen Hut und Mantel zubringen gedacht/ . . . im Januario 1686 . . . eine allgemeine Prozession gehalten werden sollte/ um Gott zu dancken . . . daß alle Unterthanen . . . zu einerley Glauben gebracht" (Marshal Schomberg is in bad straits insofar as such a gentleman is very much missed at court; up to now he has stayed, but whether in the long run this will continue remains to be seen. . . . At the end of the year, the king has tried to put everything together . . . in January 1686 he planned to hold a general procession to give thanks that all his subjects were now under one faith [*SQ* I: 347–48]).

move to Brandenburg.[138] The consequences of Schomberg's self-imposed exile are intimated four years later, in a document outlining the demands at the French surrender of the city of Bonn to the Elector of Brandenburg and his allies. Item sixteen mentions that "[a]lle deß Grafen von Schombergs Sachen sollen restituiret werden" (all things belonging to the Duke of Schomberg should be restored [*TC* IV: 65]), indicating that they had been confiscated by the state. They were, however, never restored.

This phase of European power politics constitutes part of the background of the *Frantzösische Cormantin* (1687). As was the case with Thököly, the historical narrative alone as distributed in many news reports does not suffice to make the marshal come alive and bring him closer to the reader. To add narrative drama, Happel constructs a fictional meeting between Schomberg and Cormantin on the marshal's way back from Portugal. This encounter offers the reader a rare opportunity to experience firsthand the civility and graciousness of this exceptional soldier, even under the duress of finding himself a fugitive, a wanderer, and a potential outcast. Cormantin recognizes the "Welt-beruffenen Frantzösis. Feld-Marschall/ Grafen von Schomberg" (world-famous French field marshal Duke Schomberg), and when he bows toward him to show his respect and admiration, Schomberg embraces him as if he were his son, asking what has brought him there.[139] Cormantin explains that he had fought in the Hungarian War, helping "to reduce the number of Turks," and that, in turn, he wonders about the marshal's circumstances. Schomberg allows that his time in France had passed and that he had found Portugal, theater of his early military glories, not as welcoming as he had hoped. In both cases, his religion ("meine gute Religion") made it impossible for him, as for many thousands of persecuted fellow faithful, to find a permanent home ("eine bleibende Städte"). He does acknowledge that the king had permitted him to move to Portugal, but this refuge was closed to him now. It was political shrewdness that prompted Louis XIV to attempt the re-Catholicization of France; in Portugal, it was the Inquisition that, on religious grounds, refused to grant asylum to the marshal.

Es scheinet/ replicirte der Feld-Marschall/ daß um meiner guten Religion willen/ gleich vielen Tausenden anderer Verfolgeten/ auch ich nirgends eine bleibende Städte finden kan. Der Aller-Christl. König

---

138. "[D]aß der König von Franckreich vor seiner Abreise/ des Marschalls Schomberg Resolution in des Chur-Fürsten von Brandenburg Dienst zu treten/ für guth erkläret" (Z 100/1687/82/5).

139. *FC* I: 212–13.

hat mich zwar/ auß sonderbarer Gnade/ vergönnet/ samt allem/ was mir zugehöret/ mich nach Portugall/ allwo ich weyland auch eine ansehnliche Charge bedienet/ zu erheben/ aber die Geistliche Inquisition drohete mir mit einem scharffen Prozess, ohngeachtet/ daß ich deß Königs Hertz gleichsam in meinen Händen hatte/ daß ich mich demnach auch von dannen mit den Meinigen zu weichen/ habe resolviren müssen. Mein Weg ist jetzt nach Engelland gerichtet/ was ich allda außrichten werde/ muß die Zeit lehren/ doch/ verspreche ich mir alles Gute/ weil auch selbigen Kron vor Zeiten gute Dienste von mir empfangen hat.[140]

Cormantin and the marshal share a meal, during which the conversation again reverts to the plight of the French Protestants.

Later in the novel, Cormantin's friend Trasselet tells of his journey to Rouen to find his family and his fiancée, who, it turns out, have fled from the *Dragoner* (dragoons) sent to forcibly convert the faithful. Employing a method frequently mentioned in the daily press, the *Dragoner* quartered themselves in the homes of Protestants to inflict severe economic and personal hardship.[141] Trasselet relates what he has read in the newspapers, namely, that Schomberg had gone first to England and then to Brandenburg, whose elector, Frederick William I (1620–88), appointed him privy counselor and commander in chief of the Brandenburg army ("der ihn seiner gantzen Militz alß

---

140. "It appears, responded the marshal, that because of my good religion I, like many others persecuted for their faith, cannot find a place to stay. Though the Most Christian king allowed me to take everything that is mine [i.e., movable goods] with me to Portugal, where I served some time ago, but the Inquisition threatens me with a deadly trial without considering that I had the heart of the king in my hands. Thus I had to resolve to leave along with my family. My destination is now England. What I can accomplish there, time will tell, but I am confident that things will turn out well because I have rendered good service to this crown in the past" (*FC* I: 214).

141. *FC* I: 213. The *Relations-Courir* of December 5, 1684, reported, "Das Elend der Reformirten in Languedoc . . . ist groß und erbärmlich anzuhören . . . weil mit Einquartirung der Königlichen Dragoner ihnen sehr grosse Drangsalen/ wie auch große Schatzungen . . . auferlegt werden" (the misery of the Protestants of Languedoc . . . is horrible to hear . . . because the quartering of the Royal Dragoons imposes on them great hardships and much financial loss [Z 100/1684/97/3]). On April 8, 1585, we read, "Man will in dieser Gegend (Bajonne) mit Gewalt alles Catholisch machen . . . die Reformirten von ihrem Glauben abzuziehen/ gibt und verspricht man Geld/ Aempter/ ansehnliche Heirahten und dergleichen . . . die Troupen/ welche neulich zu Bearn ankommen/ will man bey denen/ die ihren Glauben nicht verändern wollen/ einlogiren" (In this area, they want to make everyone Catholic by force . . . to turn the Reformed away from their faith they give and promise them money; and those who do not want to abjure their faith will be used as quarters for soldiers [Z 100/1685/34/5]).

Chef im Außgang deß April-Monats fürgestellet/ und seinen Sohn auch mit einer hohen Charge begnadet hat" [who installed him as chief of his whole army at the end of April and also gave his son a significant promotion] [*FC* II: 401]). The German character Franckenstein comments that France will lose many of its officers if this persecution continues. The friends agree on their empathy for the Protestants and allow that even some Catholics show pity ("welche Mitleyden mit ihnen hätten"), condemning the constant pressure on people's conscience ("Gewissenszwang") as simply inhumane (*FC* II: 401). Conforming to seventeenth-century reporting practice, the conversation shifts, without a noticeable transition, to less weighty news matters, such as women wearing men's clothing and engaging in shameless love with other women. Clearly, both the sensational and the pathetic offer reading pleasure to the novel's characters (*FC* II: 403).

But Schomberg's military exploits had not yet reached their conclusion. In 1688, the Elector of Brandenburg granted Schomberg, the most distinguished military leader of his time,[142] leave to join, as second in command, Prince William of Orange's (1650–1702) army of English, Dutch, and Huguenot troops in his campaigns in England and Ireland: "die Bataille [against Ireland] von Ihr. Kön. Maj. Selbsten/ dem Grafen Schomberg und dem Grafen von Gravamoer geführet" (the battle was led by the king himself, as well as Duke Schomberg and Duke Gravenmoer [*TE* XIII: 1301]).[143] According to Happel's narrative in the *Engelländische Eduard*, the "Geschicht-Roman auf das 1690. Jahr" (1691), the king so favored Schomberg that he "rewarded him like a king, having made him a duke and a peer of England." This does not quite reflect contemporary commentators' observation of the "little regard the king showed to that great man, the old Duke of Schomberg." When William was informed about the marshal's death, "he did not seem to be concerned."[144] The duke himself, in a posthumous fictional conversation with the Duke of Lorrain, implies that William may not have mourned his death.[145] Nevertheless, William granted Schomberg enough financial rewards to offset the losses incurred in France and Germany.[146]

In setting the scene for Schomberg's death in the *Engelländische Edu-*

---

142. "[A]ls der für den grösten Soldaten seiner Zeit ohn Wider-Rede gehalten wurde" (he was held the greatest soldier of his time, bar none [*EE* III: 368]).

143. The *Theatrum* repeatedly refers to the king as Jakob (*TE* XIII 1298, 1302), which probably was not strange to the English, who referred to his loyalists as Jacobites.

144. Both comments are quoted in Glozier, *Marshal Schomberg*.

145. Anon., *The Present State of Christendom Consider'd in Nine Dialogues Between the Duke of Lorraine and the Duke of Schomberg (done out of French)* (London: Baldwin near the Oxford Arms, 1691), unpaginated, reproduced in Glozier, *Marshal Schomberg*, 223–30.

146. Quoted in Glozier, *Marshal Schomberg*, 136.

ard, Happel stages yet another fictionalized encounter with the marshal, this time with Siegfried, one of the novel's fictional German heroes. The importance of this meeting for the novel's dramatic climax, the death of Schomberg, is twofold. First, Happel presents Siegfried as an exemplary German knight, a man of exceptional bravery in the face of the enemy, one of a number of such model cavaliers populating Happel's novels. During the siege of the Irish town of Londonderry, Siegfried captures the attention of King William, who personally congratulates and thanks him for his service. Together, they ride to the English encampment, where Siegfried meets Schomberg, who takes an immediate liking to the young officer because of his bravery, gentility, and nationality.[147] As an expression of his great respect and trust, he offers the young German a command (*EE* III: 267). However, very much like Cergely in the *Ungarische Kriegs-Roman*, who had insisted that he would rather fight as a volunteer than take orders not agreeable to him, Siegfried politely declines the offer. He chooses to remain free to lend his support according to his own decisions ("er lieber ohne Employe, bald da/ bald dorten/ wo er es am nöthigsten befinden wurde/ fechten" [he would without assignment fight here and there, wherever needed] [*EE* III: 267]).

Siegfried's meeting with Schomberg provides Happel the opportunity to introduce, ever so carefully, Schomberg's supposed fondness for Germans (owing to their bravery and sterling character)—a fondness that other reports do not seem to bear out. The numerous positive German characters Happel braids into his novels reflect not Schomberg's but the writer's predilection. As has been noted, "Schomberg conspicuously lacked any deep and lasting roots," and he did not seem guided by any abiding national sentiment.[148] Very little in his peripatetic military career suggests any great affection for his native Germany or for the German people. Though he accepted his call to service in Brandenburg, he departed for England almost immediately, doing what he always had done in his career: going where he was needed, following the call to arms.

A note in the *Nordische Mercurius* from London, dated December 16, 1689, mentions Schomberg's imminent departure for Ireland in support of the English campaign ("daß I. K. M. incliniren nach Schottland und von dannen gegen den Sommer nach Irrland zu gehen/ von wanen der Hertzog

---

147. "Der Hertzog von Schomberg warffe ebenmässig eine ungemeine Liebe auf ihn/ und liesse alle seine Bezeugungen ihme sehr wol gefallen . . . weil er nunmehr gewiß erfahren/ daß er ein Teutscher/ dannhero auch ihm sicher zu trauen wäre" (The Duke of Schomberg immediately felt a strong love for him and he accepted all his courtesies with pleasure . . . because he also now knew that he was German he knew that he could truly trust him [*EE* III: 265]).

148. Childs, "'For God and for Honour,'" 49.

von Schomberg erwartet wird" [that His Royal Majesty turned toward Scotland and from there to Ireland, from whence the Duke of Schomberg was expected]). For the climactic battle at the River Boyne, across which the fleeing James had sought refuge, the *Theatrum Europaeum* provides a detailed description of the positioning of key figures and of the battle's progress. According to the *Theatrum*, "[d]ie Teutsche Infanterie passirte am ersten biß in die Mitte/ und hielt das Feuer der Feinde ohne Schiessen auß" (the German infantry first advanced toward the middle and held the enemy's fire [*TE* XIII: 1303]). This report may indirectly have provided the anonymous continuator of *Eduard* with the information given there about the presence of German troops, a fact that lends plausibility to the fictional Siegfried's presence in Schomberg's army: German soldiers not only fought in Ireland but were also present at the moment of Schomberg's death.

The *Theatrum* is quite somber in recounting Schomberg's last moments: "Der Feind avancierte tapffer biß in das Wasser/ allwo der Herzog mit 2. Säbel-Hieben auff das Haupt/ und einem Pistolen-Schusse in den Halß/ zum höchsten Leydwesen des Königs und der gantzen Armee erleget wurde" (The enemy advanced bravely all the way into the water, where the duke took two saber strikes on the head and one pistol shot to the neck, whereupon the duke was killed, to the profound regret of the king and the whole army [*TE* XIII: 1301]). Other reports claim that one shot to the back of the head, possibly even from one of his own soldiers, killed the marshal. But whatever the details of the account, his death, at almost eighty years of age, was celebrated in the European media as heroic.[149]

Happel's *Romanisirung* offers a more emotionally charged and moving account of Schomberg's demise. In accordance with some of the versions reported, Happel describes how the marshal, leading by example, entered the river without his cuirass. In Happel's version, Siegfried, the fictional hero standing in for the historical German soldiers, tries to defend the marshal against the Irish. Schomberg is wounded in the head by an Irishman, who, in turn, is killed by Siegfried. Then, still rallying his men as they advance across the river, Schomberg is felled by two gunshot wounds to the head. Siegfried holds off the Irish long enough to allow Schomberg's *Stallmeister* to pull him, already dead, from the river (*EE* III: 270), thereby insuring a proper burial for the fallen hero at St. Patrick's Cathedral in Dublin.[150] King William's "herrliche Victorie" and the subsequent flight of James to Dublin

149. Glozier, *Marshal Schomberg*, 145.
150. Ibid., 150.

and, later, across the Channel to St. Germain was thus paid for by Schomberg's death, as "einige unbekandte und schlechte Kerls versetzten ihm
[Schomberg] einen tödtlichen Streich/ und beraubten dardurch die Welt
einer ihrer schönsten Zierde" (several unknown and bad men delivered the
deadly strike and robbed the world of its most glorious jewel [*EE* III: 370]).
William's victory is one of the few instances in which Happel (in another of
his novels, the *Ottomanische Bajazet* of 1688) articulated his political prefer-
ence: "[Es] kam die Zeitung/ daß der König JACOBUS von Engelland/
samt seiner Gemahlin und Printzen von Wallis, nach Franckreich übergan-
gen/ dem Printzen von Oranien hingegen die Regierung aufgetragen worden. Solches gönnen wir diesem redlichen Printzen ohne ENDE" (The news
arrived that King James of England with his wife and the Prince of Wales
had left for France. The government was handed to the Prince of Orange.
For this we congratulate this courageous prince).[151]

Soon afterward, the novel tells of a group of Siegfried's friends gathered to
mourn the duke's death ("als seines Wol-erfahrnen/ Alten und vortrefflichen
Generals" [*EE* III: 357–77]).[152] Rheinwald, another German, asks the novel's
English protagonist, Eduard, for a more detailed account of the duke's life
and death. Not knowing the facts, Eduard offers to read aloud from a recent
report, thereby seamlessly moving—without any sort of announcement to the
reader—from fiction to fact. The report provides the news ("Novellen") of
Schomberg's death, along with a "Lebens-Lauff." What follows is the almost
verbatim translation of a brief eulogizing biography written in English and
quickly translated into French in 1690, shortly after the duke's death. In it,
Schomberg's chaplain, Hippolyte DuChastelet de Luzancy, narrates the details
of Schomberg's life, including such details as his courageous, even Christlike
calm in the face of a terrible storm at sea on his return from Portugal in January of 1687.[153] This event, too, had been widely reported in the news.

---

151. *OB* IV: 386.

152. This military accomplishment was celebrated in many broadsheets, such as *A full account of the great victory obtained by the Protestants in Ireland, since the arrival of his Grace the Duke
of Schomberg: as is communicated by the reverend and valiant governor Walker of Chester* (London:
J. Norman, 1689).

153. "Kaum war er aus Frankreich gewichen/ . . . siehe/ da gerieht er in eine neue und
andere Gefährlichkeit/ nemlich . . . er wurde von einem . . . Sturm-Wetter überfallen . . . daß
auch die Schiff und Boots-Leuthe selbsten nicht wußten/ was darauß werden würde. . . . Seine
Gottesfurcht hatte sie auch endlich allzumahl errettet/ dan GOTT besänfftigte die Wellen/ daß
niemand umkam" (He had barely left France . . . and he encountered even more dangers . . . in
that he happened upon stormy weather . . . so that the sailors did not know what would happen
to them. . . . His fear of God did save them because God calmed the waves so that no one died

Since Happel died on May 15, 1690, and Schomberg six weeks later, on July 1, the author himself could not possibly have included the information about Schomberg's death in his novel. However, as I noted in chapter 1, we can assume that his continuator, possibly the publisher Wagner himself, completed the work, employing the information that was available by then, from sources that likely also supplied the writer of the *Theatrum* with his information. Moreover, without mentioning Happel's death, the foreword to volume 3 of the *Eduard* announces that the story will be told in the manner the reader had come to expect from this kind of novel, the *Geschicht-Roman*, "auf das noch fürlauffenden 1691. Jahr . . . den begierigen Leser in kurtzem vergnügen würde" (*EE* III: *Vorrede*).

Whoever finished the *Eduard* kept Happel's literary career alive well past his physical demise. In addition to volume 6 of the *Ungarische Kriegs-Roman* and the *Engelländische Eduard*, we find published under Happel's name the *Bayrische Max* (1692), the *Sächsische Witekind* (1693), and, even as late as 1710, the *Portugiesische Clara*. The generic model and the name of its creator clearly held sway for quite some time before being dismissed by the Romantics as a second-rate literary "Mischmasch."[154]

Conclusion

In Happel's *Engelländische Eduard*, the Duke of Schomberg's death and DuChastelet de Luzancy's panegyric provide Eduard and his friends with the occasion to examine the duke's remarkable life, "daß des ermelten Hertzogs Lebens-Lauff schrifftlich verfasset zu haben sey" (*EE* III: 357–77). Furthermore, not unlike Happel's use of media in telling Thököly's story, various print media furnished the frame for Happel, constructing his review of the century's military and religious turmoil as reflected in Schomberg's amazing

---

[*EE* II: 376]). Compare DuChastelet de Luzancy, *Abbregé de la Vie de Frederic Duc de Schomberg*, 59: "On ne remarqua aucun calme dans le visage de tous ceux qui estoient dans le Vaisseau que dans celuy du Duc de Schomberg. Il fit faire de continuelles priers a celui qui commande a la mer & aux vents. La piete les saura tous, & Dieu appaisa aussi-tot les Flots" (One saw no calmness on the faces of those in the vessel, except for the Duke of Schomberg. He encouraged all to pray continuously to him who calms the sea and the winds. Piety saved all, and God appeased the waves [WB Qu N 899g]). For the English text, see Glozier, *Marshal Schomberg*, 209–22.

154. Flemming Schock, *Die Text-Kunstkammer: Populäre Wissenssammlungen des Barock am Beispiel der "Relationes Curiosae" von E. W. Happel*, Beihefte zum Archiv für Kulturgeschichte 68 (Cologne: Böhlau, 2011), 5.

life. Although deprived of all honors and worldly possessions by Louis XIV, Schomberg never seemed to have complained, having been, according to DuChastelet de Luzancy (as quoted in the *Engelländische Eduard*), raised, in the Protestant religion, to base his actions on reason and always to remain a stranger to betrayal.[155]

While of somewhat different generations, Schomberg and Thököly commanded the attention of the European public almost simultaneously for several years. They showed up frequently in the newspapers that Happel had at his disposal and presumably read when composing his works. In fact, on March 27 and 28, 1684, they shared the same page in the *Mercurius*: Schomberg in the news from Paris as a marshal of France and Thököly in the news from Vienna as the recipient of money from undisclosed sources, presumably provided to help him continue his struggle after the Turkish defeat at Vienna. Happel deftly correlates both figures' biographies with the romances of his fictional heroes' progress through his novels. As a result, and following the prescriptions outlined by Huét and elaborated in the novel *Mandorell*, Happel raises fictional verisimilitude to the level of history in such a way as to challenge the reader to remain alert to the difference and to continue to absorb the many subtle and less-subtle interpretive nuances imbedded in these lengthy novels. In both cases, as I have shown, the rapidly growing media industry provides much of the material that goes into the production and guides consumption of news and novels.

---

155. "Er war in der Protestirenden Religion erzogen/ welche sehr vernünfftig/ und im übrigen von keine hinterlistigen Tücken weiß" (He was raised in the Protestant religion, which is very reasonable and free of all connivance [*EE* III: 374]).

THREE

Dangerous Passage

Pirates, Robbers, Captives, and Slaves

ે.

The fascination of early modern media with Imre Thököly and Friedrich von Schomberg found expression not only in newspapers but also in broadsheets, pamphlets, biographies, and, as examined in this study, novels. This fascination was based not only on the notoriety of these two men, their "star quality," but also on the fact that they represented an early modern form of globalization, of acting in the context of multiple cultural contacts—a circumstance that makes the seventeenth century so similar, in many ways, to our own. These contacts had many origins: the wars that, beginning with the Thirty Years' War, roiled all of Europe; the hegemonic efforts and successes of the Sublime Porte throughout the sixteenth and seventeenth centuries; and the burgeoning trade fueled by the competition between the major seagoing nations and trading companies, including the trade in slaves and ivory.[1]

In an expansion that was simultaneously feeding and benefiting from this development, the rapidly growing markets for and consumption of media inspired the amalgamation of fact and fiction in Happel's novels, the subject of this study. Ego-documents—both (auto)biographies and letters by individuals[2] who had spent extended periods of time in foreign cultures, whether

1. Jürgen Osterhammel and Niels P. Petersson, *Globalization: A Short History*, trans. Dona Geyer (Princeton: Princeton University Press, 2005), 31–49. See also Faruk Tabak, *The Waning of the Mediterranean, 1550–1870* (Baltimore: Johns Hopkins University Press, 2008), especially 1–29.

2. Winfried Schulze, "Ego-Dokumente: Annäherung an den Menschen in der Geschichte? Vorüberlegungen für die Tagung "EGO-DOKUMENTE,"" in *Ego-Dokumente: Annäherung an den Menschen in der Geschichte*, ed. Winfried Schulze (Berlin: Akademie, 1996).

as travelers, missionaries, captives, or slaves—tell many tales of experiencing contact with the cultural Other. Captivity narratives (discussed in this chapter), collections of news reports, and travelogues excerpted and redeployed in new collections of travel narratives and translated into multiple languages—all of these found their way into Happel's writings, whether his collections of news or his novels. That people all across Europe were eagerly reading about this multifaceted Other testifies to the broadening of mental and geographic horizons experienced by even the most sedentary reader.[3]

One of the ego-documents that circulated widely and in several languages during the second half of the seventeenth century was the autobiography of Emmanuel D'Aranda, a Spaniard from Flanders (Spanish Netherlands), who told of his capture by pirates, sale into slavery, and five years spent in Algerian captivity.[4] Johann Frisch, the German translator/editor of D'Aranda's autobiography, explains in his foreword that although he never visited Algiers in person, he made every effort to present to the reader a realistic impression of "die Beschaffenheit/ auch der Barbarn/ insonderheit derer zu Algiers Zustand und Gelegenheit" (the way the people of Barbary live, especially those in Algiers) and to move the reader to "Mitleiden gegen die Schlaven" (pity toward the slaves [dedication, 4–5]).[5] Beyond this immediate emotional appeal, D'Aranda's tale was to evoke for the reader who had never left Hamburg, let alone visited Algiers, the city and its sights. In his foreword, Frisch assures the reader that he had checked the document's facts with persons familiar with Algiers, in an effort to make sure that all locales mentioned in the text were correctly entered on the city map, "wo dieses oder jenes zufinden" (where this and that can be found).

Happel mentions D'Aranda by name and comments on the circumstances of his captivity in two of his novels, the *Spanische Quintana* (1686)

---

3. Bernhard Klein, "Randfiguren: Othello, Oroonoka und die kartographische Repräsentation Afrikas," in *Imaginationen des Anderen im 16. und 17. Jahrhundert*, ed. Ina Schabert and Michaela Boenke (Wiesbaden: Harrassowitz , 2002), 185–217; Magnus Ressel, "Hamburger Sklavenhändler als Sklaven in Westafrika," *Zeitschrift des Vereins für Hamburgische Geschichte* 96 (2011): 33–34.

4. Johann Frisch, ed., *Der Schauplatz Barbarischer Schlaverey/ eröffnet durch J. F.* (Altona: Victor de Löw, 1666), http://diglib.hab.de/drucke/gw-162/start.htm. The text is divided into three parts, beginning with D'Aranda's account (part 1). Parts 2 and 3 intermittently mention D'Aranda's experiences, which he recounts in the first person; other tales seem to be taken from additional sources relating to Algiers and the business and culture of slave trading.

5. Johann Frisch identifies the place and date of his dedication as "Altona den 10. Octob. A. 1666," indicating the geographic closeness to Hamburg.

and the *Academische Roman* (1690).[6] The influence of D'Aranda's popular account is easily discernible in several of the novels' characters who are repeatedly captured by pirates ("See-Räuber"), held for ransom, or sold as slaves. Emphasizing the authenticity of his characters' experiences in the *Academische Roman*, Happel tells of the captivity in Tripoli of a German named Klingenfeld. Among the indignities Klingenfeld has to suffer, the worst is merciless beatings on the soles of his feet, a punishment D'Aranda describes in his autobiography and for which the Turks were notorious among Christians: "Sie prügelten ihn in einem Tag wol 4. mahl/ und allemahl empfang er nicht weniger als 200. Streiche. auf die Fußsohlen/ daß er endlich gar niederfiel/ und schier in einer Ohmacht des Todes verfallen wäre" (They beat him four times in one day, and each time he received no less than two hundred lashes on the soles of his feet until he finally collapsed, passing close to death).[7] After two hundred lashes, Klingenfeld loses consciousness (*AR* II: 990) and, close to death, is handed over to a Turkish aga, whose physician, a Polish renegade, tends to his wounds. Greek merchants take pity on the German but are too afraid of the aga to help the German escape and are unwilling to lend him ransom money, so they sell him to a Jewish jeweler in Famagusta. A fellow German whom Klingenfeld had previously helped out of a difficult situation appears and pays Klingenfeld's ransom. Now free, Klingenfeld challenges to a duel the corsair who captured him. Victorious, he leaves Barbary for Alexandretta (*AR* II: 1004).[8]

Although the popularity of D'Aranda's autobiography and its influence on Happel's narratives are readily apparent, we do not know the exact number of other captive/slave narratives that circulated during the seventeenth century or how many of these Happel may have read. But public preoccupation with capture and extended captivity in non-Christian lands (a distinct possibility for early modern travelers, especially seagoing merchants)

---

6. Eberhard Werner Happel, *Der Spanische Quintana Oder Sogenannter Europaeischer Geschicht-Roman Auf Das 1686. Jahr* (Ulm: Matthaeus Wagner, 1686); Happel, *Der Academische Roman, Worinnen das Studenten-Leben fürgebildet wird* (Ulm: Matthaeus Wagner, 1690).

7. *AR* II: 989; Frisch, *Der Schauplatz Barbarischer Schlavery*, II: 110; 144: "Man solle dieser Slavin 300. Schläge unter die Fußsohlen geben"; 228: "sehen Schläge auff die blosse Fussohlen" (this slave is to receive three hundred lashes onto the soles of her feet; [they] observe lashes [being applied] to the naked soles of their feet). An especially gruesome punishment occurs at III: 298, when a slave from Hamburg, Henrich Keyser, has to hold down a fellow slave, a Frenchman, who is beaten to death for not producing the requisite ransom sum of four thousand Reichsthalers: seven hundred lashes on the soles of his feet, seven hundred on his back, and seven hundred on his buttocks.

8. Alexandretta is Iskenderun, Turkey.

is suggested by the frequent mention of slaves and captives in newspapers and news collections—such as the *Theatrum Europaeum*, Happel's *Thesaurus Exoticorum* (1688), and his earlier *Türckis. Estats- und Krieges-Bericht* (1683–84)—and by the many sermons and pronouncements about the liberation of slaves and captives that circulated in Europe. According to Linda Colley and Robert C. Davis, literary texts addressing the issues of captivity were so numerous that they all but formed a genre unto themselves, coalescing around "a miscellaneous and markedly persistent *culture of captivity*."[9] The fate of people kept enslaved (especially in the Barbary city-states of Algiers, Morocco, Tunis, Tripoli, and Salé) also received wide coverage in the German print market and specifically in the Hamburg market. Publicity was equally widespread in other big urban centers (such as London, Paris, and Amsterdam) through newspapers, broadsheets, pamphlets, church appeals, and ransom pleas.[10]

Several of Happel's novels significantly reflect this culture of captivity, enslavement, and holding for ransom. Happel thus responded to his readers' cultural interest and curiosity, much as he did when he fictionalized many of the events surrounding the Ottoman/Hungarian wars and the persecution of the French Protestants after the revocation of the Edict of Nantes in 1685. A brief survey of newspaper entries published between 1683 and 1687 yields numerous pirate-related news items.[11] For example, a notice in the Berlin *Sonntagischer Postillion* (July 5, 1683) told of 150 Algerian pirates who, with swords in hand, had stormed a village near Marseille, taking several inhabitants with them as slaves ("damit dem Säbel in der Hand in ein Dorff nahe bey Marsilien an das Land gekommen/ und haben alda etliche von ihren Sclaven mit sich genommen"). Two years later, the *Relations-Courir* of April 28, 1685, gave an account of travelers on their way to Martinique being abducted (and eventually released) by a multinational group of pirates.[12]

---

9. Linda Colley, "Going Native, Telling Tales: Collaboration and Empire," *Past and Present* 168, no. 1 (2000): 174; Robert C. Davis, *Holy War and Human Bondage: Tales of Christian-Muslim Slavery in the Early Modern Mediterranean* (Santa Barbara, CA: ABC-CLIO / Praeger, 2009), vii–xi.

10. Linda Colley, *Captives: Britain, Empire, and the World, 1600–1850* (New York: Anchor Books, 2004), 175.

11. *Nordische Mercurius, [Hamburger] Relations-Courir, Europäische Fama, Europäische Relation* (both from Altona), *Extraordinaire Relation*. For a complete list of periodical publications from Hamburg/Altona and beyond, see Holger Böning, *Welteroberung durch ein neues Publikum: Die deutsche Presse und der Weg zur Aufklärung; Hamburg und Altona als Beispiel* (Bremen: Edition Lumière, 2002), 305–12.

12. "Sie wurden . . . von diesem Seeräuber genommen/ welche auff alle Nationes kapen

In 1666, the merchant clerk turned pirate Alexander Exquemelin (discussed further later in this chapter) published an autobiography about his experiences as a pirate alongside some of the most notorious pirates of the day. Speaking to the wide circulation of such news during the sixties and early seventies of the seventeenth century, volumes 9–11 of the *Theatrum* repeatedly mention the corsairing and pirating activities of the well-known "Haupt- und Raub-Städten" (capitals and robber cities) of Algiers, Tunis, Tripoli, and Morocco.[13] On February 24, 1666, Captain Jürgen Tammas from Hamburg writes in his own hand and in secret ("eigenhändlich" and "sehr heimlich") about his imprisonment in Algiers after suffering a defeat and the loss of his ship during a sea battle against five Turkish pirate vessels ("Raubschiffe").[14] A year later, a note decries the millions in damages inflicted annually by barbarous Moors ("Barbarische Mohren") on merchants and Christian potentates.[15] To make matters worse, many Christians were taken prisoner and condemned to cruel labor as slaves.[16] In a similar way, the experience of the Spanish author Miguel de Cervantes (1547–1616), who spent five years in Algerian captivity, found its way into his narratives.[17] Yet another remarkable career of privateering, pirating, and writing travelogues comes together in the biography of Willliam Dampier, one

---

[*sic*]/ und alles was das Leben hat/ erbärmlich über Borth in das Wasser werffen. . . . Den dritten Tag . . . warff sich ermeldte Madame zu der Räuber Füssen/ und bath/ ihr Elend zu verkürtzen/ und sie eines kurzen Todes/ anstatt so vielen Elends sterben" (Z 100/1685/34/1).

13. *TE* X (1665): 95; (1667): 749; XI (1673): 478.

14. *TE* X (1666): 428.

15. Magnus Ressel, "Der Freikauf Lübecker Seeleute aus Nordafrika und die Gründung der Lübecker Sklavenkasse (1580–1640)," *Zeitschrift für Lübeckische Geschichte* 91 (2011): 123–24. For the modern reader, the word *Barbarische* presents a quandary. It could mean "barbarian," or it could mean "from Barbary."

16. "[U]nsäglich viel Christen in schnöde Dienstbarkeit zu grausamer Arbeit . . . hinweg führen" (many Christians [were] taken away [and led into] into cruel service and servitude [*TE* X (1667): 749]).

17. Cervantes spent the years from 1575 to 1580 in Algiers. Still filled with much helpful information is Ellen G. Friedman's *Spanish Captives in North Africa in the Early Modern Age* (Madison: University of Wisconsin Press, 1983), especially 57–58, 71, 120. Two recent studies, specifically Garcés's book, review in detail how much Cervantes struggled in trying to leave Algiers either by gathering enough ransom money or by flight: Maria Antonia Garcés, *Cervantes in Algiers: A Captive's Tale* (Nashville, TN: Vanderbilt University Press, 2002); Donald P. McCrory, *No Ordinary Man: The Life and Times of Miguel Cervantes* (Mineola, NY: Dover, 2002), 73–95. A more recent study by Nabil Matar points to Cervantes as having described in his *Los Banos des Argel* (1582) how, in a remarkable case of cultural transfer, Spanish captives introduced their Algerian captors to Spanish songs, musical instruments, fiestas, and "*commedias*": Nabil I. Matar, *Europe through Arab Eyes, 1578–1727* (New York: Columbia University Press, 2009), 65.

of the most famous English buccaneers (1651–1715), which is titled simply *Voyages*.[18]

An additional captivity narrative that was widely read and quickly translated was the autobiography of Alonso de Contreras (1582–1633), who had corsaired in the service of the Knights of the Order of Malta.[19] He tells of his stay on the island of Lampedusa, which, he says, was sacred to both Muslims and Christians. An image of the Virgin Mary attracted alms, money that could only be collected by the Knights of Malta, who were infamous for their corsairing and pirating on the Inland Sea, the Mediterranean. The knights would deposit the money in the Church of the Annunciation on Malta.[20] Happel's characters, reflecting many of Contreras's experiences, are frequently shipwrecked and subsequently stranded on such islands in the Mediterranean. The *Insulanische Mandorell* (1682), for instance, tells of the adventures of the protagonist and his friends and foes among the large and small islands of the Pacific and the Mediterranean.[21]

Exotic tales of captivity found eager readers wishing to be entertained at a safe distance by fictions dramatizing the experiences of captives and slaves. As he repeatedly stresses both in the prefaces to his novels and in the novels themselves, Happel wished to satisfy his readers' taste for such tales. He does so specifically (though not exclusively) in his *Geschicht-Romane*. Through tales of criminals on land and on the sea, of robbers and pirates, of people at the margins of society (*Randgruppen*) and from diverse social and ethnic backgrounds, and of characters who cross-dress and gender bend as the circumstances demand, Happel produced the narrative energy necessary to keep readers turning the pages even of his longest novels. One character among several to which I will return in chapter 4 is the intrepid heroine of the *Bayrische Max* (1692), Corinne, who is clearly modeled on the template

---

18. Gerald Norris, ed., *The Buccaneer Explorer: William Dampier's Voyages*, rev. ed. (Woodbridge: Boydell, 2008); Wolfgang Kaiser, "Negocier la Liberté: Missions Françaises pour l'échange et la rachat de captifs au Maghreb (XVIIe siècle)," in *La Mobilitè des personnes en Mediterrannée de l'Anquitité à l'époque moderne: Procedures de contrôle et documents d'identification*, ed. Claudia Moatti (Rome: École Française de Rome, 2004), 501–28.

19. Alfonso de Contreras, *Das Leben des Capitan Alonso de Contreras von ihm selbst erzählt* (Zurich: Manesse, 1961).

20. Wolfgang Kaiser, "La grotte de Lampedusa: Pratiques et imaginaire d'un 'troisième lieu' in Mediterrannée à l'époque moderne," in *Topographien des Sakralen: Religion und Raumordnung in der Vormoderne*, ed. Susanne Rau and Gerd Schwerhoff (Munich: Dölling und Galitz, 2008), 308.

21. Eberhard Werner Happel, *Der Insulanische Mandorell (1682)*, ed. Stefanie Stockhorst, Bibliothek seltener Text in Studienausgaben 12 (Berlin: Weidler, 2007).

of Grimmelshausen's Courasche.[22] After a life of crime and subterfuge as a woman who cheats and steals, usually disguised in men's clothing, she adds the element of class to her cross-dressing by adopting the identity of the valiant knight Corindo. In this role, she proves herself a virtuous companion to the novel's protagonist, Max, who pronounces at the novel's end that "Corinne hatte als Corindo gebüßt" (Corinne has done penance as Corindo [*BM* IV: 432]).

Happel's life in Hamburg, the bustling port city with its vibrant news market, provided him with easy access to the (often sensational) reports about both groups of criminals: robbers and pirates. Moreover, the far-flung information network at whose center Happel was situated helped him to negotiate for his readers the distance between the small geographic entity that was Hamburg and the huge expanse its citizens covered by trade and travel, a distance that, at different times and in various ways, harbored many threats for its seafarers, its merchants, and Hamburg's very existence as an independent city.[23] Pirates and robbers were an inescapable part of this ubiquitous threat, to be kept at bay by the vigilance of the city's inhabitants. Happel's novels convey an intense awareness of the precarious life into which his characters enter when they venture far and wide across known and unknown lands and seas.

Although a recent assessment states that sources about pirates and robbers are exceedingly rare,[24] Happel drew on many and varied source materials when making use of pirates and robbers as indispensable plot devices, not only in his novels, but in the *Relationes Curiosae*, the *Thesaurus Exoticorum*,[25]

---

22. *BM* I: 31, 63, 78ff.

23. Flemming Schock, *Die Text-Kunstkammer: Populäre Wissenssammlungen des Barock am Beispiel der "Relationes Curiosae" von E. W. Happel*, Beihefte zum Archiv für Kulturgeschichte 68 (Cologne: Böhlau, 2011), 34–46.

24. Virginia Lunsford comments, "Written and published sources are extremely rare. . . . [T]his study draws on diverse forms of cultural production, including criminal prosecution records; government pronouncements; pamphlet literature; newspapers and almanacs; contemporary books; laws and legal commentary, popular imagery, songs and poetry, and decorative arts": Virgina West Lunsford, *Piracy and Privateering in the Golden Age Netherlands* (New York: Palgrave Macmillan, 2005), 1–10.

25. Eberhard Werner Happel, *Thesaurus Exoticorum. Oder eine mit Aussländischen Raritäten und Geschichten Wohlversehene Schatz-Kammer Fürstellend Die Asiatische, Africanische und Americanische Nationes . . . Darauff folget eine Umständliche von Der Tuerckey Beschreibung . . . und sein verfluchtes Gesetz-Buch oder AKORAN* (Hamburg: Thomas von Wiering, 1688); Happel, ed., *Türckis. Estats- und Krieges-Bericht*, nos. 1–137 (1683–84).

Fig. 7. Eberhard Werner Happel's *Der Bayrische Max oder so genannter
Europaeischer Geschicht-Roman Auf Das 1691. Jahr* (1692) (Herzog August
Bibliothek, Wolfenbüttel)

the *Türckis. Estats- und Krieges-Bericht*,[26] and the *Kern-Chronica.*[27] While this chapter will focus mostly on Happel's *Geschicht-Romane*, it will also take a look at the *Insulanische Mandorell*, the *Academische Roman*, and, most important, his very first work, the *Afrikanische Tarnolast* (1667/1689), novels Happel does not identify as *Geschicht-Romane*. We will see that, even at the earlier stages in his writing career, cultural presuppositions conveyed by contemporary media reports influenced how Happel told his stories about robbers and pirates, captives and slaves.

In this chapter, I will first introduce the various and often confusing contemporary definitions of men who legally or illegally made a living chasing booty on the high seas. Second, I will review a selection of seventeenth-century texts that brought news about robbers and pirates to the early modern reader and that were probably available to Happel. This will also bring to the fore some of the political, social, and economic causes that favored the increase in national and international piracy and robberies and the impact of both on the life of men and women in Europe generally and in the Mediterranean basin in particular. Finally, I will examine several of Happel's novels, beginning with the *Tarnolast*, to see how he fictionalized the information about robbers and pirates in his narratives.

Privateers, Buccaneers, Corsairs, Pirates, and Robbers: Definitions

The geography of Happel's novels encompasses most of Europe, the Middle East, eastern Europe, the islands of the Atlantic and Indian Oceans, and the areas on both shores of the Inland Sea. The Americas remain, for the most part, outside of his narrative universe, partly because the Mediterranean trade was more in Hamburg's merchant interest than the Atlantic.[28] Accordingly, this chapter is not concerned with Atlantic piracy or the

---

26. Schock, *Die Text-Kunstkammer*, 34–46.

27. Eberhard Werner Happel, *Kern-Chronica der merckwürdigsten Welt- und Wunder-Geschichte*, 2 vols. (Hamburg: Thomas von Wiering, 1690). These volumes are arranged by years: volume 1 reports on 1618 to 1679, volume 2 on 1680 to 1690. The latter contains much information already published in Happel's novels between 1680 and 1690. It appears that the news is more or less reported as it came across his desk, including news about the Hungarian war, the persecution of the French Protestants, the activities of pirates, and many crime and wonder stories.

28. An exception is the *Insulanische Mandorell* (1682), where Happel mentions an American prince and American islands. Mandorell and Prince Cowattiar "gehen zu Schiffe nach Amerika"

African-American slave trade. Rather, it deals with the pirating and slaving that made the Mediterranean, African, Atlantic, and Asian coasts exceedingly precarious for seafarers and coastal inhabitants during the seventeenth and early eighteenth centuries.

Robbers, pirates, captives, and slaves were historically and culturally very much a fact of life for Happel and his contemporaries. They find their way into his narratives because, as we have seen in our examination of the role of media stars like Schomberg and Thököly in Happel's *Geschicht-Romane*, factual reporting, in whatever form, is never strictly separated from Happel's fiction. The cross-cultural contacts playing out in these novels tell us much about both sides: the pursuer and the pursued, the private traveler or merchant and the professional hunter of booty on land or on sea. Capture and captivity resulting from these encounters were often the beginning of a long process of commerce between different cultures, languages, and religions. Seen in this light, Happel's characters become part of the refashioning and retelling of already circulating narratives, thus opening his novels to the specific contexts and precise circumstances of his historical moment.[29]

Printed information about pirates, corsairs, and buccaneers and reports about robbers, either as gangs or as single perpetrators, was found in nearly all locations where newspapers or journals were available.[30] Furthermore, inextricably bound to such news, there emerged, in fact and in fiction, narratives about slave taking and slave trading among Christians and Muslims in the Atlantic and the Mediterranean, as among Africans, Europeans, and Asians across the continents. In other words, where there were corsairs or pirates, there were also captives, either held for ransom or sold as slaves;[31] and where there were travelers, there were also robbers, threatening citizens on both sides of the city walls, whether as pickpockets or as highwaymen who might rob or even murder. Emerging from news reports, pamphlets, and popular songs, such characters found their way into Happel's fictions.

During much of the seventeenth century and part of the eighteenth, pirates, privateers, buccaneers, or (as they are often collectively but ambigu-

---

(board a ship to America), but not much more is said after this brief mention. Eberhard Werner Happel, *Der Insulanische Mandorell (1682)*, ed. Stefanie Stockhorst, Bibliothek seltener Text in Studienausgaben 12 (Berlin: Weidler, 2007), 431 (III: 572 in original).

29. Colley, "Going Native," 176.

30. Wolfgang Behringer, *Im Zeichen des Merkur: Reichspost und Kommunikationsrevolution in der Frühen Neuzeit*, Veröffentlichungen des Max-Planck-Instituts für Geschichte 189 (Göttingen: Vandenhoeck und Ruprecht, 2003).

31. Murray Gordon, *Slavery in the Arab World* (New York: New Amsterdam Books, 1989), 44, 97–101; Tabak, *Waning of the Mediterranean*, 44, 97–101.

ously designated) corsairs operated on the early modern national and international stage with nearly as much impunity as business acumen. As Virginia Lunsford observes, "The pirate was a frightening creature whose very acts of aggression rent at the fabric of the prevailing economic and political order; moreover, their radically communitarian culture represented a revolutionary threat to early modern status quo. Not fictions, but real and horrifying threats."[32] Their presence was a fact of life as well as a fact of war. Privateers and corsairs entered into contractual agreements, so-called letters of marque, with legitimate European governments authorizing them to pursue and capture enemy vessels in the service of these governments.[33] Reflecting on the contemporary corsairing/pirating reality, a character in the *Italienische Spinelli* explains the fine points of the distinction: "Ein Caper [corsair, privateer] ist der/ so seine ehrliche *Patenta* [*sic*] hat/ darinn die Obrigkeit/ der er dienet/ ihm zu öffentlichen Krieges Zeiten/ dem Feind Abbruch zuthun/ Ordre ertheilet/ ihm auch anweiset/ was für ein Schiff er feindlich tractiren soll. . . . See-Rauber aber ist der jenige/ der entweder keiner gewissen Parthey dienet/ sondern alles was ihm fürkomt/ wegnimt/ und also keinen ansiehet/ er sey Freund oder Feind. See-Rauberey sey älter als die Caperey" (A corsair is he who has an honorable patent where the government whom he serves in wars that have been officially declared give him orders which ships he can legally attack. . . . A pirate does not serve any designated party; rather, he takes anything that comes his way without regard to friend or foe. Piracy is older than corsairing).[34]

When the fortunes of war shifted and peace treaties were signed, privateers or corsairs lost their letters of marque, upon which many of them turned to pirating in an effort to insure a steady income. The line separating pirate from privateer/corsair was blurred to such an extent that scholars such as Suraiya Faroqhi, an expert on the Ottoman Empire, and Robert C. Davis do not distinguish between the two, identifying the collective simply as corsairs/pirates.[35]

Peter Leeson's take on corsairs and pirates is a bit more nuanced. He not only maintains the distinction between privateer (*Caper*) and pirate (*Seeräu-*

---

32. Lunsford, *Piracy and Privateering in the Golden Age Netherlands*, 137.

33. In England, such "letters" were issued by the High Court of the Admiralty: C. R. Pennell, ed., *Bandits at Sea: A Pirate Reader* (New York: New York University Press, 2001), 72–74.

34. *IS* II: 271.

35. Suraiya Faroqhi, *The Ottoman Empire and the World around It* (London: Tauris, 2007), 122. Davis simply refers to them as corsairs throughout most of his study *Holy War and Human Bondage*.

ber, "sea robber") but adds a third category to the economy of corsairing: that of men who attack and rob ships mainly in the name of religion.[36] The Barbary corsairs pursued Christian ships; in turn, Christian corsairs, such as the Knights of Malta and the Knights of St. Stephen of Livorno, hunted down Muslim vessels.[37] A note in the *Relations-Courir* (Paris, January 18, 1684) says as much. It talks about an Algerian vessel that, after being stranded off the coast of Italy, was delivered of all its cargo, including 160 persons who were "made slaves" and sixty Christians who were freed.[38] When Spinelli, the protagonist of the *Italienische Spinelli* (1685), suggests that not too many pirates could be found among Christians, one of his Muslim interlocutors laughs derisively, reminding his listeners of the Knights of Malta, whom he calls some of the worst offenders in pirating: "dieselbe rauben ja stets auch Türcken und und Barbarn/ ja sie leben fast einzig und allein vom Raub" (they rob Turks and Barbarians; in fact, they completely live off robbery).[39] The *Relations-Courir* of March 6, 1685, informed its readers that news from Dalmatia indicates that the imperial troops were moving farther into Turkish territory, returning daily with much booty, and enslaving many Turks while liberating many Christians.[40]

The *Relations-Courir* of January 13, 1685, put the mutuality of slaving and hostage taking between Christians and Muslims into stark relief. It told of a Christian ship, the *Jerusalem*, that had been taken, along with 150 Christian slaves, by pirates from Tripoli. The next sentence introduces the Ritter de Tourville, who had gone to Algiers to ransom Christian captives. The Turks complained that he had brought along only Turkish slaves in bad condition and had held on to those who would bring a much larger ransom.[41]

Moreover, along with Malta and the cities of the Barbary Coast, the Italian towns of Livorno and Naples also supported active slave markets and engaged in the trade of pirated goods. Like Leeson, Wolfgang Kaiser catego-

---

36. Peter T. Leeson, *The Invisible Hook: The Hidden Economics of Pirates* (Princeton: Princeton University Press, 2009), 7.

37. Davis, *Holy War and Human Bondage*, 112–13.

38. "[D]amit man die Güter davon erhalten möchte/ und sind davon 160 Personen zu Sclaven gemacht/ und 60 Christen erlöset" (Z 100/684/6/2).

39. *IS* II: 240.

40. "[V]iel Türcken zu Sclaven/ hingegen Christliche Sclaven zu freyen Leuten machen" (Z/100/1685/19/1–2).

41. "Wir haben Zeitung/ daß 3 See-Räuber von Tripoli das Schiff Jerusalem genommen haben . . . worauff sie wol 150 Sclaven gekommen haben. . . . Der Ritter de Tourville hält sich noch umb Algiers auff/ und man sagt/ daß die Türcken daselbst klagen/ daß er nur die schlechtesten von ihren Sclaven mitgebracht hat" (Z 100/1685/4/1).

rizes privateers/corsairs as "entrepreneurs of war,"[42] persons who invested in war by supplying princes and magistrates with the military force that they were unable to muster with their own resources. He agrees with Leeson that privateering and pirating had much more in common with "a Fortune 500 company" than with a bunch of savage and wildly undisciplined outlaws combing the seas for booty.[43]

According to Leeson, yet another group of seagoing robbers, the buccaneers, were originally outlaws who had settled first on Hispaniola and then on Tortuga, an island off Hispaniola, from whence they went on their raids. By the 1660s, their reputation had spread far and wide, to such an extent that buccaneering and pirating became largely indistinguishable.[44] Alexander Exquemelin claims that buccaneers tended to govern themselves by something resembling a constitution, according to which decisions were made about where to hunt, where to rest, and how to divide the booty.[45] Leeson's description closely resembles what we read in volume 2 of the *Ungarische Kriegs-Roman* (1685), the sixth chapter of which outlines in detail how pirate ships were outfitted, what kind of booty was captured, and how this booty was distributed.[46]

Whether taken by privateers, corsairs, or pirates, booty consisted of all that was traded across the seas: sugar, leather, tobacco, and Brazil wood, as well as manufactured goods. Later, in the 1660s and 1670s, lucrative trading and pirating staples included foodstuffs such as butter, herring, salted fish, tobacco, lemons, and oranges, as well as coal, ordnance, grain, wine, brandy, vinegar, honey, beer, cotton, whale meat, and wooden and iron wares. Moreover, whether European or non-European, all parties participated as vigorously as they could in the taking of captives for ransom and for slave trading. Such captives promised a much higher return on investment than

---

42. Wolfgang Kaiser, "Negocier la liberté: Missions diplomatiques françaises pour l'échange et la rachat de captifs avec le Maghreb (XVIIe siècle)," in *La mobilité des personnes en Mediterrannée de l'Antiquité à l'époque moderne: Procedures de contrôle et documents d'identification*, ed. Claudia Moatti (Rome: École Française de Rome, 2004), 501.

43. Leeson, *Invisible Hook*, 6.

44. Ibid., 7.

45. Reviewed in the chapter "The Laws of Lawlessness: Pirate Constitutions" in ibid., 58–63. It has been pointed out that the existence of such constitutions is at the root of much romanticizing about pirate life.

46. "Der Bassa/ von jeden Preisen oder genommenen Schiff/ bekomt er den halben Schiffs-Part/ und den achten Pfennig . . . wie auch den 8. Sclaven/ ja er hat die Wahl unter denselben/ und behält die Vornehmsten für sich" (The Pasha [of Algiers] took [a fixed amount] and every eighth penny from each load . . . as well as every eighth slave; in fact, he could choose among those and took the best for himself [*UK* II: 469]).

any other goods.[47] The distribution of profits between corsair and country of contract or between pirate captain and his crew was, for the most part, highly regulated; discipline aboard ship and survival depended on it.[48] Booty was divided according to a formula that allowed for all parties to get a fair share. If prisoners were not immediately killed, such "mercy" was a result of their ransom value and not of compassion. When a crew felt shortchanged, mutiny was often the result.[49] In other words, for many of these pirate entrepreneurs, the "orderly transfer of profit" mirrored legitimate business transactions.[50]

The human component of booty significantly influenced the narrative structure and the character development in Happel's novels. In the *Spanische Quintana* (1686), for example, Happel describes piracy in some detail as one of the main sources of the thriving Mediterranean slave market. Especially savvy were the Turkish slave traders, who reportedly followed warring armies and navies to immediately purchase prisoners of war, whom they subsequently sold "like animals" in the large markets bordering the Mediterranean (*SQ* IV: 125–26).

The all-but-perpetual state of war among Muslims and Christian Europeans led to frequently changing alliances and military strategies, according to which European powers managed their hostilities against each other as well as against the states of the Barbary Coast, Algiers, Tunis, Tripoli, Salé, and Morocco. These changes further complicated the already challenging attempts to draw a clear distinction between corsair, privateer, and pirate. In addition, many European corsairs/pirates, whether or not renegades— European converts to the Muslim faith—fought as frequently under European as under Barbary banners, seeking their fortunes in alliances with the pirating cities all along the Barbary Coast.[51] As the apparent military and

---

47. C. R. Pennell, ed., *Piracy and Diplomacy in Seventeenth-Century North Africa: The Journal of Thomas Baker, English Consul in Tripoli, 1677–1685* (Toronto: Associated University Presses, 1989), 45. For detailed insight into the specifics of the Portuguese slave trade, see Linda M. Heywood and John K. Thornton, *Central Africans, Atlantic Creoles, and the Foundation of the Americas, 1585–1660* (Cambridge: Cambridge University Press, 2007), 109–69.

48. The prince who issued the letter was entitled to a percentage of the profit: Kaiser, "Negocier la Liberté," 501.

49. Lunsford, *Piracy and Privateering in the Golden Age Netherlands*, 7, 9.

50. Leeson, *Invisible Hook*, 58–63.

51. Janice E. Thomson, *Mercenaries, Pirates, and Sovereigns: State-Building and Extraterritorial Violence in Early Modern Europe* (Princeton: Princeton University Press, 1994), 43–45. An interesting and confusing exception were the Maltese corsairs, who, though, nominally confined to attacking Muslim ships, frequently included Greek (Christian) vessels among their targets (ibid., 46).

political sovereignty of Tunis, Tripoli, Morocco, and Algiers demonstrates, these cities belonged de jure under the regency of Constantinople, but the practical relationship to the Porte was somewhat murky. In fact, from about the 1620s, the city-states of the Barbary Coast behaved, in war and peace, more or less as independent entities.[52]

Those who found themselves attacked at sea always condemned their attackers as pirates, even if at war and equipped with letters of marque. In the *Academische Roman* (1690), friend and foe are sorted out simply by the nationalities of those captured. While pirates acknowledge a French captain's letter of marque on the grounds that the pirates' native Republic of Tripoli is, at present, at peace with France, they demand that all non-French persons be handed over, to be exchanged later for a good ransom ("eine ansehnliche Ransion").[53] It should be noted that Happel's dislike of the French, who habitually entered into contractual agreements not only with the Sublime Porte against the empire but also individually with the Barbary regencies, rivals his condemnation of the pirates: "also mußten die arme Gefangene/ die den Treu-losen Frantzösischen Schiffer jetzo in ihren Hertzen vermaledeyen/ in ihrem Unglück sich gedulden" (In this way, the poor prisoners, cursing the faithless French mariners, had to resign themselves to their misfortune [*AR* II: 986]).

Unlike their seagoing counterparts, robbers never had the career option of being employed in the service of legitimate governments. No country was free from the danger they represented. When describing Turkish guesthouses, the caravanseries, Tauffernier, the Jesuit confessor of General Leslie, who represented Vienna as ambassador to the Sublime Porte in 1665, mentions the need for travelers to stay in groups because "das allein-reisen dieser Orte/ absonderlich in Kauffmannschafften/ sehr gefährlich ist" (in these areas, traveling alone is very dangerous).[54] But while the influence exerted by corsairs and pirates on early European economics, politics, and intercultural

---

52. Christian Windler, "Verrechtlichte Gewalt zwischen Muslimen und Christen: Französisch-maghrebinische und spanisch-maghrebinische Beziehungen," in *Gewalt in der Frühen Neuzeit: Beiträge zur 5. Tagung der Arbeitsgemeinschaft Frühe Neuzeit im VHD*, ed. Claudia Ulbrich, Claudia Jarzebowski, and Michaele Hohkamp (Berlin: Duncker und Humblot, 2003), 325; Martin Rheinheimer, "Identität und Kulturkonflikt: Selbstzeugnisse schleswig-holsteinischer Sklaven in den Barbareskenstaaten," *Historischen Zeitschrift* 269, no. 2 (1999): 320. About Algiers's hostilities against the Netherlands while the latter were officially at peace with Constantinople, see Ressel, "Der Freikauf Lübecker Seeleute," 143; Thomson, *Mercenaries, Pirates, and Sovereigns*, 21–43.

53. *AR* II: 986.

54. Happel, *Türckis. Estats- und Krieges-Bericht*, no. 93.

contacts produced much factual and fictional information in the multiple media available to readers, contemporary facts about robbers or highwaymen are harder to come by, despite their ubiquity in Happel's fictions as well as in frequent reports about them in broadsheets, newspapers, and news collections like the *Theatrum Europaeum* or Happel's *Kern-Chronica*. Crime reports in the latter publications are usually gathered, along with weather phenomena and wonders, at the end of a given year, while newspapers, like Hamburg's *Relations-Courir*, either interspersed crime reports with their normal news accounts or moved them to the end of a page or date, as in the *Theatrum Europaeum*.

Robbers and highwaymen disquieted not only travelers but men and women in their villages and homes. Volume 7 of the *Theatrum Europaeum*, containing news of the year 1663, closes with a report about a notorious highwayman who "surpassed everything heard heretofore about an evil person, the godless, horrible murderer Melchior Hedloff."[55] After raping and murdering a pregnant woman, Hedloff cut open her belly, pulled out the fetus, tore out its heart ("ungefähr eines Daumens dick" [about the size if a thumb]), and ate it. He proceeded to rape many more women, among them "zwei Jüdinnen" (two Jewesses). On the occasion of his execution, a broadsheet of Melchior Hedloff, complete with portrait and text ("im Alter von 48. Jahr . . . Januar 14. 1654 ad vivum abgebildet" [pictured age forty-eight from life on January 14, 1654]), was widely disseminated.[56]

It is clear that criminal notoriety was a frequent topic in the newspapers of the day, from whence it found its way into Happel's novels. Some especially nefarious crimes, such as Hedloff's, were even reported several times in different newspapers. Such is the case with one attack on a coach going from Rendsburg to Hamburg, whose passengers were robbed of all their belongings and then tied to the wheels of the coach so that they would have been crushed to death had the coach moved. Among the victims who are named and, in the end, were liberated, the author mentions a well-known Jew, Abraham Michels, and his wife, who carried a goodly sum of money with

---

55. About crime reporting in the *Theatrum Europaeum*, see Gerhild Scholz Williams, "Formen der Aufrichtigkeit: Zeitgeschehen in Wort und Bild im *Theatrum Europaeum* (1618–1718)," in *Die Kunst der Aufrichtigkeit im 17. Jahrhundert*, ed. Claudia Benthien and Steffen Martus, Frühe Neuzeit (Tübingen: Niemeyer, 2006), 443–73; Matthaeus Merian, ed., *Theatrum Europaeum*, vol. 7 (Frankfurt am Main: Matthaeus Merian, 1885), 475.

56. Wolfgang Harms and Michael Schilling, eds., *Die Sammlung der Herzog August Bibliothek in Wolfenbüttel*, pt. 1, *Ethica, Physica*, and pt. 3, *Theologica, etc., Deutsche Illustrierte Flugblätter des 16. und 17. Jahrhunderts* (Tübingen: Niemeyer, 1985, 1989).

them.[57] The same incident, obviously quite notorious, appears in *Wöchentliche Ordinari Friedens- und Kriegs-Curier* of March 5, 1683.[58] However, we remain ignorant as to how exactly these criminals were organized, how they regulated their activities and interactions, and what they did with their ill-gotten gains (aside from quickly consuming them). Notwithstanding trial reports and hearsay, we are left with images and texts published in broadsheets and the sensational reports in newspapers.[59] Judging by such information, these criminals on land operated most frequently as highwaymen, in areas away from the cities and towns, or as pickpockets and thieves in towns. They attacked burghers as well as travelers, stealing their goods and money. A quick perusal of newspapers issued from 1682 to 1687 and likely read by Happel tells us of many highway robberies ("Strassen-Räuberey und Leut-Endführung"), especially of frequent attacks on postal messengers.[60] We also read much about roving gangs of soldiers who tried to make up for not hav-

---

57. Von der 9ten Woche 1683 eingekommener Zeitungen Dienstagische FAMA, 20. Februar 1683 (Z 2/1683/9 P.80.4); the *Relations-Courir* (Berlin, February 10) tells of a man who robbed and murdered a postal messenger ("Postillion-Diener") en route from Hamburg to Lentzen and was shortly thereafter caught with the money at his mother's house. The report continues that the same man had also murdered a Jew and stripped him of his clothes. Böning notes that it is often assumed (but not proven) that Happel worked as editor for the *Relations-Courir* when employed at the Wiering publishing house: Böning, *Welteroberung durch ein neues Publikum*, 73.

58. Z 98/1683/Wi-XXII/7 5./15.3.

59. "Schweidnitz/ in der perfektischen Buchdruckerey außgefertiget/ und wie daselbst/ also auch zu Breslau/ im Perfektischen Buchladen zu finden/ 1654." Harms and Schilling, *Die Sammlung der Herzog August Bibliothek in Wolfenbüttel*.

60. One example reads, "Vergangenen Sonntag ist der Berlinische Post-Botthe zwischen Trepkow unnd Lentzen . . . von hinten zu mörderischer Weise ums Leben gebracht. . . . So hat man heute die Nachricht erhalten/ daß derselbige in Halberstadt ertappt/ und gefänglich eingezogen (Last Sunday the postal messenger who was on his way from Trepkow to Lenzten was murdered. . . . Today it was learned that [the murderer] had been caught in Halberstadt and put into prison [*RC*, Hamburg, February 5, 1684; Z 100/1684/ 11/4]). This case is interesting because the paper reported a few days later that the imprisoned perpetrator was raging, attempting suicide by stabbing himself and by hitting himself with a rock. After the prisoner recovered from his wounds, the elector ordered that he be executed at the place of his crime (*RC*, February 9, 1684; Z 100/1684/14/1). Even an imperial postal messenger ("Kayserli. Postillion") was not safe from such assaults (*Eingekommener Zeitungen Dienstagischer Postillion* [Berlin], March 2, 1683 [Z 2/1683/10. P. Di./2]). The same paper reported the discovery of the messenger's letters, all opened, near Reinbeck on March 23. A quick perusal of the *Relations-Courir* of 1684–87 testifies to the frequency of such attacks. One occurred on May 22 in Utrecht. On January 4, 1684, the Berlinische Post was attacked and robbed of twenty-one hundred gold pieces; The thief was caught and put into prison (Z 100/1684/11/8). The *Relations-Courir* of February 10, 1684, reported an especially brutal murder and robbery (two thousand Gulden) of a "Postilions-Diener" between Tripkow and Lentzen. The perpetrator, described as having liberally spent his ill-gotten gain, eventually admitted that he had also murdered a Jew and pulled off all his clothes [Z 100/1684/13/4].

ing been paid: "man hat allhier niemahls so viel Strassenräuber/ als zu dieser Zeit gesehen/ sie rotten sich by 30 und 40 zusammen/ und greiffen enen jedweden ohne allen Respect an; . . . es ist aber wegen Mangel der Bezahlung der Soldaten noch zur Zeit nich viel zu ändern" (there have never been as many highway robbers as now; they are coming together in groups of thirty and forty and attacking everyone without any regard; . . . it is because of the soldiers not getting paid that this will not change for some time).[61]

The news of an attack on Hamburg merchant Hieronymus Schnittinger by a gang of nine robbers made it into several papers, in part because the gang was led by an officer ("Rittmeister"). He and an accomplice, also a Rittmeister, both identified by name, were caught, tortured, and executed for their crimes.[62] Worthy of note are the writer's observation that these crimes appear to be increasingly frequent and that many of them involve noble perpetrators, a social commentary that Happel braids into his novels.[63] Time and again, the papers report such criminal goings-on in Italy (some of them led by noblemen ["fürnehmer Banditen Häupter"]), around Venice and Naples, facts that then find their way into Happel's *Academische Roman*, where bands of highwaymen emerge as an important part of the action.[64] On June 22, 1682, it was reported from Venice that bandits had been observed on the border between Verona and Mantua and that men had been sent to keep the roads free of such criminals ("von dergleichen Strassenrauben freizuhalten").[65] Several years later, in 1687, things got so bad that the viceroy of Naples demanded that the Duke of Montecalvo, along with the criminal and civil judges, advocates, and officials of the judicial branch, appear before him to justify why nightly criminal activities could not be brought under control.[66]

---

61. *RC*, Brussels, January 9, 1685; Z 100/1685/3/7. The same difficulties arose when the French army, moving to the Spanish Netherlands, took with them so much grain and other victuals that people had nothing left to eat, leading to an increase in highway robberies ("Strassen-Räuber," *RC*, October 24, 1684; Z 100/1684/85/5).

62. Hamburg, April 31, 1685 (*Wöchentlicher Ordinarii Friedens- und Kriegs-Courier*, Nuremberg [Z 98/1685/Fr.-II/5]); the same paper brought news of a Lieutenant Mell, "welchen man vor das Haupt und Führer einer gorssen Diebischen Rotte hält/ ertappt und in gefängliche Verhafft gebracht/ er solle noch viel Geld/ Gold und kostbare Jubelen be ihm gehabt" (who was considered the leader of a large gang; he was put into prison. He was supposed to have in his possession much money, gold, and precious jewels [Z 98/1685/Fr.-XI/6]).

63. "[S]o scheint es doch gleichwol eine Sache von grosser Weitläuffigkeit zu seyn/ und darin viel Vornehme verwickelt" (Z 98/1685/Fr.-VII/7).

64. *Einkommener Zeitungen Dienstagischer Mercurius*, Naples, December 16, 1682 (Z 2/1682/2 M. Di./1).

65. *Mercurii Relation oder Wöchentliche Reichs-Ordinarii Zeitungen* (Z 11/1682/Ee 28/2).

66. "Wegen ihrer Unachtsamkeit/ daß des Nachts die gewöhnliche Ronde nicht thäten/

It appears that, most of the time, successful robbers rapidly spent their ill-gotten gains on drink, gambling, and roaming across the countryside.[67] Sometimes, however, they became almost sedentary, stowing their booty away in caves and hideaways in out-of-the-way places.[68] One of Happel's fictional robbers explains to Klingenfeld, the German protagonist of the *Academische Roman*, that he, like his companions, occupied a cave in the woods, where, after swearing an oath never to reveal the treasure troves of their comrades, they hid their horses and their booty.[69] Fictional or real, robbers, unlike pirates, generally did not offer their goods up for trade in central marketplaces. It seems that robbers or highwaymen occasionally took prisoners or captives, but there are no indications that such captives were sold as slaves, and robbers did not keep captives around for chores or for supporting other activities, unless such captives decided to become robbers themselves.

Aside from merely following criminal dispositions, men (and occasionally women) often turned to crime because of poverty, vagrancy, or war.[70] As noted, reports of such behavior can be found in the sensational news that make up the last few pages of each of the twenty-one volumes of the *Theatrum Europaeum*.[71] Happel fictionalized one such incident in his *Academische Roman*, in which a nobleman joins a band of outlaws ("Venetianischen Banditen") because, as a young student in Padua, he had found himself running with a bad crowd and subsequently had lost all his money in the company of loose women. He confesses to 283 robberies and 135 murders—23 committed by himself and 112 in the company of his gang members.[72] Defeated in a

wodurch viel Dieberey in der Stat hin und wieder begangen würden" (*RC*, April 30, 1687; Z100/1687/78/1).

67. Uwe Danker, *Räuberbanden im Alten Reich um 1700: Ein Beitrag zur Geschichte von Herrschaft und Kriminalität in der Frühen Neuzeit*, 2 vols., Suhrkamp Taschenbuch Wissenschaft 707 (Frankfurt am Main: Suhrkamp, 1988), 1:261.

68. On the organization and structuring of the gangs, see ibid., 1:276–308.

69. "Ein Jeder hat eine besondere Höhle vor sich und sein Pferd . . . auch wird ein Jeder/ der in die Gesellschaft aufgenommen wird/ zufordertst mit einem käfftigen Eyd verbunden" (*AR* I: 132).

70. Monika Spicker-Beck, *Räuber, Mordbrenner, umschweifendes Gesind: Zur Kriminalität im 16. Jahrhundert*, ed. Wolfgang Reinhard and Ernst Schulin, Rombach Wissenschaft–Reihe Historiae 8 (Freiburg im Breisgau: Rombach, 1995), 67–82.

71. *TE* X: 523–25. A report presents a family of robbers and murderers (father, mother, and son), executed in 1661 in Wohlau, Silesia, because of "'Mordtaten/ Ehebruch/ Hurerey [Vergewaltigung]/ Blutschande/ Sodomiterey/ Mordbrände und Diebstähle' verhaftet, 'peinlich verhört' und zum Tode verurteilt wurden" (523).

72. "[I]ch bin ein Edelmann aus Graubünden/ habe mich lange Zeit in Padua aufgehalten/ und bin durch unordentliche Liebe von den Studiis zu einem leichtfertigen Leben verführt worden/ welches mich gar unter die Zunfft der Räuber und Mörder hat gebracht" (I am a nobleman

duel by Klingenfeld, he confesses to having hidden his treasure away in the woods; as a gesture of repentance, he now wants to hand it over to Klingenfeld. As it turns out, such ill-gotten wealth is legally the property of the local lord, the Duke of Padua, who promptly makes a gift of it to Klingenfeld and his men in gratitude for their victory over the robber and his accomplices.[73] Reflecting the social pressures that led many men to a life of crime, the novel also tells of two bandits who confess their deeds before they are executed.

> Zwey der gefangenen Räuber verarmte Edelleute aus dem Venetianischen Gebieth wären/ die auß grossem Mangel sich unter diese Räuber-Zunfft vor einem halben Jahr begeben hätten. . . . [S]o bald sie einige Baarschafften erbeutet/ solche also den Ihrigen zugeführet hätten/ um darvon zu leben. . . . Wolten dem Handel . . . nur so lange abwarten/ biß sie ein gut Stück Geldes gemacht daß sie leben könten/ alsdann wolten sie auch ihres Lebens gehen/ und das Rauben quittiren. . . . [W]urden geköpffet/ geviertheilet/ und ihre Leibes-Theil an die Land-Strasse um die Stadt auffgehänget.[74]

The Sources

Clearly, the reality of the national and international marketplace was different for robbers than for pirates or privateers. Unlike robbers, whose land-bound life made them much less mobile, their seafaring brothers in crime ranged far and wide, seemingly able to show up anywhere at any time. Their presence was real and immediate. Thomas Heywood, the author of a contemporary tract about the famous Elizabethan pirates Clinton and Purser, says as much: "Of land-theeves I have no purpose to speake at all, but onely of those called Pirates, that is Sea-rovers; or men of Warre, but most com-

---

from Graubünden. I lived for a long time in Padua, where I fell into disreputable company, left my studies, and was led astray into a dissolute life, which finally brought me into the company of robbers and murderers [*AR* I: 130]).

73. *AR* I: 135. The *Relations-Courir* of April 30, 1687, reported that the viceroy of Naples, along with thirty "Musquetirer" and several servants, patrolled the streets of his city to help reduce street crime (*Z* 100/1687/78/1).

74. "Two of the captured robbers were noblemen from the area of Venice who joined the gangs because of dire need. . . . [A]s soon as they had gathered a few resources for their families to live on . . . they were planning to quit committing crimes. . . . [T]hey were beheaded, drawn and quartered, and their body parts were hung on the side of the road" (*AR* I: 135–36).

monly called Pirates."[75] Because ships could transport significant amounts of goods at great speed, piracy presented significantly greater "business opportunities" than robbery ever did, given the challenging logistics of traveling and of transporting goods by land. Robbers, on the whole, did not leave written records of their activities; as already noted, the most pertinent and up-to-date information about them is found in daily newspapers, to which Happel had ample access.

A telling example of pirating success in the early seventeenth century is that of the Dutchman Claes Compaen (1587–1660). Peace accords having deprived him of the legal means of making a living as a privateer, Compaen famously turned from privateering to pirating in the Mediterranean in order to ensure a reliable income for himself and his crew.[76] Toward the end of his life, he turned once again, becoming a respectable and, by all accounts, even revered citizen of his native country. Happel mentions Compaen in his *Relationes Curiosae* and in the *Italienische Spinelli*. His primary source was most likely Compaen's biography (written in Dutch), which tells about how he started as a *Freibeuter* (freebooter, i.e., privateer) in the service of the Dutch Republic.[77] Happel probably also drew on D'Aranda's *Schauplatz*, where the story is told in great detail.[78] As a pirate, Compaen was feared far and wide for his indiscriminate attacks on vessels of all kinds, no matter what their inhabitants' nationality or faith. With much booty to sell, he found safe haven in Salé and Safy, cities along the Barbary Coast with large markets for pirated goods and slaves.

D'Aranda and, subsequently, Happel (in his *Spinelli*) also mention Simon Dantzer (or de Danser or Danseker), an equally legendary pirate whose hatred for Compaen was as well-known as it was unexplained.[79] Like Compaen, Dantzer (who died in 1616) was born in Flushing in the Dutch Republic. Early in his seafaring life, he, too, privateered for the Netherlands

---

75. Thomas Heywood, *A true relation of the lives of two most famous English pyrats, [H] Purser, and [H] Clinton who lived in the reigne of Queene Elizabeth* (London: Io. Okes, 1639), chap. 4; Claire Jowitt, "Subversive Pirates? Representations of Purser and Clinton, 1583–1639," in *The Culture of Piracy, 1580–1630: English Literature and Seaborne Crime* (Aldershot: Ashgate, 2010), 17–47.

76. Leeson, *Invisible Hook*, 6.

77. *IS* II: 240–41. Claes Compaen's original occupation was privateering, the legal practice of attacking and capturing enemy ships and goods. Reports about him appear almost daily in the newspapers published in all the major European cities, such as Hamburg, Berlin, Vienna, Paris, and London.

78. Frisch, *Der Schauplatz Barbarischer Schlaverey*, II: 115–18.

79. *IS* II: 241–44.

Fig. 8. Emmanuel D'Aranda's *Schauplatz Barbarischer Schlaverey* (1666)
(Herzog August Bibliothek, Wolfenbüttel)

against Spain. After the two nations concluded a peace treaty, he became one of the most notorious and feared pirates of the late sixteenth and early seventeenth centuries.[80] Though closely associated with the Muslim pirate cities of Tunis and Algiers, Dantzer never converted, remaining loyal to his Protestant faith. In the end, this steadfastness would ultimately cost him his life: he was betrayed by the renegade community of Tunis, whose members colluded with the Jesuits of Marseille in denouncing him to the pasha as having insulted the Muslim religion. He was lured to Tunis and subsequently executed by the pasha, who had his head delivered to his ship, the *Meermin*. Frisch's *Schauplatz* tells the story a bit differently. Here, Dantzer is killed by the pasha not for reasons of faith but, rather, in an act of vengeance for having cheated the pasha out of a significant sum of money. In this scenario, too, Dantzer is beheaded, but his head is unceremoniously dumped into the ditch surrounding the pasha's castle.[81]

Happel may have gleaned additional information from widely circulating pamphlets publicizing the deeds of pirates during the early years of the century. One such report, published by the English captain Andrew Barker, describes Barker's time as a captive of the "two late famous pirates Ward and Danseker."[82] Yet another privateer mentioned in the *Spinelli* is the Englishman Sir Francis Drake (ca. 1540–96), "ein glücklicher See-Captain" and a favorite of Queen Elizabeth I (*IS* II: 273–74).[83]

No matter which way the winds of politics were blowing or who was allied with whom, what did not change throughout the seventeenth and early eighteenth centuries was the participation of privateers and pirates in ransoming captives and in slave trading.[84] The French, the British, the Mal-

---

80. Andrew Barker, *A true and certaine report of the beginning, proceedings, ouerthrowes, and now present estate of the Captaine Ward and Danseker, the two late famous pirates from their first setting foorth to this present time. . . . Published by Andrew Barker master of a ship, who was taken by the confederates of Ward and by them some time detained prisoner* (London: William Hall, 1609), n.p.; Wolfram zu Mondfeld and Barbara zu Wertheim, *Piraten: Schrecken der Weltmeere* (Stuttgart: Theiss, 2007), 119–21.

81. Frisch, *Der Schauplatz Barbarischer Schlaverey*, II: 125–30.

82. Barker briefly notes that "they have put him to death, and his Turks with him, which were about an hundred infidels, are all made slaves": Barker, *A true and certaine report*; Mondfeld and Wertheim, *Piraten*, 119.

83. G. V. Scammell, "The English in the Atlantic Islands c. 1450–1650," in *Ships, Oceans, and Empire: Studies in European Maritime and Colonial History, 1400–1750*, ed. G. V. Scammell (Aldershot: Ashgate Variorum, 1995), 299–303.

84. Heywood and Thornton's study on slave trading and corsairing begins with the tale of an Angolan slave named Angela who is captured, sold to a Portuguese trader, shipped across the Atlantic, and, shortly before reaching her destination, taken off the ship by two corsairs with

tese, the Italians, the Turks, and the Barbary states were all active in the trade, seizing men, women, and children for Mediterranean and transatlantic slavery.[85] Thus, news about piracy went hand in hand with news about captives who were either returned for ransom or sold as slaves. Narratives about their miseries were published not only in newspapers but, as previously mentioned, in (auto)biographies by and about captives. Moreover, taking captives and selling slaves were frequent themes of sermons preached and circulated in print in support of efforts to raise ransom money. Privateers who, like Compaen, had abandoned piracy for "civilian life" in their later years often felt compelled to tell their stories in order to bear witness to the realities of the privateering/pirating life.

Emmanuel D'Aranda had no such choice, certainly no agency, in his experiences as a slave. After he was captured, he suffered through five years of bondage in Algiers. As noted earlier, Happel mentions D'Aranda in volume 3 of the *Spanische Quintana*, where he recounts not only D'Aranda's experiences in Algiers but also his attempts at securing sufficient funds to buy his freedom or to become part of a prisoner exchange. His captors, erroneously assuming D'Aranda to be wealthy, held onto him in hopes of a favorable financial outcome. To avoid such a fate, wealthy captives often tried to hide their social status. They were mostly unsuccessful in this, because news of ships' passenger lists often reached the Barbary cities before the ships even left port. Pirates were usually quite savvy in ascertaining the financial potential of their captives. According to a note in the *Ungarische Kriegs-Roman* (which may also have been taken from D'Aranda), the Jews of Livorno corresponded with their brethren in Algiers, who, in turn, informed ships' captains about passengers and merchants, alerting them to the possibility of a lucrative catch.[86] Captives of lesser means, Cervantes and D'Aranda among them, could escape only by appealing for ransom money to friends and family back home. Language and cultural difficulties, the great distances, and the forbidding landscape made flight nearly impossible except by sea.

---

letters of marque from Holland and Italy, respectively; they eventually transport their booty of fifty to sixty slaves to the English colony of Virginia (Heywood and Thornton, *Central Africans, Atlantic Creoles*, 5–7). According to Heywood and Thornton, by the early seventeenth century "[s]laves had become so essential to the local economy that the (Portuguese) Crown demanded that all financial transactions be handled in slaves and not in silver money" (ibid., 113).

85. Matar, *Europe through Arab Eyes*.

86. "Ja, manchmahl weiß man in Algiers/ schon die Nahmen der Passagirer und Kauffleute/ der Soldaten und Matrosen/ wie auch die Specification der gantzen Ladung eines Schiffes" (At some point, people already know the names of the passengers and merchants, of the soldiers and sailors as well as all the specifics of the ships' cargo [*UK* II: 471]).

According to his autobiography, D'Aranda's misadventures started when he and a companion, Reinhard Salden, embarked on an English merchant ship. Close to La Rochelle, the ship was held up by a corsair, who checked their papers and warned them to be on guard because five Turkish corsairs had been observed lurking in the Channel.[87] According to D'Aranda, his captain naively trusted in the power of English warships. Moreover, he thought it impossible that Barbary pirates or corsairs from Dunkirk and the Netherlands would attack with impunity so near the English and Dutch coasts. He learned the hard way how powerful and cunning pirates were, no matter their origin. A Turkish ship soon overpowered the merchant vessel and took all on board prisoner. Among the Turkish pirate crew, D'Aranda met a renegade Englishman, who consoled D'Aranda about his fate by pointing out that such was war: one side won today, the other tomorrow.[88] In short, it appears that the renegade's reaction to his captivity was an irreligious pragmatism.

Sailing past Gibraltar, the pirates and their captives arrived at Algiers, where, as D'Aranda wistfully states, their tragedy began in earnest.[89] Once it was ascertained that ransom money was not immediately forthcoming, D'Aranda and Salden, along with the other captives, were sold to an old English renegade, who took them to his house, where they joined 250 fellow slaves. Judged neither seasoned enough yet to work as galley slaves nor rich enough to be ransomed, they were sold once again. Their new owner, a man named General Alli Pegelin (Alli Pisseling, Ali Bitchin), sent them, along with five Christian slave women, to serve his wife.[90]

Pegelin kept another dozen or so slaves in his household, along with about forty slave boys between nine and fifteen years of age, who were not allowed to leave the quarters for fear of "being debauched by the Turks."[91] Sodomy, especially with young boys, is often mentioned as widely practiced among Muslims. In fact, Linda Colley suggests that rape in Muslim captivity was a greater fear for European men than for captured European women.[92] In this context, it is clear why D'Aranda makes a special point of noting

---

87. Frisch, *Der Schauplatz Barbarischer Schlaverey*, I: 14–16.

88. Ibid., I: 16.

89. Ibid., I: 12.

90. Ibid., I: 20. Pegelin, the grand admiral of Algiers, was a renegade from Venice.

91. "[D]iese mussten nicht aus dem Hause kommen/ aus Furcht/ sie mögten von den Türken zur stummen Sünde mißbraucht werden" (They were not allowed to leave the house for fear that the Turks would abuse them with their unspoken sin). Frisch, *Der Schauplatz Barbarischer Schlaverey*, I: 54.

92. Colley, *Captives*, 129.

that Pegelin was known as an "enemy of this abominable sin," commenting that he treated the boys as a Christian potentate would his "Edel-Knaben."[93] To confirm the pervasiveness of this (to D'Aranda) abominable passion, he relates an incident where, in 1641, he witnessed a man so madly in love with a young boy yet unable to fulfill his desire that the man cut his arm with a knife and forced a slave "ohn Wiederrede" (with no back talk) to put burning coals on the wound. It is noted rather laconically that he suffered the pain with great steadfastness.[94]

The Portuguese nobleman Rotalino in the *Spanische Quintana* confirms this supposed Muslim predilection, explaining how it affected the finer points of slave pricing: "Resold slaves cost less; beautiful young women have to be virgins to yield good money. The same is true for beautiful boys since the Turks are much given to *Sodomiterey*." In Constantinople, he continues, this sin is so common that boys are bought "in bulk" (*aufkauffen*) by traders, in the hope of making much money.[95]

In the *Ottomanische Bajazet*, published two years later, Bajazet, a fictional son of the deposed Sultan Mahomet IV, describes, in some detail, the practice of the "schändliche Brunst . . . deren Namen zu nennen man einen Abscheu traget" (shameful passion . . . which to name fills one with disgust).[96] For some extra money, boys are smuggled into a place called "Krancken-Hauß"[97] by servants called *Halvagi*, who "ihren Herren junge Knaben zuführen/ und unter ihren Kleidern ins Krancken-Haus wissen zu

---

93. Frisch, *Der Schauplatz Barbarischer Schlaverey*, I: 55.

94. "So bestialische Begierde/ daß einige ihnen das Leben lieber nehmen liessen/ als dass sie ein Weib berühren solten" ([they are given to] such bestial desires that some of them rather take their own lives before they would touch a woman). Ibid., II: 165.

95. "Schon einmal verkaufte Sklaven werden unter der Hand billiger verkauft, damit der Zöllner nichts bekommt. Schöne Frauen müssen Jungfrauen sein, um viel Geld zu bringen. Dergleichen gelten die Knaben/ welche schön sind/ auch sehr viel/ weilen die Türcken der Sodomiterey gewaltig ergeben sind/ ja man findet ihrer viele . . . diese Sünde ist zu Constantinopel/ so gemein worden/ daß viel Türcken kleine Knaben aufkauffen/ um bey andern Geld zu verdienen (Resold slaves are sold more cheaply [under the table] so that the custom agents don't get any cut. Beautiful women will have to be virgins to bring much money. The same is true for beautiful boys, who are highly valued because the Turks are so much given to sodomy that many of them buy boys in great numbers to make more money) (*SQ* IV: 130–31).

96. *OB* IV: 16–19.

97. I cannot find any reference to the "Krancken-Haus" in any of the literature or in Happel's texts. There are frequent mentions of "bathhouses" for men and women, and I assume that is what Happel is talking about here (*KB* no. 65): "Des Kaysers Bäder" talks about pages ("schöne Knaben") who, scantily clad, tried to tear off the cover ("gab man den Pagen im Bade etwas um . . . daß sie sich dessen schändlich mißbraucht"), after which they had to wear something akin to a woman's skirt ("wie ein Weiber-Rock").

practiciren" (procure young boys for their masters, smuggling them into the hospital [*sic*] under their clothes).[98] The sexual perversion in which they are supposedly colluding leads men, according to Bajazet, to turn from their wives ("die den natürlichen Brauch des Weiber verlassen" [leaving natural contact with women]). Moreover, this damnable passion encourages women, especially those isolated in the seraglio, to turn to "in schändlicher Lust gegeneinader" (burning with sinful lust for each other).[99] Isolation reportedly also gave rise to a peculiar practice that the narrator finds funny ("welches Lachens werth"), namely, that cucumbers were never served whole but, instead, cut into small pieces, because it was feared that "sie möchten der gantzen mißbrauchen" (they [women] are abusing them [*OB* IV: 261]). (These cucumbers also show up in the *Thesaurus Exoticorum*, along with much of the information about same-sex passions that Happel braids into his novels.)[100] The *Türckis. Estats- und Krieges-Bericht* (1683–84) also makes mention of young boys inciting each other to sodomitic passions through sign language ("Rede-Zeichen").[101] In the same work, Happel describes members of the Turkish clergy, the *Dervis*, as men who think sodomy permissible ("die Somdomiterey halten sie für erlaubt").[102]

Happel's attention to *Sodomiterey* in many of his writings leads us to assume his and his readers' familiarity with and interest in this topic.[103] This

---

98. Further, "Ist diese unmenschliche Passion so gemein bey den Türcken/ ja durchgehends im Orient" (this inhuman passion is very common among the Turks throughout the Orient [*OB* IV: 19]). *Halvagi* ("Zuckerbäcker," makers of sweets) produced *halvas* in the second court of the Topkapi Serail, where the palace kitchens were located (Happel, *Thesaurus Exoticorum*; "vierhundert Halvagi oder Süß-Köche" in the Sultan's palace [*KB* no. 66]).

99. As an example, we read of a woman who falls in love with the daughter of an artisan, marries her, and is discovered and thrown into the sea to drown (*OB* IV: 261). This tale shows up several times in Happel's work: for example, in *TE* IV: 116. Silke Falkner reviews these "Sodomitic Pleasures" in great and knowledgeable detail in her essay "'Having It Off' with Fish, Camels, and Lads: Sodomitic Pleasures in German-Language Turcica," *Journal of the History of Sexuality* 13, no. 4 (2004): 410–27. While she examines Happel's sources for this information, she does not discuss their use in his novels.

100. *TE* IV: 121.

101. "Es werden aber auch Rede-Zeichen vielfälltig von den jungen Knaben am Hoff zu schändlicher Leibes-Reitzung mißbraucht . . . daß sie einander ihre unnatürliche Brunst mit solcher stimmlosen Sprache nicht anbieten/ noch Sodomitischen kohlen ins Herz werffen sollten" (in this way, sign language is abused for sinful bodily lust . . . [they are being watched] so that they will not abuse sign language for the incitement of sinful lust nor to throw sodomitic coals into [each other's] hearts [*KB* no. 39; Z 102/1684/39/1]); *TE* IV: 181.

102. Happel, *Türckis. Estats- und Krieges-Bericht*, no. 39, 108; Z 102/1684/39/1, 102/1684/108/1.

103. Some of this information about this supposed predilection toward sodomy comes from

is confirmed by D'Aranda's positive remarks about Pegelin's attention to keeping the young boys in his charge safe from men desiring sexual contact with them, signaling the supposed prevalence of this "custom" as well as Christians' horrified fascination with it. In 1640, yet another detailed and twice reprinted report of seven years of enslavement in Algiers was published by Francis Knight.[104] Knight's captivity narrative and an account of his time of service in Tripoli to the former English consul Thomas Baker (1677) comment on this practice, the former stating, rather wryly, that "they [his Algerian captors] are said to commit sodomy with all creatures."[105]

Along with providing information about all aspects of life in Algiers, a substantial part of D'Aranda's captivity account is devoted to the endless negotiations that eventually led to his and his companion's release, in exchange for five Muslim slaves held in Portugal. It is clear from Happel's familiarity with this text that it was not only widely circulated but also influential on the narration and genre of similar texts. Moreover, citing D'Aranda's tale in the *Quintana* lent veracity to Happel's novels: "Tapffermüthigkeit zweyer Christl. Sclaven bey ihrer Flucht. Emanuel de Airanda und noch 2. andere Sclaven haben viel zu schaffen wegen ihrer Befreying" (the courage of two Christian slaves at their flight. Emmanuel D'Aranda and two other slaves struggled much to be freed [*SQ* IV: 164]).

An additional point of interest for Happel and his readers was provided by D'Aranda's story about a failed slave uprising in 1650, under the leadership of a Hamburg native named Henrich Kayser, then reportedly living back in Hamburg. His plan was betrayed by a Spanish slave, whose hatred of the Portuguese was so intense that he preferred to stay in captivity rather than to allow a Portuguese slave to gain his freedom. In Happel's novel, the teller of this tale, a Spanish-hating Morisco, had himself experienced slavery in Algiers, at a time (1650) when slaves in Algiers numbered in the tens of

---

Thomas Sherley's *Discourse of the Turks*. In January 1603, Sherley (1564–1633/4) was captured by the Turks, to be released from captivity in Constantinople in December 1605. He reported, "For their Sodommerye they use it soe publicquely and impudently as an honest Christian would shame of companye his wyffe as they do with their buggeringe boys" (in Denison E. Ross, ed., *Thomas Sherley: Discours of the Turkes*, Camden Miscellany 16 [London: Royal Historical Society, 1936]).

104. Francis Knight, *A relation of seaven yeares slaverie under the Turks of Argeire, suffered by an English captive merchant . . . Whereunto is added a second booke conteining a discription of Argeire, with its originall manner of government, increase, and present flourishing estate* (London: T. Cotes for Michael Sparke Jr., 1640); Davis, *Holy War and Human Bondage*, 187–89.

105. Knight, *A relation of seaven yeares slaverie*, 50; Pennell, *Piracy and Diplomacy*, 62. See also Colley, *Captives*, 129; Davis, *Holy War and Human Bondage*, 23.

thousands (*SQ* I: 356). Rather than being ransomed as D'Aranda was, the fictional Quintana makes an (improbably) successful escape from Algerian imprisonment (*SQ* IV: 179).

Francis Knight also gives a vivid description not only of his own suffering but also of that of his fellow detainees. Eventually, he was able to escape, fleeing to the isle of Corfu in the company of several other captives, including a "boy from Malta." He made his way to Venice and thence to London, where he "recorded a plenary memorial of my seven yeares in bondage" (n.p.). Before describing in detail the city of Algiers, he talks movingly about the galley slaves: "Yet are they [his own sufferings] all easie in Comparison to that of the Gallies which is most inhumane and diabolicall and such as doth rather, imperverse men than Repleate any good humour in them. . . . For a drop of water they would pawne their soules, and often are constrained to drinke of the Salt Oceans; their repast at best but bread and water, and for want of sleepe are in continual extasie" (n.p.).

Just as Christians feared being sold as galley slaves, the chief dread of Muslim corsairs and pirates was capture and the prospect of living out their lives on Christian galleys.[106] As deplorable as life was for Christians on the Muslim galleys, Muslim slaves on Christian ships did not fare any better. According to Faroqhi, Matar, and Colley, Europeans enslaved Ottoman and North African prisoners well into the eighteenth century, not only to work on ships bound for the colonies, but also for labor in continental Europe itself.[107] By the end of the seventeenth century, about one-quarter of the twelve thousand galley sailors employed in the navy of Louis XIV of France were of Ottoman and Maghrebi origin.[108] As noted in chapter 2, Protestant clergy who refused to convert to Catholicism and who supported their flock in their resistance against such conversion were sent to serve on the galleys. According to numerous news reports, the Most Christian King was not troubled by this or by the fact that Muslim captives labored alongside the clergymen.[109] Louis XIV was not alone in this sober and pragmatic assessment of his military needs. The *Relations-Courir* (January 14, 1684) reported

---

106. To help outfit much-needed galleys for the imperial war effort, it was noted in the *Relations-Courir* of January 25, 1684, that imprisoned Turks and criminals were to supply the labor: "Ermelte Galleren sollen von denen gefangenen Türcken und Maleficanten gerudert/ und mit einem Regiment Soldaten versehne werden" (Z 100/1684/8/3).

107. Faroqhi, *The Ottoman Empire and the World around It*, 126–27; Matar, *Europe through Arab Eyes*, 50–59.

108. M. le Maire de Bonifacio, *La Guerre de Course en Méditerranée* (Bonificio: Les Journées Universitaire, 1999), 31.

109. Colley, *Captives*, 62.

on Vienna's vigorous efforts at outfitting a number of galleys with "gefangenen Türcken und Maleficanten," to be dispatched against the Turks.[110]

Along with the information gleaned from D'Aranda's biography and various newspaper accounts, we can safely assume that Happel was also familiar with the hugely successful autobiography of Alexander Exquemelin (1645–1707). For many years after his death, this French surgeon/pirate's story fascinated readers. After joining the French West India Company as a servant, Exquemelin was sold by the company, along with all its movable goods, when a trading agreement with the island of Tortuga (under Spanish rule) went sour. Subsequently, he was sold again, this time to a surgeon who treated him well, trained him, and set him free within a year of his sale. Not knowing where to turn or what to do, Exquemelin joined "the wicked order of pirates" for a time, before returning home in 1672. He sailed with and served under some of the most notorious pirates of the age, such as Henry Morgan (1635–88), Pierre le Grand, Michel the Basque, and François Nau, known as L'Olonois (1630–71).[111] Upon abandoning pirating, Exquemelin settled in Amsterdam and wrote a book about his experiences. Originally published in Dutch in 1678, Exquemelin's book was soon translated into German (1679) and English (1684)[112] and, by all accounts, enjoyed a wide readership.[113]

Pirates, captives, and slaves occupied early modern discourses in yet another way. Throughout the seventeenth century, European rulers of the states most affected by piracy and slave trading—England, Spain, and the Netherlands—frequently circulated proclamations against piracy and the taking of captives for ransom. In part, D'Aranda's and Exquemelin's autobiographies fulfill a similar role, resembling other texts issued during the seventeenth century that pleaded for the return of former slaves or those still held captive. The former wished to alert the world to their suffering, the latter to remind people of their duty to raise the money to ransom slaves from captivity.[114]

---

110. Z 100/1684/8/4.

111. Alexandre Oexmelin [Alexander Exquemelin], *Die Americanische See-Räuber: Entdeckt, in gegenwärtiger Beschreibung der grössten . . . verübten Räuberey und Grausamkeit* (Nuremberg: Christoph Riegels, 1679). The English translation appeared in 1684: John Esquemeling, *The Buccaneers of America: In the Original English Translation of 1684* (New York: Cosimo Classics, 1684), 53–58, 79–120.

112. Esquemeling, *Buccaneers of America*.

113. Mondfeld and Werheim, *Piraten*, 125–26.

114. One of them is Francis Brooks, *Barbarian cruelty being a true history of the distressed condition of the Christian captives under the tyranny of Mully Ishmael, Emperor of Marokko, and*

Happel's familiarity with the administration of ransom money can be assumed, since, as a busy seaport and trading hub, Hamburg was one of the first cities to establish a slave account (*Sklavenkasse*), a sort of insurance in case of capture.[115] Already in 1622, such an account was administered by a Hamburg shipping enterprise, initially to help only German sailors. Later, the Admiralty founded its own *Sklavenkasse*,[116] and other cities, such as Lübeck (in 1627), established accounts into which sailors on vessels bound for France, Spain, and Portugal paid money to ensure their ransom should such be needed.[117]

In addition to publicizing the plight of captives and rousing relatives at home to donate money for their redemption, official publications also outlined the rules governing the collection of ransom. Typically, the authors beseeched their listeners or readers to remember the suffering of those languishing in captivity or laboring as slaves. In 1609, King James I of England (1566–1625) published an eloquent address entitled *A Proclamation against Pirats*.[118] A missive issued in 1650, the *Act for the Redemption of Captives*, suggested that, not unlike the *Sklavenkassen*, moneys were to be collected on all goods traded, according to a fixed schedule, for purposes of ransom: "duty on Goods and Merchandizes Exported and Imported into, and out of our Realm. . . . Rates established by the Authority of the present Parliament . . . levyed and paid over and above the said Custome and subsidy." In case such decrees were not heeded, the Act reminded the reader that such fees were to be employed for the redemption of captives.[119]

King of Fez and Macqueness in Barbary (London: Printed for I. Salisbury at the Rising-Sun in Cornhil, 1692).

115. Magnus Ressel, "The North European Way of Ransoming: Exploration into an Unknown Dimension of the Early Modern Welfare State," *Historical Social Research* 35, no. 4 (2010): 128–30.

116. Rheinheimer, "Identität und Kulturkonflikt," 324.

117. Ressel, "Der Freikauf Lübecker Seeleute," 123–56.

118. James I, King of England and Wales, *Proclamation against Pirats* (London: Robert Barker, printer to the Kings most excellent Maiestie, 1609).

119. This Act of Parliament spelled out in detail how much duty was to be imposed on goods traded in and out of English ports: "The Kings Maiestie . . . is resolued and hereby declareth, that such punishment shal be inflicted on him or them so offending," namely 1. Take ships upon the Sea; 2. Come into any of his ports with stolen goods; 3. Those who supply "any Pirate or Sea-rouer" shall also be punished; 4. All grievances such as described above shall be heard without delay, and finally, 5. "No Ship or goods taken from any of his Maiesties friends, shalbe deliuered vpon any other order, than vpon proofe made, or certificate exhibited in said Court of the Admiraltie, to the end that a Record may be kept of all such restitutions made to strangers, to serue of occasion shall require" (Anon., "An Act for the Redemption of Captives; Ordered by the Parliament, That this Act be forthwith Printed and Published," in *Hen: Scobell, Cler. Parl.* [London, 1650], n.p.).

However, while relatives often frantically pleaded for help and while the Crown verbally inveighed against the taking of captives for ransom, the English government itself generally felt little obligation to ransom captives who were employees of large trading companies. Thus, the financial burden, especially for the less well-to-do, was frequently borne by religious groups and private individuals.[120] Most active among these were the orders of the Mercedarians and Trinitarians (absent from Protestant England, but operating in Spain and France), whose members raised the requisite money by leading processions.[121] Frequently, members of these orders were charged with not only delivering the ransom money but also returning or exchanging the captives. Most successful among them was the English Trinity House, a charitable organization established by Henry VIII to help sailors, travelers, and explorers in need. Trinity House was also authorized to issue ransom permits, "patents for collection," which it did by the score in an effort to control fraud and theft.[122] During the second half of the seventeenth century, when the pressure to raise redemption money increased significantly, the Privy Council, supported by the royal family, and the archbishop of Canterbury and the City of London began several campaigns to raise funds, some of them very successful.[123] When the necessary resources to ensure the release of the captives could not be immediately procured, as was the case with D'Aranda and Cervantes, relatives traveled far and wide begging for money to ransom their loved ones.

After efforts at reclaiming captives failed and years had passed, captives often abandoned any hope of returning to the land of their birth, thus being forced to make the land of their captivity their home. Reflecting this reality, Spinelli, the hero of Happel's novel of the same name, rescues an aged English slave and returns him to his hometown. The man's response to this good deed is not exactly what one might expect: he is less than enthused at the prospect of having to rebuild his life in a country grown foreign to him over many years. He tells his "liberator" that he would prefer to spend the

120. Daniel J. Vitkus and Nabil Matar, eds., *Piracy, Slavery, and Redemption* (New York: Columbia University Press, 2001), 29; Ressel, "Der Freikauf Lübecker Seeleute."

121. Vitkus and Matar, *Piracy, Slavery, and Redemption*, 54. Collections were taken in Spanish and French parishes, and money was raised in processions led by the Redemptionist fathers (Spain and France); the same happened among Muslims from taxation and donations. These organizations also sent Catholic fathers to the Barbary states to hand over the money and then to return with the redeemed captives. See also Colley, *Captives*, 80.

122. Vitkus and Matar, *Piracy, Slavery, and Redemption*, 25.

123. In 1670, responding to a "charity brief" issued by the King's Printer, over 21,500 pounds was raised. Many others, though not quite as successful, were to follow. See Colley, *Captives*, 76.

rest of his life in Barbary, whose customs and way of life were more familiar to him now than his former home (*IS* II: 308–11). Such reactions must not have been infrequent. Colley cites the example of three Englishmen who, after being ransomed, decided to stay in Algiers and voluntarily convert to Islam.[124] Of four hundred Englishmen identified in September 1669 as being held captive in Algiers, many were listed as "old slaves." In 1668, an English captain was recorded as having been enslaved from 1652 to 1668.[125] Other studies set the numbers much higher and the time of captivity much longer, noting that as many as seven thousand men and women from Britain and Ireland may have been enslaved in North Africa between 1622 and 1642. This is corroborated by Colley's estimate of five thousand Britons and Irishmen held in captivity between 1660 and 1710.[126] Still other studies set the number even higher, suggesting that by the mid-seventeenth century, there may have been between eight thousand and forty thousand slaves in Algiers.[127] In the *Spanische Quintana*, one of the characters confirms this estimate, informing his listeners that "wie man es jüngst außgerechnet/ machen sie gegenwärtig eine Summa von 36000 Menschen. In Algiers allein 25000" (as was recently counted, there are at the present time thirty-six thousand people in slavery, of those twenty-five thousand alone in Algiers), representing a truly international group of "Christen auß Franckreich/ Italien/ Spanien/ Engelland/ Teutschland/ Flandern/ Holland/ Griechenland/ Ungarn/ Pohlen/ Sclavonien/ und Rußland" (*SQ* IV: 114).

Further supporting this information about captives are files recently unearthed in the archives of the Vatican Library.[128] These files contain *litterae hortatoriae*, letters of supplication, directed at the Holy See. They afford us yet another glimpse at the experiences of captives in need of ransom, at pleas for help with collecting ransom money, and at petitions that highlight the vigorous and often desperate attempts undertaken to redeem captives held in Muslim lands during the last third of the sixteenth century. The files include not only letters from soldiers and civilians captured by Turks, as well as letters from the captives' relatives, but also letters from Muslims

---

124. Ibid., 118; Ressel, "Der Freikauf Lübecker Seeleute," 134–35.

125. Vitkus and Matar, *Piracy, Slavery, and Redemption*, 14, 15. Davis gives even higher numbers, in *Holy War and Human Bondage*, 60–62.

126. Colley, "Going Native, Telling Tales," 171–72.

127. Rheinheimer, "Identität und Kulturkonflikt," 321.

128. Wipertus E. Rudt de Collenberg, ed., *Esclavage et Rançons des Chréstiens en Méditerranéel (1570–1600): D'après les Litterae Hortatoriae de l'Archivio Segretto Vaticano* (Paris: Le Leopard d'Or, 1987).

who had converted and needed assistance in bringing their families to the Christian West.[129] Identifying places of capture as well as location and length of captivity, the records construct, in their sparse and dry entirety, a rich image "of the Mediterranean as a region where captivity, and its twin sisters, piracy and privateering, sustained the interface between Islamic and Christian societies."[130] In this, they allow a glimpse, however sparse, at the Muslim experience in European captivity.[131]

Sermons were yet another medium that provided material for Happel's novels. Of the many sermons on the subject of the "Redemption of Captives," one published in 1637 by Charles Fitz-Geffry may suffice as a typical example of the genre.[132] The frequent pillaging and slaving along the English coast prompted Fitz-Geffry to write on the theme of compassion toward captives. More specifically, he deplores the fate of the people of the village of Baltamore along the Cornish coast, which was often raided in the middle of the night by Turkish pirates. According to Fitz-Geffry, these pirates captured whole families: "suddenly their houses were broken up, they were hauled out of their beds, the husband, wife and children every one fast bound . . . carried away . . . and afterward so separated as not suffered to meet again."[133] In Happel's *Spinelli*, this is the fate visited on the young protagonist, who is abducted while herding his father's sheep and subsequently sold into slavery.[134]

Fitz-Geffry compares biblical bondage to the suffering of modern-day captives, reminding his audience that no person and no place were safe. As long as Turkish and Algerian ships turned up in their "harbours mouths," all people were in danger of being "merchandized" in the Turkish "Men-

---

129. Ibid., 3.

130. Matar, *Europe through Arab Eyes*, 39.

131. For an excellent introduction to this little-researched area, see Markus Friedrich, "'Türken' im Alten Reich: Zur Aufnahme und Konversion von Muslimen im deutschen Sprachraum (16.–18. Jahrhundert)," *Historische Zeitschrift* 294 (2012): 329–60.

132. Charles Fitz-Geffry, *Compassion towards Captives Chiefly Towards our Brethren and Country-men who are in miserable bondage in Barbarie Preached in Plymouth, in October 1636* (Oxford: Leonard Lichfield for Edward Forrest, 1637).

133. Ibid., n.p. Sometimes whole families were captured, in which case the father was allowed to return to Europe to raise the ransom money. See Vitkus and Matar, *Piracy, Slavery, and Redemption*, 15.

134. Happel, *Der Italienische Spinelli*. Spinelli was a shepherd's son from northern Italy. His parents had been impoverished by the plundering bandits and pirates but were of the nobility; when the father grew old, the twelve-year-old Spinelli took over the herd of two hundred animals. Working close to the coast, Turkish raiders captured him and others. The Turks divided the captives among themselves and sold the Christians, young Spinelli among them. His master set him to cutting stones (*IS* I: 186–288).

markets," sold like horses at a fair, and, worse, "turning Turkes" while in bondage. Fitz-Geffry cites a letter sent by a captive, a steadfast husband, to his "widow," reassuring her that he would never "turn Turke" and warning her to keep their son from becoming a seaman, lest he suffer the same fate as his father. Fitz-Geffrey urges readers to donate money "according to every man's ability towards the redeeming & reducing them [the captives] home" or else to support the captives' wives and children at home. In the 1630s, the activities of Algerian corsairs who attacked the English and Irish coast, capturing and holding inhabitants for ransom, prompted a parliamentary levy in trade to finance such ransoms.[135] Later in the century, newspapers, most notably the *Relations-Courir*, carried many items about the redemption of Christian slaves, often in exchange for Turkish captives.[136]

Along with his warnings, Fitz-Geffry reminds his audience that, despite the constant dangers and challenges, they should consider themselves fortunate because they can read their news about conflagrations in all parts of Europe "at leasure" in the "Gazette, the Corante, Gallobelgicus" while remaining relatively safe at home. Unlike the people in France, the Palatinate, Bohemia, and Germany, who were always living under the shadow of war, his readers (the dangers to the English coastal areas notwithstanding) still "stand safe on the shore while we see others tossed in the sea." "Happy are the people that are in such a case," he says, "but not happy if insensible of their brethrens unhappiness" (26). Clearly, perusing one's daily newspaper had become a ritual relied upon for vital information as well as for a measure of comfort, reminding the reader that the fate of others was always just a little bit worse than one's own. Fitz-Geffry closes by urging his readers to be generous, reminding them of the king's letters of patent authorizing collections on behalf of the captive brethren.[137]

Reports, sermons, and appeals on the topic of slaves and captives highlight yet another cultural phenomenon associated with piracy and slaving previously mentioned, namely, the fact that many Christians in captivity "turned Turk," that is, converted to the Muslim faith or became (in the language of the day) "renegades." We heard about D'Aranda's benefactor, Alli Pegelin, a renegade from Venice who succeeded in being appointed to a lead-

---

135. Colley, *Captives*, 105.

136. One example among many (August 21, 1685) tells of two ships that had arrived at Toulon from Tripoli with "180 Christen-Sclaven/ und die 10 Türckischen Geisel/ welche alda so lange biß die übrigen Sclaven auch erlöset sind/ bleiben sollen" (Z 100/1685/74/1).

137. "His Majesties letters of patent in our captive brethrens behalf were larger than any granted heretofore for other collections." Fitz-Geffry, *Compassion towards Captives*, 31.

ing position in the Algerian admiralty. Conversions are frequently reported and criticized in contemporary Christian writings, and many found their way into Happel's novels. One such case is that of the Irish-born pirate Garzella, who "turned Turke" and was "beschnitten" (circumcised). He rescues Quintana and his companions after their ship is damaged in a storm and the "Christenhunde" (Christian dogs) are left by the Muslim sailors to their fate (*SQ* III: 294). Garzella assures his captives that he will keep them safe, but only as long as he is guaranteed a generous ransom for them. In the end, when freed, his Christian captives execute him for his pirating crimes (*SQ* IV: 230).

Though rarely reported in the news of the time, the conversion of a Muslim to Christianity constitutes an important part of the *Ottomanische Bajazet*.[138] At the novel's happy conclusion, Bajazet is baptized. He swears allegiance to the king of Hungary, upon which the German emperor invests him with land in Dalmatia (*OB* IV: 230, 384). Newspapers occasionally reported on the public's encounters with Muslim converts, as does an account in the *Relations-Courir* (June 4, 1684). It tells of a young Turk, a pasha's son, who was led by several officers on horseback through Vienna and Linz. No further comment is given. The *Relations-Courir* (September 16, 1685) described in a bit greater detail how a rather large number of Turks, men and women of differing ages, were led through Regensburg on their way to several courts. Among them was a young boy of six years, "ein kleiner Sohn des Bassa von Ofen."[139] The *Kern-Chronica* of February 1688 reported the baptism in Magdeburg of a young Turkish man.[140]

Ransomed captives or freed slaves were often queried about their Barbary experiences. Aside from securing information about Barbary military preparedness, investigators, no matter what their nationality, were always very interested in the numbers, names, and lives of converts to Islam.[141] The *Quintana* reports that Tunis alone was estimated to have had three to four thousand male and six to seven hundred female renegades among its citizens (*SQ* IV: 109). According to a Swedish pirate who had lived for a long time among the Muslims, many of these renegades fully participated in the life of the Barbary cities of Algiers, Tunis, Tripoli, and Salé, as well as

---

138. Though few baptisms are recorded, Markus Friedrich mentions some that occurred in midcentury in the German-speaking areas: Friedrich, "'Türken' im Alten Reich: Zur Aufnahme und Konversion von Muslimen im deutschen Sprachraum (16.–18. Jahrhundert)," 341–42.

139. Z 100/1685/90/5.

140. Happel, *KC* II: 22. 1688.

141. Vitkus and Matar, *Piracy, Slavery, and Redemption*, 32–40.

of Constantinople, as traders, corsairing captains, and Janissaries.[142] Thomas Baker, English consul in Tripoli from 1677 to 1678, writes in a journal about "renegades" he had met or heard of who served in the powerful position of captain (called *rais*) in command of corsairing ships for the Barbary states. Among the thirteen *raises* mentioned, he identifies five renegade Christians, six Turks, a Kulughli (a native of Tripoli), and a "Moor," most likely an Arab.[143]

Whether fact or fiction, renegades converted either under duress after being captured and enslaved or, especially if captured at a very young age, voluntarily after they had lost all hope of ever returning home. Of special interest here is the military recruiting system that filled the ranks of the Janissaries, the elite Turkish fighting force, by collecting boys from families in areas in tribute to Constantinople.[144] Such forced recruiting, known as *Knabenlese* (*devşirme*), was institutionalized during the seventeenth century, although it was said to have started as early as the sixteenth century.[145] Happel (and, one must assume, his readership) was clearly fascinated with this "custom," for he elaborates on it in the *Krieges-Bericht* as well as the

---

142. "Ein Schwede, der lange in der Barbarey gelebt und auf Raub war und alle Raubnester auch kannte/ setzete sich näher herbey/ und begunte seinen Bericht mit folgenden Worten: "Über die Schiffe: schnell, aber im Sturm nicht gut; deshalb im Winter im Hafen" (A Swede who had lived in Barbary for a long time and participated in piracy and knew all of the hiding places sat nearby, and he began his report with the following words . . . [*SQ* IV: 107]). The Swede reported that their ships were fast but not good in stormy weather, which was why they stayed in port in the winter.

143. Pennell, *Piracy and Diplomacy*. Baker speaks of intense power struggles between the renegade *raises* and the Turks that lasted throughout the century (32–33). For earlier (sixteenth-century) examples, see Tijana Krstic, *Contested Conversions to Islam: Narratives of Religious Change in the Early Modern Ottoman Empire* (Stanford: Stanford University Press, 2011).

144. Raised as Muslims, these elite soldiers, housed in barracks, were forbidden to drink alcohol or gamble or to marry before leaving the corps. Their sons were not allowed to enter the corps, and any wealth accumulated during time of service was returned to the corps. This elite group eschewed individualism, defining itself as a brotherhood of fighters totally devoted to their military code of honor, which meant, in effect, service to the sultan. See Bodo Hechelhammer, "Das Korps der Janitscharen: Eine militärische Elite im Spannungsfeld von Gesellschaft, Militär und Obrigkeit im Osmanischen Reich," *Militär und Gesellschaft in der Frühen Neuzeit* 14, no. 1 (2010): 42. See also Baki Tezcan, *The Second Ottoman Empire: Political and Social Transformation in the Early Modern World*, Cambridge Studies in Islamic Civilization (Cambridge: Cambridge University Press, 2010), 198–210.

145. Jateen Lad, "Panoptic Bodies: Black Eunuchs as Guardians of the Topkapi Harem," in *Harem Histories: Envisioning Places and Living Spaces*, ed. Marilyn Booth (Durham: Duke University Press, 2010), 154; Tezcan, *Second Ottoman Empire*, 47, 204; Charles H. Parker, *Global Interactions in the Early Modern Age, 1400–1800* (Cambridge: Cambridge University Press, 2010), 60–63.

Thesaurus Exoticorum, braiding this information into the *Ottomannische Bajazet* as well. Hiding his identity under the name Oltrano, the fictional Bajazet reviews, in considerable detail, the role of the *Christenkinder* sent to Constantinople either as prisoners of war or as presents to the pasha.[146] In their ninth or tenth year, the most beautiful among the boys were selected, through a series of rigorous training exercises, for service in the most important administrative positions in the empire.[147] Becoming a renegade in this way was, as Thomas Graf confirms, not merely "a religious and spiritual but a legal and political act."[148] According to Lad, the boys became "symbolic sons of the Sultan,"[149] and those who survived indoctrination and instruction were molded into administrators or elite soldiers who joined the sultan's Janissaries and Spahi.[150] The importance of this military elite is repeatedly mentioned in the *Krieges-Bericht* and in the *Thesaurus Exoticorum*: "Es ist gar gewiß/ daß der Sultan eine gewaltige Armee zu Land auffbringen kan/ deren Stärcke bestehet meist in den Janitscharen und Spahi, jene werden wie auch diese auß . . . den den christlichen Kindern genommen. . . . Erstreckt sich die Anzahl zu Constantinopel . . . leicht über 12 000" (It is true that the sultan can call up a huge army on land whose strength consists mainly of Janissaries and Spahi chosen from among the Christian children. . . . In Constantinople they easily number . . . twelve thousand [*ThEx* II: 50; *KB* nos. 10–13]). Moreover, the *Thesaurus* observes that these troops were so privileged and, in some instances, so powerful that they occasionally attempted to remove the sultan and establish a government to their own liking ("die Regierung ihres Gefallens einzurichten").[151] It was said that eight to ten thousand of them lost their lives in the siege of Vienna (1683).[152] The next year, the *Relations-Courir* reported that fourteen thousand of these elite troops, Janissaries as well as

---

146. *OB* I: 248–77 (also in *Türckis. Estats- und Krieges-Bericht* and *Thesaurus Exoticorum*).

147. No effort was spared to train these boys, called *Ichoglans*, for their future tasks: "zu den höchsten Ehrenstellen/ und ansehnlichen Aemtern zu gelangen/ so erdulden sie mit Gedult/ all solche Barbarisch Tractament der Verschnittenen" (they reached the highest places of honor and very respected offices. Thus they suffered with great patience the cruel treatment of the eunuchs [Happel, *Türckis. Estats- und Krieges-Bericht*, no. 75]).

148. Thomas Graf, "A Sample of Renegades Active ca. 1560–1610," paper presented at the AHA conference, Boston, January 6–9, 2011, 2. I am grateful to Thomas Graf for sending me a copy of his presentation.

149. Lad, "Panoptic Bodies," 154.

150. Spahi: "die beste Reuterey/ geübet in allerhand Gewehr/ und ein rechter Kern des Sultans Land-Milice zu Pferde" (The best horsemen practiced in the use of many weapons, and they were the very core of the sultan's militia on horseback [*ThEx* II: 50; *KB* no. 13]).

151. Tezcan, *Second Ottoman Empire*, 213–23.

152. Hechelhammer, "Das Korps der Janitscharen," 45.

Spahi, were gathered in Ofen (Buda) as the city was besieged by the imperial army.[153] The *Türckis. Estats- und Krieges-Bericht* from Vienna for July 14 and 23, 1684, told of four thousand Janissaries (*KB* no. 93). In November, the conflict still not resolved, the support of the Janissaries was mentioned once again, as it is on numerous occasions in the *Krieges-Bericht.*[154]

It is clear that, toward the end of the century, the sovereigns of the most powerful European trading nations recognized piracy as a grave international challenge. Consequently, in an effort to gain a semblance of control over this menace, they entered into nonaggression pacts not only with each other but also with the pirating states of Barbary, Tunis, Morocco, Tripoli, and Constantinople. For the most part, however, long-term success eluded them because pirates did not abide by contractual agreements between states. A news story from July 1683 informed readers that pirates from Tripoli had broken a peace treaty with France, as had those associated with the Sublime Porte and Tunis, bringing the number of pirate ships in the Mediterranean to dangerously high levels. This piece of bad news prompted the editorial comment that merchant ships should be provided with convoys "wie die Holländer zu thun pflegen" (as the Dutch are wont to do) to secure safe passage. Stressing the seriousness of the pirate threat, the story, explaining the Dutch way of protecting its merchant fleet, informed readers that, in addition to the warships already dispatched, twenty vessels would be added, "nebst unterschiedlichen Brandern/ und alle Galleren mit Galliotten" (with many kinds of vessels).[155] A news note from July 14 of the same year recalls yet another peace ratified between Algiers and France, part of which involved the exchange of six hundred slaves.

Because of Happel's *Standortgebundenheit* (the fact that he lived and wrote in Hamburg), he occupied a front-row seat in the drama of pirates and slaves as it played out nationally and internationally on the high seas and in the coastal areas.[156] Keenly concerned about the safety of all merchant ships, especially its own, the City of Hamburg maintained a powerful fleet that included ships serving as convoys for the protection of merchant vessels against pirate attacks.[157] In a brief note, Happel describes how, in 1686, he

---

153. *RC*, July 12, October 22, 1684; Z 100/1684/82–86/7.

154. "Wie dann erst den 24 passato 200 Janitscharen/ mit viel Proviant/ zu Wasser sich in Ofen practisiret haben" (As two hundred Janissaries with many provisions moved toward Ofen [*RC* 89, November 2, 1684; Z 100/1684/89/8]).

155. Von der 33. Woche 1683, *Einkommener Zeitungen Sontagische Fama*, Berlin.

156. See the introduction to Schock, *Die Text-Kunstkamme.*

157. Ressel, "Der Freikauf Lübecker Seeleute," 131–34.

inspected the newest addition to the fleet, the proud new flagship the *Wappen von Hamburg II*.[158] He had reported in the *Kern-Chronica* of October 10, 1683, how the original *Wappen* was destroyed by fire and the subsequent explosion of all its ordinance in the Bay of Cadiz. To describe the horrific event, Happel reproduces in full a letter from a friend detailing the dramatic demise of the vessel.[159]

The need for security measures against pirates, such as convoys of ships, was clear. In the 1680s, the Hamburg *Relations-Courir* underscored the brazenness of Algerian pirates, who conducted raids all the way up into the English Channel. From Toulon (*RC*, May 7, 1687), we hear that Turkish robbers were doing much damage along the coast ("Die Türckischen Räuber thun auff dieser Küste sehr grossen Schaden").[160] Not only did their presence threaten commercial maritime traffic, but they pillaged and robbed areas along the coast, as described in a report of "[so] die 6 Algierischen Räuber mit Wegnehmung der Schiffe vor ihre Küste verüben/ sintemal dieselbe alles ohne Unterscheid berauben" (six Algerian robbers who had stolen ships along their coast and who are robbing everybody they can get their hands on).[161] Four days later, on June 7, we read about the Algerians marauding along the Channel ("Die Algierischen Räuber vagiren noch im Canal"). The same publication told of several English slaves who had been captured in the previous year and were now employed as *Steuerleute* on a Turkish vessel. The immediacy of the pirating threat prompted the Dutch to outfit a fast ship to deliver a warning to the merchant fleet returning from the West Indies ("nicht weniger als 6. andere auß West-Indien mit grossen Contanten erwartende Schiffe zu warnen"). On June 20, a report from Amsterdam noted that "die Algierischen Räuber lassen sich noch dan und wan auf unsern Küsten sehen/ weil sie doch alle aus England kommende Paquet Bothe anhalten. . . . Weil aber bereits etliche von unsern Kriegs-Schiffen ausgelauffen sind/ wird hoffentlich die See von diesen Buben bald befreyet werden" (the Algerian pirates have been sighted once or twice along our coasts because they are lying in wait for English package boats. We hope that our warships can soon be under way to hopefully free the sea from these criminals).[162] Of

---

158. Schock, *Die Text-Kunstkammer*, 40.

159. Happel, *KC* II: 87, 1683.

160. Z 100/1687/73/3.

161. *Relations-Courir*, Nieder-Elbe, June 3, 1687; Colley, *Captives: Britain, Empire, and the World, 1600–1850*, 50. Colley tells of brazen raids by Algerian corsairs at the English west coast, on the Channel Islands, and up to the coast of Ireland.

162. *RC*, Hamburg, June 20, 1687.

additional interest is a note in the same paper informing readers that the ships from Barbary ("Barbarischen Schiffen") were manned, for the most part, with Dutch renegades ("Holländische Renegaden"). The paper gave an account of a young renegade who, on arriving in his hometown along the Dutch coast, inquired about a certain widow, who turned out to be his mother. His brother asked him why he had "turned Turk," something the brother insisted he would never have done himself. We do not know what the young renegade offered as an explanation, but he reportedly intervened with his commander so that the local Dutch fishermen, rather than being captured and sold into slavery, were treated to a nice meal.

Surveying several issues of the *Relations-Courir* published in Hamburg from 1683 to 1685, we find almost daily mention of pirates and the taking of captives.[163] As avid in his consumption as in his production of news, Happel selected many items from these newspapers for reemployment in his *Relationes Curiosae* (1681–91), his histories, and his novels.[164] In addition, I have shown that Happel had at his disposal, in German, the contemporary (auto)biographical accounts written by former pirates/corsairs, captives, and slaves, many of which he incorporated into his fictions. In turn, his work was widely read and copied by others, even decades after his death. In 1728, Captain Charles Johnson (identified by Manuel Schonhorn as a pseudonym for Daniel Defoe) cited volume 3 of the *Relationes Curiosae* as one of the sources for his history of piracy and slavers, quoting the chapter "Über Seeräuber, die in Hamburg bestraft wurden" (About pirates who were punished in Hamburg [589]).[165] Johnson/Defoe praises Happel's flu-

---

163. Böning, *Welteroberung durch ein neues Publikum.* I here give a few examples: despite the peace between France and Algiers, the pirates took two ships along the coast of St. Malo (*RC*, February 8, 1684; Z 100/1684/11/3); a Dutch corsair captured a French merchant ship along the coast of England (*RC*, August 14, 1684; Z 100/1684/66/3); Soliman Aga, one of the most feared pirates, was defeated and killed, and twelve Christian slaves were liberated (*RC*, September 1, 1684; Z 100/1684/77/2); Constantinople ordered all pirates ("Räuber") of Barbary to outfit as many ships as possible to attack the Christians ("wider die Christen zu agiren") (*RC*, October 8, 1684; Z 100/1684/85/3).

164. Eberhard Werner Happel, *E.G. Happelii Grösste Denckwürdigkeiten der Welt oder so genannte Relationes Curiosae*, vol. 3 (Hamburg: Thomas von Wiering, 1687); Happel, *Der Spanische Quintana*; Happel, *Dess Teutschen Carls/ Oder so genannten Europäischen Geschicht-Romans auf das 1689. Jahr* (Ulm: Matthaeus Wagner, 1690); Happel, *Dess Engelländischen Eduards/ Oder so genannten Europäischen Geschicht-ROMANS, auf das 1690. Jahr . . .*, 4 vols. (Ulm: Matthaeus Wagner, 1690); Happel, *Academische Roman-*.

165. Carl Johnson, *Schauplatz der Englischen See-Rauber*, trans. J.M. [Joachim Meyer] (Goslar, 1728); Charles Johnson [Daniel Defoe], *A General History of the Pyrates* (1724), ed. Manuel

ency in Dutch, noting that Happel had taken his information about Claes Compaen, the pirate turned respectable citizen, directly from Dutch sources ("zitiert Holländischer Sprache beschrieben, woraus *Happelius* in Relat. Curos. 3. Theil. p. 603 einen Auszug gemacht, aus dem wir dieses wieder genommen" [n.p.]).

The Dutch Republic was notorious for employing privateers who then became pirates when their legal permits ran out. During what is known as the golden age of piracy (1650–1730), the first generation of privateers (1650–80) was made up of the "mostly Protestant sea dogs of England, northern France, and the Netherlands," who mainly hunted ships destined for Catholic Spain.[166] We cannot say for certain whether Happel spoke English. Considering Hamburg's close proximity to England and Happel's demonstrated familiarity with English politics, history, and culture, we can assume that he had, at the very least, a solid reading knowledge of the language. Both the *Relationes* and Happel's novels make use of English primary sources, such as travel reports and chorographies, signaling a detailed knowledge of English political, cultural, and economic affairs.[167] In addition, Happel also published extensively and directly on English matters and, in 1689, put out a translation of a tract on English criminal law.[168] Finally, as I have noted elsewhere in this study, Happel points out with pride, in the foreword of the *Ungarische Kriegs-Roman*, that several of his works had been translated, presumably into English or Dutch.[169]

Thus, Francis Drake, whom Happel, as previously mentioned, calls "ein glücklicher See-Captain" in his *Spinelli*, bears at least a passing resemblance to a very successful fictional pirate turned privateer in the service of the Spanish crown, the Duke of Tarsis (*IS* II: 273–74). In response to a feud, the king of Spain had confiscated the duke's possessions and land, whereupon the duke, joined by a number of "christlichen Corsaren," takes to sea

---

Schonhorn (Mineola, NY: Dover, 1999). Schonhorn identifies Defoe as the author in a postscript, "Note on the Author and the Text," 709–12.

166. Marcus Rediker, *Villains of All Nations: Atlantic Pirates in the Golden Age* (Boston: Beacon, 2004), 8.

167. Schock, *Die Text-Kunstkammer*, 144–66; Eberhard Werner Happel, *Fortuna Brittannica: oder Brittanischer Glücks-Wechsel: Fürstellend Eine kurtzbündige Beschreibung aller Königen von Engelland/ und des schier stets unglücklichsten Hauses Stuart* (Hamburg: Thomas von Wiering, 1689).

168. Happel, *Fortuna Brittannica;* Henry Care, *Draconica Oder Ein Außzug aller Englischen Poenal-Gesetze,* trans. Eberhard Werner Happel (Hamburg: Thomas von Wiering, 1689).

169. *UK* I: *Vorrede.*

and becomes rich pursuing merchant ships, especially in the area of Calabria and Apulia.[170] Concerned about the duke's pirating activities, the king offers him a pardon and, shortly thereafter, asks him and his corsairs for help against the Ottomans and Algerians attacking the Spanish fortress of Oran. In response to the duke's overwhelming success against the pirates, the king not only inducts him into the Order of the Golden Fleece but also installs him as commander of the royal fleet, at an annual salary of twenty thousand ducats.[171] Spain's dealings with Oran did indeed include such a siege and a victory at sea over the Turks, in 1568.[172]

Fictionalizing Pirates, Robbers, and Slaves

Creating narrative tension by using "real" information in the service of fictional plots, the twists and turns of Happel's stories lead the reader on marvelous expeditions, whose attractions he frequently underscores in the forewords (*Vorreden*) to his novels. The *Quintana* serves as an example: "Die Historie ist ein solch nützlich Werck/ daß wir ohne dieselbe/ wie blinde Leute/ gleichsam im Finstern tappen würden/ darum ist es hoch nöthig/ daß man die Geschichten unserer Zeit fleissig aufzeichnet/ welches von diesem auf dies/ von jenem auf andere Weise geschiehet. Ich habe mir die Romanische Weise hiebey am bequemsten düncken lassen/ und lebe der Versicherung/ es werde der geneigte Leser seine Belustigung haben" (History is such useful work that without it we would be like the blind trying to find our way in the dark. Therefore, it is necessary that all tales from our time are written down, which happens in different ways. I have found that the way of romance is the most fitting [for me] and I am living assured that

---

170. "Lieffen die Banditen Hauffen-Weiß zu ihm/ also/ daß sich ein Jeder in der Gegend von Calabrien und Apulien vor dem Printzen de Tursis fürchtete; kam zu viel Geld und alle Schiffe zahlten Schutz" (Bandits joined them in droves so that everybody in the area of Calabria and Apulia was afraid of the Prince of Tarsis. He gathered great wealth, and all ships had to pay protection [*AR* I: 402]).

171. "[I]hm nicht allein den berühmten Orden deß güldenen Flüß/ sondern darneben ein Königl. Patent übersandte/ darinn er zu einem Admiral über eine Esquadre Königlicher Kriegs-Schiffe unter einer jährlichen Gage von 20 000. Dukaten bestellet wurde (He did not only bestow the Golden Fleece on him, he also gave him a royal promotion, which meant he was made an admiral of the royal war fleet with the yearly pay of twenty thousand ducats [*AR* I: 405]).

172. At the siege of Oran in 1556, Ottoman troops from Algiers besieged the Spanish garrison. The siege, by land and sea, was unsuccessful. More than a decade later, on July 14, 1568, John of Austria (the illegitimate son of Charles I and thus the paternal half brother of King Philip II) led a flotilla of thirty-three galleys against the Algerians.

it will give pleasure to the honored reader ([*SQ* I: *Vorrede*]). More specifically, in the foreword to the third book of the *Quintana*, he explains that "[d]er Leser wird diesem Quintana nebst der *Romanisirung* nicht allein denckwürdige Geschichten deß abgelebten Jahres/ sondern auch fürnehmlich die Spanischen und Portugallischen Materien kürtzlich beysammen finden/ so ist auch dieses Werck hin und wieder mit Lehr-reichen und nützlichen Discursen von allerhand lieblichen Sachen nicht anders/ als eine Tafel mit vielerhand Gewürtz und Confituren/ gleichsam bezuchert" (the reader will find in this *Quintana*, aside from romance, not only all the memorable stories of this past year but also about Spanish and Portuguese matters. Moreover, this work contains here and there informative and useful discourses of many enjoyable matters comparable to a table laden with many spices and sweet confections [*SQ* IV: *Vorrede*]).

This foreword to book 3 of the *Quintana* assures the reader that Happel did not simply repeat any given information. Rather, he strove to integrate it into the narrative logic of his tales: "Ordnung in die Information zu bringen und nicht jede Kleinigkeit zu berichten . . . [Ich] habe mich sothaner Schrifften und Documenten bedienet/ die deßfalls zu beyden Seiten publiciret/[173] und öffentlich in Druck sind kommen" (to bring order into this information and not to relate any minor item . . . I employed texts and documents that speak to both sides of the conflict and have been made publicly available).

Already in the *Afrikanische Tarnolast*, Happel's first novel (begun in the fall of 1666 but not published until 1689), pirates and robbers represent an essential element of the plot's construction. The novel begins with the story of the Mauretanian prince Tarnolast and the Portuguese princess Clara, "worinn Gar seltzame Glücks-Veränderungen/ höchst-verwunderliche Ebentheueren/ insonderheit aber die Africanische Sachen grossen Theils angeführet/ auch sonst allerhand leßwürdige Dinge fürgebracht werden" (wherein are told strange turns of fate, wondrous adventures, especially African matters and many things worthy of reading).[174] In this novel, Happel identifies yet another important theme that was to appear alongside the tales of slaves and captives: that of traversing borders and, in the process, encountering non-European societies and cultures.

---

173. In this case, he speaks about "die Hamburger-Belagerung ist eine von den Wichtigsten/ welche ich also eingeführet habe" (the siege of Hamburg by Denmark, about which he attempts to report as impartially as possible as not to annoy his readers).

174. Eberhard Werner Happel, *Der Afrikanische Tarnolast* (1689), ed. John D. Lindberg, 4 vols., Bibliothek des Literarischen Vereins in Stuttgart 305–8 (Stuttgart: Anton Hiersemann, 1982), title page.

Prince Tarnolast's travails carry him across many such cultural barriers. We meet him as he rides out to hunt on a horse that had been presented to his father by the Tunisian king, Muley Asses, in gratitude for the father's help against the famous Algerian pirate Barbarossa.[175] Even if Happel, after the publication of D'Aranda's autobiography, can assume his audience's familiarity with this name, the Barbarossa of Happel's fiction turns out to be a bit different from the historical one.[176] A native of the city of Mytilene on the island of Lesbos, the historical Barbarossa began his seafaring life rather modestly, commanding only one ship. He soon had several ships and many men under his control, most of whom volunteered to serve under his command.[177] He agreed to help the king of Algiers against Spain but instead murdered the king and had himself crowned in his stead; thus, as Defoe notes, "a Thief became a mighty King."[178] Subsequently, he conquered the city of Tunis (1534), which was one of the pirate strongholds along the Barbary Coast in Happel's time.

His father's good deed does not help Tarnolast, and his hunt takes an unhappy turn. He is captured by Arab robbers, who take him to Tunis, the place "woselbsten die See-Räuber ihre grosse allgemeine Ablage hielten" (where even pirates stored many of their goods).[179] Traveling by land from Tunis to Tripoli and from there by ship to Egypt, they are attacked by pirates. Thus, already in his very first novel, Happel introduces the reader to abduction, enslavement, and pirating, as well as the economic and personal hardships that will constitute one of the mainstays of his later novels. The robbers battling the pirates appear to be losing until Tarnolast, their captive, requests

175. "[S]einem Vater vom König Muley Asses aus Tunes, wegen seines geleisteten Beystandes gegend den grossen Algirischen Rauber T . . . Barbaroussa war verehret worden" (which was given to his father in gratitude for the support he had rendered to the king of Tunis against the famous pirate Barbarossa [AT I: 2]). Muley Asses could be either Muhammad IV or Muhammad V, depending on when the adventures are supposed to have taken place. Hayreddin Barbarossa or Barbarossa Hayreddin Pasha (1478–1546) was an Ottoman admiral who dominated the Mediterranean for decades. He was born on the island of Lesbos (Mytilene) and died in Constantinople.

176. Emmanuel D'Aranda, *Schauplatz Barbarischer Schlaverey* (Altona: Victor de Löw, 1666). 21. D'Aranda reviews Barbarossa's career, starting with his success as a pirate (together with his brother) and including his conquest of Algiers and Tunis, after which he called himself king of Algiers: "Anno 1515, gemeldeten Harjaden oder Barbarossam, das er sie [the Algerians] in seinem Schutz nehmen und von den Castilianern befreien solte. Beydes geschach" (In the year 1515, the just-mentioned Harjaden or Barbarossa [said] that he would protect [the Algerians] and liberate them from the Castilians).

177. Johnson [Defoe], *A General History of the Pyrates*, 30–31.

178. Ibid., 666. Defoe identifies *The Turkish History . . . by Richard Knolles* (1687) as his source.

179. *AT* I: 562.

a sword from the leader of the gang, Loriaga, so that he might participate
in the fight. Tarnolast "wants to know how much he could surpass both"
the robbers and the pirates with his fighting skills (*AT* I: 16). Ultimately,
the robbers prevail. In gratitude, Loriaga henceforth treats Tarnolast with
great politeness, liberating him from his chains and taking him along on a
pilgrimage to Mecca and Medina. But Loriaga's luck eventually runs out.
During a horrific storm, he is swept into the Red Sea and drowns. Upon
reaching Aden, the robbers fail to show Tarnolast the same gratitude their
captain had; they sell him and his horse for four thousand *aspers*, prompting
one of Happel's very few editorial comments: "so sahe man doch wol was vor
ein tückisch/ verrätherisch untreu Volck die Araber seynd" (this made clear
what a treacherous, unfaithful people the Arabs are [*AT* I: 17]).

As noted in the introduction, already at this early stage in his writing
career, Happel shows the signature traits that would later attract high praise
from the writer and philosopher Christian Thomasius. One of the interlocutors in Thomasius's review of the *Tarnolast* approvingly comments on the way
in which the text heightens the reader's enjoyment by joining chorography,
travel narratives, and the news of the day with his romances.[180] Thomasius
applauds that Happel "allegationes [fictions] gar artig mit in die Umständen
der Geschichte [gemischt]/ daß dieselbige und deren Wahrscheinlichkeit
dadurch nicht *turbiret* werde" (mixed fictions very effectively with historical facts so that the verisimilitude was in no way disturbed).[181] In addition,
he highlights Happel's talent at describing exotic cultures and customs. In
Thomasius's eyes, this sets Happel apart from lesser writers who present
"Spanische/ Türckische/ Africanische/ Persische Liebes-Geschichte . . . als
wenn man mitten in Paris wäre" (Spanish, Turkish, African, Persian love
stories . . . as if they took place in the middle of Paris).[182] Even Happel's
many (fictional) love stories (*Liebesgeschichten*) do not offend the reader's
sense of *Wahrscheinlichkeit*.[183] Nor does the African prince Tarnolast appear
like a European nobleman; "derowegen dörffte man auch seine *inventions*

---

180. About chorography, see Barbara J. Shapiro, *A Culture of Fact: England, 1550–1720*
(Ithaca: Cornell University Press, 2000). Stockhorst notes that, while generally positive, Thomasius distances himself from some of the praise and criticism by putting it into the mouths of two
interlocutors, claiming that he, Thomasius, never read the whole novel, because he was too busy
reviewing Lohenstein's *Arminius* (in Happel, *Der Insulanische Mandorell*, 651).

181. Christian Thomasius, "Eberhardi Guerneri Happelii Africanischer Tarnolast," in *Frei-
mütige, lustige und ernsthafte, jedoch vernunftsmässige Gedanken oder Monatsgespräche . . .* , ed.
Christian Thomasius (1689; repr., Frankfurt am Main: Athenaeum, 1972), 703.

182. Ibid., 736.

183. "Nicht gar zu offenbahr wieder die Wahrscheinlichkeit anstoßen" (not militating too
much against verisimilitude [ibid., 734]).

nicht nach den Europäischen manieren ausmessen" (thus it would not do to measure his inventions with European measures).[184]

To return to the text, Tarnolast is sold to an aga, who treats him well in every way other than setting him free. Recognizing the quality of this slave, who identifies himself only as a nobleman from Mauretania, the aga employs him to instruct his daughters in foreign languages and cultures (*AT* I: 18). Predictably, Vermuth, one of Tarnolast's students, falls in love with the prince, who returns her affection. When Tarnolast saves her from a lion, the aga frees him from bondage, under the condition that he remain at court (*AT* I: 22). The couple's happiness seems complete until Tarnolast is offered the crown of the kingdom of Madagascar [*AT* I: 29]. He accepts, and before he sets out for Madagascar, he promises to marry Princess Vermuth upon his return. Alas, Tarnolast's departure turns out to be the beginning of a long and convoluted detour that includes multiple shipwrecks, enemy attacks, sojourns on abandoned islands, and meetings with strange peoples, whose women inevitably fall in love with him.

After one of those shipwrecks, Tarnolast and his fellow travelers seek refuge on an island. This quiet moment in the action offers the castaways ample opportunities to tell the stories of their lives and loves. These interludes serve two narrative functions. First, they aid the reader in navigating the text's ever more complicated events and relationships. Second, they allow for a momentary pause in the narrative flow, concentrating attention on a single character and providing clarification of his or her position in the emerging story.

As a consequence of one such conversation, Tarnolast decides to convert to Christianity. (It is worth noting here that Muslim converts to the Christian faith are never dismissed as renegades in Happel's novels or in the newspapers.) By converting, Tarnolast gives up the crown of Madagascar (which is forbidden to Christians), forsakes Vermuth, and risks his own father's disapproval. In response to these events and apprehensions, rather than settling in one place and into one social setting or role, Tarnolast (and the reader) roams far and wide across continents and seas until he arrives in France. There, in Brittany, he accepts an offer from one of his fellow travelers to accompany a shipload of goods returning from East India on their way to Orléans. He hopes that this job will earn him enough money to attend the University of Orléans, one of the finest institutions of higher learning in France ("allervornehmste in Frankreich" [*AT* I: 35]).[185]

---

184. Ibid., 377.

185. This point is made again in the *Academische Roman*, where university life, only touched on here, is joined with an entertaining illustration of early modern higher education.

After many changes in scenery, geographic location, mood, and mind, the potential marriage no longer being a subject of concern, Tarnolast's father calls his son home. On his way there, Tarnolast travels through Italy. Attacked by robbers, he is not only victorious over them but also liberates several prisoners, who speak an African language. One of the robbers, an African from Algiers named Tassibal, begs for mercy, which Tarnolast grants him, while also accepting him into his service. As it turns out, far from being a mere robber, Tassibal emerges as Ariontes, prince of Guinea. Such changes in fortune are indispensable stylistic requisites in seventeenth-century novels, and in Happel's, as we have already observed, these changes are often brought about by encounters with robbers and pirates. Allowing for much narrative diversity, such plot devices offer Happel numerous occasions to highlight the moral fortitude of his protagonists, who frequently experience significant reversals in social station or are compelled to deal with persons of seemingly lower status who later emerge as anything but socially inferior.

Over the course of the *Afrikanische Tarnolast*, robbers and pirates bring about many trials and tribulations by way of identity confusion, be it of gender, class, familial relationships, or ethnicities. These developments introduce the reader to diverse peoples from faraway lands, many of whom turn out to be less alien than assumed. The African Tarnolast, for example, though decidedly un-European, is frequently described as exceedingly beautiful. With fair, curly hair ("sein Gold-gelb oder etwas weißliches von selbst gekrausseltes Haar" [his golden-yellow or even white-flecked and curly hair] [*AT* I: 107]) and "unmenschliche Schönheit" (superhuman beauty), he is seemingly an earthly angel favored by God ("an diesem himmlischen Menschen hat wol Gott und die Natur ihr Meister-Stück rechtschaffen bewiesen" [with this divine person God and Nature have contracted a masterpiece] [*AT* I:112]). This "color blindness" conforms to a fluidity of racial labeling that seems to apply only to the non-European Other. Contemporary captivity narratives tell of Moors who are diverse in color, whereas Arabians and Barbarians (inhabitants of Barbary) are described as white and tawny, respectively.[186] Of course, Europeans, male or female, never appear as black and are described as beautiful more often than not.

It is important to note that, already in Happel's very first novel, female characters are very much part of the travel and captive narrative and, in this role, are accorded extraordinary agency. Scoletha, the sister of Ariontes, is

---

186. "The subjects of the emperor of Morocco do all call themselves Moors, though they are of diverse nations and colors. . . . These [barbarians] are white, another sort of Arabians . . . are tawny." Colley, *Captives*, 108–9. Colley cites a seaman and former captive, John Whitehead.

an excellent example of this determined activism, which can involve hiding one's gender (whether male or female) by cross-dressing, as well as taking on different class roles. Princess Scoletha is accompanied by a servant girl who turns out to be the noblewoman Erlabis, who was abducted from her home at a very young age and forced into captivity in North Africa. We meet Scoletha as she makes the independent and courageous decision to journey (geographically quite incorrectly) across the sea to surprise her fiancé, Calander, in his native Congo, rather than waiting to be fetched by him as his bride. To protect herself against the hazards of the journey, Scoletha dons men's clothing and weapons: "wie ich dann von Jugend auff mit Pfeilen und Schwerdt wohl umzugehen fleissig gelernet hatte" (from the time of my youth I have learned to use arrows and sword [*AT* II: 444]).

Cross-dressing joins pirating in complicating what was to be a joyous bridal journey. Attacked by pirates, Scoletha and her attendants, also wearing men's clothing and armor, join the fight, swords valiantly in female hands. Outnumbered, they are taken prisoner, at which juncture Scoletha and her fellow captives pretend to be Guinean noblemen (*AT* II: 446). Not surprisingly, the pirates put all of them but Scoletha to work as oarsmen. From the information circulating about both Muslims and Christians taken captive, we know that readers would have been well informed about the harshness of such a fate.[187] For the most part, however, the captain, "ein ansehnlicher junger Herr" (a handsome young man), treats his captives reasonably well, assigning them work alongside his crew (*AT* II: 447). The physical strength of these noblewomen seems to be an expression of the verisimilitude so much praised by Thomasius. Like Scoletha, many of Happel's female characters disclose that they grew up as tomboys, practiced in the use of arms and in horseback riding and clearly unafraid of traveling to faraway and unfamiliar places, be it alone or with only a female companion. (I will discuss some of the roles of such female characters in Happel's novels in greater detail in chapter 4.)

Alongside his fictional heroines, Happel mentions several historical examples of what he often calls *Amazoninnen*, by which he means strong and combative women. In the *Frantzösische Cormantin* (1688), one character

---

187. "Captivity, and its twin sisters, piracy and privateering, sustained the 'interface between Islamic and Christian societies—a point of regular contact for all classes.' . . . [C]aptivity narratives provide a limited understanding of the Muslim experience." Matar, *Europe through Arab Eyes*, 39, quoting Robert I. Burns, "Piracy as an Islamic-Christian Interface in the Thirteenth Century," *Viator* 11 (1980): 165.

recalls with admiration the famous cross-dressing Spanish Basque soldier Catalina de Erauso (1592–1650), who fled a nunnery and, in men's clothing, went to fight wars in Europe and in the New World. Citing one of his many sources, Pietro Della Valle's *Viaggi* (translated into German as *Eines Vornehmen Römischen Patritii Reiss-Beschreibung in Unterschiedliche Theile Der Welt* in 1674), Happel informs the reader that the king awarded her eight hundred crowns yearly for her service (*FC* III: 158).[188]

After Cormantin is shipwrecked on the Congolese coast, Happel introduces the reader to a martial woman every bit as impressive as Catalina or the Thökölin. At the court of the king of Congo, Cormantin meets the beautiful (fictional) princess Taxinda, who, like many of Happel's heroines, resembles an Amazon in her physical beauty and her prowess. At the same court, Cormantin also encounters a Jesuit priest who tells him about the historical Angolan queen Anna Xinga (1583–1663).[189] (The similarity between the names is obvious.) Rehearsing contemporary reports, the Jesuit praises the historical queen's courage as much as he condemns her supposed cruelty, by explaining "daß es unter den Mohren auch viele tapffere Frauns-Personen gibt . . . werden wir daselbst [in Angola] erstarren müssen/ über die unvergleichliche Thaten einer welt-bekandten Mohrischen Prinzessin/ welche sich daselbst ums Jahr Christi 1645. durch ihre glückliche Waffen so berühmt gemacht/ als sie billich wegen ihrer abscheulichen Grausamkeit und Zauberey tadeln war" (that among the Moors there are indeed many brave women . . . they would be amazed by the incomparable deeds of one world-renowned Moorish princess who, in the year 1645, became famous because of luck in war just as much as she was justifiably criticized because of her cruelty and for practicing magic" [*FC* II: 127]). To add to such rumors, he recounts that she was said to have preferred men's clothing and that she insisted that her men wear women's clothing. It is a matter of historical record that Anna Xinga personally led her troops into battle against the

---

188. Stephanie Merrim, "Catalina de Erauso: From Anomaly to Icon," in *Coded Encounters: Writing, Gender, and Ethnicity in Colonial Latin America*, ed. Jeffrey A. Cole, Francisco Javier Cevallos, Nina Scott, and Nicomedes Suárez-Araúz (Amherst: University of Massachusetts Press, 1994), 178; Isabel Hernandez, "From Spain to the Americas, from the Convent to the Front: Catalina de Erauso's Shifting Identities," *L'Homme: Europäische Zeitschrift für feministische Geschichtswissenschaft* 22, no. 1 (2011): 71–84; Pietro della Valle, *Eines vornehmen Römischen Patritii Reiss-Beschreibung in unterschiedliche Theile der Welt* (Geneva: Widerhold, 1674). Della Valle lived from 1586 to 1652.

189. Anna Xinga is (Ana de Sousa) Nzinga or (Njinga) Mbande (those are the most common spellings, but there are many others).

Fig. 9. Anna Xinga (1583–1663) (Herzog August Bibliothek, Wolfenbüttel)

Portuguese and preferred to be called "king" rather than "queen." Moreover, records show that she demanded that her husband wear women's clothing, thus underscoring her role as king.[190]

News reports of Anna Xinga's many battles with the Portuguese colonizers and her efforts at playing Portuguese slave and ivory trading interests against those of the Dutch commented on her successes as much as on her losses.[191] News about her from Amsterdam (*Wöchentliche Zeitung*, April 11, 1648) noted not only the enmity between the Netherlands and Portugal in the Central African slave trade but also the queen's ability to negotiate a precarious path between these two colonial powers: "aus Angola verlautet/ daß die unsern [the Dutch] daselbst eine grosse Victoria erhalten/ und in die 2000. Schwarze und Portugesen geschlagen; so hette die Königin von Conga mit den unsern ein Bündniß gemacht/ und der Portugesen Feind seyn/ sich erkläret" (from Angola we hear that ours [our soldiers, the Dutch] have achieved a great victory and defeated two thousand black and Portuguese troops. [It is said] that the queen entered into a treaty with us and declared herself an enemy of the Portuguese).

In Happel's novel, Cormantin is appointed general in the Congolese army, "nicht ohne Widersprechen" (not without opposition). While serving in this role, he falls in love with Princess Taxinda (*FC* II: 185). Her brother, Prince Canati, supports the union, but native tradition does not allow for such a marriage. Her angry father has Taxinda beheaded (or so it seems) and forces Cormantin to leave Congo aboard a Portuguese ship. During the journey, the ship's captain entertains his passengers with tales of the wild exploits of Roeck the Brazilian, tales Happel most likely took from Exquemelin's autobiography, translated into German in 1678 (*FC* I: 194).[192]

---

190. Heywood and Thornton, *Central Africans, Atlantic Creoles*, 131. Heywood and Thornton's study is an excellent source for the details of the Angolan queen's life and her dealings with the Portuguese and Central African slave trade.

191. "Es scheinet so/ daß die Holländer den Krieg gegen die Portugesen (welche den Holländern die Insul Angola abgenommen haben/ von wannen die ElephantsZähn in grosser Menge kommen) fortsetzen wollen" (it appears that the Dutch have once again started the war against the Portuguese, who had taken from them the island of Angola [*sic*], from which much ivory [is being shipped] [*Wöchentliche Zeitung*, Frankfurt, June 16, 1649, 10:2–3]). The same newspaper reported on August 25, 1649, about negotiations between Portugal and Spain concerning the "Oeffnung des Kauf- besonderheit des Schlaven-Handels zwischen ihnen beyderseits . . . welches diesem Königreich [Portugal] zu großem Vortheil gedeyen kan, und sonderlich weiln die von Angola nun wieder gäntzlich unter dem Gehorsam unseres Königs gebracht" (opening of trade, specifically the slave trade between them . . . which will bring great advantage to the Portuguese, especially because the Angolans have now been returned to the obedience of our king [Nr. 155]).

192. Esquemeling, *Buccaneers of America*, 69–70.

In keeping with the drama associated with cross-dressing already observed in Happel's very first novel, Taxinda (now described as "Congische Taxinda") reappears at Cormantin's court at the end of the novel as the "Mohrische Ritter Lind" (*FC* IV: 384), her father having merely staged her execution. Canati would still like his sister and Cormantin to marry, but, in a fate typical of Happel's Amazons, Taxinda dies in combat before vows can be exchanged. All is not lost, however, as she had already installed Cormantin as the sole heir to her fortune of gold, jewels, and other precious items. In this, the story follows a narrative pattern frequently employed by Happel, by which his penniless but virtuous and highborn heroes gain great wealth without having to marry women from foreign shores.

Powerful and fearless women, whether or not in cross-dress, seem to have had a strong appeal for Happel and his audience. Chapter 2 introduced us to Imre Thököly's wife, the valiant Thökölin, whose cross-dressed combat alongside her husband at Munkács made for a dramatic, if fictionalized, moment in the *Ungarische Kriegs-Roman*. Her life and times coincided with those of other strong female leaders who supplied exciting content for the seventeenth-century news media, such as Sweden's Queen Christina (1626–89) and the legendary Queen Anna Xinga. In fact, Happel lived in Hamburg in the early 1670s, when Queen Christina came through several times on her way to and from Stockholm. During one of those sojourns, she visited with Duke Friedrich of Holstein-Gottorp, a maternal relative.[193] Happel had served as a tutor with a noble family in the environs of the ducal court, whose chamber of wonders he had admired. Not unlike Happel's historical and fictional *Amazoninnen*, Christina was reported to have loved "manly" pursuits like hunting and horseback riding.[194] It was said that she repeatedly rejected what she considered the yoke of marriage, leading to much speculation about her sexual orientation.[195]

Returning to Scoletha, one of the *Tarnolast*'s heroines, and her attendants, we find them, along with their fellow pirates, still sailing the seas, attacking ships and dividing the spoils among themselves. Rising to the

193. Veronica Buckley, *Christina, Queen of Sweden: The Restless Life of a European Eccentric* (New York: HarperCollins, 2004), 165–66.

194. Ibid., 18–21, 324n19; Elisabeth Waghall, "Eine Königin in den Zeitungen: Königin Christina von Schweden als Beispiel frühneuzeitlicher Nachrichtenvermittlung," *Daphnis* 37, nos. 1–2 (2008): 302–32.

195. Pfufendorf said, "Doch war sie schon damals resolviert/ sich unter das Joch des Ehestandes nicht zu begeben" (However, she was resolved never to bow to the yoke of marriage). See Waghall, "Eine Königin in den Zeitungen," 316n38. I return to this theme in chapter 4.

challenge of multilingual communication among the pirates, Scoletha over-
comes the language barrier by teaching herself to speak Arabic. After five
months at sea, they finally approach a big island, which Scoletha recognizes as England. The suggestion that they attack and rob a small coastal
town is rejected by an old pirate, who warns that these English are wary and
would break the pirates' necks as soon as they saw them. Moreover, they are
reminded that England recently has entered into a peace treaty with Algiers,
"welches zu stören uns übel gelingen möchte" (which we would not succeed
in disturbing [*AT* II: 447]).

As the reader has come to expect, and in keeping with the generic presuppositions of these novels, complications continue to dog the characters.
Scoletha's gender is finally discovered by a pirate who happens upon her
asleep and partially uncovered (*AT* II: 448). Not wanting to squander the
value of this privileged information by sharing it with his companions, he
suggests that he would be willing to keep her secret if she would consent to
give in to his desire. This suggestion is anything but acceptable to Scoletha,
who proceeds to kill him with a small bread knife (*AT* II: 449). Then, show-
ing great presence of mind, she puts the pirate's own large knife into his left
hand in such a way that the point is embedded in his wound, suggesting to
the captain that her attacker had committed suicide (*AT* I: 449).

This captain, however, appears to have different worries. When they
make ready for an encounter with yet another merchant vessel, he confides
to Scoletha that he will give up pirating and free her and all the other captives if they help him to victory in this last fray. She assents and soon finds
herself fighting against a young nobleman who might have defeated her had
he not already been severely wounded. After the pirates are once again victorious and take over the merchant ship, she takes the young man prisoner.
Eventually, after Scoletha has returned safely home and told her friends
about her adventures, it becomes clear that the young man (not surprisingly to the reader who has become accustomed to Happel's surprise moves)
is her fiancé, Calander, then barely twenty-one and of "Herren Standes"
(noble birth). As her prisoner, he pretends to be a German nobleman, but
she realizes from his conduct that he must be more distinguished than that,
for he cannot refrain from giving commands (*AT* II: 452). Returning to the
communication challenges on the ship, we hear that Calander and the ship's
German captain speak only Latin and German. The captain is a commoner
("gemeinen Geschlechts") from the powerful merchant city of Hamburg
("eine mächtige Handelsstadt/ so sie Hamburg nenneten") who had been

retained with his crew for the protection of the vessel (*AT* I:452).[196] Scoletha already knows Latin, and she learns German during the seven months they spend together on the ship.[197] Though only peripherally a topic of our study, languages and language learning frequently surface as a plot device and a topic of discussion in Happel's novels.[198]

Still cross-dressed, Scoletha had also become best friends with the chief of the pirates ("Obriste Räuber"), prompting him to offer her a high position among his crew. She declines, pointing out that his men would resent such a promotion. As noted, he had confessed in confidence his disillusionment with his pirating life. Having been abducted at age three from his African home, a narrative complication familiar to us from contemporary reports and from the use Happel made of it in later novels, the pirate chief does not know anything about his family, except that he is of noble birth (*AT* II: 453).[199] Now twenty-three, he has gathered sufficient wealth to leave his life of crime and find a position that will allow him to fight for an honest wage and an honest cause. Scoletha, sensing her chance to regain her freedom, promises to take him with her to Guinea should she ever be free to return there. His crew members, who seem to be of like mind, agree that those of them who are married, tired of pirating, and want to quit this life ("wann sie zur See sich müde geraubet hatten") should go and live on a small island in the Canaries ("unter deß Canarischen Regenten Botmässigkeit/ weil sie bishero keinen Herrn erkennet" [they agreed to become subjects of the regent of the Canary Islands since they had not recognized any power over them up to now] [*AT* II: 453]). The single men should go with Scoletha to Guinea. She promises them on her knightly honor (she is still dressed as a man) to provide for them at her parents' court. Calander agrees to go to Lisbon to buy the German captain's freedom for a generous ransom. Clearly, then, chivalry, far from being a purely Christian virtue, is an internationally recognized quality, as much at home in Guinea as in Germany. In Happel's fictions, it is also gender neutral.

---

196. "Diese Beede kunten keine als die Lateinische/ so mir auch zimlich bekandt war/ und ihre Mutter-Sprache die Teutsche" (these two spoke only Latin, with which I was familiar, and their mother tongue, German).

197. The fact that a native from Congo and his intended bride should speak Latin does not seem to raise eyebrows, either in the writer or (presumably) in the reader.

198. A brief discussion of this issue is forthcoming in my essay "Early Modern Translation and Transfer: Mixing but (Not) Matching Languages," which will appear in a collection edited by Bethany Wiggin.

199. Suffering the same fate as Spinelli, Quintana, and Cormantin from their European homes.

But before Scoletha and her companions are out of harm's way, more mishaps befall them. Still disguised as a man, Scoletha encounters yet another pirate. Though they are ignorant of each other's identity, he later turns out to be her brother Ariontes. He is victorious over her and sells her to an old widow, who, hoping to help Scoletha in securing her ransom, agrees to write a letter on her behalf (*AT* II: 459). Unfortunately, the old woman dies before Scoletha can be freed, and she winds up in the household of an unkind man whose wife falls in love with her, thinking her a man. Such unfortunate outcomes of cross-dressing and gender mix-ups frequently occur in Happel's novels, as we have already observed. Here, it prompts Scoletha to reveal her true gender to the husband, who quickly sells her to an Arab, who, in turn, puts her on a ship as a galley slave (*AT* II:462). Finally, just when she is about to be killed by her captors, she is rescued by a man in disguise, who turns out to be none other than our hero, Prince Tarnolast.

Safely home, Scoletha entertains her friends, who listen with rapt attention to the tale of the pirate captain's return to the path of righteousness ("sie möchte hierinne wohl alles umständlich erzehlen" [she was implored to tell everything in the greatest detail] [*AT* II: 449]). Familiar with contemporary pirate writings, we now know that Happel's readers were aware that this tale had been taken directly from life, from the biographies, the ego-documents, of and by men like Claes Compaen, William Dampier, and Alexander Exquemelin. Likewise, Happel frequently makes use of the familiar narrative theme of youthful abduction by pirates, as noted in Scoletha's interaction with the pirate captain. Happel's *Spinelli* also begins with the kidnapping of the protagonist at a young age—in this case, twelve (*IS* I: 286). Barely escaping circumcision and thus irrevocably "turning Turk," Spinelli is sold and resold a number of times, until he finally gains his freedom in exchange for his courageous defense in Muslim service (*IS* I: 296).

Here, once again, fiction meets fact. Such raids were frequent along the Mediterranean coast, and I have already reviewed the training and the life that such youthful captives received in Constantinople if they were not sold as slaves outright.[200] Had Happel not had a different narrative scheme, the life of Cormantin, the protagonist of the novel by the same name, might have followed the same familiar pattern. Cormantin, too, was snatched from his home at a young age, so young that he had no memory of his parents (*FC* II: 49). Sold and resold, he spent time in the service of Tafiletta, the notorious king of Tunis, whose true story Cormantin tells, assuring his listener—

---

200. See "Fear of the Horizon," in Davis, *Holy War and Human Bondage*, 75–103.

after he had overcome all these hardships and rejoined his friends—that whatever else they had heard about this infamous man had more in common with a novel than with his life.[201]

The evolution of the formula of being abducted and reunited with family, lovers, or friends believed to be lost in the context of pirate/robber narratives is reflected in the *Italienische Spinelli*, the *Spanische Quintana*, and the *Frantzösische Cormantin*, as well as the *Ottomanische Bajazet*, in which Happel seems to have profited, once again, from D'Aranda's autobiography. In addition, the *Quintana* also returns to yet another of D'Aranda's stories. This one tells, in great detail, of a Christian captive, a Dominican monk named Joseph, who was treated like a son in his master's house. Unable to raise enough money for ransom, however, Joseph gave in to the sins of the flesh, so "daß er nicht allein den schönen Weibern nachhinge sondern auch . . . sich nicht scheuete den Türckischen Greuln nachzuhängen/ so/ daß kein Knabe vor ihm sicher war" (that he did not only covet beautiful women, he also was not ashamed to pursue the Turkish horror [i.e., sodomy]).[202] Ultimately, Joseph is punished with one hundred lashes to the soles of his feet and put to death at the stake—not for his sexual exploits (as the reader might have expected), but, rather, for having maligned the Muslim faith.[203]

Among the locales prominent in D'Aranda's narrative that also play an important role in Happel's novels is the *Baing* or *bain*, a barracks of sorts for slaves and captives, located in a kind of enclosed street complete with taverns and shops.[204] In the *Cormantin*, Happel provides details about what he calls the "BAINS oder GEFANGEN-HÄUSER in der Stadt" (*bains*, or prison

201. "Ich habe denselben Traktat gelesen/ derselbe aber gleichet mehr einem Roman als einer wahrhafftigen Geschichte" (I have read this document. It sounds more like a novel than like the story of his real life [*FC* II: 54]). French, English, and German translations of Tafiletta's biography were circulating widely. Rashid Mawlai, *Warhaffte und merckwürdige Geschichts-Erzehlung von Tafilette, dem grossen Bestreiter und Kayser der Barbarey; aus der englischen in die frantzösische/ und aus solcher in die teutsche Sprache übersetzt* (Nuremberg: Johann Hoffmann, 1670). Tafiletta is Moulay al-Rashid (1631–72), sultan of Morocco from 1666 to 1672. He has been called the founder of the Alaouite dynasty.

202. *SQ* I: 3621; Frisch, *Der Schauplatz Barbarischer Schlaverey*, III: 273–79.

203. Joseph is relegated to one of Pissiling's *bains*: "in diesem bain hat ihn Airanda gekennet/ der ihm dies Zeugnuß giebet/ er sey gelahrt und wolredend gewesen/ aber dabey lustig und gern bey Geselschafft" (D'Aranda got to know him in his *bain*, and he can testify to the fact that he [Joseph] was learned, well spoken, and with all that also funny and a good sport). Frisch, *Der Schauplatz Barbarischer Schlaverey*, III: 274).

204. The word *bain* comes from the Italian *bagno* (as on D'Aranda, *Schauplatz Barbarischer Schlaverey*, 57, referring to the *bagno* in Livorno). I am using Happel's version of the word, especially as *bagnio* has other meanings in English (originally "bathhouse," usually "brothel").

houses, in the city), whose two to three thousand inhabitants are in service to the well-to-do Turks.[205] We read that Christians, almost all of them slaves, from France, Italy, Spain, England, Germany, Flanders, Holland, Greece, Hungary, Poland, Slovenia, and Russia totaled twenty-five thousand people (*FC* II: 301).[206] In the *Thesaurus Exoticorum*, Happel informs his readers that Algiers had six such *Sklaven-Kerker*, and he makes special mention of "Alli Peglins Bain," which, at the time Happel's source was written, had fallen into disrepair along with its master ("mit seinem Herren gefallen"). However, as the report cited by Happel continues, this sad state of affairs would soon be corrected, because there were too many prisoners in need of housing.[207] The *Quintana* has a former slave estimate that the number of slaves may have even been higher in 1650: "als ich vor 35. Jahren in Algiers im Sclavenstand lebete/ zehlete man über 48. 000 Sklaven" (when I lived as a slave in Algiers thirty-five years ago, they had about forty-eight thousand slaves [*SQ* I: 356]). Escaping by land was impossible for those not fluent in the native languages,[208] especially given that an escapee's shaved head and slave clothing and the iron ball attached to his waist would make him easily recognizable. The only chance to get away was by sea (*SQ* 4:132).

Recounting his years in the *bain*, D'Aranda tells of a life of abnormal normalcy, in which an old Italian slave sells goods and D'Aranda himself is put to work turning the wheel to raise water from a well; he is verbally punished by the guard when he is too slow. According to the *Krieges-Bericht*, "die Blutsaure Arbeit der Sclaven zu beschreiben/ ist so unmüglich/ alß schwer es ist/ dieselbe außzustehen" (to describe the sheer hardship of slave work is as impossible as it is to suffer it [*KB* no. 64]). According to D'Aranda, the men amused themselves with drinking, whoring, and the heinous sin of sodomy with young slaves.[209] Slaves ("Schlaven und Galeebuben") from many nations lived together and interacted closely while playing quite different roles according to their religion. The prisoners were Christian, as were the tavern owners (*Taverniers*); the customers were Turkish pirates and soldiers

---

205. "Bains oder Gefangen-Häusern in der Stadt wol 2. biß 3000. ohne die/ welche noch in vermögenden Türcken-Diensten stehen" (*bains* or prison houses in the city that held between two and three thousand slaves who served the well-to-do [*FC* II: 30]).

206. Davis, *Holy War and Human Bondage*, 194–95ff.

207. "[W]ird aber vermuthet/ daß er/ weil die Barbaren überhäuffig viel Gefangene täglich bekommen/ wieder werde zurechte gemacht werden" (it is believed that he will be reestablished because the barbarians keep capturing so many prisoners[*TE* I: 50].

208. Happel reviews in detail Pietro della Valle's descriptions of languages spoken in Turkey, in Happel, *Türckis. Estats- und Krieges-Bericht*, no. 59 (Z 102/1684/59/1).

209. Frisch, *Der Schauplatz Barbarischer Schlaverey*, I: 57.

("die Gäste sind Türckische Seeräuber und Soldaten").[210] Apparently, in the *bains* of Algiers, Muslims and Christians interacted freely, even playing tricks on each other. The able-bodied slaves went out to work in the morning and returned to the *bain* at night. If the oppression got too severe, the slaves rebelled against their Muslim masters, ensuring that the abuse, on the whole, did not become overly brutal or deadly, since such treatment would have led to a loss of labor.[211]

In the *bain*, where so many nationalities lived in such close proximity, control over language emerged as an existential need. D'Aranda describes the inhabitants as speaking what is called a lingua franca ("Franco, welches die gemeine Sprache unter den Schlaven und Türcken" [Franco, which is the common language among slaves and Turks]), a kind of Creole of Italian, Spanish, French, and Portuguese.[212] Survival demanded participation in this lingua franca, demanded translation.[213] Speaking it was not only vital for communication, whether among slaves or between slaves and masters, but also helped to establish a group consciousness that aided the captives in distinguishing between insiders and outcasts.[214] Slaves and captives who were conversant in this discourse were included in the group; for those who were not, punishment could be merciless, often consisting of the already mentioned floggings on the soles of the feet: "Diejenige Sclaven/ die erst neue ankommen/ und weder die Sprache noch die Sitten dieser Barbarn verstehen/ werden Wild genannt/ und durch Schläge zahm gemacht/ wie die unvernünfftigen Bestien" (newly arriving slaves who did not know the language or the customs of these barbarians were called wild animals and tamed with beatings like beasts without reason [*UK* II: 472]).[215] *Wilt* or *Wild* referred to those who still wore European dress or were unaccustomed to the work of a slave.[216]

---

210. Davis, *Holy War and Human Bondage*, 200–202.

211. For an informative and detailed description, see Friedman, *Spanish Captives in North Africa*, 60–61, 85. Her portrayal confirms what we read in D'Aranda.

212. Frisch, *Der Schauplatz Barbarischer Schlaverey*, I: 59; Windler, "Verrechtlichte Gewalt zwischen Muslimen und Christen," 325.

213. Doris Bachmann-Medick, *Cultural Turns: Neuorientierungen in den Kulturwissenschaften*, Rowohlts Encyclopädie 55675 (Hamburg: Rowohlt, 2006), 251.

214. Rheinheimer, "Identität und Kulturkonflikt," 344.

215. Windler, "Verrechtlichte Gewalt zwischen Muslimen und Christen," 325; *UK* II: 472: "In Algiers [ist] die sogenannte Franckische Sprache im Schwang/ welche auß Portugiesisch/ Frantzösisch/ Welschn/ fürnehmlich aber auß der Spanischen zusammengesetzt ist/mittels welcher die Sclaven und Barbarn einander ziemlich verstehen" (In Algiers they speak the so-called lingua franca, which is put together from Portuguese, French, Italian, and mainly Spanish. With it the slaves and barbarians can effectively communicate).

216. "Laß das bleiben du Hund/ du bist noch wilt" (Leave this alone, you dog, you are

The economy of the *bains* depended on there being someone to mediate between the motley crew assembled in this form of prison and those on the outside who might be able to procure ransom money. This role was often played by Jews, who, forbidden to own slaves themselves, traded slaves and earned money by facilitating the ransoming of wealthy captives. Rheinheimer cites a letter sent home from a northern German enslaved in Algiers who asked his family to send money to deliver him: "er habe mit dem Juden gesprochen, so die Schlafen hier löset" (he had spoken with the Jew who frees slaves around here).[217] According to Happel, Jews were afforded "ihre besondere Obrigkeit" (their special authority) among the Muslims based on their linguistic dexterity and cultural flexibility (*UK* II: 471). They were not only tolerated but indispensable: "weil die durch die gantze Welt ein fertige Correspondentz unterhalten/ ja manchmahl weiß man in Algier/ schon die Nahmen der Passagirer und Kauffleuten/ der Soldaten und Matrosen/ wie auch die Specification der gantzen Ladung eines Schiffs/ ehe dasselbe einmah die See erreichet" (because they had a ready correspondence throughout the whole world, so that sometimes in Algiers they already know the names of the passengers and merchants, soldiers and sailors, as well as the cargo, before they leave).[218] We read that Jews were believed to live in all countries across Europe and to communicate to their compatriots in Algiers and Livorno every detail ("alles Haar Klein") about the travelers on each vessel crossing the Mediterranean. (Like Algiers and other cities in North

---

still [a wild beast]); "Sie nanten ihn wilt; weil er noch seine Spanische Kleidung trug/ worbey ein jeder merken könnte/ das er neulich erst angekommen" (they called him wild because he was still wearing Spanish clothes, which signaled that he had arrived only recently). Frisch, *Der Schauplatz Barbarischer Schlaverey*, I: 60, 63.

217. Rheinheimer, "Identität und Kulturkonflikt," 335. D'Aranda (Frisch, *Der Schauplatz Barbarischer Schlaverey*, II: 174) also mentions Jews as being forbidden to buy slaves: "Er (ein Jude namens Ciscas) liess durch einen Türcken ihm einen Schlaven kauffen (weil die Juden selbst keine Schlaven kauffen oder halten müssen) (He [a Jew named Ciscas] had the Turks by a slave for him [because the Jews are not allowed to buy or keep slaves themselves])." About the involvement of the Jewish Ergass family of Livorno in the ransoming of Jewish and Christian slaves, see Francesca Trivellato, *The Familiarity of Strangers: The Sephardic Diaspora, Livorno, and Cross-Cultural Trade in the Early Modern Period* (New Haven: Yale University Press, 2009), 292n55.

218. *UK* II: 471: "Diese Juden machen auch grossen Profit durch die Wechseln von den gelösten Sclaven/ sie selber aber därffen keine Sclaven halten" (the Jews make profit much from the exchange of freed slaves since they themselves are not allowed to keep slaves); Frisch, *Der Schauplatz Barbarischer Schlaverey*, II: 36: "Sie werden hie gerne geduldet/ weil sie nicht allein grosse Handlung mit den Christen in Italien und ander Ohrten treiben; sondern auch ihre Correspondenten durch die gantze Christenheit haben/ so daß die Türcken durch sie grossen Gewin in Außwechslung der Schlaven geniessen" (They are tolerated because they don't only trade with Christians in Italy and other places, but they also entertain correspondences throughout the whole of Christianity).

Africa, as well as Constantinople, Livorno had a *bain*, or *Bagno*, in which several thousand Muslim slaves were housed.)[219] There were also influential Jewish merchant families—such as the Mendes family of Constantinople, confidants of several grand viziers[220]—who could employ their commercial networks all across Europe and the Middle East to facilitate ransom dealings.

In volume 2 of the *Ungarische Kriegs-Roman*, one of the main characters, the Albanian nobleman Cergely, is briefly imprisoned in the *bain* of Constantinople, the famous "Christen-Kercker."[221] Happel gives the specific date of June 1683. In December of this year, the new grand vizier, Kara Ibrahim Bassa, assumed his rule over the Ottoman court.[222] Before Cergely and his friends make their escape, Happel takes a moment to describe this *Christen-Kercker* to his readers as a "grossen Sclaven-Kercker/ welchen man Bainum auf Türckisch zu nennen pfleget. Wer zu Constantinopel gewesen ist/ wird wissen/ daß diese Christen-Kercker einen Jammer-vollen Spectacul machen" (a great slave prison, which in Turkish is called *Bainum*. Whoever has visited Constantinople knows that these prisons for Christians are a pitiful spectacle to behold [*UK* II: 304–13]). Constructed as a tower several stories high, it was said to hold about two hundred prisoners of many nations ("verschiedener Nationen"). Happel takes care to depict Cergely and his friends as fortunate enough not to be tortured or shackled, unlike the other prisoners, kept in a large dungeon below the tower, "welche aber in Kercker-Fesseln liegen/ müssen sich in Löchern/ als wilde Thiere behelfen" (who are lying in chains in these holes like wild animals).

Happel's description of this dungeon is based on the report of the man who accompanied the "Keyserlichen Ambassdeur/ Herrn Graf Walter Leßle/ Anno 1665 nach Constantinopel gangen/ redete davon also" (imperial ambassador Duke Walter Leslie in the year 1665 and reported about it).[223] This man

---

219. Trivellato, *Familiarity of Strangers*, 82.

220. Gabor Agoston, "Information, Ideology, and the Limits of Imperial Policy: Ottoman Grand Strategy in the Context of Ottoman-Habsburg Rivalry," in *The Early Ottomans: Remapping the Empire*, ed. Virginia Aksan and Daniel Goffman (Cambridge: Cambridge University Press, 2007), 82. Equally notorious for their language ability are the Jewish physicians ("weil sie viel umbher reisen/ und allerhand Sprachen verstehen" [because they travel much they understand many languages] [*KB* no. 44; Z 102/1684/44/1).

221. While still identified as a *bain*, the *bain* of Constantinople seems different from the one in Algiers, much more like a conventional prison than a ghetto or barracks.

222. Kara Ibrahim Pasha, also known by the Turkish name Bayburtlu Kara Ibrahim Paşa, was grand vizier of the Ottoman Empire from December 15, 1683, until November 18, 1685. See also Günter Kettermann, ed., *Atlas zur Geschichte des Islam mit einer Einleitung von Adel Theodor Khoury* (Darmstadt: Wissenschaftliche Buchgesellschaft, 2001), 109.

223. Walter Leslie (1607–67), field marshal in 1658, was invested in 1666 with the Order of

is not named in the *Ungarische Kriegs-Roman*, but in the *Türckis. Estats- und Krieges-Bericht*, Happel identifies him as Leslie's confessor ("Beichtvater"), Paul Tauffernier (Taffernier).[224] While in Constantinople, Tauffernier was allowed to visit the Christian slaves, even those in the dungeon, in accordance with fulfilling his spiritual duties toward the prisoners.[225] Tauffernier recounts his meeting with hundreds of noblemen of various nationalities who were locked up in the towers, eagerly awaiting ransom and letters from home: "Die Brieffe ihrer guten Freunde erweckten sie gar vom Tode/ Und die Hoffnung frey zu werden war ihnen das Leben selbst" (Letters from good friends raised them practically from their deathbeds, and the hope to be set free was to them life itself [*UK* II: 311]).

In the *Thesaurus*, Happel returns to the "Christen-Kärcker," describing it as divided into two parts, one called "Seven Towers," the other the *Bainum* (*ThEx* II: 131). Rather than being locked up in these ugly jails ("häßliche Kärcker"), a few of the slaves and other prisoners, recognizable by clothes and hairstyle, were allowed to walk around town; they "tragen ihre Frey-heit elendiglicher Weise herum" (pathetically carry around with them their "freedom").[226] Happel points out that such a "Sclaven-Kercker" also existed in other Turkish cities, including Ofen (Buda), the capital of Ottoman Hungary, giving the modern reader a clear indication that this part of Hungary was indeed Turkish to him.[227]

Happel returns to the Algerian *bain* in his *Academische Roman*, where his treatment of it alternates between serious social and historical commentary

---

the Golden Fleece in recognition of defeating the Ottomans in 1665. As imperial ambassador, he traveled to Istanbul to conclude the peace treaty with Sultan Mehmet (Mahomet) IV.

224. In this report, he tells about his stay with Leslie in a caravanserai, which he describes as "ein schönes uns Reisenden angenehmes Gebäude . . . ein Königl. Stall mit grossem [*sic*] Pracht erbauet" (a beautiful building, very pleasant for travelers . . . a royal stable built in great splendor [*KB* no. 93]).

225. *UK* II: 309, 311. Under normal circumstances, the Jesuits living in Galata tended to the prisoners. Galata was the part of town where most Orthodox and European Christians lived and where the embassies were located. A similar fate befell the ambassador of Rudolf II, Eustachius Prancker, who spent three years in captivity, at the galleys as well as in the infamous "Black Tower." Amazingly, it was not until 1597—after his release—that Prancker "turned Turk." See Graf, "A Sample of Renegades Active ca. 1560–1610," 3.

226. Familiarity with Constantinople's *bain* can be deduced from a brief note in the *Relations-Courir* of December 6, 1685, which reported what turned out to be a rumor, namely, that Thököly was brought to Constantinople and imprisoned in the "Gefängnuß zum 7 Thür-men" (Z 100/1695/135/7).

227. *UK* II: 311.

and comic action reminiscent of Till Eulenspiegel's pranks (1515).[228] Troll and Venereus, two of Klingenfeld's clownish friends (one a fool, the other a lover), are captured by pirates on their way to Famagusta and sold as slaves. Troll becomes the property of Christians[229] from Syria, who apparently treated Christian slaves a bit more gently than did the Muslims: "bey weitem nicht so strenge halten/ wie die Türcken" (they were not watched nearly as harshly as the Turks [*AR* II: 1022]). Venereus and Troll, however, misbehave and, as punishment, are forced to leave their relatively comfortable existence in their owners' home for a *bain*, shackled and desperately hoping to be ransomed. But this *bain* is a bit different than others Happel presents elsewhere to his readers. The inmates are reasonably well fed and provided wine, for which they have to pay a weekly "Speise-Geld." (To the two men's chagrin, hard liquor ["Brandwein"] is off-limits, for fear that its consumption would lead to fighting among the inmates.) Troll and Venereus share their quarters with a diverse group of prisoners, including a "Maronitischer Pfaff" (Maronite priest) who, outside the walls, had been keeping three wives; an officer who had committed arson in surrounding villages; and a merchant imprisoned for nonpayment of debts. The latter colludes with the man in charge, the *Wirt*, by tattling to him about every mischief the other inmates were planning (*AR* II: 1023).

Surely most amusing to the reader is a young Muslim prisoner locked up because he had married a girl against her parents' will and fathered a child with her. The randy young bride frequently visits him ("diese als eine geile Dame, kam nur/ um bei ihm zu schlafen" [because this lecherous woman only visited to have sex with him]). Because the conjugal visits take place in

---

228. Till Eulenspiegel was a trickster figure whose tales were disseminated in popular printed editions collecting lightly connected episodes that recounted his career as a wanderer who played tricks on the unsuspecting, tricks that occasionally carried a moral message and social criticism. Happel was familiar with Eulenspiegel's tales, which he mentions when warning students not to spend too much time with inferior books: "Es müssen aber die Studenten nur gute Bücher lesen/ am Anfang wenige/ hernach meherere/ und müssen sich nicht zu viel verlieben in die Amadys/ Eulenspiegel/ Garten-Gesellschafft/ Rollwagen/ Grillen-Vertreiber" (Students should read only good books, a few in the beginning and then increasingly more. And they should not fall in love with the Amadis, Eulenspiegel, Garten-Gesellschaft, Rollwagen, Grillen-Vertreiber [*AR* II: 862]).

229. "[D]enn es ist zu wissen/ daß allhier ein Christlicher Printz auß dem Geschlecht der alten Drusi wohnet [der in Syrien viel Land besaß] und denen etliche sind die die Christlichen Sclaven an sich handeln/ und bey weitem nicht so strenge halten/ wie die Türcken" (It should be said that a Christian prince of the lineage of the ancient Drusi lived here, who kept slaves whom they treated better than did the Turks [*AR* II: 1023]). Happel may be confusing Syriac Christians with Muslims of the Druze faith, which began as a movement in Ismailism and was influenced by Greek philosophy and gnosticism.

full view of all the other prisoners, their desires have to remain unfulfilled ("nichts Eheliches fürnehmen könten" [nothing of a marital nature could be undertaken] [*AR* II: 1027]). Troll and the student lover Venereus resolve to help out their fellow inmate. To prevent the guards' unwanted attention, they cover a corner with a coat, behind which the couple can achieve some privacy. Venereus then sits down at the table with Olearius's very popular *Persische Reisebeschreibung* before him,[230] borrowed from a German renegade in town. As he reads, he frequently bursts out with convoluted and loud explications of the illustrations adorning the tract, distracting the guards long enough for the couple to consummate their affections (*AR* II: 1028).[231] Happel's admiration for Olearius and his public's familiarity with his travel writing could not have been employed more effectively and amusingly in this narrative context.

The two jokesters also organize food deliveries, beat up other inmates, and play practical jokes that would have made Eulenspiegel proud. Just as the contemporary reader would have expected, no *Eulenspiegelei* can pass without a bit of scatological humor. Troll and Venereus, in solitary confinement right above the kitchen of their warden, cut a hole in the floor of their cell, and in the morning, they pour the contents of their *Topf* (chamberpot) through the hole, right onto the warden's clothing (*AR* II: 3031). After they are ransomed by a friend, an Italian prince, the prince and their friends are so amused at these prisoners' adventures that they "vor Lachen die Bäuche halten" (laugh until they had to hold their sides [*AR* II: 2050]). Life as a slave apparently could have its lighter moments.

Conclusion

In the *Afrikanische Tarnolast*, his first novel, Happel constructed a narrative template that he would employ in many of his later novels. Contacts with

---

230. *Beschreibung der muscowitischen und persischen Reise* (Schleswig, 1647; several enlarged editions, 1656, etc.).

231. "Venereus breitet eine grosses Buch vor sich aus/ so er von einem Teutschen/ der allhier wohnete/ geliehen bekommen/ darinn die Persische Rayse-Beschreibung des Herrn OLEARII war/ sobald er solches auf den Tisch geleget/ begunte er die Kupffer-Stücke zu expliciren . . . Troll aber . . . redete sehr laut. . . . Unter diesem Lärm nahm der Mann seine Frau" (Venereus opened the big book in front of him, which he had borrowed from a German who lived in town. It described the Persian travels of Herr Olearius. As soon as he had placed it on the table, he began to carefully explicate the engravings. . . . Troll, however, spoke with a loud voice, and with all this to-do, the man could get to his wife [*AR* II: 1028]). See Gerhard Dünnhaupt, "Adam Olearius (1599–1671)," in *Personalbibliographien zu den Drucken des Barock*, ed. Gerhard Dünnhaupt, Hiersemanns bibliographische Handbücher 3 (Stuttgart: Hiersemann, 1991), 2979–3004.

the exotic Other, who becomes familiar, a friend even, during the course of the experience provide important content for his tales. Chivalric conduct proves the same the world over, human qualities are recognized no matter what the faith of the adversary, and pirating yields resources sufficient to finance a life after piracy. Courageous noblewomen readily choose to cross-dress to accomplish physically challenging tasks like traveling to and in foreign countries, where they are in danger of being captured and sold as slaves. In his first novel, Happel hones the skills and many of the techniques that would characterize his subsequent work, most notably the employment of sources from multiple print media, most prominent among them newspapers, pirate biographies, histories, ransom sermons, and proclamations for the release of captives. Reflecting the experiences of seventeenth-century readers, these contemporary news reports contained examples of outlandish identity swaps, cruel treatment of captives, and extraordinary slave stories, all of which found their way into his novels.

As one would expect, with his career advancing, Happel became increasingly more accomplished in his craft. He shortened the chapters of his novels, made chapter headings more concise, and created ever more nuanced characters (if not as multilayered and psychologically complex as we find in novels of succeeding centuries) who are ever more logically tied into his narratives. In other words, we find that the action of his later novels is more tightly controlled and that the locales, though exotic, conform more closely to what was known at the time from travel reports, chorographies, histories, and the ubiquitous newspapers.

In the next chapter, I will move from reviewing the historical facts employed in his novels to the *Romanisirungen*, the fictions. I will show that they, too, though not "history," are not far removed from the times and places of seventeenth-century realities.

FOUR

Losing Direction

Romance and Gender Confusions

໕▲

Methodological Assumptions

In the preceding chapters, we explored the role of the media and contemporary history in the construction of Happel's novels. The other element of Happel's history and romance dichotomy, the *Romanisirungen*, will occupy us in this one.

After Happel settled in Hamburg, the *Afrikanische Tarnolast* languished in publication limbo while its author began writing novels, histories, and very successful collections of news and knowledge, such as the *Relationes Curiosae* (1681–91).[1] All of his novels are long, mostly consisting of at least four volumes around four hundred pages each; the *Ungarische Kriegs-Roman* extends to six volumes. Hoping to increase his sales volume by maintaining his loyal readership, Happel often advertised a novel as being built on its predecessor, as he does when introducing the *Bajazet* (1688).

Auf diese Weise habe ich meinen Jährlichen Geschicht-ROMAN angerichtet/ und wechselt derselbe alle jahr solcher Gestalt um/ daß er allemahl einen neuen TRACTAT absolviret/ und solcher Gestalt handelt der Italiänische SPINELLI den Italiänischen Estat, samt den Geschichten deß 1685.sten Jahrs ab; Diesem folgt über das 1686.

---

1. The two *Geschicht-Romane*, the *Italiänischen Spinelli* (1685) and the *Spanische Quintana* (1686), are part of the most productive period of Happel's professional life, which also includes the *Frantzösische Cormatin* (1687), the *Ottomanische Bajazet* (1688), the *Teutsche Carl* (1690), the *Engelländische Eduard* (1691), and the *Ungarische Kriegs-Roman* (1685–97).

ste Jahr der Spanische QUINTANA, welcher/ nächst den principal-
esten Historien desselben Jahrs/ den Spanischen Estat durchgehet;
Der Frantzösische CORMANTIN commentiret über die Actiones
deß 1687.sten Jahrs/ und stellet dem Liebhaber zugleich die Frantzösische Estats- und andere Materien für. Jetzo folget der Ottomannische BAJAZET, ein Geschicht-ROMAN über gegenwärtiges 1688.
ste Jahr.[2]

Alternatively, he reminds his readers that they are about to read a novel in
the manner of past productions. Thus, the *Frantzösischen Cormantin* begins,
"Ich fange anjetzo einen Geschicht-ROMAN auf gegenwärtiges 1687. Jahr
an/ darinn ich die Ordnung und Weise/ wie in dem SPINELLI und QUIN-
TANA unterhalten werde" (I will now start the *Geschicht-Roman* for this
present year 1687, in which I will entertain you in the same way as I did with
the *Spinelli* and the *Quintana* [*FC* I: *Vorrede*]). In the introduction to the
Teutsche Carl (1690), Happel not only repeats the history/romance duality
but also tells his detractors to do a better job of writing themselves if they are
able. Clearly exceedingly confident about his popularity with his readers, he
tells them what they will find in his works: "Merck-würdige Begebenheiten
an ihrem Ort/ und zu ihrer Zeit/ auf Historische/ das ist/ Unpartheyische
Weise/ eingeführt werden/ und zwar Alles unter einem Lieblichen Helden-
Roman, welche Schreibens-Art/ so viel ich annoch mercke/ den meisten
Liebhabern meiner Wercken am Besten gefallen/ obgleich ein oder anderer
scheel-sichtiger Momus die Nase darüber runtzelt/ und deßwegen/ daß er
überklug seyn/ und aller redlichen Leute Schrifften tadeln wil" (Amazing
events will be introduced according to their proper time and place and in a
neutral way. All of it will be presented in a lovely heroic novel the kind of
which has, so far, pleased all my readers even if this or that envious critic
wrinkled his nose over it only because he thinks he is overclever and has to
criticize everything other people write [*TC* I: *Vorrede*]).

In the introduction to part 3 of the *Engelländische Eduard* (1691),[3] Hap-

---

2. "Thus, I have produced every year a Geschicht-Roman changing each one so that it
would be a new product. In this way, the *Italiänische Spinelli* treated Italy along with the events
of the year 1685. This was followed, in 1686, by the *Spanische Quintana*, which presents Spanish
matters along with the most important stories of that year. The *Frantzösische Cormantin* comments on the actions of the year 1687 and presents information to those who like to hear about
the French state as well as other matters. This is now followed by the *Ottomanische Bajazet*, a
Geschicht-Roman treating this current year" (*OB* I: *Vorrede*).

3. *EE* III: 125–29.

pel reaffirms his narrative scheme, saying that he writes novels that join history and romance, fact and fiction, to delight and entertain his readers: "Es bleibet aber der Author nicht nur bey der blossen Romanisirung; sondern ist bemühet/ unter diesem Liebes- und Helden-Gedichte/ auch die vornehmsten Handlung- und Verrichtungen so wol im Kriegs- als auch andern Sachen/ grosse Feld- und See-Schlachten/ Belager- und Eroberungen der Städten/ wie sie mit der Warheit übereinkommen/ ohne Zusatz/ oder Jemanden Nachtheil/ wie es einem *Historico* geziemet/ Unparteyisch/ und wie sie sich hin und wieder zugetragen/ auf eine ebenmässige nicht unangenehme Manier/ mit einzuflechten."[4] He apologizes should anything other than the truth have slipped into the narrative, stating that he has done all he could to avoid such a misstep; if one has occurred, the fault, in all probability, is to be found in his sources: "So auch/ wider bessers Hoffen/ dieses Jahrs-Geschichten betreffend/ etwas/ das mit der Warheit nicht völlig übereinstimmete/ eingeschlichen seyn solte/ wolle der Günstige Leser solches keines Weges dem Authori, sondern denen sonsten für Authentisch gehaltenen Berichten und publiquen Schriften zumessen" (In case something not completely true concerning this year should have slipped in, I would beg of the reader to not hold it against the author but against those authentic and public reports [from which he took his stories] [*EE* III: *Vorrede*]). He is confident that any reasonable and independent reader will be fully capable of separating fact from fiction: "Dann/ was Romanische Außziehrungen seyen/ das wird ein jeder verständiger Leser selbsten von der eigentlichen Geschichte zu unterscheiden wissen" (for what is romantic decoration each reasonable reader should easily understand [*EE* III: *Vorrede*]).

By 1691, the year the *Engelländische Eduard* was published, Happel had died. Nevertheless, a third novel, the *Bayrische Max*, relates events of the year 1691 and was published in 1692. Clearly, the author/publisher applied Happel's successful fact/fiction formula to ghostwriting this and subsequent novels. As I already noted, the most insistent expression of compliment to the dead writer as well as the expert exploitation of the dead writer's fame is found in the *Ungarische Kriegs-Roman*. While Happel completed volumes 1 through 5, volume 6 did not appear until 1697. It is introduced along with a foreword by an anonymous writer. While still alive, Happel had advertised volume 5 of

---

4. "However, the author will not limit himself by presenting the tale in a romantic way, he also will try to combine this story of love and heroes with matters of war and other important things such as battles on land and sea, sieges, conquests of cities, as they conform to the truth without any additions or doing harm to anyone. This is as it behooves a *Historico*, to tell the story impartially and as this and that took place, in an even, pleasant manner" (*EE* III: *Vorrede*).

the *Kriegs-Roman* several times (in preceding novels), making clear that he was producing both the *Ottomannische Bajazet* and the *Frantzösische Cormantin* concurrently with the *Ungarische Kriegs-Roman*.[5] In fact, in the respective prefaces, he announces that he was holding back information in order not to spoil the reader's pleasure when he or she returned to the *Kriegs-Roman*: "Es ware beinahe dahin kommen/ daß unsern CORMANTIN ungemeinen Gloire in Morea theilhafftig gemacht/ . . . wann ich nicht bey Zeiten mich eines andern besonnen/ in Erwegung/ daß es sich nicht gezieme/ einen ROMAN mit dem andern/ also viel weniger diesen Geschicht- mit dem Ungarischen Roman zu vermengen" (It would have almost reached the point where our Cormantin would have gained inestimable glory in Morea if I had not changed my mind just in time, thinking that it would not do to mix [the narrative] of one novel up with another, even less the former with this *Ungarische Roman* [*FC* III: *Vorrede*]). In 1697, the anonymous continuator's *captatio benevolentia* explains that he had taken it upon himself to complete Happel's novel even though he knew his writing could never measure up to Happel's literary artistry (*UK* VI: *Vorrede*). Yet another anonymous continuator, the author of the *Der Sächsische Witekind* of 1692, also takes the opportunity of the foreword to make an appearance under Happel's name, in this way validating and affirming his writerly authority as "Happel" to his readers: "Der Sächsische WITEKIND/ Oder so genannter Europaeischer Geschicht-Roman, Auf Das 1692. Jahr; In welchem/ Nach Ahrt deß Italiänischen SPINELLI, Spanischen QUINTANA, Frantzösischen CORMANTINS/ Ottomanischen BAJAZETS/ Teutschen CARLS/ Engelländischen EDUARDS und Bayrischen MAX, in einer Liebes- und Helden-Geschichte/ die Denck-würdigsten Begebnüssen/ Kriegs- und Politischen Staats-Sachen/ Glücks- und Unglücks- auch hohe Todes-Fälle/ Hoch-Fürstliche Beylager/ Schlachten/ Belager- und Eroberungen/ etc. dieses Jahrs unparteyisch beschrieben werden" (The *Sächsischen Witekind* or so-called European Geschicht-Roman for the year 1692, in which, according to the model of the *Spinelli, Quintana, Cormantin, Bajazet, Carl, Eduard,* and *Max*, all memorable matters of war, politics, fortunes and misfortunes, deaths of the highborn, noble weddings, battles, sieges, and conquests are reported in a neutral way [*Vorrede*]).[6]

---

5. "Schier-künfftig hast du auch zu sehen den Vierdten Theil/ oder Beschluß dieses Romans [*OB*]/ welchem so dann auf dem Fuß gleichsam folgen wird der Fünffte oder Letzte Theil des Ungarischen Kriegs-Romans/ in dessen Außfertigung wir jetzo begriffen sind" (Pretty soon you will see the fourth and final part of this novel, upon which will immediately follow volume 5 of the Ungarische Kriege-Roman, with which we are busy as we speak [*OB* III: *Vorrede*]).

6. Eberhard Werner Happel, *Der Sächsische Witekind/ Oder so-genannter Europaeischer Geschicht-Roman. Auf das 1692. Jahr* (Ulm: Matthaeus Wagner, 1692).

Whoever the actual authors were, we soon realize that Happel's and his continuators' complex narratives can only be appreciated if they are read carefully and repeatedly, in order to keep control of the many narrative strands intertwined in complicated ways. Having explored Happel's emplotment of facts in his fiction, much of it based on contemporary media, I will now turn to reviewing specifically the construction of the *Romanisirungen*, his romances, to which he so frequently refers. To avoid confusion, I will concentrate only on the vagaries, trials, and tribulations of the lead characters in his romances. This will make it easier for us to explore the narrative construction of their action. We will see that none of the men or women is what we would call a "realistic" figure in the modern sense. Yet, as the action unfolds, we observe Happel's considerable acuity in introducing us to the emotions and personalities of his actors.

It is important to remember, first, that although part of the *romanische Handlung*, the "action of romance," Happel's characters move through these narratives while confronting and dealing with the historical, social, scientific, and cultural realities of their world, which together make up what I, following George Lakoff's lead, have elsewhere called "experiential realism."[7] According to Lakoff, experiential realism, or, as he also calls it, experientialism,[8] is characterized first by "a commitment to the existence of the real world" in which the characters, in this case Happel's men and women, act and move.

Second, there must be the recognition that "reality places constraints on concepts," even if fictional. This means that Happel's fictional characters act within the realities of their environment, not in some fairyland. Theirs is a world of wars, piracy, slavery, ransoms, religious conflicts, travel, and courtly diversions, as well as of encounters and conflicts with peasants and people of many different national, ethnic, and racial backgrounds. Additionally, his characters do not accept notions of the "scientific" or "wondrous" in their conversations without questioning them.[9] The occasional intrusion of magic into the action is vigorously discussed, even if clear pronouncements for or against its efficacy are missing.[10]

7. Gerhild Scholz Williams, *Defining Dominion: The Discourses of Magic and Witchcraft in Early Modern France and Germany*, Studies in Medieval and Early Modern Civilization 6 (Ann Arbor: University of Michigan Press, 1995), 18.

8. George Lakoff, *Women, Fire, and Dangerous Things: What Categories Reveal about the Mind* (Chicago: University of Chicago Press, 1987), xv.

9. Favorites among those are discussions about animal/human procreation, magical mirrors, bloody rains, and other such wonders.

10. I have dealt with the early modern magic/science dichotomy in Gerhild Scholz Williams, *Ways of Knowing in Early Modern Germany: Johannes Praetorius as a Witness to His Time*

Third for our purposes (fourth for Lakoff), there has to be "a commitment to the existence of a stable knowledge of the world," a knowledge that, in the case of Happel's novels, accounts for the important role of news, chorographies, travel narratives, and the many other items of early modern knowledge that keep the characters talking.[11]

While Lakoff's methodology relies on cognitive and linguistic assumptions about how we know what we know, he attempts "to bring together some of the evidence for the view that reason is embodied and imaginative."[12] In this investigation of Happel's romance action, I am interested in experiential realism, or experientialism, as a critical instrument that allows us to see how Happel's fictional characters navigate a world in tune with and based on contemporary realities as presented in the print media. For the purposes of a critical assessment of Happel's *Romanisirungen*, Lakoff's experientialism will help clarify the ways in which Happel shapes the categories and classifications that, in turn, help readers to articulate, organize, and name his characters' interaction with society and to accept that interaction as true. Thus, experientialism represents the totality of Happel's world as his characters confront the broadly constructed Other. It defines under which specific conditions, when, and why characters are able to accept mental constructs such as foreign cultures, in all their linguistic and ethnic complexity, as real, true, and accessible, as is the case when, for example, they experience slavery in a Muslim country. Finally, for this study, experiential realism conforms to what Thomasius praises as Happel's ability to construct narrative verisimilitude when he places his characters into a specific cultural environment, be it their own or the unfamiliar and foreign. In other words, Lakoff's categories help us understand life as it is experienced by the seventeenth-century reader and consistent with the "ways in which the collective cultural inventory of meanings and meaningful external forms . . . is spread over a population."[13] As we have explored in chapters 2 and 3, the assumption of a "stable knowledge of the world" (Lakoff's fourth point) is reflected in the rapid evolution of print journalism, in the increasing production and consumption of

(Aldershot: Ashgate, 2006), 111–68. Lakoff's third aspect of experientialism is of less interest and importance to us here. He mentions that there must be "a conception of truth that goes beyond the internal coherence" (*Women, Fire, and Dangerous Things*, 15).

11. For example, in an extended critique of the educational shortcomings of university professors, the *Academische Roman* enumerates that beyond canon law, they should know biblical geography, chorography, and topography (*AR* I: 237).

12. Lakoff, *Women, Fire, and Dangerous Things*, xvii.

13. Ulf Hannerz, *Cultural Complexity: Construction and Corrosion* (Chicago: University of Chicago Press, 1992), 7.

newspapers, journals, *Theatra*, and encyclopedic literature.[14] The "fiction" of these novels, the *romanische Handlungen* in which Happel's men and women participate, would not have been so popular if it did not fit with the experiential realism of the seventeenth-century readers.

Following his often-repeated formula of amalgamizing history and fiction to construct narrative verisimilitude, the experiential realism ("wahre beglaubigte Geschichte und mögliche wahrscheinliche Erfindung" [true history and truly proven invention]) of these novels is further guided by three constants affecting the lives of the characters, their friends, and their foes.[15] To recap, the characters are, first and foremost, avid consumers of news reports, a characteristic confirmed by the countless instances in these novels when they express the wish to read newspapers, have them read to them, and/or comment on what they have read or heard. Second, news about the internal and external politics and conflicts roiling the European continent and beyond prompts the characters to move from one political and military arena to another, occasionally changing allegiances along the way. Third, as they journey across Europe and beyond, they encounter strangers and distant Others—Tartars, Russians, Circassians, Turks, Asians, and Africans—and they intermittently find themselves compelled to shed their national prejudices. Or they find those prejudices confirmed, as is the case when they meet up with Frenchmen or Italians, offering Happel a platform for his sometimes rather unashamedly articulated anti-*Welsch* bias.

Moreover, several of the novels introduce a fourth aspect, the dramatic encounters with members of the lower classes, most often peasants. These encounters allow Happel to showcase his and presumably his seventeenth-century readers' negative predispositions toward peasants, highlighting much of seventeenth-century stereotyping of class and gender. In fact, given the occasional positive comments about the truly Other (the Turk, the African, or the Asian woman or man), it is easy to see that it is much more challenging for the actors—and presumably Happel's seventeenth-century readers—to overcome class differences than the differences of ethnicity or race.

Thus, the amalgam of history and romance elaborated in Happel's novels influences the characters' actions and, therewith, the progress of the narrative as the actors face the challenges posed by gender mix-ups, culture

14. Williams, *Ways of Knowing in Early Modern Germany*, 1–25.

15. Wilhelm Vosskamp, *Romantheorie in Deutschland: Von Martin Opitz bis Friedrich von Blanckenburg*, Germanistische Abhandlungen (Stuttgart: Metzler, 1973), 11. Vosskamp cites Wilhem von Stubenberg, Birken, and Zesen.

clashes, and conflicts of class. Specifically, Happel's observations about the disparities between love among the peasants and love among the nobility allow a glimpse at early modern assumptions about gender and class. Moreover, we note once again that few, if any, of Happel's novels proceed without pirates or robbers furnishing important narrative elements as the action moves along. Frequently separated and reunited, the characters are forced to confront strangers in strange lands and to handle existential crises of social and sexual displacement, allowing the reader to explore the strengths and weaknesses of his or her own reactions. Europe and the areas beyond metamorphose into an expansive matrix of geography and politics overlaid with a network of personal allegiances, faithful friendships, fiery passions, and cruel betrayals. In all the varieties of human experiences to emerge as topics in Happel's novels, the news media (consumed by his characters in endless variations) constantly serve to broaden the mental horizon of the reader, who, through reading, himself or herself becomes a traveler.[16]

In these novels, travel is the domain of young men and women; the old or even middle-aged (most often parents, nursemaids, relatives, or other persons of authority) remain sedentary, unfit for the excitement of the road, for the challenges of new lives, new loves, and new battles. In a world filled with political and military turmoil, these elders (even if not old in age) represent the stability to which the young return after their trials. They provide the voice of experience as they reminisce about their own travails and romances of long ago. In the end, their very presence stabilizes the gender roles that are so often rendered ambiguous in Happel's novels.

All of this brings up the question of why Happel's young people travel so much. Young men's voluntary or involuntary peregrinations are often prompted by reading about political events in faraway places or by joining friends who are themselves in search of adventure. When asked, for example, to formally join an army (whether imperial, English, or French), the protagonists usually decline, preferring to come and go as they please and to serve in wars of their own choosing.[17] At other times, they are compelled

---

16. "[N]eben den großen Unkosten/ auch einer gefährlichen Rayse dahin/ überheben/ wann er uns dieselbe . . . durch eine Beschreibung gleichsam vor Augen stellet" (Aside from the great cost, travel is also dangerous, so [it is very helpful] if we can just read about it [*EE* III: 223]). See Percy G. Adams, *Travel Literature and the Evolution of the Novel* (Lexington: University Press of Kentucky, 1983), 63.

17. In chapter 1, Siegfried rejects the offer of William of Orange, as does Cergely when asked to join Caprara before Munkács. The same is true for the valiant Moor Zolfiar in the *Ungarische Kriegs-Roman*: "Er wuste wol/ daß der unvergleichliche Mohr ein handverster Ritter war/ . . . daß er vor einen von den allertapffersten Cavalliern passiren kunte/ er wuste gar wol/

to search for lovers who are lost or presumed dead. Young women generally travel for pleasure, to escape unwanted male attention, or, like their male counterparts, to find a missing lover or husband-to-be. Both young men's and young women's travels are regularly complicated by political changes or by challenges in their personal lives that require them to move to different locales along the way, occasionally disguising themselves as people of the opposite sex or a different social class.

It is a challenge for the contemporary reader to follow the vagaries of these characters through the many episodes intertwining politics, history and romance, fact and fiction. However, the variations on the themes of separation, misfortune, and disguises—including, but not limited to, changed identities and cross-dressing practiced by both men and women—are presented with great imaginative verve and narrative energy. In this, Happel's novels reflect the seventeenth-century discussion about "true factual history and seemingly true fiction" that is considered the foundation of the novel.[18] The fictional aspects of Happel's *Romanisirungen* are embedded in the characters' experiential realism, which, in turn, controls the narrative evolution of these novels. They contribute to the narrative tension and direct the reader toward the eventual resolution, the "teaching moments" that, along with the entertainment, constitute the value of these novels as well as their claim to authority as teaching tools.[19] So confident is Happel in the success of his formula that he challenges critics to add whatever they wish to what he has written: "Solte sich nun jemand finden/ er sey wer er wolle/ der da Lust hätte/ eine oder andere Materie gerne in unserm Geschicht-Roman angeführet und abgehandelt zu wissen/ der hat mich allemahl zu seinen bereitwilligen Diensten/ und kann sothane Materie entweder an mich/ allhier nach Hamburg/ oder nach Ulm an den Verleger senden/ so soll die Sache schon geschehen/ was recht ist/ ohne daß wir uns vorbehalten/ in keine Partheylichkeiten einiger massen eingeflochten zu werden" (Should anyone be found, whoever he may be, who would like to see such material treated in the *Geschicht-Roman*, he would find me a willing helper to do so. He only needs to send me the materials either to me here in Hamburg or to my

---

daß er ein Voluntair, und unter keinem Regiment engagiret oder verbunden war/ dannen-hero erwählete er ihn zu seinem Beystand in dieser fürhabenden Schlacht" (He knew full well that the incomparable Moor was a true knight . . . that he could pass for one of the bravest cavaliers; he knew well that he was a volunteer and that he was not engaged with nor tied to any regiment; therefore he chose him to stand by him in the upcoming battle [*UK* IV: 587]).

18. Vosskamp, *Romantheorie in Deutschland*, 12–17.

19. Ibid., 60.

publishers in Ulm and I will see to it that the matter is taken care of with the assurance that no partiality will get into the text [*IS* I: *Vorrede*]).

In the following sections of this chapter, I will explore three aspects that are especially prominent in the romance action of Happel's novels. These are the narrative variations of friendship, the dramatic potential of cross-dressing and gender-bending, and, finally, the conflicts raised by love: high, low, and in between.

Beautiful Friends

As I noted in chapter 3, even in his first effort, the *Afrikanische Tarnolast*, Happel presented his *Romanisirungen* embedded in facts. We hear about the Ottoman siege of Vienna, about Mediterranean piracy and slavery, and, as the title would lead us to expect, much about the African states along the Atlantic, especially Guinea and Angola, which, according to one of the characters, used to be called Congo.[20] We are told that, with the help of the Portuguese, the son of the king, himself named Angola, had won the rule over the land whose name he changed to his own. We also hear about the brutality of the *Lusitanische* (Portuguese) governor, whose son is described as attacking Tarnolast without provocation. This incident alludes to the often-tense relationship between the Africans and the Portuguese on the west coast of Africa, especially Congo and Angola, during the first half of the seventeenth century.[21] At this stage in Happel's career, however, these facts do not yet dominate the action as clearly as in the later *Geschicht-Romane*. Contemporary history is certainly present in the *Tarnolast*, but it rarely rises to the surface of the action or to a position of parity with the fiction as it will in the later novels.

As we follow the characters on their seemingly endless series of (mis)adventures, we do encounter, as I have pointed out, much cross-dressing and gender-bending, and we meet martial maidens of a variety of ethnic backgrounds. Another theme woven throughout the fabric of the *Tarnolast* is that of multiple friendships expressed and experienced with much emotional intensity, whether between members of the same sex or between men and women. One of the characters, Princess Calandis, puts it

20. There are now two Congos (neither of which is Angola), and one of them shows up later in this chapter.

21. Linda M. Heywood and John K. Thornton, *Central Africans, Atlantic Creoles, and the Foundation of the Americas, 1585–1660* (Cambridge: Cambridge University Press, 2007), 109.

succinctly when she is about to suffer separation from her friend Reolisca, who is departing for Tunis: "Wann sich nahe Vewandte scheiden sollen/ so gehet's ihnen durchs Hertz/ wann sich aber die allerbeste Freunde von einander trennen/ so kan keiner von denen selben auß hefftiger Bestürtzung weinen" (When close relatives have to depart, it affects the heart; however, when true friends have to take leave of each other, they are so stricken that they are unable [even] to cry [*AT* I: 493]). In other words, the pain of separation so paralyzes the friends that they are unable even to shed tears.

Such moving scenes between women notwithstanding, at heart Happel's books are about men, which means that many of the most intriguing friendships he describes are those between men. The European Renaissance was well acquainted with heterosexual men writing about their passionate, even intimate love for other men.[22] As Merry Wiesner has noted, "same-sex attachments were often regarded as signs of virility" as long as they went along with masculine honor, strength, and military prowess.[23] Happel's novels chronicle several male friendships, some of them doubly fascinating because they involve men of different races. Such is the case in the *Tarnolast*, whose protagonist attracts friends not only because of his superior manly qualities but also because of his exceptional beauty. Beauty, as we will see, is the indispensable ingredient for attraction, whether between members of the opposite or the same sex. We encounter this ingredient in the *Ottomanische Bajazet* (1688) when Arbiel, a Greek knight, comes upon a group of Arabs and Turks engaged in a fight. The Turks are led by a handsome young knight barely twenty-three years old, his eyes ablaze with generosity and courage ("geführt von einem ansehnlichen Türckischen Jüngling/ dem die Großmüthig- und Tapfferkeit auß den Augen helle genug herfür leuchtete" [*OB* I: 19]). Arbiel joins the fight on the Turkish side, helping to assure them of victory. In gratitude, Oltranto, their young leader, "completely turns his heart" to Arbiel, who Oltranto says must henceforth always ride at his side. Arbiel politely expresses his appreciation while pointing out that he is a European Christian, a piece of information Oltranto waves aside, assuring Arbiel of his lifelong brotherly devotion: "[er] sich im Allergeringsten nicht kehrete/ sondern darbey bliebe/ daß er ihn Lebens-lang nicht weniger/ als seinen leiblichen Brudern/ lieben wolte" ([he] did not care in the least but

---

22. Todd W. Reeser, *Masculinities in Theory: An Introduction* (Oxford: Wiley-Blackwell, 2010), 2.

23. Merry E. Wiesner, *Women and Gender in Early Modern Europe*, ed. William Beik, 2nd ed., New Approaches to European History (Cambridge: Cambridge University Press, 2000), 306.

insisted that all his life he would love him like a brother [*OB* I: 20]). This friendship is doubly remarkable since it turns out that Oltranto is the Turkish emperor Mahomet's son with a Christian woman, Eumenia (*OB* III: 265).

An equally transcultural friendship binds Cergely and Zolfiar, a character who appears early in the *Ungarische Kriegs-Roman* under a different name and who is actually the African prince Orlian ("dann mein Vatter ist der grossse Neguz von Mohrenland/ und ich bin der Erb-Printz ORLIAN" [for my father is the great Neguz of the land of the Moors, and I am the successor to the throne Orlian]). His noble qualities, beauty, and valiant spirit are in no way affected, it appears, by the fact that he is dark-skinned (*UK* I: 84). With his close friend Cergely, he travels to Venice and Vienna, from whence they go their separate ways, Cergely moving on to Munkács (as we read in chapter 2) and Zolfiar returning to Venice, where he plans to lend his support in the imperial fight against the Ottomans (*UK* III: 385).[24] Along the way, he renders support to Count Königsmarck (1665–94) against the Turks. Like Caprara recognizing Cergely's innate virtue and valor, the count acknowledges that Zolfiar is "ein handvester Ritter/ . . . daß er vor einen von den allertapffersten Cavalliern passiren kunte/ er wuste gar wol/ daß er ein Voluntair, und unter keinem Regiment engagiret oder verbunden war/ dannen-hero erwählete er ihn zu seinem Beystand in dieser fürhabenden Schlacht" (a true knight . . . so that he could pass for one of the most renowned cavaliers. He knew that as a volunteer he did not have to fight for any one regiment except the one he had chosen to give his support to [*UK* IV: 586]). He leaves the novel's action and the reader after performing one more valiant deed: on his way back to his homeland, he rescues a handsome lady, the wife of the Pasha of Lepanto, from an attack by robbers in the woods (*UK* IV: 229).

Returning to Tarnolast, we find that confirmation of his beauty comes to the reader in many ways. When Jacob Cartier, a French sailor, first lays eyes on Tarnolast, he stares at him ("sahe ihn lange Zeit steiff an"), completely enraptured by his beauty ("war wegen seiner Schönheit . . . fast entzücket" [*AT* I:32]). Later, when Tarnolast turns up shipwrecked on the Madagascan shore, two sisters, the king's daughters, come upon the sleeping hero and

---

24. Happel included a detailed report on the Venetian/Turkish conflict in his *Thesaurus Exoticorum. Oder eine mit Aussländischen Raritäten und Geschichten Wohlversehene Schatz-Kammer Fürstellend Die Asiatische, Africanische und Americanische Nationes . . . Darauff folget eine Umständliche von Der Tuerckey Beschreibung . . . und sein verfluchtes Gesetz-Buch oder AKORAN* (Hamburg: Thomas von Wiering, 1688), pt. V: 114–66.

are mesmerized by his exquisite good looks, made all the more alluring by his naked upper body ("die große Zartheit des schönsten Leibes" [*AT* IV: 1026]). At this point, the story comes full circle: we remember that Tarnolast had originally been designated king of Madagascar, an honor he was forced by law to forgo after his conversion to Christianity.

Effusive praise is also directed at one of Tarnolast's companions, the German knight Florus, because of his manly blond beauty. We meet him amid a group of admiring "Mohren," among them the African king Hereochus, who gaze upon him as if he were an angelic vision. The king especially "kunte den frischen Florus nicht genug ansehen/ als welcher ein gantz halb Englische Gestalt/ gegen den Mohren zu rechnen hatte/ sintemal er allein ein Nordischer Europeer unter allen . . . war" (could not take his eyes off Florus, who appeared to him like an angel compared to the Moors, especially since he was the only northern European among them [*AT* III: 741]). A member of the German imperial nobility, Florus is not only beautiful but also learned. This handsome and articulate German knight, a politically astute reader of newspapers, belongs to a cast of German characters who will appear under different names in most of Happel's subsequent novels. Valiant, courteous, and (frequently) also very shy toward women, they are often given the role of teachers, delivering the chorographies that make up much of the instructional content of Happel's novels. Other characters in the novel often comment on the special bond that Florus shares with Tarnolast and Prince Oran ("die beiden Haupt-Fürsten"), a bond that makes the three appear like blood brothers ("als wie leibliche Brüder" [*AT* III: 797]).

Clearly, Florus and German characters of like disposition are more often friends of men than lovers of women. This is confirmed by yet another such character, Klaur, the resident German know-it-all in the *Italienische Spinelli* (1685). After the novel's protagonists find and marry their desired partners (at the end of four long volumes), we read that "Klaur aber nahm ihm beständig für/ der Liebe abgesagter Feind zu seyn/ biß zu seines Lebens Ende" (Klaur, however, was completely resolved never to give into feelings of love until the end of his life [*IS* IV: 399]).

On another occasion that serves to demonstrate the impact of exceptional male beauty on those present, the Duke of Florence acknowledges the African Tarnolast, described as moving through town like an angel who had come down to earth. He recognizes him as a man of noble birth, even though, as so often is the case in these novels, Tarnolast travels under an assumed name. His friend, the Portuguese Prince Oran, kisses him, exclaiming that God and Nature had created a masterpiece in this heavenly person (*AT* I: 112–14). In the ensuing narrative, Prince Oran expresses his great affection for Tarnolast by always wanting the two of them to dress alike. They are described as resembling each other like brothers, even though Oran is said to be of darker complexion and hair color than the African Tarnolast, whose white skin and blond, curly hair are the object of much fascination among the men and women they meet (*AT* I: 121). Later in the narrative, however, when Oran is traveling among the people of Angola, Princess Fialalla admires his "whiteness," exclaiming that she had never seen such a pale and delicate person ("dann einen solchen weissen zarten Menschen hatte sie die Tage ihres Lebens nicht gesehen" [*AT* IV: 951]). Once again, the gradations in skin color tend, as we noted in chapter 3, to catch the attention of the novel's actors without necessarily signaling negative characteristics.

Remaining with passionate friendships between men, we note that Oran's attachment to Tarnolast is described as so intense that he is loath to let him out of his sight, "dann seine innerliche Liebe und recht brüderliche Treu war gegen ihn so groß/ daß er seine Gesellschafft zu entbehren/ eine gantze Woche zu sein dauchte" (for his love and his truly brotherly faithfulness toward him were so great that he did not want to be apart from him for a week [*AT* I: 212]). Somewhat later, when Oran and Tarnolast share a bed, they talk all night about Tarnolast's missing bride, Clara. In the morning, Tarnolast leaves without saying good-bye, which prompts Oran to search everywhere for him "der ihm lieber war/ als die gantze Welt" (whom he loves more than the whole world), but in vain (*AT* I: 483). Tarnolast's charisma seems to extend to all with whom he comes into contact. Adding to his stable of devotees, Ariontes, king of Guinea, is also described as a very close friend ("vertrauliche Freundschaft"), so much so that they, too, share the same bed. This is judged proper by the narrator since they are said to be social equals ("in Betrachtung sie einander in Hoheit fast gleich" [*AT* I: 418]), even if Ariontes is wealthier in land and goods.

Not everyone, however, appreciates Tarnolast's beauty. The archbishop of Toledo, overcome by it as well as by Tarnolast's expert lute playing (he "stunde unterdessen als unbewegliches Bild und betrachtete als ein Entzuckter diesen köstlichen Lautenisten" [stood motionless as a painting and stared as if bewitched at this lovely lutist]), offers Tarnolast not only a gorgeous necklace but also an officer's post in his army. This prompts the other officers to insult Tarnolast by disparaging his "weibische Schönheit" (effeminate beauty). They suggest that he should wear women's clothing in order to draw even greater attention to his "grosse[n] Schönheit" (*AT* I: 174). Combat ensues, in which, of course, Tarnolast trounces his foes, proving again that manliness, not effeminacy, is reflected in his beauty as well as in his valor.

Toward the conclusion of the novel, it is by their beauty and valor that Tarnolast and his long-lost brother Dovial recognize each other after fighting a duel to an indeterminate end. The good looks of both men amaze onlookers: "unser Fürst [Oran] verwunderte sich dermassen über die Schönheit/ welches nach abgelöstem Helm nicht mehr verborgen war" (our prince was so amazed at his [Tarnolast's] beauty no longer hidden under the helmet now loosened [*AT* IV: 1169]).

As if this gorgeousness were not enough, Tarnolast has other assets as well. Finding him among a group of knights of different nationalities, they are amazed ("entsetzten sie sich") to hear him converse with each of them in his own language, African as well as European. This conforms to what we have heard about the great admiration directed at Friedrich von Schomberg for his knowledge of many languages. Clearly, such ability was considered a noble virtue, adding to the verisimilitude as the characters traverse many lands and meet many diverse people.

Reading the *Afrikanische Tarnolast*, we note (as I have previously mentioned) that all the basic narrative structures that Happel will employ in subsequent novels are already in place, if not yet quite developed. There will be different locales, more emphasis on contemporary history, more chorographic information, and more transfer of factual knowledge as Happel himself gains more control over story and character development by using more concise, more precisely formulated chapter headings and shorter chapters. He will also employ increasingly detailed indexes or tables of content to help orient the reader. The need for such organizing aids is already apparent to him in the *Tarnolast*, where the brief chapter headings barely suffice to guide the reader through each content-rich chapter. Responding to the need to periodically catch his reader up to the story, Happel twice constructs situations that allow him to list for review all of the characters. In both cases, he gathers them in the formal narrative setting of a meal, giving him the chance to reintroduce them by name: "Hiermit tratten sie insgesamt in den Grossen Eß-Saal" (thus they all entered the dining hall [*AT* III: 871]). Shortly thereafter, when the actors disperse to pursue their various passions and tasks, they are once again identified by name, adventure, and goal of their travels (*AT* III: 898–99). At the very end of the novel, we are told the names of our heroes ("die unsrigen") for one last time, as they disband to return home ("reiseten ein jeder nach seinem Orth wieder nach Haus" [each traveled to his home] [*AT* IV: 1209]).

We assume that this kind of closure was what Happel's readership expected. Some of his other novels describe how now married couples gather for conversations and newspaper readings; the marital pairing, however, is not always an even two and two. We encounter another unexpected variation on the theme in a story dealing with yet one more male friendship, told by Goribald, one of the protagonists of the *Bayrische Max*. The narrator announces his tale as true and as having taken place not long ago in France ("die sich in Wahrheit noch nicht lange zugetragen" [*BM* IV: 200]). Raising the expectations of his audience, Goribald hesitates to tell his story, for fear that they will find its French foolishness ("Frantzösischen Alfenzereyen") too annoying for listening. But because bad weather keeps the company indoors ("wegen übeler Witterung" [*BM* IV: 200]), he finally relents and shares it with them.

Goribald's is a story where romantic love and male friendship conflict, converge, and, in the end, find an unexpected ending. It is the tale of two noble, brave, and learned cavaliers, Flavigny and Sainte Columbe ("vornehme/ tapffere/ und wegen sonderbarer Klugkeit und hohem Verstand/ beruffene Cavalliere" [noble, courageous cavaliers known for their intelligence and reason]), who are deeply devoted to one another ("eine im höchsten Grad vertrauliche Freundschafft" [an abiding friendship] [*BM* IV: 201]). They tell each other everything and, having found women to be of ever-changeable minds ("wanckelmüthig"), decide to swear off love and marriage for good, only keeping company with each other. Their renunciation is not without its challenges, and both struggle mightily to overcome love's mortification ("deß Frauenzimmers Mortification"). But in the end, they renew their vow ("versprachen einander von neuem") to remain single (*BM* IV: 201).

Predictably, a visit to the house of a friend, the father of an exceedingly beautiful daughter of thirteen or fourteen years, changes everything. While it first appears as if the two *Sonderlinge* are completely oblivious to the charms of beautiful Justine, Flavigny falls in love (he "durch die Augen wegen der schönen Justine Feur gefangen" [had caught fire through his eyes because of this beautiful Justine] [*BM* IV: 202]). After the girl's father dies, the two men continue visiting the widow and her daughter, whose mourning black renders her even more beguiling to them. Love's revenge for his decision to disdain the love for a woman renders Flavigny helpless; he becomes Love's slave ("der Liebe Leibeigener" [*BM* IV: 203]). Though he hides his affliction from Columbe, the pact between them is effectively severed ("der gemachte Bund mit seinem Freu[n]de ware nun gebrochen"). Columbe notices the discomfort and changes in mood in his friend, but he fails to understand them. He accepts as true every "erdichteten Vorwand" advanced by Flavigny, who flees to Paris and thence to war without admitting the true reason for his flight. He returns after two years of service in the French king's army in Alsace, more in love with Justine than ever (*BM* IV: 204). He is determined to admit his love and openly break his vow to his friend, no matter how much Columbe might chastise or mock him (*BM* IV: 205).

Meanwhile, Columbe has given in to his parents' entreaties and agreed to get married. The two friends confess to each other their mutual decision to abandon their promise, a decision they both now find completely agreeable—until Flavigny learns that Columbe has married Justine. What follows is a psychologically revealing three-step between the two men and the completely unsuspecting Justine. The quandary between hoping against hope that his love might find fulfillment and the torture he suffers as he considers the potentially cruel betrayal of his most faithful friend drives Flavigny to the brink of despair. An unexpected turn, however, offers an equally unexpected solution, not without a quick nod to French/German prejudices: unable to explain Flavigny's strange melancholy, Justine suspects that he may have fallen in love with a German princess but does not want to admit to such passion, for fear of being mocked ("auß Furcht außgelacht zu werden" [*BM* IV: 210]). In other words, a German princess was clearly an unlikely object of a French nobleman's attraction. Goribald's German listeners have their own take on this tale. They confess that had the protagonists not been noblemen, they would not have believed that a Frenchman could have demonstrated such patience, hiding his love for such a long time ("deren Natur zuwider/ so lange hinter dem Berge/ und ihre Liebe verborgen zu halten/ sich auch mit so langer Gedult zu quälen" [contrary to nature hiding for such a long time and, with long patience, torturing himself] [*BM* IV: 212]).

Finally, after a year of misery, Flavigny writes a letter disclosing the truth to Justine, which she shares with her husband. At this point, a variation on the theme of male best friends introduces yet another twist to this story. Columbe is deeply affected by this disclosure—less, however, by his wife's predicament than by his friend's despair ("nicht so sehr in Ansehung seiner Frauen/ als wegen der Verzweiflung seines Freundes" [*BM* IV: 213]). This revelation leads to a most unexpected turn: Columbe reveals that he married Justine only to do his friend a favor. Furthermore, contrary to the deep love he feels for his friend, his affection for his wife is neutral at best ("lebte mit ihr etwas kaltsinnig/ da er hingegen seinen Freund auf das höchste liebete" [213]). He blames Justine for his friend's suffering and thus treats his wife with increasing coldness and indifference. In the meantime, Flavigny has fled all company, seeking refuge at his estate located a significant distance from Paris ("daselbsten einsam lebte/ und alle Gesellschafften flohe" [he lived there in solitude, avoiding all company] [*BM* IV: 214]).

Visiting his friend at his hiding place, Columbe, wishing nothing more than to assure himself of his friend's affection ("Zuneigung"), reveals not only that he does not love his wife but that he would rather spend his life with his friend than with a woman he does not love ("lieber sein Leben mit einem Freund so ihme lieb ware zu bringen/ als mit einer Frau/ die er nicht liebte/ leben wolte" [*BM* IV: 216]). He stays with Flavigny for several months, making no effort to hide his disdain and contempt toward his wife, who finally decides to enter a nunnery. After several more twists and turns in this unlikely story, Columbe admits to impotence and thus his inability ever to love a woman ("auß einigem Mangel der Natur/ niemahlen eine herztliche Zuneigung zu dem weiblichen Geschlecht haben können" [*BM* IV: 222]). In other words, despite three years of marriage, Justine has remained a virgin, a fact that opens the door to annulment and remarriage. Eagerly encouraged by Columbe, Justine and Flavigny confess their love for each other and, after allowing for the appropriate time to pass, exchange marriage vows. The threesome lives happily ever after—together: "Sainte Columbe . . . lebet nun mit seinem Freunde und Justinen in der allervollkommensten Verständnüß/ beide letztere aber in höchstvergnüglicher Liebeszufriedenheit" [Sainte Columbe . . . now lived with his friend and Justine in complete harmony, the latter in happy fulfillment of their love] [*BM* IV: 226]). Friendship does indeed come in many forms in Happel's novels.

Cross-Dressing

In chapter 3, we reviewed cross-dressing in the context of the *Tarnolast*'s slaving narrative. In the context of Happel's *Romanisirungen*, cross-dressing joins intense male friendships and the worship of noble male and female beauty as yet another narrative device of great dramatic power and versatility. In her recent survey of women warriors in German literature, *Beauty or Beast*, Helen Watanabe-O'Kelly has explored the experiential realism implicit in the woman warrior as a cross-dresser who breaks the cultural convention demanding that clothing conform to the gendered body. Thus, the cross-dresser, whether male or female, destabilizes cultural norms, bringing uncertainty or even chaos to social interactions.[25] Watanabe-O'Kelly devotes

---

25. Helen Watanabe-O'Kelly, *Beauty or Beast? The Woman Warrior in the German Imagina-*

a chapter of her book to the martial maiden, the "unbecoming" woman or cross-dresser, as one example of the "manly" woman whose strength and virtue emerge as being very much like that of a man's. One of those warrior maidens is the female protagonist of Andreas Heinrich Bucholtz's (1607–71) lengthy novel *Herkules und Valiska* (1659–60). Less "classy" but no less fascinating is the titular heroine of Hans Jakob Christoph von Grimmelshausen's novel *Courasche* (1670), also set during the Thirty Years' War.[26]

Bucholtz and Grimmelshausen, both Happel's contemporaries, constructed heroines whose spunk, manly courage, and dexterity with all manner of weaponry, as well as the ease with which they move about in man's clothing, made them readers' favorites—Courasche to this very day. Unlike Courasche, however, whose sexual appetites are very pronounced (even voracious), Bucholtz's Valiska remains virginal until wed. After having been married for some time, she hosts a tournament dressed as an Amazon, engaging in manly deeds that would be considered far beyond a woman's strength.[27] Already familiar with the *Amazonninen* in Happel's novels, we know that as a special class of woman, Amazons possess strength equal to or exceeding that of a man. Dressing as an Amazon enables (empowers) these martial women to display this strength, which would otherwise be condemned as unwomanly. In addition, not unlike Happel's Eduard and Edmunda (to whom I will turn momentarily), Herkules and Valiska are described as so completely interchangeable in their virtue, courage, and beauty that they become "two aspects of the same person, and together they make up one perfect human being," merging the masculine and feminine in such a way that cross-dressing loses its (mis)identifying power.[28]

In the *Bayrische Max* (published posthumously in 1692), Happel's *Geschicht-Roman* for "sonderbare Liebhaber/ und curieuse Gemüther" (special lovers and the curious), we encounter the intrepid Corinne, "ein Muster eines Gottlosen/ boßhafften und abgefäumten Weibes; Raachgi-

---

tion from the Renaissance to the Present* (Oxford: Oxford University Press, 2010), 183–203 and bibliography; also see Reeser, *Masculinities in Theory*, 35–37.

26. Hans Jakob Christoph von Grimmelshausen, *Lebensbeschreibung der Erzbetrügerin und Landstörzerin Courasche* (1670), ed. Klaus Haberkamm and Günther Weydt, Universalbibliothek 7998 (Stuttgart: Reclam, 2001). Grimmelshausen's *Courasche* also influenced a later work that Happel had seen (he mentions it in his *Relationes Curiosae* [1685]), *Falsette/ Das ist eine Beschreibung einer Ertzbetrügerin* (1686). See Dieter Breuer, "In Grimmelshausen's Tracks: The Literary and Cultural Legacy," in *A Companion to the Works of Grimmelshausen*, ed. Karl Otto Jr. (Rochester: Camden House, 2003), 240; Watanabe-O'Kelly, *Beauty or Beast?*, 198–202.

27. Watanabe-O'Kelly, *Beauty or Beast?*, 193.

28. Ibid., 192.

eriges/ ungetreues/ arglistiges und verschlagenes Frauenzimmer" (a model of a godless, mean, scheming woman; vengeful, unfaithful, conniving, and sly bitch)—in short, a character very much constructed in the image of Courasche,[29] bearing a striking resemblance to Grimmelhausen's heroine in character, action, and even biography. We meet Corinne as she is attending as a maid ("Cammer-Mensch") to the wife of Lord Dumpart, a nobleman attached to the English court. She gained employment in the Dumpart household by misrepresenting herself as a French Protestant fleeing persecution in her homeland. (Her tale thus highlights the fact that along with many honest and desperate refugees came others who abused peoples' goodwill toward those hurt by the French persecutions.) In this new position, Corinne is about to get into serious trouble with her mistress and Lord Dumpart. Bribed with presents and sweet words by the dissolute knight Furfant, she helps him enter the chamber where the traveling Lady Dumpart has fallen asleep while waiting for her carriage to be repaired. Furfant surreptitiously slips into the lady's chamber, ready to kiss her lips and touch her breasts ("buhlerisch betasten" [*BM* I: 38]), which the lady has inadvertently left exposed. Lady Dumpart awakens with a start and, with loud cries, tells him to be gone. Before obeying, he blames his misdeed on his well-established passion for the lady. Corinne's role in the assault is discovered by the German knight Teuto, who thwarts Furfant's dastardly intent. But as Lord Dumpart makes ready to punish her, Corinne implores him and his friends to listen to her story, which reads very much like Courasche's biography.

A "schlaues und durchtriebenes Weibes-Bild" (scheming and conniving woman), Corinne has no trouble spinning her tale for her eager audience. Constructing herself as only partially responsible for her trespasses, she pities and blames herself as a toy in Fortuna's hands, a mirror of inconstancy, vessel of shame, and blemish on the face of the female sex (*BM* I: 71). Like Courasche, she is of noble birth, but her innately bad character led her to waste all her good fortune. Exceedingly beautiful, she was married off early on by her parents to a much older man. This often-used narrative ploy affords Happel a chance, as it does many writers of his time, to blame young women's early marriage to much older men for much immorality among married women, whose desires in such ill-conceived matches remain unfulfilled.

In Corinne's case, she immediately takes up with multiple lovers—if platonically, as she insists. Nonetheless, her husband soon tires of her affairs

29. *BM* I: 31, 63, 78ff.

and places her in a nunnery, from which she flees with the help of an army captain. She gets pregnant, is sold into slavery, and becomes a prostitute. While pursuing this profession, she picks up an illness, possibly syphilis (or "the French disease"), which temporarily ravages her beauty and puts her into a hospital. The attending physician turns out to be the perfect match for her: a French cavalier by birth, well read and intelligent, he is a person of less-than-sterling qualities, "arglistig und abgefäumt/ von schlechter Treu und Aufrichtigkeit/ im Werck ein Betrüger/ und seiner Profession nach ein Räuber und Beutelschneider" (manipulative and cunning, unfaithful, in all his works a cheat and by profession a robber and pickpocket [*BM* I: 180]). He teaches Corinne everything he knows, and dressed and cross-dressed as two wandering pilgrims ("wallfahrende Einsiedler"), they go about flim-flamming the unsuspecting public, especially women who fall in love with the man they take Corinne to be. Under her rough male exterior, her female masculinity signals to them something delicate and well mannered, which prompts them to commit all kinds of foolishness ("und begiengen hunder-terley Thorheiten" [*BM* I: 85]). Here, then, we are entertained by another of Happel's favorite narrative effects regarding cross-dressing: in projecting a beguiling masculinity, Corinne awakens inappropriate passions in her female audience. Nevertheless, she and her partner in crime are eventually caught; he is executed, while she is thrown into prison, from which she escapes with the help of a troupe of actors. She begins a new life as "Comoe-diantin," wandering from town to town. Along the way, she marries a *Mar-quetenter*, who leaves her his wealth upon his death. Tired of the wandering life and after having learned, she says, that virtue alone brings happiness, she quits the troupe and sets out for England, where, as already mentioned, she pretends to be a Protestant refugee. In this role, she deceitfully garners much goodwill and assistance ("genosse unter diesem Schein/ auch vielfältige Gut-thaten" [*BM* I: 88]).

Coming to the end of her story, Corinne asks forgiveness from her audi-ence, most importantly Dumpart. Rather than insisting that she go to court and be punished for her crimes, he tells her to be gone and never to return (*BM* I: 90). The reason for this seemingly strange generosity is Dumpart's pragmatic wish not to have himself or his wife dragged through a lengthy trial, which would cause boundless gossip.

This would seem to be the end of the story (*BM* II: 327). But the tale does not end with this development. Instead, while cleaning out Corinne's room, Lady Dumpart finds the correspondence between Corinne and Fur-fant, which describes the whole story of their misdeeds. Then Teuto and

Lord Dumpart encounter Corinne again, once more hiding in man's clothing. Along with several peasants, she has watched a duel between Teuto and the English knight Gram. She falsely denounces the victorious Teuto to the surrounding peasant crowd as a Catholic spy, whereupon he is taken prisoner and brought to London to be put on trial (*BM* I: 178ff). Not only is Corinne's lie discovered, but the court also finds out about her role in a conspiracy to kill the king of England. She is imprisoned, at which point it seems that Happel intends to leave her to her fate ("wir überlassen sie anjetzo ihrem Richter/ in der Hoffnung/ sie werde nach Verdienst ihrer Wercke abgestrafft warden" [we will leave her now to her judge in the hope that she will be punished in accordance with her deeds] [*BM* I: 184]).

But once again the narrative strands separate and rejoin in unexpected ways. Corinne surfaces some time later when two officers get into a fight, each claiming to have been her husband in a former life (*BM* II: 323). This prompts another one of Happel's rare authorial comments: that one should not be surprised at the "schnelle Gemüths-Aenderung der Soldaten-Weiber" (how quickly soldier's women change their minds). If they lose their man in battle today, they will come to terms ("sich engagiret") with the loss tomorrow or the day after and marry again, all of which confirms that nothing is more inconstant than a woman's mind ("nichts variablers als Menschen-bevorab Weiber-Sinn ist"). Bringing his reader along in the story, Happel tells us that Corinne flees London and, in the company of English soldiers, crosses the Channel on her way back to the Spanish Netherlands. She reconnects with the *Musquetirer* who, in years past, had callously hired her out as a whore. Infuriated over this past ill treatment, she attacks him with a knife. Further on, she meets the captain who had freed her from the cloister. He loses his life fighting another man over her. All these conflagrations lead Max to suspect that the "Ertz-Bösewichtin Corinne" is the one behind all this bloodshed. But before his hunch can be confirmed, she escapes, "weil sie zu gute Freunde hatte/ die ihr durchhalffen/ weil sie ihnen/ wie gar wol zu vermuthen/ auch manchen guten Reuter-Dienst geleistet" (because she had many good friends who helped her because she, as might be surmised, had served [serviced] them with many a good ride [*BM* II: 327]). The double entendre suggests that she will once again disappear among the soldiers, servicing them as she has in the past.

For the time being, Max and several of his friends decide to join King William's English campaign. Along the way, they rescue a noble Frenchman, Corindo, from attacking robbers. Impressing them with his good manners, he joins the group (he "in so weniger Zeit sich schon ziemlich bey ihnen eingeschmeichelt und in guten credit gesetzet" [in a short time had talked himself into their good graces] [*BM* II: 344]). Corindo introduces himself as "ein geborner Frantzoß/ eines vorrnehmen Kauffmann's Sohn/ aber jetzo seiner Eltern und größten Theils seines Vermögens/ weil seine Eltern Hugenotten gewesen waren/ beraubet seye" (a Frenchman by birth, a wealthy merchant's son whose parents had lost most of their fortune because they were Huguenots [*BM* III: 106–7]). Not until the end of the novel is Corindo outed as Corinne by two of the protagonists, Theodelinde and Mariana. Once again, the turmoil brought about by the movement of Protestant refugees across borders and countries had supplied a credible story (as noted in chapter 2) supporting the experiential realism of Corinne's life.

When Corinne, a beautiful woman once again, joins the company on Max and Theodelinde's wedding day, one of the characters, Flenston, recognizes her. In a fit of rage, he tries to kill her, calling her a "verfluchte Bestie" (cursed beast) and accusing her of trying to disturb honest people's peace: "dein gottloses Gifft noch weiter außbreiten/ nachdem Franckreich/ Engelund Niederland/ dessen schon so viel geprüffet" (you have spread your godless poison far enough after you have spread it already across France, England, and the Netherlands [*BM* IV: 431]). Max and his friends, however, decide that her valiant deeds in men's dress make up for the crimes she committed in the past. All is thus forgiven, and she is welcomed to join Max and Theodelinde's court (*BM* IV: 432).

Unlike Courasche, who dies an ignominious death, Corinne, by the penance she has done as a "man," returns to the life of wealth and virtue rejected in her youthful sexual rebellion. Her adventurous and, in parts, criminal life affords the reader a glimpse at her repeated changes in gender and social milieu as she transforms herself from privileged and pampered daughter of wealthy parents to fake physician, cheating moneylender, and traveling actor. Should the reader desire to recall Corinne's evil life at its worst and thus doubly appreciate her conversion, Happel directs us to the twenty-fifth chapter of the second book ("25. Cap. Deß 2. Theils") for a recap (*BM* IV: 432).

These examples of switches in social and gender performance demonstrate that though Happel's is indeed a man's world, his heroines are occasionally able (however briefly) to leave their assigned station in life for the world of the Other, be it as member of the opposite gender or of a different social milieu. Another of these travelers in the realms of early modern female masculinity is Tescola, one of the many cross-dressing women who populate the *Ungarische Kriegs-Roman*. We come across her in volume 5, the last volume written by Happel himself. Like many of Happel's protagonists we have observed, Tescola is very much at ease entertaining her friends with the details of her adventures (*UK* V: 858). One of those has her, as the reader might expect, shipwrecked on her way to Constantinople. She is picked up by Cossacks, who made the area around and across the Black Sea very unsafe at that time. She escapes and travels to Poland, hiding in Polish men's clothing and carrying a gun. From there, she proceeds to Vienna, resolved to lend support against the Ottoman siege. In this role, she rescues Cergely from an attack by a huge aga ("Baum-starcken Aga"), cutting off his hand with her sword—a very martial maiden indeed. Thereafter captured by Turks and sold and resold several times, she ends up first in Syria and then in Gaza, where, still in men's dress under the name of Tesco, she serves as a soldier, guarding the ramparts of Gaza for a Christian Palestinian prince. Threatened by Turks with either "Beschneidung" (circumcision) or death by burning for wearing green (a crime for infidels), she is rescued by the valiant Moor ("ansehnlicher Mohr") Zolfiar, a noble African prince from Nubia who is also a Christian. (We remember him as the beautiful Moor who, as Orlian, befriends Cergely early in the *Kriegs-Roman* [*UK* V: 862–65]). All ends with yet another cross-dressing twist: Tescola, still dressed as a man, agrees to do combat with the Princess Basky, Cergely's love interest, to help decide who will be Cergely's bride ("Dann ich hatte mir vorgenommen/ selber in einen Amazonischen Habit bey dem Kampff zu erscheinen/ und mit ihr zu kämpffen" [I had decided to appear in Amazonian dress and face her in combat] [*UK* V: 863]). The cross-dressed man becomes the Amazon Tescola, who, as the martial maiden, defeats Princess Basky (also dressed in Amazon garb) to win the hand of her love, Cergely.

With this happy ending, Happel seems to assume that he has reached the end of the Hungarian story. But far from it: the war had not yet reached its end, and after Happel's death, the anonymous continuator picked up where he left off, again separating and finally reuniting the long-suffering couples.

Love: High and Low

By the mid-1680s, Happel had refined the narrative template he applied to the romantic actions of his novels to the point that he could refer to it as something that his audience expected and liked. The women and men populating his novels are young and either noble or the children of wealthy merchants. They are single, as are the men and women whom they meet and lose and meet again. Happel's *Geschicht-Romane*, however, are not family romances in the traditional sense. When parents or elders do show up, their appearance usually serves to clear up some confusion about a character's real parents (*Max*), to provide the impetus for a character to leave home (*Eduard*), or to supply information that can only be obtained from a person who, by staying home, is familiar with past history.

The female characters, of noble birth or from wealthy bourgeois families, are resourceful, courageous, and well educated. They hold their own in the endless conversations that fill the pages of Happel's novels; in fact, a few among them are praised for their extraordinary learnedness.[30] The *Academische Roman* introduces the reader to several examples of female erudition. Following Happel's model of German learnedness, one of the protagonists, the German Klingenfeld, whom we have already met several times, encourages two young women to demonstrate to their audience their ability to speak Latin. To help them overcome their reticence, he tells them about the famous Carola Catharina Patina, whose beautiful Latin oration upon the lifting of the Ottoman siege in 1683 amazed everyone in Vienna ("über den glücklichen Entsatz der Stadt Wien" [about the fortuitous delivery of the city of Vienna] [*AR* I: 276]).[31] One of the two women, Ilmene (who later turns out to be a man in cross-dress), adds that many a German prince was eager to get to know this learned lady. Ilmene introduces herself as a noblewoman from Greece, which clearly eases the challenges of keeping up appearances.

A discussion about the nature of love follows, which ends with the observation that, because they live a freer life, Egyptian and German women are much less lustful than Italian and French women. The ensuing conversation about learned women past and present introduces the famous Spanish poetess Eloisa Sigea (1522–60), whom the novel credits with knowing Latin, Greek, Hebrew, Syrian, and Arabic.[32] Klingenfeld vigorously rejects the rumor that this devout and learned woman had written an ugly book about love ("ein häßliches Liebes-Buch"). Moreover, her sister Angela is said to have been equally learned (*AR* I: 283).

The novels' highborn young men and women do not, however, remain

---

30. One of them is certainly the Thökölin (whom I discuss thoroughly in chapter 2).

31. Charlotte-Catherine and Gabrielle-Charlotte Patina of Paris were a mother and daughter who resided in Padua. Charlotte-Catherine (Carola) wrote poetry and a number of essays, the most famous among them being an oration on the lifting of the siege of Vienna (1683).

32. One of the first works of Western erotic fiction, *Dialogues of Luisa Sigea*, was falsely attributed to her.

only among themselves. During the course of their travels, away from the comforts of home and friends, they occasionally are faced with challenging predicaments brought about by encounters with peasants and other characters of the lower classes. Such encounters frequently end up being potentially dangerous for them. Though untrained in the art of combat, peasants tend, if provoked or suspicious, to gather in groups, often armed with weapons or farm implements just as lethal as swords or guns.

Peasant girls whom the protagonists meet along the way are generally described as passionate and very direct in the pursuit of what they see as their potential or even promised partner and as not given to delaying the gratification of their desires. Although several of them do show themselves to be faithful, steadfast, and resourceful, the line demarcating the social difference between them and the leading male and female characters is clearly drawn and insurmountable. For example, even when a peasant girl saves a young nobleman's life and falls deeply in love with him, any promises of marriage that the young man extends in return for her help are not expected to be kept. Class represents "true" social value, and thus, regardless of ethnicity or culture, members of the upper classes (except for those who pretend, like the knight Furfant) remain paragons of virtue and beauty, while peasants are seen as unrefined and unhandsome. The two may mingle sexually, but never romantically.

It can be said (tipping a cap to the spaghetti Western of old) that Happel's female characters come in three types: "the good, the bad, and the ugly." Like Corinne/Corindo, some of them metamorphose from one category into the other and back again during the course of the narrative. An example is Maestra, a female lead in the *Spanische Quintana*. The death of her father forces her to obey the advice of her mother and of the king of Portugal (at whose court her father had served) to marry the noble and wealthy Prince Rotalino. Shortly after the wedding, she seems to change, at least in Rotalino's mind's eye, from a beautiful woman into an ugly hag: "Ich kan selber es nicht sagen/ wie sobald ihre Schönheit abgenommen/ daß sie ihre Rosenfarbe verlohr/ unter dem gantzen Gesicht erblassete/ und gantz runtzelig ward. Solches erweckte in mir einen Widerwillen gegen Maestra . . . daß ich sie bald hernach auß einem/ wiewohl mir unbekannten/ innerlichen Trieb/ nicht mehr vor meinen Augen sehen konnte noch wollte" (I cannot say how her beauty diminished so soon so that her rose color disappeared and her whole face grew pale and that she became all wrinkly. This raised such an aversion in me that I soon did not want to see her anymore, for some reason that was not clear to me [*SQ* I: 7–8]). Later, it turns out that

Rotalino's aversion is caused by a spell cast on her by a witch, on behalf of a woman who was herself in love with Rotalino.[33] This is yet another occasion when adversity—whether brought about by difficult family circumstances; malevolent magic; or encounters with pirates, robbers, or inclement weather—keeps the characters moving. Undeterred by this misfortune and unbeknownst to Rotalino, Maestra shadows him for several years as he travels far and wide in an attempt to find himself. She hides in various disguises, including cross-dress, while her husband wanders all across Europe in the company of other cavaliers who search for women and adventure.

Ignoring his marriage vows, Rotalino gets into romantic entanglements with several women, all of whom, as it turns out, are Maestra in disguise. She conceives two children as a result of these encounters with a husband who does not recognize her as his wife and thus commits adultery in his heart. Maestra leaves the two children to be raised by a trusted friend. But she does not stop here. Traveling in cross-dress because of the insecure roads, she accepts the position of administrator at the court of the Duke of Ferreine in Algarve (a province in Portugal)—thus demonstrating that she is clearly capable of filling a man's position at court. When she and Rotalino meet once again, she saves him from murderous thugs, proving her valor to be as exceptional as her administrative talents and fidelity (*SQ* IV: 288–89).

Love and magic mix once again in the *Spinelli*, when the title character has a dramatic encounter with a beautiful woman who turns out not to be what he assumes. Traveling in Italy, a friend introduces Spinelli to a charming and learned lady, describing her as "eine der gelahrtesten Damen/ so die Welt jemahlen herfürgebracht" (one of the most learned ladies ever born into this world [*IS* I: 111ff.]). Of course, Spinelli's curiosity is piqued; he wishes to meet and get to know her better. Seeming to return the attraction, she takes him to a room whose walls are adorned with many "Geschichtbilder" (murals depicting historical events), another room furnished with splendid cabinets, and a third room filled with magnificent statues. All the while, he hears music played on exquisite instruments (*IS* I: 113). Stunned by the apparent wealth conveyed by these chambers of wonder, Spinelli watches, enthralled, as she opens yet another cabinet. To his horror, it is filled with skeletons, some with the flesh still clinging to their bones. As they move out of the cabinet toward him, he strikes at them but, unable to wound them,

---

33. The wife of a farmer admits that she had started the whole thing because of another woman who had been in love with Rotalino. But Maestra's constant prayers had forced her to abandon her magic spells (*SQ* IV: 273).

must flee to another room. The next morning, he realizes that he had seen an apparition, the work of a ghost who dwelled in the rooms, unused for many years because a murder had been committed there. Ever since, the ghost and his female companion have haunted the castle (*IS* I: 114), bearing witness to their deadly love through potentially deadly magic.[34] Spinelli moves on, but not without his servant mocking him about his apparent cowardice in the face of ghostly encounters.

The peripatetic life of Happel's characters, whether pursued voluntarily or not, lends great narrative openness to his novels. The women characters in particular gain extraordinary agency and freedom of movement from this openness. While men experience foreign culture in war or travel, women in cross-dress experience men's roles (as a kind of foreignness) before they ever even leave their native countries. For both sexes, cross-dressing (either by compulsion or by design) or hiding their identities by taking on different names and social roles broadens the horizon of the narrative geographically, socially, and sexually.

Extreme and unforeseen consequences sometimes follow from such pretending. Spinelli saves one of his friends, Don Severino, along with a Muslim woman, Salari, from slavery. Very much in love with Severino, Salari agrees not only to marry him but also to be baptized in order to return with him to his Christian homeland. Shortly after gaining his freedom, however, Severino, now again assuming his true noble persona, is reunited with his true love, Mardi, whom he had believed dead. Rejected, abandoned, and unable to return to her homeland, Salari commits suicide, one of several violent and, in baroque novels, not unfamiliar reactions of women betrayed by their lovers. Far from living happily ever after, however, Severino and Mardi also die, killed by random bullets on the day of their wedding ("am Tage des Beylagers ohngefehr erschossen" [*IS* I: 344]). No explanation is offered aside from the sad fact, commemorated with a beautiful funeral and a moving sentiment inscribed on their gravestone.

Two novels we have already encountered several times, the *Teutsche Carl* and the *Engelländische Eduard*, also combine history, politics, and passion with extensive travels across Europe.[35] The action of both novels unfolds around two pairs, Carl and Cyclaste and Eduard and Edmunda, respectively, who, in complicated and life-threatening ways, become entangled with lech-

---

34. "Monsters come with the house." David R. Castillo, *Baroque Horrors: Roots of the Fantastic in the Age of Curiosity* (Ann Arbor: University of Michigan Press, 2010), xiii.

35. Eberhard Werner Happel, *Dess Teutschen Carls/ Oder so genannten Europäischen Geschicht-Romans auf das 1689. Jahr* (Ulm: Matthaeus Wagner, 1690).

erous members of their own class as well as with peasants. Peasants mostly stay close to home, but when they do travel, they frequently create havoc for any strangers they encounter. Birlot, one of the characters in the *Bayrische Max*, describes peasants as beasts who behave properly only when under the firm control of their master: "[Birlot] wuste wol/ daß/ wann man unter der Bauren Hand und Gewalt/ man denselbigen gute Worte geben müsse/ so man anders ohne Beschimpffung oder Schaden von ihnen zu kommen gedencket/ weilen durchgehends/ aller Orthen und Enden/ kein ärgeres und bestialischeres Volck und Gesinde ist/ als die Bauren/ wann sie sehen/ daß sie einigen Gewalt oder Vortheil über jemand . . . haben" (He [Birlot] knew well that when one is in the hand of the peasants one has to speak nicely to them so that one can get away from them without being cursed or getting into any other trouble, maybe even being hanged. That is because there is far and wide no worse riffraff than peasants if they think they have power over you [*BM* III: 140]). When peasants love, Happel tells us, they do so foolishly, never comprehending that their passions directed at those beyond their social station will always remain unrequited.

Still, when noblemen and noblewomen travel, often in disguise, they frequently find themselves in situations where they are forced to ask for and accept assistance. In return and always under duress, they make promises that they have no intention of keeping. Such disingenuous dealings with those beneath their station predictably lead to dangerous entanglements and amusing and occasionally threatening encounters. For the modern reader, who is just as likely to feel empathetic toward the betrayed peasant as appalled by the peasants' ill-placed desire, these situations tend to evoke contradictory emotions.[36]

Peasant love as described by Happel, oriented toward immediate sexual fulfillment and swift marriage, is circumscribed by village morality, which, in turn, is upheld by the expectations of family and community. If accepted under false premises and left unrequited, peasant love turns quickly into aggressive possessiveness and vengefulness. Noble love, including passionate friendship, covers a much wider spectrum of emotional and physical responses and experiences. Noble lovers and friends suffer long separations or traverse great distances before the destined happy ending can be reached. Sometimes a nobleman, such as the knights Furfant and Hardiknut, will

---

36. In addition, when broken promises find their way into the local courts, the straightforward, if brutal, sense of justice of the locals contrasts sharply with the courtliness and polite legal argumentation of the noble traveler.

exhibit impatience, sometimes to the point of forcing the consummation of a romantic or even sexual encounter in conflict with the required trial time. He might not acknowledge or respect mutual desire, thus signaling a serious lack of character and morals that will eventually exact the appropriate punishment. In other words, noble birth does not, in and of itself, confer nobility of character and action. As we see in Furfant, Corinne's flimflamming French physician, Corinne herself, and Eduard's lecherous father (discussed later in this chapter), incestuous, illicit, violent desires, as well as cheating and betrayal, are also found among the highborn—though, in Happel's novels, not as frequently and reliably as a steadfast loyalty that perseveres through long absences and encounters with all kinds of temptations.

Even in the unambiguous division between high- and low-class lovers, Happel occasionally introduces some fine-grained distinctions. The most memorable among them involve two peasant girls—one German, one English—who play a significant role in the *Teutsche Carl*. They are Cyclaste's companion Ursula and an unnamed English country girl. Both represent an exception to the prohibition against crossing the seemingly unbridgeable divide between the romantic responses of the nobility and those of the peasants. Their genuine faithfulness and resourcefulness in love are rewarded in the end, though not with the object of their desires.

Before we meet the novel's protagonist, Carl, his childhood friend and companion Baldrich tells us that his own tale is so entwined with Carl's as to be inseparable: "Deß Carl und meiner Begebenheiten sind demnach dergestalt in einander verknüpffet/ daß keine ohne die andere völlig mag begriffen werden" (Carl's and my experiences are interwoven in such a way that neither can be understood without understanding both [*DC* I: 322]). Baldrich, however, is not privileged with any knowledge of Carl's true identity as a baron, knight, or *Reichs-Graf* (*DC* I: 335). At this point, we learn only that Carl travels disguised as a wealthy English merchant's son. Confirming Happel's strong pro-English sentiments, his detailed knowledge of English history and politics, and his support for the Protestant cause, Carl is described as being in good standing at the court of William of Orange. Highlighting the ease with which he moves on the European stage, Carl also strikes up a friendship with the French dauphin and, while on his way to Paris, saves his life. Considering the strongly critical comments throughout the novel that are directed at the rapacious war of destruction and conquest carried out by Louis XIV in the Palatinate during the late 1680s, this fictional friendship is worthy of note. French cruelties, broken treaties, and deceptions are described in great detail in the *Teutsche Carl* and several of the other *Geschicht-Romane*: "Der Frantzosen Greuel in der Pfalz wird erzehlet (the horrible deeds of the French in the Palatinum are told [*DC* II: 313]); Kayserliche[s] Commissions-Decret. Frantzosen den Stillstand vom 15. August 1684 nicht beachtet . . . gegen alle Gött-Geist- und Weltliche Rechten/ Münster- und Nimwegischen Friedens-Schlüsse (Imperial decree: the French have disregarded the truce of August 15, 1684 . . . against all divine, spiritual and worldly rights, the Peace of Münster and Nimwegen [*DC* I: 336]). It is rare for Happel to suggest that a Frenchman is worthy of friendship.

In Paris, Carl meets Cyclaste, the daughter of the wealthy French merchant Valcour, who is also Carl's personal banker. At this stage, the narrative closely resembles the popular French novel *L'Illustre Parisienne* (1679) by Sieur de Prechac, a nobleman and author of novels at the court of the Duke of Orléans.[37] Prechac's novel tells of a duke's son, disguised as a wealthy merchant's son from Hamburg, who stays as a guest at the house of a prosperous Paris banker. The banker's daughter, Blanche, falls in love with the young man and, after his departure, follows him to his homeland. We can assume that Happel was familiar with the novel, which appeared in four German translations between 1680 and 1734.[38] Like Happel's novel, the French "original" entertains the reader with a series of misunderstandings and disguises characteristic of what Singer calls a "comedy of errors" (*Verwechslungskomödie*).[39]

Happel's novel transcends the comedic character of its model, however, situating the romantic story (as always) within the context of contemporary history and culture. In addition to his expert intertwining of history and romance, Happel directs his reader to "seek out this world in order to learn" rather than to find respite in the escapism of mere comedy.[40] While we find comedic situations and comic characters in several of his novels, comic action as such rarely dominates the main stage. When Happel does introduce a comic character—except in the *Academische Roman*, which contains several—he apologizes to his readers, insisting that he does so only in response to readers' demands. Concerning Horuch, Spinelli's comic side-

---

37. Herbert Singer, *Der deutsche Roman zwischen Barock und Rokoko* (Cologne: Böhlau, 1963), 22–29.

38. Ibid., 29.

39. Ibid., 26.

40. Urs Herzog, *Der deutsche Roman des 17. Jahrhunderts: Eine Einführung*, Sprache und Literatur 98 (Stuttgart: Kohlhammer, 1976), 88. See the discussion of Huet and Happel in the introduction.

kick, and Lompyn, Cergely's comic companion in the *Ungarische Kriegs-Roman,* Happel tells his readers that while he may have promised not to employ such characters again, he did not feel bound by his word.

> Gleichwie wir den lustigen Horuch im Außgang deß Spinelli haben ruhen lassen/ also wird wieder derselbe/ noch seines Gleichen eine andere lustige Person/ so bald auf unsern Theatro erscheinen/ weil mich bedencket/ es ruffe mir jemand ins Ohr/ daß sich sothaner Schreib-Art keine possierliche Person schicken wolle. Jedoch/ so fern ich vermercke/ daß man Horuch oder Lompyn nicht gar ungerne gehöret/ bin ich an Zusage eben nicht so sehr gebunden/ noch ein sothaner Sclav meiner Worten/ daß ich dieselbe/ dem günstigen Leser zu Gefallen/ nicht allemal retractiren könte.[41]

Returning to Carl, Cyclaste predictably falls in love with him, assuming him to be the wealthy heir of a London banker. Carl, however, seems less immediately affected by romance. The two enjoy a pleasant time together conversing and playing at *Ringelreiten,* a form of nonlethal jousting. (This foreshadows Cyclaste's martial abilities, which will come into play later in the novel.) Soon Carl bids Cyclaste good-bye, without revealing his true identity. Shortly after Carl's departure, the lovesick Cyclaste secures her parents' permission to set out for England to become his bride (*DC* IV: 2). Her father is very much taken by this union, because, while outwardly a practicing Catholic, he is at heart an upright Protestant ("aufrichtiger Reformirter"), descended from ancient French Protestant nobility, who converted to Catholicism to save his family and his fortune (*DC* IV: 8).[42] As we noted in chapter 2, the revocation of the Edict of Nantes in 1685 had made living openly as a Protestant in Catholic France dangerous, if not impossible.

Carl's disguise as a banker's son convinced the family that Cyclaste, because of her ancient nobility, would bring the greater social prestige to the

---

41. "Just as we left the funny Horuch at the end of the *Spinelli,* we will not very soon have a funny person like him appear on the stage of our theater, because I feel that someone is telling me that such a person is not appropriate for our story. However, as far as I can tell, you have liked to hear about Horuch and Lompyn, so I am not bound by my promise, neither am I a slave to my words so much that I cannot please my dear reader [with such a story] (*IS* IV: *Vorrede*).

42. "Valcour Adel aus Piedmont . . . woselbst seine Vorfahren der Religion halben außgewiesen worden/ und habe er sich endlich in Paris niedergelassen/ auch mit Handelschafft ein Ehrliches gewonnen/ bey jüngster Reformation aber habe er m[it seinem gantzen Haus sich der Römisch-Catholischen Religion begeben müssen/ jedoch nur nach dem äusserlichen Schein/ weil er und die Seinigen annoch im Hertzen gut Reformirt wären" (*DC* II, 43).

match. This incorrect assumption—Carl is in fact the scion of highest German nobility—does not prevent their marriage when they finally find each other. But in acknowledgment that Cyclaste is the social inferior, their union will be morganatic, or "an die lincke Hand" (*DC* IV: 367). Even with such restrictions, however, the marriage would not even be possible if she were not of a noble family, albeit at some historical distance.[43]

Before this happy conclusion is reached, however, many adventures await the peripatetic Cyclaste. Resting in a farmhouse during her travels across Germany, she meets a peasant girl, Ursula, who tells her of her German fiancé, Baldrich—who turns out to be Carl's companion and confidant. Practiced in riding horses and handling weapons, Ursula joins Cyclaste as a servant as much as a companion. Both women are memorable examples of female self-determination and courage, the hallmarks of Happel's heroines. During their journey across Germany and on to England in search of Carl and Baldrich, they allow the reader to witness the destruction visited by the French soldiers on the cities of Bonn, Worms, Heidelberg, and Mainz along the Rhine, affording Happel yet another opportunity to condemn the cruelty and treachery of the French troops (*DC* III: 342–78, IV: 25–65).

Baldrich, too, has been seeking Carl, from whom he had been separated during some of the many conflagrations visited on the actors in Happel's novels. On the way, he gets into one predicament after another, several of them calling for the help of women to extricate him from his tight spots. Accepting the promises of his affection, two women offer him help on the way. One is an unnamed English maid. After he manages to escape from her, he falls in with the German peasant girl Ursula, whom Cyclaste meets later on her wanderings in search of Carl. Having sought refuge from French soldiers, Ursula offers Baldrich the cramped quarters of her parents' cottage, and specifically her bed. This temporary hiding place forces him to spend the night lying very close to her. Fearing he might be delivered to the soldiers, who might suspect him of being a German spy and kill him, he promises to marry her. Before dawn breaks, he attempts to escape, but he is thwarted by Ursula's passion, her vigilance, and his own fear of her brothers. When it comes down to the alternative of marrying her or being taken prisoner by the French, the choice is easy: he tells the French "in ihrer Sprache" that Ursula is crazy and that they had better take him away (*DC*

43. A morganatic marriage is a marriage between people of unequal social rank, which prevents the passage of the husband's titles and privileges to the wife and any children born of the marriage. It is referred to as a left-handed marriage because the groom holds his bride's right hand with his left hand, instead of his right, in the wedding ceremony.

II: 351). Once in the clear, aided by his language skills, Baldrich predictably disappears, not counting on the determination of both young women to eventually find him.

Meanwhile, Carl's travels take him across a much more expansive geography, namely, to the far reaches of Tartary, Muscovy, and Turkey. He narrowly escapes castration at the Turkish court and marriage proposals by a Circassian and a Tartar princess, who follow him all the way to Germany. Dressed in men's clothing, they participate in a tournament hosted by Carl's brother, Christian, and sadly end up killing one another in a duel (*DC* IV: 356). As they breathe their last, they install Carl as the heir of their distant wealthy lands, thus simultaneously bearing witness to the depth of their passion and acknowledging Carl's knightly superiority. Time and again, men and women accept Carl as peerless and perfect in every way. In his person, the negative German stereotype of the drunkard and loudmouth, often mentioned in Happel's novels, finds its worthy counterweight. As one of the two women marvels, "man hat uns von den Teutschen erzehlet/ daß sie lauter ungeschickte grobe Leute wären/ und nun finden wir an euch/ mein Herr/ ein rechtes Muster der Leutseeligkeit/ der Höflichkeit/ und der Tapfferkeit" [we have been told about the Germans that they were all rough and uncouth people, and now we find in you, my lord, a true example of affability, courtliness, and courage] [*DC* IV: 254]).

During his travels in the far reaches of eastern Europe and Central Asia, Carl meets Syrenia, wife of the Tartar prince Melik, whom he saves from a raging bear. As a result of the struggle, he suffers a serious leg wound, which modesty forbids him to allow Syrenia to see—in vain, of course, for she insists on dressing his wound, mesmerized by his snow-white thigh.[44] Of martial and Amazonian spirit, Syrenia has been adept at throwing the spear and handling the bow and arrow since her youth and is thus familiar with the mishaps that can befall the valiant fighter, male or female.[45] Her very direct approach to the stranger Carl is the perfect counterpoint to Carl's modesty, his very gentle and feminine masculinity.

While the idea of genetic selection was still many centuries in the future, Syrenia attempts an early version of it. Her husband Melik, due to some damage ("Schaden") about which only she knows, is impotent. She loves him and does not want a divorce, but she does want an heir. In her straight-

---

44. "[E]inen guten Theil seines Schnee-weissen Ober-Beins/ zu sehen bekam" (*DC* IV: 294).

45. "[I]n dem Wurff-Spieß und Bogen von Jugend her wol geübet hatten" (from my youth I have practiced with bow and sword [*DC* IV: 291]).

forward way, she asks Carl to provide her one: "gönnt mir einen Erben von Eurer vollkommenen Person . . . ich verlange einen solchen Edlen und Tugend-reichen Sohn zur Welt zu bringen/ wie ihr seyd" (please allow me to have an heir by you and your perfect person . . . I desire to give birth to such a noble and virtuous son like you [*DC* IV: 295–96]). They do make a fitting couple, their masculine and feminine virtues perfectly complementing each other. As Carl blushes profusely, insisting ever so politely that he cannot accept her "modest proposal," she presents him with a note in her husband's own hand, saying that he allows Carl to sleep with his wife ("dannenhero hat er mir nicht allein erlaubet/ bey euch zu schlaffen . . . sondern auch diese Briefflein unter seiner eigenen Hand zugestellet" [*DC* IV: 297]). The note reassures Carl that the prince expects his wife "einen Sohn zu erwerben/ welcher für einen rechtmässigen Erben und Nachfolger von mir soll aner-kannt und erzogen werden" (to give birth to a son who will be my rightful heir and successor, fully acknowledged by me and raised accordingly [*DC* IV: 297]). Carl, now in a rather casual way, shares his potency, leaving the ideal of German masculinity to live on in faraway Tartary: "hiermit küssete er sie etliche mahl/ und leget sich zu ihr. Hernach stunden sie wieder auf/ setzten sich zu Pferde . . . und ritten miteinander wieder zurück" (thus he kissed her several times and lay down next to her. Afterwards they rose, climbed on their horses, and rode home together [*TC* IV: 298]).

Though Syrenia's initiative seems a bit forward for seventeenth-century social conduct, we should remember that Happel is presenting her and the other princesses whom the protagonists meet in faraway lands as different from German noblewomen, though no less high-class. We remember that Christian Thomasius had commended Happel for his sensitivity toward the sexual and cultural "otherness" of foreign women, insisting that what we would reject as sexual aggressiveness must not be taken amiss, "ob es gleich unserem *decoro* zuwiderlieffe" (even if it was against our way of behaving)[46]

While his encounters with Tartars and Circassians are keeping Carl busy, Cyclaste's travels to eventual marital bliss continue to be fraught with dan-gers, most often in the form of predatory men. The anxious reader, however, is reassured to learn that, like so many of Happel's heroines, Cyclaste is by no means defenseless. Confronted by four drunken peasants set on doing her harm (they "sie unverschämter weise betasten wolten" [wanted to touch

---

46. Christian Thomasius, "Eberhardi Guerneri Happelii Africanischer Tarnolast," in *Frei-mütige, lustige und ernsthafte, jedoch vernunftsmässige Gedanken oder Monatsgespräche* . . . , ed. Christian Thomasius, Athenaeum Reprints (1689; repr., Frankfurt am Main: Athenaeum, 1972), 737.

her in insulting ways] [*DC* IV: 12]), she defends her virtue by attacking two of them with her sword, inflicting serious wounds. Stunned that a woman could even look at blood without fainting, let alone fight so fiercely, the peasants bring charges against her before the local duke. In an especially amusing take on Happel's cross-dressing theme, they accuse her and her companion, Ursula, of cross-dressing, of being men in woman's clothing ("in Weibes-Kleidern verstellte Soldaten" *DC* IV: 13). Her prowess would be doubly unacceptable to the peasants if she were truly a woman. To the peasants' shame, an examination by "an honest woman" proves them wrong.

More danger ensues in the person of the local duke (and judge) himself, who becomes annoyingly demanding of Cyclaste's affection ("der ihr gewaltig um ihre Liebe anlage" [*DC* IV: 17]). In his arrogance, he decides to take advantage of Cyclaste's presumably defenseless state as a woman traveling accompanied only by a female companion. He devises a plan by which he might make her his own: rather than raping her outright, he arranges for a tourney, the prize of which would be Cyclaste's hand. But the two women handily outsmart him. They are helped by the duke's aged mother, who disapproves of her son's misplaced passion and uncourtly conduct. They disguise themselves as knights (suited in armor provided by the cavalier's mother) and, their identity thus concealed, take part in the tourney. To the chagrin of the hapless duke, Cyclaste and Ursula beat him and his friends at their own game (*DC* IV: 20) and continue on their journey.

At the German court of Carl's brother Christian, Cyclaste finally finds Carl. The two peasant girls also find the object of their affection, coming face to face with Baldrich, their presumed but elusive groom. Though completely devoted to Carl, Baldrich, it turns out, is much less faithful to the women who saved his life (*DC* I: 9). Far from keeping his promises to at least one of the girls, Baldrich has once again lost his heart to another unsuitable girl: the "fürstliche Prinzessin" Atrobinta. She stands socially as high above him as the two peasant girls seem to be beneath him (*DC* IV: 363). Attempting to flee with his new love in "schlechten und unbekandten Kleider" (bad and unrecognizable dress), Baldrich is mortally wounded by his pursuers, Atrobinta's brothers. At this point, Ursula and the English girl recognize him as their long-lost fiancé. They throw themselves over his wounded body, each trying to pull the other away from him (*DC* IV: 365). Turning their anger at him toward each other, they tear at each other's hair in furious assertion of their claims. (Peasant girls in Happel's works always claw and tear, mostly at their own kind.) During all this uproar, Baldrich breathes his last ("welcher darunter so unmächtig ward/ daß er sich endlich auf die Seite warff/ und seinen Geist auffgabe" [who fainted, turned to his side, and finally gave up the ghost] [*DC* IV: 365]), leaving three grieving women behind. The fight is described as funny but is only laughable if one fails to consider Baldrich's sad fate and the women's disappointment ("gienge es an eine lustige Balgerey/ über welche die andern wol hätten lachen mögen/ wenn das schmerzliche Empfinden des Unglücks/ so den redlichen Baldrich überfallen/ sie nicht darvon abgehalten hätte" [Then started an amusing fight about which others might well have laughed if the painful understanding of honest Baldrich's misfortune had not kept them [from laughing] [*DC* IV: 365]). Clearly, the novels' noble characters (and, presumably, its seventeenth-century readership) are unable to credit peasant women with genuine feelings of love and could not imagine them as deserving of any serious empathy. Baldrich, however, remains *redlich* (virtuous), despite having betrayed these women who saved his life and who, in following him, demonstrated their own *Redlichkeit* (virtuousness).

The passion of the two peasant girls is as immediate as it is ignorant of the social chasm that separates both of them from their lover. At the end of their journey, they are rewarded nonetheless for their faithfulness and good sense by being invited to join Carl's and Cyclaste's household, leaving the rough and uncouth peasant world for the elegance of the court (*DC* IV: 374). Cyclaste becomes Carl's bride, even if only in a morganatic marriage, a "Heirat an die linke Hand."

The story of the *Engelländische Eduard* also unfolds via gender confusion, cross-dressing, and romantic mix-ups, as the tale follows the two main characters, Eduard and Edmunda, on their circuitous journey toward a happy ending. Hiding their sexual and social identities, they, too, run into trouble with all manner of peasants, robbers, and pirates. At the outset of the novel, we meet Eduard disguised as the noblewoman Celinde, lost with his (or her) page in the Scottish woods near their destination, Edinburgh. They come upon the noble Sylvian, his wife, and their two adult sons, who offer the travelers shelter from the hardships of the road. What seems at first to be a happy coincidence turns out otherwise.

Sylvian ("ein in Liebes-Händel nicht unerfahrener Cavallier" [a cavalier practiced in matters of love]) and his sons all fall in love with the beautiful Celinde. Sylvian would like to seduce her right then under his own roof but is fearful of his wife's wrath ("wurde auch etliche mahl Sinnes aufzustehen/ vnd sie in ihrem Bethe zu besuchen/ hätte es auch ohne Zweifel gethan/ wann er sich nicht vor der Albela scheuen müssen/ mit Gewalt sich etwas unterstehen/ war nicht rathsam" (he thought several times of getting up and visiting her in her bedroom but was afraid of Albela were he to try/force anything untoward [*EE* I: 19]). The two sons, for their part, don robbers' disguises and attack Celinde as she continues toward Edinburgh. Defending herself with skill unexpected from a woman, she kills one of them, and Sylvian, rushing to her defense (in hopes of being rewarded with affection for his bravery), unknowingly kills the other. When he realizes that he has killed his own son, Sylvian is horrified and, violently denouncing his fate, commits suicide (*EE* I: 31). This family drama is but one instance of a gender mix-up with fatal consequences. These mix-ups are brought about by inappropriate, even violent sexual desire directed by older men at young women; by married women pining for attractive, cross-dressed strangers; and by confusion over gender and social identities that leads to destructive passions and, sometimes, unhappy endings.

Upon reaching Edinburgh, Celinde abandons her disguise, revealing herself as the English nobleman Eduard—beautiful, valiant, gentle, and very well educated. While the reasons for his cross-dressing remain a mystery until quite deep into the novel, the fact that a "woman" is fully capable of defending herself, even killing an attacker, is in no way censured. Elsewhere in Happel's novels, we have seen the same prowess in Cyclaste, Scoletha, the two Eastern princesses, the Thökölin, and Ursula. In his novels, noblewomen are frequently accomplished in the use of sword and pistol and, as we saw in the *Teutsche Carl*, show dexterity on horseback. Edmunda, Eduard's love interest, explains her swordsmanship as a product of her innate fearlessness, in which she says she differs from other women: "weil ich nun mit tapffern jungen Leuthen täglich umgienge/ und den Degen ein wenig verstunde/ kriegte ich nach und nach auch eine mehere Courage und Hertzhafftigkeit/ daß ich mich nicht leichtlich für etwas entsetzete/ noch/ nach Weiblicher Blödigkeit/ eine Gefahr groß achtete" (because I was daily surrounded by brave young people and was practiced in the use of a sword I gained more and more courage and strength so that nothing frightened me easily, nor did I fear danger just because of feminine weakness [*EE* IV: 338]).

In placing the Celinde/Eduard episode at the very beginning of this novel, Happel effectively reemploys the narrative technique we already encountered in the *Carl* and other earlier novels. His fictional characters, male and female, navigate the challenges posed by global and local geographies and events with remarkable equanimity and flexibility, even if for reasons hard for the reader to fathom. Across Europe and beyond, they visit foreign cities and strange lands to prove their valor, satisfy their thirst for novelty, test their loyalties, and seek out other equally peripatetic companions of both genders.

Following the principle of partial and thus titillating disclosure, Happel waits until the second book to tell his readers why Eduard is in need of disguise. It turns out that his fortitude has been sorely tested by his father, Hardiknut, who drove him away from court because he favored his younger son, the unprincipled and conniving Canut. He also desired Eduard's beloved Edmunda for himself, "weil er eine nicht geringe Liebes-Flamme (*ungeachtet er schon wol bey Jahren [emphasis mine]*) in seinem Herzen gegen sie hegete/ und/ um solcher Ursach willen seinen Sohn Eduard/ dessen gegen Edmunden tragende Liebe ihme nicht allerdings unbekandt/ desto gehässiger ware" (because, despite his advanced age, he harbored a passionate love for her, and since he knew of his son's love [for Edmunda], he bore him no small portion of ill will [*EE* III: 133]). Toward the end of the narrative, during a nocturnal romantic muddle at an especially precarious moment, Eduard inadvertently kills the disguised Canut, another victim of mistaken identity (*EE* IV: 156–70). Terrified, Eduard flees not only the scene but the country as well. Once on the road, he seeks to distract himself with sightseeing and reading the news.

Just as Eduard disguised himself as a woman, Edmunda escapes Hardiknut by disguising herself as a man, taking the name Emedund. These parallel cross-dressings confer on the lovers a degendered quality: they seem to slip in and out of gender roles with such skill and ease that it almost puts their individual gender identity into question.[47] Whether in masculine or feminine dress, they are beautiful, always attracting the passionate (if inappropriate and inconvenient) attention of members of the apparently opposite (but, in fact, same) sex. Far from providing the desired protection, their cross-dressing works so perfectly that it repeatedly gets them into troubling, potentially violent situations. Thus, when Edmunda metamorphoses from a beautiful woman into a beautiful man, she attracts much unwelcome attention from women.

Shortly after Edmunda feels from Hardiknut, she is vigorously pursued by a (nameless) village girl. Before we come to this point in Edmunda's adventure, we have learned that this girl is the daughter of a fisherman from whom Edmunda/Emedund had sought help after a shipwreck. After Edmunda/Emedund has paid the fisherman in advance for his help, the fisherman attempts to push Edmunda/Emedund back into the sea, hoping to extract more money for a second rescue. Edmunda/Emedund deftly derails this plan by throwing the fisherman overboard and severing several of his

---

47. Watanabe-O'Kelly, *Beauty or Beast?*, 190–93.

fingers so that he cannot climb back into the boat (*EE* IV: 3ff.). Reaching shore and seeking refuge for the night, Edmunda/Emedund enters a hut that turns out to belong to the very same fisherman, who arrives later, cursing the stranger who had thwarted his plan for quick money. His daughter, immediately attracted to the handsome stranger, hides him, not only from her father's rage, but also from the angry mob whom her father gathers to find the culprit (*EE* IV: 11). Although already betrothed to a young peasant, the girl mistakenly thinks that her assistance will make the beautiful stranger not only grateful but also willing to become her husband. Edmunda/Emedund is deeply offended by the girl's unseemly affection for a man who, aside from being a woman, is also far above the girl's social station. But unable to escape without the girl's help, she/he acquiesces to the girl's request for a kiss, hoping it will temporarily satisfy her—to little avail, it turns out. Like the peasant girls in love with Baldrich, the girl faithfully waits for her "lover's" promised return. Meanwhile, her mother alternately beats her for her foolishness and praises her for (as she assumes) selling her virginity so dearly.[48]

Wandering about the countryside, not knowing which way to turn, Edmunda/Emedund is discovered by several peasants searching for him, suspecting that he wants to evade the promised marriage. They try to take him prisoner but are prevented by a local nobleman named Stilpo, who is much impressed by the stranger's courage and ease with the sword. The peasants press their case at the ducal, that is, Stilpo's, court, where they accuse Edmunda/Emedund of having violated the girl, stolen her clothes, and taken the bride away from her intended groom (*EE* IV: 233). These accusations anger Edmunda/Emedund, who strikes the girl's lover ("der Dirnen Buhle") so hard that blood flows from his mouth and nose. Meanwhile the girl, still in love with Edmunda/Emedund, asserts her right to him by placing a big "peasant kiss" on his lips ("einen schön dölpischen Bauern-Kuß"). In response, Edmunda/Emedund loses all decorum and hits the girl across the mouth, to the amusement of all present (*EE* IV: 233). Equally angered by all this is Stilpo's wife, Serena, who has also fallen for the beautiful and, by all appearances, noble stranger. She recoils at the idea that the peasant girl's coarse lips should besmirch such an angelic face (*EE* IV: 234). Clearly, Edmunda/Emedund cannot win for losing, as getting rid of one woman in love threatens to deliver him into the desirous arms of another.

Upon hearing of Edmunda/Emedund's predicament, Duke Stilpo pro-

---

48. Because "sie ihr Pussilage so wohl angeleget/ ware deßwegen nicht mehr so hart erbittert/ als Anfangs" (*EE* IV: 23).

nounces him innocent of the peasants' charges, rejecting the girl's claims to him. Serena, however, now presents the greater romantic challenge. Without hesitation, she vigorously presses upon Edmunda/Emedund her obviously unchaste affection (*EE* IV: 270–71). Cornered in the bedroom and desperately trying to escape Serena's advances, the panicked Edmunda/Emedund rips open his shirt—rather, her shirt—revealing her "white breasts" to the stunned Serena. Only then does the lovesick wife regain her senses, moving swiftly from carnal desire for Edmunda/Emedund to fervent friendship for Edmunda. Informed by a servant girl of the events seemingly transpiring in the bedroom, Stilpo arrives to find the two women asleep in each other's arms on Emedund/Edmunda's bed. In a jealous rage, he wants to kill him/her, until he realizes his error and apologizes for the confusion. Serena's guilty passion for the beautiful man she assumed the stranger Edmunda/Emedund to be remains hidden and unpunished, whereas the servant girl who had tried to alert Stilpo to his wife's indiscretion must take her leave.[49]

Things turn out differently for Eduard's father, Hardiknut, whose unseemly desire for the much younger Edmunda and equally blind love for his worthless son Canut started the whole drama. Confronted with the shocking revelation that Eduard is not his son and that Edmunda, the object of his passion, is actually his daughter, he is overcome by fear, horror, hate, fury, vengeance, and anger to such an extent that he suffers a paroxysm and drops dead on the spot. Hardiknut's passion for Edmunda had already implied a degree of incest—she was, after all, his son's betrothed. As it turns out, had Hardiknut had his violent way with her, the relationship would have been incestuous to an even greater degree.

In the *Bayrische Max*, a very conscious struggle involving an incestuous brother-sister passion is woven into the whole of the narrative. One of the protagonists, Erich, finds himself forced by his father to enter into marriage with an underage but very wealthy girl. Erich refuses, not only because he loves another woman, but because, as he points out, he and the girl love each

---

49. "Ob schon Serena an ihrem Gemahl sich ziemlich vergriffen/ so muste desto weniger Stilpo Sünder seyn . . . und bey seyner Serena sich außsöhnen lassen/ . . . Das Kammer-Mensch aber/ . . . muste/ wiewol in gewisser Maß/ unschuldig das Bad aussauffen/ und in höchster Ungnad ihren Dienst quittieren . . . so stünde auch noch dahin/ ob einem in Diensten Stehenden zukommen könne/ seiner Herrschafft Beginnen außzuspähen/ und an den Tag zu bringen" (Even though Serena had done badly by her husband, Stilpo was made out to be the villain, and he had to try to make up with Serena. . . . The servant girl, though innocent of the whole thing, had to suffer the consequences and was chased from her job in disgrace . . . one would have to think whether it is appropriate for a servant to spy on her masters and bring to light their misdeeds [*EE* IV: 333]).

other like brother and sister, and such a union would amount to a kind of "Blut-Schande."[50] Even more inappropriate is the attraction between Max and his sister, Theodelinde. This passion surfaces in a conversation between two of Max's friends, Erich and Firant, who remark on the siblings' extraordinary closeness. Erich observes that he would like to find out more about Theodelinde and Max, because he cannot quite decide if Theodelinde is Max's sister or his lover ("ich nimmer recht eigentlich weiß/ ob ich Ruhmbemeldte Fräulein für Maxen Schwester oder seine Liebste betrachen soll" [*BM* III: 66]). A few pages later, Erich repeatedly expresses his amazement at the depth of their attachment, stating that if he did not know for sure that they were siblings, he would have been compelled to believe that they were lovers ("so hätte ich glauben müssen/ daß sie sonsten Verliebte wären" [*BM* III: 71]). Clearly, the deep attachment and resulting emotional turmoil inflicted on both siblings is so intense that others around them not only notice it but feel compelled to discuss it. This situation is complicated by the fact that Theodelinde seems unable to hide her jealousy when Max interacts with other women, specifically with Mariana, for whom Max's close friend Goribald feels deep affection. Erich perceptively comments on his inability to describe the strange emotions of envy and jealousy existing between the two pairs of sisters and brothers, "die ich/ meine Herren/ nicht beschreiben/ noch deren eigentliche Ursach außsinnen und begreiffen kan/ von dergleichen sie auch schwerlich werden gehöret/ oder gelesen haben" (which I, my lords, cannot describe nor find out the real meaning of which they would have hardly heard or read about [*BM* III: 73]).

Independently of each other, Max and Theodelinde, too, are concerned about their relationship. They acknowledge to themselves the depth of their attachment in the strongest and most desperate terms. In their thoughts, they speak of flames of passion pulling them toward each other while reason pushes them away. They complain of Nature, who cruelly treats them like a stepmother, making them love what they should despise ("dasjenige zu lieben/ was dir selbsten ein Greuel und Scheusal ist . . . eine Blutschänderische/ von aller Welt höchst-sträfflich gehaltene und verfluchte

---

50. Under these circumstances, the marriage would be "nicht anders/ als eine Art von Blut-Schande/ und ist der Natur fast unmöglich" (nothing but a kind of incest and in nature almost impossible [*BM* I: 259]). For more on the incest motif in seventeeth-century writings, see Gerhild Scholz Williams, "Sensationslust, Tabu und Scham: Öffentlichkeit und Berichterstattung im 17. Jahrhundert; Thurneysser, Pierre de Lancre, *Theatrum Europaeum*," in *Tabu: Über den gesellschaftlichen Umgang mit Ekel und Scham*, ed. Anja Hesse et al., Braunschweiger kulturwissenschaftliche Studien 1 (Berlin: Kulturverlag Kadmos, 2009), 75–101.

Zuneigung" [to love what you hate and despise . . . an incestuous attraction by all the world condemned as and thought punishable by law] [*BM* III: 209]). Expressions of violent yet sinful desire are followed by the most tender assurances of respect and affection, which even the most vile passion could never defeat.

This emotional conflict continues during the frequent separations brought about by Max's travels and adventures, and it is shared by Theodelinde's cogitations at home. The matter is complicated by the false rumor of Max's death and the ardent courting of Theodelinde by a doppelgänger, also named Max and in every way the negative image of the *Bayrische* Max. In a complete emotional meltdown, the *Bayrische* Max confesses his unnatural and supernatural love ("wider- und übernatürliche Liebe" [*BM* IV: 229]) to his friend Goribald. The language he employs is that of compulsion, of complete inability to resist this passion ("Es zwingt mich aber ein gantz anderer als brüderlicherr Geblüths- und Liebes-Triebe hierzu" [However, I felt compelled by feeling that is very different from a brotherly love or attraction]). Goribald, far from registering shock or censure, instead expresses compassion and affection, saying, "hier ist für wahr guter Raht theuer" (in this, good advice is hard to come by). Unable to imagine a solution other than death, the two friends agree that they had better return home to await their fate (*BM* IV: 230). After many more challenges that postpone his return for a long time, Max arrives, sword in hand, to avenge the inappropriate advances of the false Max toward his sister. Shortly thereafter, in a classic deus ex machina moment, an old nursemaid reveals that, many years ago, she had supplanted a weak and dying child with a foundling, the *Bayrischen*—the real—Max. He is not his parents' child by blood and thus not Theodelinde's brother. The couple's marriage, now perfectly in order and accompanied by several others, closes the novel.

Conclusion

After we explored, in chapters 2 and 3, the relationship of media and contemporary history with the action in Happel's novels, we came away with a clearer understanding of how Happel employed and emplotted the second dimension of his narrative model, namely, his fictions (*Romanisirungen*). We noted that he never tires of pointing to the narrative dichotomies between his romances and his facts, his histories. Exploring this duality, Happel guides readers to the desired goal, the conveyance of knowledge that is both intellectual and emotional. He repeatedly assures his "blind" readers that he wants to make them see, not only what is knowable by way of facts, but also what can be felt by way of empathy and emotion. He wants his readers to grow in their understanding of the endless varieties of passions—of love and hate, fear and joy, friendship and enmity—as much as he wants to open their eyes to the revelation that the feared Other will emerge as, in many ways, not unlike that which is familiar.

Happel's novels typically end with the main characters returning from whence they had started their explorations or finding a home with the appropriate partner. Ideally, these points of return are marked by weddings. The couples, now settled safely and comfortably in their familiar surroundings, amuse themselves with "allerhand Zeitungen und Gesprächen" (reports from across the German lands) about a sea battle between the Dutch and the English or yet another victory of the Turk over the empire (*EE* IV: 399–400); or, as in the *Teutsche Carl*, banquet guests are entertained with all the news of the year's end.[51] The reader leaves the stage to the happy couples in their fictional bliss and returns to the theater of real-world news and politics.

---

51. "Als der Cavallier diesen Brief abgelesen hatte/ forscheten die beyden Printzen/ ob er nicht anders von neuen Zeitungen/ zum Beschluß des Jahres/ mitzutheilen hätte? Worauf sich dieser folgender Gestalt heraußließ: Am 9. Decembris ward der neugebohrne Königl. Printz von Portugal . . . zu Lissabon getauffet" (The cavalier read the letter, and he asked the prince about the news in the paper at the end of the year. Upon which he told about the newborn Prince of Portugal who had been baptized on December 9). This is followed by reports about a storm in Augsburg, an earthquake in Austria, and an imperial defeat at the hands of the Tartars and the Turks (*DC* IV: 370).

Conclusion

✎

I conclude this exploration of Happel's novels with a brief look at a character who, *in nuce*, contains all the aspects that come together to make Happel's novels such an intriguing subject for study: the synergies of facts and fiction (*historia/Romanisirung*) and, in the context of both, the entertaining complications that arise in these narratives from the mix-ups of gender, class, and nationalities. To wrap up my examination of media and the novel, I will introduce one last historical person who significantly interacted with fictional characters in one of Happel's earlier novels, the *Insulanische Mandorell* (1682), several of whose characters we have met in the preceding chapters. In this novel, Happel moved beyond the European-Mediterranean-African theater to China and the islands off China's southeastern coast, especially Formosa (Taiwan) and Quemoy.[1] The *Insulanische Mandorell* is not yet called a *Geschicht-Roman* but, rather, is subtitled *Eine GEOGRAPHische und POLITIsche Beschreibung Aller und jeden INSULN Auff dem gantzen Erd-Boden/ Vorgestellet In einer anmüthig und wohl-erfundenen Liebes- und Helden-Geschichte.*[2] Nor does it display quite the writerly control that

---

1. This is not Happel's first foray into the Far East, which began with his *Der Asiatische Onogambo: Darin Der jetzt-regierende grosse Sinesische Käyser Xunchius. Als ein umbschweiffender Ritter vorgestellet/ nächst dessen und anderer Asiatischer Printzen Liebes-Geschichten und ritterlichen Thaten/ auch alle in Asien gelegene Königreiche und Länder . . . kürtzlich mit eingeführt werden/ Eberhard Werner Happel* (Hamburg: Naumann, 1673), the very much fictionalized story of the Emperor Xunchius (Shunzhi), whom Adam Schall, one of the most famous Jesuit missionaries to China, instructed in European science and the Christian faith. Xunchius also appears in Happel's *Thesaurus Exoticorum* (*TE* I: 27).

2. Eberhard Werner Happel, *Der Insulanische Mandorell (1682)*, ed. Stefanie Stockhorst, Bibliothek seltener Text in Studienausgaben 12 (Berlin: Weidler, 2007), frontispiece.

Happel would exert over the narrative development in his later novels. Otherwise, however, the *Mandorell* exhibits all the characteristics that we have come to identify as hallmarks of Happel's ensuing novelistic oeuvre.

There is, first and foremost, the fictionalization of a historical person, here the famous Chinese pirate Coxinga (1624–62), who established his rule over Formosa and Quemoy.[3] While not yet as seamlessly woven into the narrative development as in later novels, the basic ingredients are already present. There is the transnational cult of celebrity that grew up around Coxinga and his father, Zhing Zhilong (1604–61), notorious under his Christian name, Nicholas Iquan, who was himself a leader of pirates and privateers and was called the king of South China.[4] Iquan shows up very early in the *Mandorell* as the "See-Held Iquon auß China," who, according the Sumatran princess Ziriska, was forced to turn to piracy ("Seeraub") because of poverty caused by misfortune ("ein Heroischer Fürst/ ehe er Armuth leydet" [*AT* I: 49]). No man in the whole of the Orient, we read in the *Mandorell*, was as powerful and feared as Iquan's son, Coxinga, who ruled the seas between China, Japan, and Formosa as leader of a fleet of countless ships (*AT* I: 13).[5] According to reports and tales about him, Coxinga was "surpris-

---

3. The rather confusing biography of Coxinga has been unraveled by Jonathan Clements in *Coxinga and the Fall of the Ming Dynasty* (Phoenix Mill: Sutton, 2004). Clements made use of some of the same sources cited by Happel in the introduction to the *Thesaurus Exoticorum*, namely, Johan Nieuhof, *Die Gesantschaft der Ost-Indischen Geselschaft in den Vereinigten Niederländern an den Tartarischen Cham und nunmehr auch Sinischen Keiser: verrichtet durch die Herren Peter de Gojern und Jacob Keisern; darinnen begriffen die aller märckwürdigsten Sachen, welche ihnen auf währender Reise vom 1655. Jahre bis in das 1657. aufgestoßen* (Amsterdam, 1666), 23, 127, http://digi.ub.uni-heidelberg.de/diglit/nieuhof1666. See also Frederick Coyett, *Das verwarloste Formosa oder Warhafftige Erzehlung/ wie durch Verwarlosing der Niederländer in Ost-Indien das Eyland Formosa von dem Chinesischen Mandorin und Seerauber Coxinja überrumpelt . . . worden* (Nuremberg: Christoph Endters, 1677); Clements, *Coxinga and the Fall of the Ming Dynasty*. The historical Coxinga was born in 1624 as Zheng Sen in Hirado, Japan, Nagasaki prefecture, to Zheng Zhelong (Iquan), a Chinese merchant and pirate. A successful and famous military leader, he supported the deposed Ming dynasty against the Manchu invaders. Defeated, he withdrew to Formosa (Taiwan), from which he expelled the Dutch after a nine-month siege. He died in 1662 on Formosa. His name derives from the appellation *Guoxingy* (Lord of the Imperial Surname).

4. Clements, *Coxinga and the Fall of the Ming Dynasty*, 4; John L. Cramner-Byng and John E. Wills Jr., "Trade and Diplomacy with Maritime Europe, 1644–c. 1800," in *China and Maritime Europe, 1500–1800: Trade, Settlement, Diplomacy, and Mission*, ed. John E. Wills Jr. (Cambridge: Cambridge University Press, 2011), 188; Charles H. Parker, *Global Interactions in the Early Modern Age, 1400–1800* (Cambridge: Cambridge University Press, 2010), 42–43.

5. Details about the contemporary writings concerning Ming and Quing China and the role of Coxinga and his father can be found in three recent essays by Anna Busquets Alemany: "Dreams in Chinese Periphery: Victorio Riccio and Zheng Chenggong's Regime" (forthcoming); "Other Voices for the Conflict: Three Spanish Texts about the Manchu Conquest of China"

ingly cosmopolitan."[6] He had a Japanese mother and African and Indian attendants, as well as black former slaves (brought in by the Portuguese) among his troops; he also kept and sold captives as slaves.[7] True to Happel's blending of history and romance, the novel's lovers, Coxinga and Podolla, frequently appear disguised, changing their appearances as often as their gender identities. During the course of the narrative, they meet several times without recognizing each other.

Happel gathered information about the pirate-king Coxinga from several sources. Among these are travel narratives (which he enumerates in the preface to the *Thesaurus Exoticorum*) and the news publications available to him, even if these were not always chronologically correct.[8] A careful reading of the *Mandorell* also reveals that Happel found his most important source in the German translation of the Dutch report about Coxinga's siege of Formosa (1662), *Das verwarloste Formosa*. This report was written in 1675 by the last governor of the island, the Swedish-born Frederick Coyett, and

---

(forthcoming); and "El imperio maritimo de la familia Zheng en el contexto del Japón Tokugawa y la China en transición Ming–Qing," in *Itinerarios, Viajes y Contactos Japón-Europa*, ed. Pilar Garcés García and Lourdes Terrón Barbosa (Frankfurt am Main: Peter Lang, 2013). I am very grateful to Professor Busquets Alemany, who generously shared with me her research on an area of Chinese history that clearly influenced German novel writing but that lacked substantive literary and historical exploration until recently. See also John W. Witek, "Catholic Mission and the Expansion of Christianity, 1644–1800," in Wills, *China and Maritime Europe*, 38.

6. Clements, *Coxinga and the Fall of the Ming Dynasty*, 5.

7. Ibid., 208. Throughout his life as a military commander, he kept a group of freed black slaves from Africa, the feared Black Guards, whom he and his father before him had purchased from the Portuguese for loyal protection (79–80). He is shown with his guards in an illustration in Olfert Dapper's *Gedenkwuerdige Verrichtung der Niederlaendischen Ost-Indischen Gesellschaft in dem Kaiserreich Taising oder Sina . . . wobey alles dasjenige was auf dem Sinisischen See-Strandel und bey Tajovan, Formosa, Aimuy und Quemuy, unter dem Befehlhaber Balthasar Bort, im 1662. und folgenden Jahre vorgefallenl erzaehlet wird* (Amsterdam: Jacob von Meurs, 1676). The image is reproduced in Clements, *Coxinga and the Fall of the Ming Dynasty*, 153.

8. As I mentioned in note 3, Happel also cited Nieuhof, *Die Gesantschaft der Ost-Indischen Geselschaft*. Dapper's *Gedenkwuerdige Verrichtung* contains a map of Quemoy and surroundings that, in the lower right corner, identifies the subject as "On the Island which now a kingdom used the famous Pyratese Iquan [the father, GSW] and Kocksinga to Resord" (http://resolver. sub.uni-goettingen.de/purl?PPN615812651). The *Extra Ordinari Mittwochs Post Zeitungenl Anno 1665* reported "Auß Cölln/ vom 18. September," on the basis of a letter from The Hague, that the Dutch had defeated the "beschraiten Rauber Coxinga . . . darauff die Stadt Formosa wieder eingenommen." Coxinga was dead by then, and the newspaper most likely meant Zheng Jing, Coxinga's eldest son, who was often referred to as Coxinga. After his father's death, Zheng Jing assembled a large pirate fleet and sailed in the area of the Philippines. Busquets Alemany mentions several of these reports in "Other Voices for the Conflict."

Fig. 10. Frederick Coyett's *Das verwarloste Formosa* (1677) (Herzog August Bibliothek, Wolfenbüttel)

was translated into German in 1677.[9] From Coyett's description, Happel also extracted much of the chorographic information about Formosa as well as about Japan, which he then included in the *Mandorell*.[10]

Loyal to the Ming dynasty, Coxinga had been driven out of northern China by the invading Manchus (1644). In turn, he chased the Dutch out of Formosa, not out of hatred toward them but, as the *Mandorell* has it, because he and his loyalists needed to find a home base from which to plan the expulsion of the "Tartaren" (Manchus) from the north (*IM* II: 413). In the novel, the story of the fall of Formosa to Coxinga's siege prompts the comment that "derjenige/ so diese Sinesen Commandirete/ und von ihnen zum Könige erwehlet/ heisse Coxinga, ein tapferer Soldat/ und alles was er anfinge/ gienge ihm gücklich von statten" (the one who commanded these Chinese and whom they had chosen as their king is named Coxinga, a brave soldier, and all he touched turned out well [*IM* II: 413]). A Dutchman who listens to this description offers a different opinion, calling Coxinga a "liederlichen Gesell" (unsavory person) who, like his father, had amassed a fortune through piracy. This assessment is countered by a Chinese listener, who praises Coxinga as a liberator, "ein Erlöser des Vaterlandes" (a deliverer of the fatherland), who, born from an ancient Chinese royal family and having assembled a large fleet, was now poised to drive the Manchus out of China.[11] These comments reflect Jonathan Clements's assessment that "the Manchus and the Dutch called Coxinga a pirate, the English and Spanish called him a king. His Chinese countrymen called him both, depending on their mood."[12]

As he would do when writing about the encounters of his fictional characters with the historical celebrities Thököly and Schomberg, Happel constructs a fictional meeting between Coxinga and the novel's protagonist, the Englishman Mandorell, and his companions, after the latter arrive on Formosa. The splendor of Coxinga's attire and of his court leaves them speechless (*IM* II: 429). In a narrative twist that will become an important element in Happel's later novels, these actors realize that they had unknowingly encountered Coxinga several times in the past in various knightly disguises and, of course, also in cross-dress, as the valiant princess and *Amazonin*

---

9. Coyett, *Das verwarloste Formosa*.

10. IM I: 383–91.

11. "Er ist aus uhraltem Geschlechte der SINESISCHEN Könige entsprossen . . . hat sich nur unter den Holländern versteckt . . . jetzt hat er Truppen gesammelt um die MONARCHIE DES TARTARN IN CHINA übern Hauffen zu werfen" (*IM* II: 413).

12. Clements, *Coxinga and the Fall of the Ming Dynasty*, 5.

Tisca. At the novel's end, Coxinga and Princess Podolla get married, with the exemplary, widely traveled English knight Mandorell in attendance. This is not at all in congruence with historical fact, as the historical Coxinga died at age thirty-eight on Formosa, never able to regain a foothold in mainland China.

The *Mandorell* tells the story of Coxinga, still considered a hero in present-day China and Taiwan,[13] with considerable historical accuracy, including the expulsion of the Dutch from Formosa. It does occasionally appear that, in the fictionalizing process, Happel blends into one character Coxinga; his father, Iquan; and his son, Jing—in part, to be fair to Happel, because his sources seem also to mix them up. Despite this confusion, Happel's tale of Coxinga's life and actions comes across to the reader as a story of an extraordinary individual. The novel, following the rules rehearsed in Happel's translation of Pierre Daniel Huét's tract on the novel (1670), changes "ein verwirrendes Misch-Masch [*sic*] ohne Ordnung und annehmlichkeit" (a confusing mess without order or comfort) into "Kunst/ nach gewissen Regeln geschrieben" (art following certain rules [*IM* II: 433]).

Following this prescription, Happel begins and ends his novels that followed the publication of the *Mandorell* by reporting on and, at the same time, fictionalizing his world. Writing in Hamburg and letting his imagination roam across large parts of the known world, he addresses readers who, like he, are avid consumers of print products, newspapers, travel reports, chorographies, and broadsheets. Like the writings of many of his contemporaries, his novels are characterized by what I elsewhere have called "textual hybridity," which evolved toward the second half of the seventeenth century into a distinctly new medium, the highly popular novel. While paying his respect to Huét's ideas by translating Huét's tract and including it in the *Mandorell*, Happel moved on to his own special kind of fact/fiction amalgamation. What Schock identifies as multiple use of his sources (*Mehrfachverwertung*) becomes much more than a time-saving and money-producing device. It emerges, in fact, as the signature trait of Happel's work. Moreover, Happel did more than produce "novel translations" as he transferred English and French models into German. True to the time and place in which he lived and fully aware of the readerly appetite of his public, he presents in his texts diverse ways of knowing that open into diverse ways of telling in the context of a literary German readership. Working very closely, geographi-

---

13. Clements prints a photograph of a Chinese propaganda print from 1955 that shows Coxinga's expulsion of the Dutch from Taiwan.

cally and creatively, with and for the successful Hamburg publisher Wiering, Happel, like many fellow authors, presents himself as an expert user and consumer of news, as an interpreter of multiple cultures and peoples, and as a teller of countless stories of loves lost and found and of women playing at being men and vice versa. His familiarity with and dependence on the writings of contemporaries in many different genres assisted him in constructing his multivolume novels and capacious compendiums of knowledge and news, as he offered his readers historical, geographical, political, social, and emotional knowledge.

As Happel constructs images of faraway worlds and spins tales of exotic experiences, his characters confront and respond to the world in a way that, as outlined in chapter 4, we found persuasively theorized in George Lakoff's experiential realism, or "experientialism."[14] Reading these novels with Lakoff's methodological assumptions in mind, we realize how effectively Happel integrates fact and fiction, and we are able to follow the evolution of the narrative methodology that proves fundamental to his novels. In other words, Lakoff's experientialism provides us the instrument that allows us to empathetically monitor Happel's fictional and factual characters as they navigate through his (hi)stories. The fictional aspects of these novels, the *romanische Handlungen*, in which Happel's men and women participate, could only have assumed the popularity they did because they fit within the experiential realism of his seventeenth-century readers.

Hence we find that Happel's narrative universe encompasses, without contradiction, great diversities of race, gender, class, and nationality. Germany, Europe, the world around the Mediterranean Sea, and the lands further afield reveal themselves to Happel's readers as effortlessly as do the private worlds of men and women who traverse these worlds, whether by their own free will or as subjects of the actions of others. Happel's art directs the reader's gaze to men and women who, through the multiple masks the author employs, slip with ease in and out of gendered identities, even if the results of such "slippages" occasionally challenge the reader's comprehension in unanticipated ways. In the end, the control of the writer over his way of telling allows the reader to access all of Happel's worlds and to come away with knowledge about many varieties of Others. Some of these are distant in geography and culture, such as the Africans and Asians to whom he

---

14. Gerhild Scholz Williams, *Defining Dominion: The Discourses of Magic and Witchcraft in Early Modern France and Germany*, ed. Marvin B. Becker, Studies in Medieval and Early Modern Civilization 6 (Ann Arbor: University of Michigan Press, 1995), 18.

introduces his readers, as well as the exotic kings, queens, knights, burghers, and peasants that populate his works. Some, such as the Hungarian rebel or the marshal of France, become Others by their notoriety, their extraordinary lives, or their celebrity, even if they remain culturally and experientially much closer to Happel's readers.

As Happel grows increasingly accomplished in his art, his novel writing, the depiction of his characters (in no way could we call it character development) and his characters' cultural commentaries guide his readers through vast geographies toward encounters with people who act, suffer, and love, for all their differences, much as his readers do. His novels intertwine the astonishing with the horrific, the sexual with the social, fact with fiction. For all their baroque heft as expressed through the histories they tell, their excessive length, and their elaborate story lines, these novels are, to the patient reader, historically enlightening, intellectually appealing, and emotionally instructive, even though they do not consistently contribute and conform to what we today would consider the logical progression of the narrative and the psychologically realistic evolution of characters. The reader's frustration at such "failings" quickly gives way to fascination as he or she follows Happel through the breadth and depth of his oeuvre and the vagaries of his characters' lives. Once accustomed to Happel's variety and multiplicity of sources, characters, and locales, the reader follows Happel's lead as he imposes order on a mass of information with the help of various structuring devices, such as indexes, chapter summaries, and intertextual narrative repetitions, all of which keep us safely engaged in his narratives even when they seem perilously close to disintegration.

In the end, the narrative intricacies of Happel's novels present an intriguing challenge to readers, past or present. We must patiently follow his often complicated and sometimes tortuous narrative paths as he seeks ways to help us empathize with his literary and epistemological goals, his moral agenda, and his coming to terms with the world he inhabited. Happel narrates and warns, criticizes and cajoles. He teaches and entertains as he guides his readers through (un)familiar worlds and introduces them to (un)familiar peoples and customs, all the while helping them recognize that the strange is not really so strange if looked at closely and with a reasonably open mind. This, once again, conforms to a sentiment that he offers in the form of a question in the foreword of the *Thesaurus Exoticorum*, "ob woll jemand sagen möchte/ es ware bey den Wilden und barbarischen Leuthen nichts zu sehen oder zu lernen" (whether anyone can say that we could not learn or see anything [useful] even when observing wild and barbaric people). In his age of turmoil, the seventeenth century, the news he so amply employs tells him and his readers that human existence is unpredictable yet fascinating and is certainly not always terrifying. History and Happel, as a *Historico* ("the best in the world," by the assessment of his publisher Matthaeus Wagner),[15] not only teach but, along with fiction, affirm that, even under the worst of circumstances, people want to know about what goes on in the world and in the lives of other peoples and cultures. They will buy the books produced by writers who understand how to engage readers' curiosity without compromising their own duty to instruct. Thus, along with Happel's writerly skills, the novel matured toward the dominating literary expression it was to become in the nineteenth century.

---

15. Eberhard Werner Happel, *Historia Moderna Europae, Oder eine Historische Beschreibung dess Heutigen Europae* (Ulm: Matthaeus Wagner, 1692), *Voransprache*.

Bibliography

ॐ

Adams, Percy G. *Travel Literature and the Evolution of the Novel*. Lexington: University Press of Kentucky, 1983.

Agoston, Gabor. "Information, Ideology, and the Limits of Imperial Policy: Ottoman Grand Strategy in the Context of Ottoman-Habsburg Rivalry." In *The Early Ottomans: Remapping the Empire*, edited by Virginia Aksan and Daniel Goffman, 75–103. Cambridge: Cambridge University Press, 2007.

Anon. "An Act for the Redemption of Captives; Ordered by the Parliament, That this Act be forthwith Printed and Published." In *Hen: Scobell, Cler. Parl.* London, 1650.

Anon. *The Present State of Christendom Consider'd in Nine Dialogues Between the Duke of Lorraine and the Duke of Schomberg (done out of French)*. London: Baldwin near the Oxford Arms, 1691.

Anon. *Warhafftige Eigentliche Original Bildnüs Nebst Denkwürdiger und Ominöser auführlicher Lebens-Beschreibugn/ des gebohrnen Ungarischen Grafen Nunmehro aber/ von Ottomannischen Porten/ bereits erklärten Fürsten Emerici Tökeli . . . Dabei zu finden auch das Manifest und Bildnüs Abaffi des Fürsten aus Siebenbürgen. . . .* 1683.

Bachmann-Medick, Doris. *Cultural Turns: Neuorientierungen in den Kulturwissenschaften*. Rowohlts Encyclopädie 55675. Hamburg: Rowohlt, 2006.

Bahlcke, Joachim, ed. *Glaubensflüchtlinge: Ursachen, Formen und Auswirkungen frühneuzeitlicher Konfessionsmigration in Europa*. Berlin: LIT, 2008.

Barker, Andrew. *A true and certaine report of the beginning, proceedings, ouerthrowes, and now present estate of the Captaine Ward and Danseker, the two late famous pirates from their first setting foorth to this present time. . . . Published by Andrew Barker master of a ship, who was taken by the confederates of Ward and by them some time detained prisoner*. London: William Hall, 1609.

Baron, Samuel H., ed. *The Travels of Olearius in Seventeenth-Century Russia*. Stanford: Stanford University Press, 1967.

Beetz, Manfred, and Herbert Jaumann, eds. *Thomasius im literarischen Feld: Neue Beiträge zur Erforschung seines Werkes im historischen Kontext*. Tübingen: Niemeyer, 2003.

Behringer, Wolfgang. *Im Zeichen des Merkur: Reichspost und Kommunikationsrevolution in der Frühen Neuzeit.* Veröffentlichungen des Max-Planck-Instituts für Geschichte 189. Göttingen: Vandenhoeck und Ruprecht, 2003.

Behringer, Wolfgang. "Veränderung der Raum-Zeit-Relation: Zur Bedeutung des Zeitungs- und Nachrichtenwesens während der Zeit des Dreissigjährigen Krieges." In *Zwischen Alltag und Katastrophe: Der Dreissigjährige Krieg aus der Nähe*, edited by Benigna von Krusenstjern and Hans Medick, 39–83. Veröffentlichungen des Max-Planck-Instituts für Geschichte. Göttingen: Vandenhoeck und Ruprecht, 1999.

Bonifacio, M. le Maire de. *La Guerre de Course en Méditerranée.* Bonificio: Les Journées Universitaire, 1999.

Böning, Holger, ed. *Deutsche Presse: Bibliographische Handbücher zur Geschichte der deutschsprachigen periodischen Presse von den Anfängen bis 1815.* Vol. 1. Stuttgart: Frommann-Holzboog, 1996.

Böning, Holger, ed. "Weltaneignung durch neues Publikum: Zeitungen und Zeitschriften als Medientypen der Moderne." In *Kommunikation und Medien in der Frühen Neuzeit*, edited by Johannes Burkhardt, 105–37. Historische Zeitschrift Beiheft 41. Munich: Oldenbourg, 2005.

Böning, Holger, ed. *Welteroberung durch ein neues Publikum: Die deutsche Presse und der Weg zur Aufklärung; Hamburg und Altona als Beispiel.* Bremen: Edition Lumière, 2002.

Bono, Salvatore. *Piraten und Korsaren im Mittelmeer: Seekrieg, Handel und Sklaverei vom 16. bis 19. Jahrhundert.* Translated by Achim Wurm. Stuttgart: Klett-Cotta, 2009.

Boone, Joseph A., and Nancy J. Vickers, eds. "Celebrity, Fame, Notoriety." Special issue, *PMLA* 126, no. 4 (2011).

Breuer, Dieter. "In Grimmelshausen's Tracks: The Literary and Cultural Legacy." In *A Companion to the Works of Grimmelshausen*, edited by Karl Otto Jr., 231–69. Rochester: Camden House, 2003.

Brooks, Francis. *Barbarian cruelty being a true history of the distressed condition of the Christian captives under the tyranny of Mully Ishmael, Emperor of Marokko, and King of Fez and Macqueness in Barbary.* London: Printed for I. Salisbury at the Rising-Sun in Cornhil, 1692.

Buckley, Veronica. *Christina, Queen of Sweden: The Restless Life of a European Eccentric.* New York: HarperCollins, 2004.

Burckhardt, Johannes, and Christine Werckstetter, eds. *Kommunikation und Medien in der Frühen Neuzeit.* Historische Zeitschrift, Beiheft 41. Munich: Oldenbourg, 2005.

Burgess, Douglas R., Jr. *The Pirates' Pact: The Secret Alliances between History's Most Notorious Buccaneers and Colonial America.* New York: McGraw-Hill, 2008.

Burns, Robert I. "Piracy as an Islamic-Christian Interface in the Thirteenth Century." *Viator* 11 (1980): 165–78.

Busquets Alemany, Anna. "Dreams in Chinese Periphery: Victorio Riccio and Zheng Chenggong's Regime." Forthcoming.

Busquets Alemany, Anna. "El imperio marítimo de la familia Zheng en el contexto del Japón Tokugawa y la China en transición Ming–Qing." In *Itinerarios, Viajes y Contactos Japón-Europa*, edited by Pilar Garcés García and Lourdes Terrón Barbosa, 197–200. Frankfurt am Main: Peter Lang, 2013.

Busquets Alemany, Anna. "Other Voices for the Conflict: Three Spanish Texts about the Manchu Conquest of China." 2013.

Care, Henry. *Draconica Oder Ein Außzug aller Englischen Poenal-Gesetze*. Translated by Eberhard Werner Happel. Hamburg: Thomas von Wiering, 1689.

Cartledge, Bryan. *The Will to Survive: A History of Hungary*. New York: Columbia University Press, 2011.

Castillo, David R. *Baroque Horrors: Roots of the Fantastic in the Age of Curiosity*. Ann Arbor: University of Michigan Press, 2010.

Cenner-Wilhelmb, Gisela. "Feind oder zukünftiger Verbündeter? Zur Beurteilung der politischen Rolle der Emerikus Thököly in den grafischen Blättern seiner Zeit." In *Das Osmanische Reich und Europa 1683 bis 1789: Konflikt, Entspannung und Austausch*, edited by Gernot Heiss and Grete Klingenstein, 54–70. Wiener Beiträge zur Geschichte 10. Munich: Oldenbourg, 1983.

Childs, John. "'For God and for Honour': Marshal Schomberg." *History Today* 38, no. 7 (1988): 46–59.

Clements, Jonathan. *Coxinga and the Fall of the Ming Dynasty*. Phoenix Mill: Sutton, 2004.

Colley, Linda. *Captives: Britain, Empire, and the World, 1600–1850*. New York: Anchor Books, 2004.

Colley, Linda. "Going Native, Telling Tales: Collaboration and Empire." *Past and Present* 168, no. 1 (2000): 170–93.

Contreras, Alfonso de. *Das Leben des Capitan Alonso de Contreras von ihm selbst erzählt*. Zurich: Manesse, 1961.

Coyett, Frederick. *Das verwarloste Formosa oder Warhafftige Erzehlung/ wie durch Verwarlosing der Niederländer in Ost-Indien das Eyland Formosa von dem Chinesischen Mandorin und Seerauber Coxinja überrumpelt . . . worden*. Nuremberg: Christoph Endters, 1677.

Cramner-Byng, John L., and John E. Wills Jr. "Trade and Diplomacy with Maritime Europe, 1644–c. 1800." In *China and Maritime Europe, 1500–1800: Trade, Settlement, Diplomacy, and Mission*, edited by John E. Wills Jr., 183–254. Cambridge: Cambridge University Press, 2011.

Dammann, Günther. "Fakten und Fiktionen im Roman bei Eberhard Werner Happel, Schriftsteller in Hamburg." In *Hamburg: Eine Metropolregion zwischen Früher Neuzeit und Aufklärung*, edited by Johann Anselm Steiger and Sandra Richter, 461–75. Metropolis: Texte und Studien zu Zentren der Kultur in der Frühen Neuzeit. Berlin: Fink, 2012.

Danker, Uwe. *Räuberbanden im Alten Reich um 1700: Ein Beitrag zur Geschichte von Herrschaft und Kriminalität in der Frühen Neuzeit*. 2 vols. Suhrkamp Taschenbuch Wissenschaft 707. Frankfurt am Main: Suhrkamp, 1988.

Dapper, Olfert. *Gedenkwuerdige Verrichtung der Niederlaendischen Ost-Indischen Gesellschaft in dem Kaiserreich Taising oder Sina . . . wobey alles dasjenige was auf dem Sinisischen See-Strande/ und bey Tajovan, Formosa, Aimuy und Quemuy, unter dem Befehlhaber Balthasar Bort, im 1662. und folgenden Jahre vorgefallen/ erzaehlet wird*. Amsterdam: Jacob von Meurs, 1676.

D'Aranda, Emmanuel. *Schauplatz Barbarischer Schlaverey*. Altona: Victor de Löw, 1666.

Davis, Lennard. *Factual Fictions: The Origins of the English Novel*. New York: Columbia University Press, 1983.

Davis, Robert C. *Christian Slaves, Muslim Masters: White Slavery in the Mediterranean, the Barbary Coast, and Italy, 1500–1800.* London: Palgrave Macmillan, 2004.

Davis, Robert C. *Holy War and Human Bondage: Tales of Christian-Muslim Slavery in the Early Modern Mediterranean.* Santa Barbara, CA: ABC-CLIO / Praeger, 2009.

Della Valle, Pietro. *Eines vornehmen Römischen Patritii Reiss-Beschreibung in unterschiedliche Theile der Welt.* Geneva: Widerhold, 1674.

300 Jahre Hugenotten in Hessen: Herkunft und Flucht, Aufnahme und Assimilation, Wirkung und Ausstrahlung; Ausstellung, Museum Fridericianum, Kassel, 12. April bis 28. Juli 1985. Kassel: Weber und Weidemeyer, 1985.

DuChastelet de Luzancy, Hippolyte. *Abbregé de la Vie du Frederic Duc de Schomberg . . . Par Monsr. de Luzaney, Ministre d'Harwich & Chapelain du feu de Duc de Schomberg.* La Haye: Jean Aelberts, Marchand Librairie, près la Cour, 1690.

Duchhardt, Heinz. *Europa am Vorabend der Moderne, 1650–1800.* Edited by Peter Blickle. Handbuch der Geschichte Europas 6. Stuttgart: Eugen Ulmer, 2003.

Dünnhaupt, Gerhard. "Adam Olearius (1599–1671)." In *Personalbibliographien zu den Drucken des Barock,* edited by Gerhard Dünnhaupt, 2979–3004. Hiersemanns bibliographische Handbücher 3. Stuttgart: Hiersemann, 1991.

Dünnhaupt, Gerhard, ed. *Personalbibliographien zu den Drucken des Barock.* Hiersemanns bibliographische Handbücher 3. Stuttgart: Hiersemann, 1991.

Egenhoff, Uta. *Berufsschriftstellertum und Journalismus in der Frühen Neuzeit: Eberhard Werner Happels Relationes Curiosae im Medienverbund des 17. Jahrhunderts.* Presse und Geschichte 33. Bremen: Edition Lumière, 2008.

Esquemeling, John. *The Buccaneers of America: In the Original English Translation of 1684.* New York: Cosimo Classics, 1684.

Falkner, Silke R. ""Having It Off" with Fish, Camels, and Lads: Sodomitic Pleasures in German-Language Turcica." *Journal of the History of Sexuality* 13, no. 4 (2004): 401–27.

Faroqhi, Suraiya. *The Ottoman Empire and the World around It.* London: Tauris, 2007.

Fata, Marta. *Ungarn, das Reich der Stephanskrone, im Zeitalter der Reformation und Konfessionalisierung: Multiethnizität, Land und Konfession, 1500–1700.* Münster: Aschendorff, 2000.

Fitz-Geffry, Charles. *Compassion towards Captives Chiefly Towards our Brethren and Country-men who are in miserable bondage in Barbarie Preached in Plymouth, in October 1636.* Oxford: Leonard Lichfield for Edward Forrest, 1637.

Francisci, Erasmus. *Der blutig-lang-gereitzte/ endlich aber Sieghafft-entzündete Adler-Blitz Wider den Glantz deß barbarischen Sebels/ vnd Mord-Brandes.* Nuremberg: Johann Andreae Endters, Seel. Söhne, 1684.

Friedman, Ellen G. *Spanish Captives in North Africa in the Early Modern Age.* Madison: University of Wisconsin Press, 1983.

Friedrich, Markus. "'Türken' im Alten Reich: Zur Aufnahme und Konversion von Muslimen im deutschen Sprachraum (16.–18. Jahrhundert)." *Historische Zeitschrift* 294 (2012): 329–60.

Frisch, Johann, ed. *Der Schauplatz Barbarischer Schlaverey/ eröffnet durch J. F.* Altona: Victor de Löw, 1666.

A full account of the great victory obtained by the Protestants in Ireland, since the arrival of his Grace the Duke of Schomberg: as is communicated by the reverend and valiant governor Walker of Chester. London: J. Norman, 1689.

Gallagher, Catherine. "The Rise of Fictionality." In *The Novel: History, Geography, and Culture*, edited by Franco Moretti, 337–63. Princeton: Princeton University Press, 2006.

Garcés, Maria Antonia. *Cervantes in Algiers: A Captive's Tale*. Nashville, TN: Vanderbilt University Press, 2002.

Geulen, Hans. *Erzählkunst der frühen Neuzeit: Zur Geschichte epischer Darbietungweisen und Formen im Roman der Renaissance und des Barock*. Tübingen: Lothar Rotsch, 1975. .

Glozier, Matthew. *Marshal Schomberg (1615–1690), "The Ablest Soldier of His Age": International Soldiering and the Formation of State Armies in Seventeenth-Century Europe*. Brighton: Sussex Academic Press, 2005.

Glozier, Matthew, and David Onnekink, eds. *War, Religion, and Service: Huguenot Soldiering, 1685–1713*. Politics and Culture in North-Western Europe, 1650–1720. Aldershot: Ashgate, 2007.

Gordon, Murray. *Slavery in the Arab World*. New York: New Amsterdam Books, 1989.

Graf, Thomas. "A Sample of Renegades Active ca. 1560–1610." Paper presented at the AHA conference, Boston, January 6–9, 2011.

Grimmelshausen, Hans Jakob Christoph von. *Lebensbeschreibung der Erzbetrügerin und Landstörzerin Courasche*. 1670. Edited by Klaus Haberkamm and Günther Weydt. Universalbibliothek 7998. Stuttgart: Reclam, 2001.

Hammond, Brean, and Shaun Regan. *Making the Novel: Fiction and Society in Britain, 1660–1789*. New York: Palgrave Macmillan, 2006.

Hannerz, Ulf. *Cultural Complexity: Construction and Corrosion*. Chicago: University of Chicago Press, 1992.

Happel, Eberhard Werner. *Der Academische Roman, Worinnen das Studenten-Leben fürgebildet wird*. Ulm: Matthaeus Wagner, 1690.

Happel, Eberhard Werner. *Der Afrikanische Tarnolast*. 1689. Edited by John D. Lindberg. 4 vols. Bibliothek des Literarischen Vereins in Stuttgart 305–8. Stuttgart: Anton Hiersemann, 1982.

Happel, Eberhard Werner. *Der Asiatische Onogambo: Darin Der jetzt-regierende grosse Sinesische Käyser Xunchius. Als ein umbschweiffender Ritter vorgestellet/ nächst dessen und anderer Asiatischer Printzen Liebes-Geschichten und ritterlichen Thaten/ auch alle in Asien gelegene Königreiche und Länder . . . kürtzlich mit eingeführt werden/ Eberhard Werner Happel*. Hamburg: Naumann, 1673.

Happel, Eberhard Werner. *Der Bayrische Max oder so genannter Europaeischer Geschicht-Roman Auf Das 1691. Jahr*. Ulm: Matthaeus Wagner, 1692.

Happel, Eberhard Werner. *E. G. Happelii Grösste Denckwürdigkeiten der Welt oder so genannte Relationes Curiosae*. Vol. 3. Hamburg: Thomas von Wiering, 1687.

Happel, Eberhard Werner. *Dess Engelländischen Eduards/ Oder so genannten Europäischen Geschicht-ROMANS, auf das 1690. Jahr. . . .* 4 vols. Ulm: Matthaeus Wagner, 1691.

Happel, Eberhard Werner. *Fortuna Brittannica: oder Brittanischer Glücks-Wechsel: Fürstellend Eine kurtzbündige Beschreibung aller Königen von Engelland/ und des schier stets unglücklichsten Hauses Stuart*. Hamburg: Thomas von Wiering, 1689.

Happel, Eberhard Werner. *Der Frantzösische Cormantin, Oder so genannter Europæischer Geschicht-Roman, Auf Das 1687. Jahr: Worinnen Man nächst denen Angelegenheiten deß Königreichs Franckreich/ die fürnehmste Schlachten/ Belagerungen/ Wunder . . .*

und was sonsten . . . passiret . . . in einer wol-erfundenen Liebes- und Helden-Geschichte leß-würdig fürgestellet/ Everhardus Guernerus Happelius. . . . Ulm: Matthaeus Wagner, 1687–88.

Happel, Eberhard Werner. *Historia Moderna Europae, Oder eine Historische Beschreibung dess Heutigen Europae*. Ulm: Matthaeus Wagner, 1692.

Happel, Eberhard Werner. *Der Insulanische Mandorell (1682)*. Edited by Stefanie Stockhorst. Bibliothek seltener Text in Studienausgaben 12. Berlin: Weidler, 2007.

Happel, Eberhard Werner. *Der Italienische Spinelli/ oder so genannter Europaeischer Geschicht-Roman/ Auff das 1685. Jahr*. Ulm: Matthaeus Wagner, 1685.

Happel, Eberhard Werner. *Kern-Chronica der merckwürdigsten Welt- und Wunder-Geschichte*. 2 vols. Hamburg: Thomas von Wiering, 1690.

Happel, Eberhard Werner. *Mundi Mirabilis Tripartiti: Oder Wunderbaren Welt In einer kurtzen Cosmographia Fuergestellet*. Vol. 2. Ulm: Daniel Bartholomaeus, 1708.

Happel, Eberhard Werner. *Der Ottomanische Bajazet, oder so genannter Europaeischer Geschicht-Roman Auf Das Jahr 1688*. . . . Ulm: Matthaeus Wagner 1688.

Happel, Eberhard Werner. *Der Sächsische Witekind/ Oder so-genannter Europaeischer Geschicht-Roman. Auf das 1692. Jahr*. Ulm: Matthaeus Wagner, 1692.

Happel, Eberhard Werner. *Der Spanische Quintana Oder Sogenannter Europaeischer Geschicht-Roman Auf Das 1686. Jahr*. Ulm: Matthaeus Wagner, 1686.

Happel, Eberhard Werner. *Dess Teutschen Carls/ Oder so genannten Europäischen Geschicht-Romans auf das 1689. Jahr*. Ulm: Matthaeus Wagner, 1690.

Happel, Eberhard Werner. *Thesaurus Exoticorum. Oder eine mit Aussländischen Raritäten und Geschichten Wohlversehene Schatz-Kammer Fürstellend Die Asiatische, Africanische und Americanische Nationes . . . Darauff folget eine Umständliche von Der Tuerckey Beschreibung . . . und sein verfluchtes Gesetz-Buch oder AKORAN*. Hamburg: Thomas von Wiering, 1688.

Happel, Eberhard Werner, ed. *Türckis. Estats- und Krieges-Bericht*. Nos. 1–137. Hamburg: Thomas von Wiering, 1683–84.

Happel, Eberhard Werner. *Der Ungarische Kriegs-Roman*. 6 vols. Ulm: Matthaeus Wagner, 1685–97.

Harms, Wolfgang, and Michael Schilling, eds. *Die Sammlung der Herzog August Bibliothek in Wolfenbüttel*. Pt. 1, *Ethica, Physica*, and pt. 3, *Theologica, etc., Deutsche Illustrierte Flugblätter des 16. und 17. Jahrhunderts*. Tübingen: Niemeyer, 1985, 1989.

Hechelhammer, Bodo. "Das Korps der Janitscharen: Eine militärische Elite im Spannungsfeld von Gesellschaft, Militär und Obrigkeit im Osmanischen Reich." *Militär und Gesellschaft in der Frühen Neuzeit* 14, no. 1 (2010): 33–58.

Hernandez, Isabel. "From Spain to the Americas, from the Convent to the Front: Catalina de Erauso's Shifting Identities." *L'Homme: Europäische Zeitschrift für feministische Geschichtswissenschaft* 22, no. 1 (2011): 71–84.

Herzog, Urs. *Der deutsche Roman des 17. Jahrhunderts: Eine Einführung*. Sprache und Literatur 98. Stuttgart: Kohlhammer, 1976.

Heywood, Linda M., and John K. Thornton. *Central Africans, Atlantic Creoles, and the Foundation of the Americas, 1585–1660*. Cambridge: Cambridge University Press, 2007.

Heywood, Thomas. *A true relation of the lives of two most famous English pyrats, [H] Purser, and [H] Clinton who lived in the reigne of Queene Elizabeth*. London: Io. Okes, 1639.

Huet, Pierre-Daniel. *Traite de l'origine des romans: Faksimiledrucke nach der Erstausgabe von 1670 und der Happelschen Uebersetzung von 1682 mit einem Nachwort von Hans Hinterhaeuser. . . .* Stuttgart: Metzler, 1966.

Jacob, Margaret C. *Strangers Nowhere in the World: The Rise of Cosmopolitanism in Early Modern Europe.* Philadelphia: University of Philadelphia Press, 2006.

James I, King of England and Wales. *Proclamation against Pirats.* London: Robert Barker, printer to the Kings most excellent Maiestie, 1609.

Johnson, Carl. *Schauplatz der Englischen See-Rauber.* Translated by J.M. [Joachim Meier]. Goslar, 1728.

Johnson, Charles [Daniel Defoe]. *A General History of the Pyrates.* 1724. Edited by Manuel Schonhorn. Mineola, NY: Dover, 1999.

Jowitt, Claire. *The Culture of Piracy, 1580–1630: English Literature and Seaborne Crime.* Aldershot: Ashgate, 2010.

Kaiser, Wolfgang. "Negocier la Liberté: Missions Françaises pour l'échange et la rachat de captifs au Maghreb (XVIIe siècle)." In *La Mobilité des personnes en Mediterrannée de l'Anquitité à l'époque moderne: Procedures de contrôle et documents d'identification,* edited by Claudia Moatti, 501–28. Rome: École Française de Rome, 2004.

Kettermann, Günter, ed. *Atlas zur Geschichte des Islam mit einer Einleitung von Adel Theodor Khoury.* Darmstadt: Wissenschaftliche Buchgesellschaft, 2001.

Killy, Walter, with Hans Fromm, eds. *Literaturlexikon: Autoren und Werke deutscher Sprache.* Vol. 4. Gütersloh: Bertelmanns Lexikon, 1989.

Kintzinger, Marion. *Chronos und Historia: Studien zur Titelblattikonographie historiographischer Werke vom 16. bis zum 18. Jahrhundert.* Wolfenbütteler Forschung 60. Wiesbaden: Harrassowitz, 1995.

Klein, Bernhard. "Randfiguren: Othello, Oroonoka und die kartographische Repräsentation Afrikas." In *Imaginationen des Anderen im 16. und 17. Jahrhundert,* edited by Ina Schabert and Michaela Boenke, 185–217. Wiesbaden: Harrassowitz, 2002.

Knight, Francis. *A relation of seaven yeares slaverie under the Turks of Argeire, suffered by an English captive merchant. . . . Whereunto is added a second booke conteining a discription of Argeire, with its originall manner of government, increase, and present flourishing estate.* London: T. Cotes for Michael Sparke Jr., 1640.

Kontler, László. *A History of Hungary: Millennium in Central Europe.* New York: Palgrave Macmillan, 2002.

Köpeczi, Béla. *Staatsräson und Christliche Solidarität: Die ungarischen Aufstände und Europa in der zweiten Hälfte des 17. Jahrhunderts.* Vienna: Böhlaus Nachf., 1983.

Krstic, Tijana. *Contested Conversions to Islam: Narratives of Religious Change in the Early Modern Ottoman Empire.* Stanford: Stanford University Press, 2011.

Lachenicht, Susanne. *Hugenotten in Europa und Nordamerika: Migration und Integration in der Frühen Neuzeit.* Frankfurt am Main: Campus, 2010.

Lad, Jateen. "Panoptic Bodies: Black Eunuchs as Guardians of the Topkapi Harem." In *Harem Histories: Envisioning Places and Living Spaces,* edited by Marilyn Booth, 136–77. Durham: Duke University Press, 2010.

Lakoff, George. *Women, Fire, and Dangerous Things: What Categories Reveal about the Mind.* Chicago: University of Chicago Press, 1987.

Leeson, Peter T. *The Invisible Hook: The Hidden Economics of Pirates.* Princeton: Princeton University Press, 2009.

Lendvai, Paul. *The Hungarians: A Thousand Years of Victory in Defeat.* Translated by Ann Major. London: Hurst, 2003.

Lock, Gerhard. *Der höfisch-galante Roman des 17. Jahrhunderts bei Eberhard Werner Happel.* Würzburg: Konrad Triltsch, 1939.

Lohsträter, Kai. "Alles Kriegstheater? Das 'Theatrum Europaeum' im Kontext der Kriegberichterstattung des 17. Jahrhunderts." Paper delivered at Interdisziplinärer Workshop des DFG-Projekts "Welt und Wissen auf der Bühne: Die Theatrum-Literatur der Frühen Neuzeit," March 12–13, 2011, University of Kassel, Germany.

Lüneburg, Anton Ulrich Herzog zu Braunschweig und. *Die durchleuchtige Syrerinn Aramena.* 6 vols. Nuremberg: Hofmann, 1669–73.

Lüneburg, Anton Ulrich Herzog zu Braunschweig und. *Die durchleuchtige Syrerinn Aramena.* 1669. Pt. 1. Edited by Blake Lee Spahr. Facsimile of the 1st ed. Bern: Lang, 1975.

Lunsford, Virginia West. *Piracy and Privateering in the Golden Age Netherlands.* New York: Palgrave Macmillan 2005.

Matar, Nabil I. *Europe through Arab Eyes, 1578–1727.* New York: Columbia University Press, 2009.

Matchlesse Crueltie, declared at large in the ensuing History of the Waldensians. . . . Wherein is related their Original and Beginning. . . . Likewise, Hereunto is added an exact Narrative of the late Bloody and Barbarous Massacres. . . . London: Edward Brewster, at the Crane in Pauls Church-yard, 1655.

Mawlai, Rashid. *Warhaffte und merckwürdige Geschichts-Erzehlung von Tafilette, dem grossen Bestreiter und Kayser der Barbarey; aus der englischen in die frantzösische/ und aus solcher in die teutsche Sprache übersetzt.* Nuremberg: Johann Hoffmann, 1670.

McCarthy, John A. "The Gallant Novel and the German Enlightenment (1670–1750)." *Deutsche Vierteljahrschrift für Literaturwissenschaft und Geistesgeschichte* 59 (1985): 47–78.

McCrory, Donald P. *No Ordinary Man: The Life and Times of Miguel Cervantes.* Mineola, NY: Dover, 2002.

Meid, Volker. *Die deutsche Literatur im Zeitalter des Barock: Vom Späthumanismus zur Frühaufklärung, 1570–1740.* Geschichte der deutschen Literatur von den Anfängen bis zur Gegenwart 5. Munich: Beck, 2009.

Meierhofer, Christian. "Allerhand Begebenheiten: Happels *sogenannte Europaeische Geschicht-Romane* als Wissensfundus." In *Polyhistorismus und Buntschriftstellerei: Populäre Wissensformen und Wissenskultur in der Frühen Neuzeit,* edited by Flemming Schock, 230–53. Frühe Neuzeit 169. Berlin: De Gruyter, 2012.

Merian, Matthaei Sel. Erben, ed. *Theatri Europaei Continuati Dreyzehender Theil/ Das ist: die Fortsetzung Denck- und Merckwurdiger Geschichten/ Welche/ ihrer gewohnlichen Eintheilung nach/ an verschiedenen Orten durch Europa . . . vom Jahr 1687, an biss 1691. sich begeben und zugetragen. . . .* Vol. 13. Frankfurt am Main: Johann Goerlin, 1688.

Merian, Matthaeus, ed. *Theatrum Europaeum.* Vol. 1. Frankfurt am Main: Matthaeus Merian, 1662.

Merian, Matthaeus, ed. *Theatrum Europaeum.* Vol. 7. Frankfurt am Main: Matthaeus Merian, 1685.

Merrim, Stephanie. "Catalina de Erauso: From Anomaly to Icon." In *Coded Encounters: Writing, Gender, and Ethnicity in Colonial Latin America*, edited by Jeffrey A. Cole, Francisco Javier Cevallos, Nina Scott, and Nicomedes Suárez-Aráúz, 177–205. Amherst: University of Massachusetts Press, 1994.

Molnár, Miklós. *A Concise History of Hungary*. Translated by Anna Magyar. Cambridge: Cambridge University Press, 2001.

Mondfeld, Wolfram zu, and Barbara zu Wertheim. *Piraten: Schrecken der Weltmeere*. Stuttgart: Theiss, 2007.

Moretti, Franco, ed. *The Novel*. Vol. 2, *Forms and Themes*. Princeton: Princeton University Press, 2006.

Moretti, Franco, ed. "Theory/History." Paper presented at the conference "Theories of the Novel," Brown University, October 2007.

Newman, Jane. *The Intervention of Philology: Gender, Learning, and Power in Lohenstein's Roman Plays*. Edited by Paul T. Roberge. University of North Carolina Studies in the Germanic Languages and Literatures 122. Chapel Hill: University of North Carolina Press, 2000.

Nieuhof, Johan. *Die Gesantschaft der Ost-Indischen Geselschaft in den Vereinigten Niederländern an den Tartarischen Cham und nunmehr auch Sinischen Keiser: verrichtet durch die Herren Peter de Gojern und Jacob Keisern; darinnen begriffen die aller märkwürdigsten Sachen, welche ihnen auf währender Reise vom 1655. Jahre bis in das 1657. aufgestoßen*. Amsterdam, 1666.

Norris, Gerald, ed. *The Buccaneer Explorer: William Dampier's Voyages*. 1994. Rev. ed. Woodbridge: Boydell, 2008.

Nunberg, Jeffrey. "Data Deluge." Review of *The Information: A History, a Theory, a Flood*, by James Gleick. *New York Times Book Review*, March 20, 2011, 10–12.

Oexmelin, Alexandre [Alexander Exquemelin]. *Die Americanische See-Räuber: Entdeckt, in gegenwärtiger Beschreibung der grössten . . . verübten Räuberey und Grausamkeit*. Nuremberg: Christoph Riegels, 1679.

Osterhammel, Jürgen, and Niels P. Petersson. *Globalization: A Short History*. Translated by Dona Geyer. Princeton: Princeton University Press, 2005.

Paas, John Roger, ed. *The German Political Broadsheet, 1600–1700*. Vol. 11, *1683–1685*. Wiesbaden: Harrassowitz, 2011.

Parker, Charles H. *Global Interactions in the Early Modern Age, 1400–1800*. Cambridge: Cambridge University Press, 2010.

Pennell, C. R., ed. *Bandits at Sea: A Pirate Reader*. New York: New York University Press, 2001.

Pennell, C. R., ed. *Piracy and Diplomacy in Seventeenth-Century North Africa: The Journal of Thomas Baker, English Consul in Tripoli, 1677–1685*. Toronto: Associated University Presses, 1989.

Praetorius, Johannes. *Adunatus cometologus; Oder ein Geographischer Cometen Extract. . . .* Leipzig: Johann Wittigau, 1665.

Prange, Carsten. *Die Zeitungen und Zeitschriften des 17. Jahrhunderts in Hamburg und Altona: Ein Beitrag zur Publizistik der Frühaufklärung*. Hamburg: Hans Christians, 1978.

Rediker, Marcus. *Villains of All Nations: Atlantic Pirates in the Golden Age*. Boston: Beacon, 2004.

Reeser, Todd W. *Masculinities in Theory: An Introduction*. Oxford: Wiley-Blackwell, 2010.

Ressel, Magnus. "Der Freikauf Lübecker Seeleute aus Nordafrika und die Gründung der Lübecker Sklavenkasse (1580–1640)." *Zeitschrift für Lübeckische Geschichte* 91 (2011): 123–58.

Ressel, Magnus. "Hamburger Sklavenhändler als Sklaven in Westafrika." *Zeitschrift des Vereins für Hamburgische Geschichte* 96 (2011): 33–69.

Ressel, Magnus. "The North European Way of Ransoming: Exploration into an Unknown Dimension of the Early Modern Welfare State." *Historical Social Research* 35, no. 4 (2010): 125–47.

Rheinheimer, Martin. "Identität und Kulturkonflikt: Selbstzeugnisse schleswig-holsteinischer Sklaven in den Barbareskenstaaten." *Historischen Zeitschrift* 269, no. 2 (1999): 317–69.

Ross, Denison E., ed. *Thomas Sherley: Discours of the Turkes*. Camden Miscellany 16. London: Royal Historical Society, 1936.

Roßbach, Nikola, and Thomas Stäcker, with Flemming Schock, Constanze Baum, Imke Harjes, and Sabine Kalff, eds. *Welt und Wissen auf der Bühne: Die Theatrum-Literatur der Frühen Neuzeit. Repertorium*. Wolfenbüttel: Herzog August Bibliothek, 2011. http://diglib.hab.de/edoc/ed000132/startx.htm.

Rudt de Collenberg, Wipertus E., ed. *Esclavage et Rançons des Chréstiens en Méditerranéel (1570–1600): D'après les Litterae Hortatoriae de l'Archivio Segretto Vaticano*. Paris: Le Leopard d'Or, 1987.

Scammell, G. V. "The English in the Atlantic Islands c. 1450–1650." In *Ships, Oceans, and Empire: Studies in European Maritime and Colonial History, 1400–1750*, edited by G. V. Scammell, 295–317. Aldershot: Ashgate Variorum, 1995.

Scattola, Merio. "Roman und praktische Philosophie in der Tradition der Gelehrtengeschichte." In *Kultur der Kommunikation: Die europäische Gelehrtenrepublik im Zeitalter von Leibniz und Lessing*, edited by Ulrich Johannes Schneider, 293–317. Wolfenbütteler Forschungen 109. Wiesbaden: Harrassowitz, 2005.

Schmitt, Stefanie. *Inszenierungen der von Glaubwürdigkeit: Studien zur Beglaubigung im späthöfischen und frühneuzeitlichen Roman*. Münchner Texte und Untersuchungen zur Deutschen Literatur des Mittelalters 129. Tübingen: Niemeyer, 2005.

Schock, Flemming. "Reading Others: Intertextuality in Early Modern Popular Writing (Eberhard Werner Happel's *Relationes Curiosae*)." Unpublished manuscript.

Schock, Flemming. *Die Text-Kunstkammer: Populäre Wissenssammlungen des Barock am Beispiel der "Relationes Curiosae" von E. W. Happel*. Beihefte zum Archiv für Kulturgeschichte 68. Cologne: Böhlau, 2011.

Schomberg, Friedrich von, and Marquis de Ruvigny. *The Humble Petition of the Protestants of France Lately presented to His Most Christian Majesty*. London: L. Curtis, 1685.

Schulze, Winfried. "Ego-Dokumente: Annäherung an den Menschen in der Geschichte? Vorüberlegungen für die Tagung 'EGO-DOKUMENTE.'" In *Ego-Dokumente: Annäherung an den Menschen in der Geschichte*, edited by Winfried Schulze, 11–29. Berlin: Akademie, 1996.

Schuwirth, Theo. *Eberhard Werner Happel (1647–1690): Ein Beitrag zur deutschen Literatur des 17. Jahrhunderts*. Marburg, 1908.

Segal, Ronald. *Islam's Black Slaves: The Other Diaspora*. New York: Farrar, Straus and Giroux, 2001.

Shapiro, Barbara J. *A Culture of Fact: England, 1550–1720*. Ithaca: Cornell University Press, 2000.

Singer, Herbert. *Der deutsche Roman zwischen Barock und Rokoko*. Cologne: Böhlau, 1963.

Smith, Pamela H., and Benjamin Schmidt, eds. *Making Knowledge in Early Modern Europe: Practices, Objects, and Texts, 1400–1800*. Chicago: University of Chicago Press, 2007.

Spicker-Beck, Monika. *Räuber, Mordbrenner, umschweifendes Gesind: Zur Kriminalität im 16. Jahrhundert*. Edited by Wolfgang Reinhard and Ernst Schulin. Rombach Wissenschaft–Reihe Historiae 8. Freiburg im Breisgau: Rombach, 1995.

Strassner, Erich. *Zeitung*. Grundlagen der Medienkommunikation 2. Tübingen: Niemeyer, 1997.

Tabak, Faruk. *The Waning of the Mediterranean, 1550–1870*. Baltimore: Johns Hopkins University Press, 2008.

Tatlock, Lynne. "The Novel as Archive in New Times." *Daphnis* 37, nos. 1–2 (2009): 351–73.

Tatlock, Lynne. "Selling Turks: Eberhard Werner Happel's *Turcica* (1683–1690)," *Colloquia Germanica* 28, nos. 3–4 (1995): 307–37.

Tatlock, Lynne. "*Thesaurus Novorum*: Periodicity and Rhetoric of Fact in Eberhard Werner Happel's Prose." *Daphnis* 19, no. 1 (1990): 105–35.

Tezcan, Baki. *The Second Ottoman Empire: Political and Social Transformation in the Early Modern World*. Cambridge Studies in Islamic Civilization. Cambridge: Cambridge University Press, 2010.

Thomasius, Christian. "Eberhardi Guerneri Happelii Africanischer Tarnolast." In *Freimütige, lustige und ernsthafte, jedoch vernunftsmässige Gedanken oder Monatsgespräche . . .*, edited by Christian Thomasius, 697–806. 1689. Repr., Frankfurt am Main: Athenaeum, 1972.

Thomson, Janice E. *Mercenaries, Pirates, and Sovereigns: State-Building and Extraterritorial Violence in Early Modern Europe*. Princeton: Princeton University Press, 1994.

Thorel-Cailletteau, Sylvie. "The Poetry of Mediocrity." In *The Novel*, vol. 2, *Forms and Themes*, edited by Franco Moretti, 64–94. Princeton: Princeton University Press, 2006.

Tracy, James, ed. *The Rise of Merchant Empires: Long-Distance Trade in the Early Modern World, 1550–1750*. Studies in Comparative Early Modern History. Cambridge: Cambridge University Press, 1990.

Trivellato, Francesca. *The Familiarity of Strangers: The Sephardic Diaspora, Livorno, and Cross-Cultural Trade in the Early Modern Period*. New Haven: Yale University Press, 2009.

Vickers, Joseph A., and Nancy J. Boone. "Introduction: Celebrity Rites." In "Celebrity, Fame, Notoriety," special issue, *PMLA* 126, no. 4 (2011): 900–12.

Vitkus, Daniel J., and Nabil Matar, eds. *Piracy, Slavery, and Redemption*. New York: Columbia University Press, 2001.

Vosskamp, Wilhelm. *Romantheorie in Deutschland: Von Martin Opitz bis Friedrich von Blanckenburg*. Germanistische Abhandlungen 40. Stuttgart: Metzler, 1973.

Waghall, Elisabeth. "Eine Königin in den Zeitungen: Königin Christina von Schweden als Beispiel frühneuzeitlicher Nachrichtenvermittlung." *Daphnis* 37, nos. 1–2 (2008): 302–32.

Wahrenburg, Fritz. *Funktionswandel des Romans und aesthetische Norm: Die Entwicklung seiner Theorie in Deutschland bis zur Mitte des 18. Jahrhunderts.* Studien zur allgemeinen und vergleichenden Literaturwissenschaft 11. Stuttgart: Metzler, 1976.

Warner, William B. *Licensing Entertainment: The Elevation of Novel Reading in Britain, 1684–1750.* Berkeley: University of California Press, 1998.

Watanabe-O'Kelly, Helen. *Beauty or Beast? The Woman Warrior in the German Imagination from the Renaissance to the Present.* Oxford: Oxford University Press, 2010.

Weber, Ernst, ed. *Texte zur Romantheorie.* Vol. 1. Munich: Fink, 1974.

Wiedemann, Conrad. *Der galante Stil 1680–1730.* Deutsche Texte 11. Tübingen: Niemeyer, 1969.

Wiesner, Merry E. *Women and Gender in Early Modern Europe.* Edited by William Beik. 2nd ed. New Approaches to European History. Cambridge: Cambridge University Press, 2000.

Wiggin, Bethany. *Novel Translations: The European Novel and the German Book, 1680–1730.* Signale: Modern German Letters, Cultures, and Thought. Ithaca: Cornell University Press, 2011.

Williams, Gerhild Scholz. *Defining Dominion: The Discourses of Magic and Witchcraft in Early Modern France and Germany.* Studies in Medieval and Early Modern Civilization 6. Ann Arbor: University of Michigan Press, 1995.

Williams, Gerhild Scholz. "Formen der Aufrichtigkeit: Zeitgeschehen in Wort und Bild im *Theatrum Europaeum* (1618–1718)." In *Die Kunst der Aufrichtigkeit im 17. Jahrhundert*, edited by Claudia Benthien and Steffen Martus, 443–73. Tübingen: Niemeyer, 2006.

Williams, Gerhild Scholz, ed. *Mothering Baby: On Being a Woman in Early Modern Germany; Johannes Praetorius's "Apocalypsis Cybeles: Das ist Eine Schnakische Wochen-Comedie (1662)."* Medieval and Renaissance Texts and Studies. Tempe: Arizona Center for Medieval and Renaissance Studies, 2010.

Williams, Gerhild Scholz. "Sensationslust, Tabu und Scham: Öffentlichkeit und Berichterstattung im 17. Jahrhundert; Thurneysser, Pierre de Lancre, *Theatrum Europaeum.*" In *Tabu: Über den gesellschaftlichen Umgang mit Ekel und Scham*, edited by Anja Hesse et al., 75–101. Braunschweiger kulturwissenschaftliche Studien 1. Berlin: Kulturverlag Kadmos, 2009.

Williams, Gerhild Scholz. "Staging the News: The Theater of Passions and Politics in Eberhard Werner Happel's *Dess Englischen Eduards* (1690/1)." In *Dimensionen der Theatrum-Metapher in der Frühen Neuzeit: Ordnung und Repräsentation des Wissens*, edited by Flemming Schock et al., 369–89. Hannover: Wehrhahn, 2008.

Williams, Gerhild Scholz. *Ways of Knowing in Early Modern Germany: Johannes Praetorius as a Witness to His Time.* Aldershot: Ashgate, 2006.

Wills, John E., Jr., ed. *China and Maritime Europe, 1500–1800: Trade, Settlement, Diplomacy, and Mission.* Cambridge: Cambridge University Press, 2011.

Windler, Christian. "Verrechtlichte Gewalt zwischen Muslimen und Christen: Französisch-maghrebinische und spanisch-maghrebinische Beziehungen." In

Gewalt in der Frühen Neuzeit: Beiträge zur 5. Tagung der Arbeitsgemeinschaft Frühe Neuzeit im VHD, edited by Claudia Ulbrich, Claudia Jarzebowski, and Michaele Hohkamp, 325–41. Berlin: Duncker und Humblot, 2003.

Witek, John W. "Catholic Mission and the Expansion of Christianity, 1644–1800." In Wills, *China and Maritime Europe, 1500–1800*, 135–83.

Zeiler, Martin. *Herrn Martin Zeillers/ Wolseeliger Gedächtnüß Epistolische SchatzKammer: Bestehend Von Siebenhundert und Sechs Sendschreiben/ Worinnen Allerhand köstliche Schätze/ unterschiedlicher Künsten und Wissenschaften/ schöner anmutiger und nutzlicher Historien/ lehr-reicher Fragen . . . zu finden seynd.* Ulm: Matthaeus Wagner, 1683.

Zenner, Gottfried, ed. *Novellen aus der gelehrten und curiösen Welt.* Frankfurt am Main: Augustus Boetius, 1692.

Index

☙

Page locators in *italics* indicate figures.